Hermann Grossmann
Hand of the Cause of God

Dr Hermann Großmann

16.02.1899 - 07.07.1968

Susanne Pfaff-Grossmann

Hermann Grossmann
Hand of the Cause of God

A Life for the Faith

Hartmut Grossmann

Reflections on my Father

GEORGE RONALD
OXFORD

George Ronald, Publisher
Oxford
www.grbooks.com

© Verlag Ralf Ackermann, Rothenberg 2009
All Rights Reserved

A catalogue record for this book is available from
the British Library

ISBN 978-0-85398-531-0

Typesetting: Katharina Ackermann
Cover design: SteinerGraphics
Printed in England by Cromwell Press Group

CONTENTS

Preface vii

PART I A LIFE FOR THE FAITH

1	Childhood and Early Youth	3
2	The First World War	8
3	Encounter with the Bahá'í Faith	13
4	Anna Hartmuth	17
5	First Endeavours on Behalf of the Beloved Cause	21
6	Esperanto	34
7	The Years up to 1937	40
8	Pilgrimage to Haifa	48
9	Interdiction under the National Socialists	54
10	The Renewal of Bahá'í Activities, 1945-1948	71
11	The Five Year Plan, 1948-1953	95
12	Appointment as a Hand of the Cause of God	105
13	Anna Grossmann	114
14	The Tireless Scholar	124
15	Launching the Ten Year Crusade	135
16	Elsa Maria Grossmann	140
17	The First Five Years of the Ten Year Crusade, 1953-1957	151
18	Second Pilgrimage, 1957	163
19	The Passing of the Guardian, Shoghi Effendi	169
20	Return to South America, 1959	181
21	South American Pillars of the Universal House of Justice	194
22	Last Journey to South America, 1962	211
23	The Most Great Jubilee, 1963	220
24	Final Years and Passing	225

Appendices

1 Religion and Science *A Talk by Hermann Grossmann, December 1957*	237
2 List of Published Books, Booklets and Articles by Hermann Grossmann: A Selection	243

PART II   REFLECTIONS ON MY FATHER

Instead of an Introduction	249
The Tablet from 'Abdu'l-Bahá	252
The Seeker	257
The Hand of the Cause of God	260
The Advocate of God	263
The Administrator	266
The Systematist	270
The Visionary Artist and Thinker	274
The Educator	278
A German Bahá'í Teacher in France	281
My Parents	285
Glossary	293
Bibliography	297
References	299
Index	313

PREFACE

Encouraged by my brother Hartmut Grossmann, then Counsellor at the International Teaching Centre in Haifa, I began in 1994 to research the life of my father, the Hand of the Cause of God, Dr Hermann Grossmann. First, I surveyed and organized his vast archives together with the religious literature that he had bequeathed to the National Spiritual Assembly of the Bahá'ís of Germany and which is currently stored at the National Office in Hofheim am Taunus. The more I delved into these records, the more present he became and the closer I felt to him. In all his works and manuscripts he came to life again. I saw him once more as the loving father, the educator of his children, a person often tired and overworked, the indefatigable teacher drawing from his inexhaustible fund of knowledge, and the scientific labourer who dealt with each subject in the Faith systematically. He reflected on a single issue for days, approaching it from ever new perspectives. Above all, he was an inspiring Bahá'í teacher who explained problems in a way that led to their solution logically. He would discuss everything that was on his mind with my mother. Without her he would not have achieved what he did. She shared everything with him: his griefs, his worries, but also his moments of joy. She was a true consort.

Naturally, this biography is very personal. The memories of my parents are so present in my mind that it is impossible to write in a detached, objective way.

For the benefit of those readers who are less well acquainted with the Bahá'í Faith, I would like to offer the following brief outline:

Bahá'u'lláh, the Central Figure of the Bahá'í Faith and the Manifestation of God for this age, was born in Persia in 1817. In 1863 He publicly declared that He was the Messenger whose coming all Prophets of the past had foretold and whose advent marked a new outpouring of the Divine Will. After many years of imprisonment, exile, deprivation and physical suffering He died in 1892. Today His Shrine in Bahjí, near 'Akká, in Israel, is regarded by His followers as the holiest spot on earth. Bahá'u'lláh revealed a vast number of Writings. They proclaim the unity of mankind, a unity in diversity. The purpose is to overcome whatever creates divisions between people and to promote the unification of the human race.

In His Testament Bahá'u'lláh appointed His eldest Son, 'Abdu'l-Bahá, as Interpreter and Expounder of His Writings. After 'Abdu'l-Bahá was at last released from prison, following the Young Turk uprising in 1908, He was able to undertake travels to different countries in Europe and North America, in order to spread His Father's teachings. In His Will and Testament 'Abdu'l-Bahá appointed His eldest grandson, Shoghi Effendi, as 'Guardian of the Cause of God'. Under the leadership of Shoghi Effendi the Bahá'í Cause spread throughout the world. Today, there is hardly any country or territory that does not count some followers of the Bahá'í Faith among its inhabitants. The teachings of Bahá'u'lláh have taken firm root worldwide and are being applied through social and economic projects that promote the welfare of humanity. In this way, the Bahá'ís are providing an increasingly corrupt, desolate and despairing world with a way out of its misery through the teachings of the new Manifestation of God, thus bringing about fundamental change.

Bahá'u'lláh Himself designated some of His most faithful followers as 'Hands of the Cause of God'. In His Will and Testament 'Abdu'l-Bahá wrote:

> The obligations of the Hands of the Cause of God are to diffuse the Divine Fragrances, to edify the souls of men, to promote learning, to improve the character of all men and to be, at all times and under all conditions, sanctified and detached from earthly things. They must manifest the fear of God by their conduct, their manners, their deeds and their words.[1]

The same high standards of character and dedication were also required of those who were appointed Hands at a later date. 'Abdu'l-Bahá raised four believers posthumously to this noble rank. Similarly, the Guardian, Shoghi Effendi, honoured ten Bahá'ís after their passing by appointing them to this position. In December 1951, for the first time, Shoghi Effendi appointed a contingent of twelve living Bahá'ís as Hands, and in February 1952 seven more. Between 1952 and 1957 five were appointed to replace those who had passed away. Finally in October 1957, shortly before his death, Shoghi Effendi appointed a last contingent of eight believers to this high rank. Thus at the time of Shoghi Effendi's passing in November 1957 the total number of Hands of the Cause was twenty-seven. Designated in his last message to the Bahá'í world as the 'Chief Stewards of Bahá'u'lláh's embryonic World Commonwealth', this

PREFACE

body of twenty-seven Hands of the Cause was entrusted with the task of preserving the unity and purity of the Bahá'í Faith until, in 1963, it passed its sacred obligation on to the newly elected 'Universal House of Justice', the highest institution of the Bahá'í Faith.

It was my niece, Anke Grossmann, who suggested that this biography should be written. Since she and her family were at the time living as Bahá'í pioneers in Chita, east of Lake Baikal in the Far East of Russia, and their adverse living conditions did not allow her to conduct the necessary research, she sought the assistance of her parents, my brother Hartmut Grossmann and my sister-in-law Ursula Grossmann. Thus began the task of gathering together reports from friends who had known Hermann and Anna Grossmann while they were still alive. During a visit to Haifa, Anke Grossmann arranged for the interviews quoted in this book. The valuable contributions made by Ian Semple, long-time member of the Universal House of Justice, Martin Aiff, René Steiner, Hermine and Massoud Berdjis, and Harry Liedtke, to name but a few, are warmly acknowledged. In no lesser degree I am obliged to Mas'úd Khamsí, Fred Schechter, Athos Costas, Donald Witzel, Ursula von Brunn, Gilbert Grassely, Sabino Ortega and Oscar Salazar for their very vivid accounts of the journeys of the Hand of the Cause in South America.

I also wish to thank Anneliese Bopp, who was for many years a Counsellor at the International Teaching Centre in Haifa, my sister-in-law Ursula Grossmann, Bernhard Westerhoff, who researched the material for the chapter on Esperanto, as well as Gisela von Brunn, my daughter Katharina and my son-in-law Ralf Ackermann, who lent their untiring help and support. I am also indebted to Sigrun Schaefer for her assistance with the proofreading and her valuable advice.

Finally, I wish to express my sincere thanks to all who remain unnamed but who contributed generously to this biography.

Soon after the release of Hermann Grossmann's biography in the summer 2001, it was decided to publish it in English as well so as to embrace a larger readership. Dr Geraldine Schuckelt translated the book. I thank my niece Barbara Maknoni for the book's stylistic revision and my daughter Katharina and my son-in-law Ralf Ackermann for their indefatigable and indispensable help. Also I wish to thank to Maralynn Dunbar for translating the Spanish parts and above all I want to say a very special word of appreciation and gratitude to Ian Semple for his valuable looking review and comments. Finally I want to thank May Hofman for her excellent and patient work as editor.

HERMANN GROSSMANN

I hope that this book will help to preserve the memory of my father and bring him closer to those who never had the privilege of meeting him.

Susanne Pfaff-Grossmann
Böbingen, 2001, 2008

*Yield thee thanks unto God
that thou hast been enabled to rend the veils asunder,
to gaze on the beauty of the Sun of Reality,
and to walk in the path of the Kingdom.*

'Abdu'l-Bahá to Hermann Grossmann,
9 December 1920

PART I

A Life for the Faith

Susanne Pfaff-Grossmann

*With love and thanks to my husband
Emil Pfaff*

CHAPTER 1

CHILDHOOD AND EARLY YOUTH

Hermann Grossmann was born on España Street in Rosario de Santa Fé in Argentina on 16 February 1899. The vicar of the parish of Esperanza de Santa Fé entered his name in the parish register as the fourth child of Curt Grossmann and his wife Johanna *née* Mongsfeld on 13 June 1899. The families of both his parents had been Protestants for many generations. Curt and Johanna Grossmann were both of German descent. In the middle of the 19th century Johanna Grossmann's parents had fled from the hunger and poverty that prevailed in their respective homelands of Saxony and Holstein in Germany. After the privations and dangers of a long sea voyage lasting many weeks they had reached Argentina, where they intended to start a new life. There it was possible for an industrious man to learn a new profession and he was not condemned to remain forever in the social class into which he had been born. Thus, Johanna's father became a lithographer, but died at the age of only 37 during a yellow fever epidemic; he became infected with the disease while selflessly caring for others who were suffering from it. All the adult male members of the large family died of yellow fever during that time. Johanna Grossmann's mother, Susanna Mongsfeld, Hermann Grossmann's grandmother, was left widowed, unprovided for, and with three small children. Nevertheless, from that time onwards she became the focal point and driving force of the family, dedicating herself with energy and self-sacrifice to the task of bringing up her children. Her grandchildren later knew her by the affectionate name of 'Coca'.

Hermann Grossmann's father, Curt Grossmann, was among the more recent immigrants. His family came from Wörmlitz near Halle in Germany, where his forefathers had worked as farm labourers on an estate. Curt Grossmann was born in 1865 in Dresden-Neustadt; after the early death of his father he, as the eldest son, had the duty of providing for his mother and his four brothers and sisters. In those days the only way to escape from poverty and hunger was to emigrate. He decided to seek his fortune in Argentina. There he prospered, and while still a young man succeeded in working his way up to a senior position in a prominent company in Rosario. He introduced a form of shorthand for the Spanish language which facilitated the taking of notes during lectures and dictation. This innovation made him well known in the Spanish-speaking world. His hard work and his natural capabilities brought him both wealth and renown, so much so that he was able to choose a wife from a respected upper middle-class family. He was tirelessly engaged in promoting the welfare of his adopted country. So greatly was Curt Grossmann respected that when his grandson (then Counsellor) Hartmut Grossmann visited Rosario in February 2000 on behalf of the Bahá'í World Centre in Haifa he was received by the Lord Mayor and other civic dignitaries, who hailed him as the descendant of one who had performed unforgettable services to the city a hundred years earlier. Even the well-known football club 'Rosario Central' presented him with a T-shirt bearing its emblems, Curt Grossmann having been one of its founding members.

Hermann Grossmann's parents enjoyed a happy marriage in which the different aspects of their characters complemented each other to make a harmonious whole. His mother was a kind and loving person; his father was conscientious and possessed a strong sense of duty. They taught their children to be open-minded and receptive towards new ideas. Indeed, they laid the spiritual foundations that later enabled Hermann and Elsa Maria Grossmann to spontaneously accept the Message of Bahá'u'lláh.

Of the four children born to Johanna and Curt Grossmann, one son died a few days after birth. Rudolf, the elder of the two surviving sons, became an outstanding Hispanic scholar at the University of Hamburg. The daughter, Elsa Maria, born in Rosario in 1896, dedicated her life wholly to the Bahá'í Faith; she became a Knight of Bahá'u'lláh for the Frisian Islands and a highly skilled translator of English into German. Hermann, or Germán as he was called at home in Argentina, was the youngest child.

The three children were artistically and intellectually very gifted. In this regard they certainly owed much to their artistic, sensitive and intelligent grandmother, Susanna Mongsfeld, their dear Coca, who understood well how to awaken and develop the talents of her grandchildren. She was the centre of calmness within the family, providing a warm sense of security and harmony for the three children

CHILDHOOD AND EARLY YOUTH

while they were growing up. As a deeply religious person, she constantly tried to plant the seeds of this spirituality in their hearts. Many of her poems reveal an intense longing for God. One such is the following, which she wrote in September 1905 at the age of 62:

Ich harre Dein

Ich harre Dein in Jugendfreuden,
Du gabst sie mir.
Du Vater gibst ja Lust und Leiden.
Ich danke Dir.

Ich harrte Dein, als Stürme nahten,
Du warst mein Hort.
Hast mich geführt auf rauhen Pfaden,
Du treuer Gott.

Ich harrte Dein und Deiner Güte,
Herr hat gewacht.
Du hast bewahrt mich und behütet,
Trotz Sturm und Nacht.

Ich harre Dein im Silberhaar.
Der Tag sich neigt.
Du Gott der himmlische und wahre,
Mir Frieden reich.

Ich harre Dein. O gib den Frieden
Mein Gott bald mir.
Lass bald von Freud hienieden
Mich ruhn bei Dir.

I trust in Thee

While Thou didst grant me the pleasures of youth,
I trusted in Thee.
Father, for the joys and sorrows Thou bestowest
I thank Thee.

I trusted in Thee when storms were approaching
Thou wert my refuge.
Thou didst guide me over stony paths,
Thou one true God.

I trusted in Thee and in Thy goodness,
O vigilant Lord.
Thou didst keep me safe and shielded
while nightly storms were raging.

With silvering hair I trust in Thee,
when now the light of day is dimming.
Thou God of all things heavenly and true,
grant me Thy peace.

Grant me soon Thy peace, O my beloved Lord.
I trust in Thee.
Release me soon from earthly joys and sorrows
that I may find my rest in Thee.

The children attended the German school in Rosario. When Hermann Grossmann left this school after four years, in 1908, he had been the most successful pupil in his class. The unrestrictive and progressive atmosphere of this school, which could only have thrived in a liberal and multi-cultural country that was proud of its independence, made a lasting impression upon the young boy. He was indebted to his Argentine childhood for profoundly shaping his character, and throughout his life he regarded Argentina as his true home. Not once did he consider relinquishing his Argentine nationality; he was proud of it. When, during his military service in the German army, he was subjected to discrimination on account of his nationality, he wrote indignantly to his sister, 'I would never dream of giving up my citizenship of a country that shows such great promise ... I am first and foremost an Argentinian.'

Hermann Grossmann's father felt a growing urge to return to his native country, Germany. He pondered over this question for a long time, paying a visit to Germany in 1905 before finally deciding to return with his family. They left Argentina in 1909 and settled in Hamburg, a major North Sea port. Curt Grossmann purchased a partnership in a firm that manufactured fine cardboard, with headquarters in Waldmichelbach (Odenwald) in southwestern Germany. He became managing director of the company's factory in Wandsbek near Hamburg, one of six factories owned by the firm. Three of the other factories were in Waldmichelbach, one was in Ruhla in Thuringia and the sixth was in Altkinsberg near Eger (today Cheb), in what is now the Czech Republic.

From 1909 to 1911 Hermann Grossmann attended the secondary school near the Lübeck Gate in Hamburg. For the 10-year-old a painful period of adjustment to new circumstances began. His new teachers turned out to be narrow-minded and intolerant, displaying the attitudes and characteristics that typified the Wilhelminian period in Germany. The German government had found an effective way to suppress the influence of liberal-minded, progressive and, hence, 'troublemaking' teachers: they were simply transferred to German schools in other countries. But it was precisely teachers of this kind who had so profoundly influenced Hermann during his childhood in Rosario. In the spring of 1911 he transferred to high school, the 'Oberrealschule auf der Uhlenhorst zu Hamburg', and graduated from there in January 1917 with the German university entrance qualification, the 'Abitur'.

CHAPTER 2

THE FIRST WORLD WAR

When the First World War broke out in August 1914 the family was cut off from relatives and friends, and Coca's plans to visit them had to be abandoned. In 1916 Curt Grossmann acquired the civic rights of the city of Hamburg, allowing his family automatically to become German citizens while retaining their Argentine nationality. But as a German citizen, Hermann Grossmann was now faced with the threat of conscription into military service and involvement in the war. His renowned and revered physics teacher, Ernst Grimsehl, had already been killed in 1914 during a vain assault in Flanders (near Langemark), together with all the students of his final-year class. Professor Grimsehl was the founding editor of a comprehensive physics handbook, which even today, extended and revised, is still in print and has been an important reference work for physicists for many decades. He was an enthusiastic teacher and one who was able to ignite enthusiasm in his pupils. He aroused in Hermann a life-long interest in the natural sciences, thereby laying a firm foundation in him for grasping the rapid developments in physics that were revolutionizing man's conception of the universe. This was later to become a frequent theme in his lectures.

In April 1917, at the age of eighteen, Hermann Grossmann was recruited and passed as being physically fit for military service. The carefree life of learning, excursions and enjoyment in the company of friends came to an abrupt end. In June he was sent as an infantryman in a troop transport to Heitersheim in Baden in the south of Germany, far away from the region familiar to him. Worried that the youth of Hamburg – already seen at that time as unreliable and rebellious – would cause trouble, the military authorities of the German Empire made sure that the recruits were sent to places far from their homes. To those with insight it was by now evident that in this dreadful war, which had already claimed millions of lives, the tide of Germany's fortunes was turning.

Nevertheless, Hermann Grossmann decided to pursue a military career and therefore joined the army as an officer cadet. In November 1917, after a short period of training, he was transferred to the front in France. As a mere 18-year-old he was now confronted with the horrors of trench warfare, rearguard action and hand-to-hand combat. Friend and foe alike, the soldiers lay without shelter in holes and trenches which they had quickly dug themselves, using small spades, to have at least a little bit of protection from enemy fire. During the day the English aircraft would circle overhead, discovering the soldiers and shooting at them. They were mercilessly exposed to heat, cold, rain and snow, and they suffered from a constant gnawing hunger because ration carriers were hindered by enemy fire from reaching the troops. The lack of food left them tired and sometimes utterly exhausted. To his diary he confided his distress, fear and despair while recording stark facts, writing descriptive prose, composing poems, and making drawings in an attempt to free his soul from the impact of these dreadful experiences.

Essenfassen

Berin Enenholen. 1917.

On 23 September 1918 he recorded the following in his diary:

Es krampft mein Herz in dumpfer Qual:
Gott, Vater! steh mir bei!
Wo ist der Weg zu Deinem Licht?
Bang such ich, doch ich find ihn nicht –
Die Kraft bricht mir entzwei.

My heart is cramped with numbing pain,
God, Father, stand by me!
Where is the way to Thy light?
I search, but it escapes my sight –
This torment is tearing me in two.

My soul awoke one morning and was appalled to see its shadow in the light of day. Only in the light itself is clarity; only light has no shadow. And I desired to be a part of that light, so as not to have to tremble before myself again.

But now for a long time I have been searching for the way, the way that will lead me upwards. Yet I search in vain, for the closer I seem to come to that light, the further I seem to be thrown back into regions where there is only shadow ...

O God, how thorny is Thy way! Thou dost crush us into naught ere Thou dost raise us up to Thee. How heavily do my wrongdoings weigh upon me! Ever since I came to know Thee, I have regarded myself as the lowest of worms and am ready to endure the fate Thou hast meted out to me, even should I be trodden underfoot by the lowest mob. At times, when no one sees me, I lay myself down and bewail the lost paradise to which no angel will lead us back.

Hermann Grossmann contracted an infectious skin disease on one of his legs. This was successfully treated in a military hospital, but as soon as he had recovered he was sent back to the front. His company had suffered many casualties, both dead and wounded. In his diary he described how wounded comrades, crying and groaning, lay between the trenches and how all too often it was impossible to rescue them. Those responsible for first aid would go to pick up the wounded but often returned unsuccessfully because they had come under enemy fire. He saw humans and animals killed by the effects of poison gas. He and his comrades once had to seek shelter in a trench in which there still lingered the remnants of these lethal gas clouds. It was a horrifying and merciless war. Then came the day when the dead could no longer be replaced and his company had to be disbanded. Hermann survived unwounded, and was promoted to the rank of officer trainee. On 15 October 1918 he recorded in his diary: 'In these last days of the war our thoughts are focused entirely on the prospect of peace. We wait with expectancy and hope. Let our hope not be in vain!'

Shortly afterwards, on 11 November, the killing finally came to an end. An armistice was declared, and the diary closes with a pencil drawing of the three crosses of Golgotha, on which the shape of the Crucified One is lightly sketched.

Years later, after he had become a Bahá'í, Hermann Grossmann prefaced his diary with the following words:

Dreams and hopes were my companions when I began this logbook. The dreams died as the light of day was too bright and the hopes perished in the face of what seemed to be the truth.

Later I found out what was really true and within that truth new dreams and hopes were born. In Thee all things have been gloriously fulfilled.

One last terrible experience still awaited the dejected, physically and mentally tormented returnee. When the soldiers arrived in Hamburg, there was no jubilant crowd to cheer them as there had been when they had marched out to war, no one decorated their guns any more. Mutinying marines assailed them with verbal abuse, spat at them and tore the epaulettes off their uniforms. The inhabitants of Hamburg were starving and freezing. The trees that had lined the streets had been chopped down for firewood. Hamburg was living through the 'turnip winter' in which no one had more than the bare minimum to eat. The black market flourished. A whole generation of young people sank into despondency and despair. The old world and its order had collapsed; traditional values had vanished. Hermann Grossmann asked himself whether hatred, destruction and endless misery could be the meaning of life.

Later, Elsa Maria Grossmann would relate how before this time her brother Hermann had always been a cheerful and carefree soul. But now he had become a different person, often plunged into dark despondency. She and her mother tried in vain to help him relax and provide him with some diversion. At last his depression became so deep that he could bear life no longer and was ready to end it. Only the vision of his mother, which he suddenly beheld at that decisive moment, and the unexpected visit of a friend, jolted him back. From then on he became a despairing seeker.[2]

As a start to his search, engagement with a political party, the Deutsche Volkspartei, proved to be only a brief intermezzo. It was, after all, not what he was looking for.

At this critical time he was a student at the Polytechnikum, a technical college in Köthen in Saxony, where he intended to study papermaking technology.

CHAPTER 3

ENCOUNTER WITH THE BAHÁ'Í FAITH

Hermann Grossmann soon realized that studying technical subjects did not really appeal to him, so in his second semester at Köthen, in 1920, he transferred to the University of Leipzig in order to study economics.

Throughout this time the agitation in his soul persisted, and his reflections culminated in the idea that human society must be undergoing a process of development. God had created man out of love. He must also have intended man to have the capacity for further development. Indeed, He had shown this to be the case in the past, for He had sent into the world such Messengers as Abraham, Moses and Christ. Perhaps now He would send another Revealer of His Word who would establish a new order for the world – a Christ returned, who would release mankind from its terrible suffering.[3]

Let his sister, Elsa Maria, tell us what happened at this time:

> At about the time when his studies [in Leipzig] were coming to an end, a friend told Hermann about a forthcoming lecture at the 'Theosophical Society', thinking that it might interest him, and so my brother went there. The speaker on that evening was a Mr Harlan Ober, who, along with his wife, Grace, was on a return journey from Haifa. The Obers had been visiting 'Abdu'l-Bahá, who had asked them specially to go to Leipzig. Hermann was very much attracted by the spirit that this couple had brought with them from Haifa. Mr Ober announced that he and his wife would be staying in Leipzig for a few weeks and that people were welcome to visit them in their hotel at any time if they wished to ask any questions about his talk on the Bahá'í Faith. Some people who were more or less interested in the Faith did indeed come.[4]

Anna Grossmann, his future wife, later recounted how Hermann Grossmann frequently spoke about this providential encounter in 1920:

The meeting had already begun when he arrived, and as he entered the rather dimly lit hall the bright figure of a woman stood out. She was standing at the lectern and saying that 'all people are the leaves of one tree and the flowers of one garden'. He was immediately convinced of the truth of her words. Later she approached him and ventured to say: 'I feel I have spoken for you.' 'Certainly,' he replied, 'but please tell me what it's all about.'

It is interesting to note that on the same evening Mrs Lina Benke also spontaneously accepted the Bahá'í Faith, followed only a short time later by her husband, Adam Benke. Soon all three of them, in order to learn more about this new religion, made daily visits to Alma Knobloch, who at that time was staying in Leipzig.[5]

Alma Knobloch had been living in the United States of America and had become a Bahá'í there. In 1907 'Abdu'l-Bahá had asked her to go to Germany as a pioneer and help with the propagation of the Faith. She taught the Faith for many years; during the First World War she gave up her American citizenship so as to be able to stay with her German friends. Her activities in Germany left their traces in Stuttgart, Hamburg, Leipzig and many other towns.[6] Adam Benke, as will be seen later, sacrificed his life for the Cause of Bahá'u'lláh whilst he and his wife Lina were teaching the Faith in Sofia, the capital of Bulgaria.

For now, however, let us go back to August 1920 and listen again to the reminiscences recorded by Elsa Maria Grossmann. She tells us that one day her brother announced he was coming to Hamburg:

> I was waiting in the main station in Hamburg, anxiously expecting the arrival of my brother. For some time his life had been very clouded by the terrible experiences of the war. Imagine how surprised I now was to see the change in him, to see how he jumped down from the train and hurried towards me with such youthful energy and enthusiasm. As we made our way over the long platform to the exit, he related all that had happened during those eventful weeks in Leipzig. Having left the station, we deliberately walked home so as to have enough time to talk about this new religion. When we arrived home, Hermann told our mother about his experiences. Very calmly she asked, 'Hermann, are you quite sure that these are not the teachings of a false prophet?' 'Yes, Mother, certainly!', my brother replied, 'it is Christ who has returned.' To this my mother responded quite simply, 'Well, my son, if you're firmly convinced of this, then you must follow your chosen path – and rest assured that I will help you in whatever ways I can.'[7]

At the same time as Hermann Grossmann became a Bahá'í, Adelbert Mühlschlegel, unknown to him at that time, but later to become his friend and fellow wayfarer, also spontaneously accepted the Bahá'í Faith.[8]

After two semesters Hermann Grossmann left the University of Leipzig and in October 1920 he enrolled in the Faculty of Law and Political Science at Hamburg University, where on 16 February 1923, at the close of the 1922/23 winter semester, his studies culminated in a doctoral examination. The doctoral thesis he submitted bore the title 'Artificial leathers and their usage in the shoe industry of Pirmasens, particularly during the war and the post-war years'.

Thirty years later his daughter, Susanne Grossmann, successfully completed her finals for a university degree in physics. Dr Grossmann wrote to her from Vienna, where this news had reached him:

> My dear girl,
> ... I must tell you how happy I am to hear this good news. Not that I ever doubted that you would succeed, but I did have doubts as to whether it was right of me to encourage you to go to university when it seemed that you were sometimes discouraged or would rather have chosen an easier way without all that intensive studying. One reason for my encouragement may have been that I saw myself succeeding through you, as well as the fact that my own wishes would be realized if you could achieve what for me was never possible, namely to follow a course of studies that really suited my inclinations. At that time I had no one to advise me about studying at university. My father was anxious that I get my education finished and enter his factory. Two semesters, plus one interim semester in Leipzig, was all I could manage. Later I had to divide my time between business and attending evening lectures. I'm sure it wouldn't really have been necessary to do everything this way. On the other hand, perhaps it was good for me to go through all of that ... So now maybe you'll understand why I wanted so much to help you children with your education, to advise you, to work with you, and to ensure that you'd be able, with pleasure and satisfaction, to tackle all the difficult tasks which even the most attractive course of study can present. Now you've achieved your goal ... my heartfelt thanks, my dear girl, that you've been so steadfast and have succeeded in fulfilling one of my greatest wishes!
>
> Lots and lots of love. Let me take you in my arms and kiss you a thousand times.
>
> Your faithful father

Hermann Grossmann had once cherished the idea of becoming a painter.

HERMANN GROSSMANN

He was strongly influenced by the school of Professor Lichtwark, a well-known art educationalist in Hamburg and the Director of the city's Museum of Fine Arts. In Leipzig he successfully completed a course on art history given by Professor Wackernagel. During this period he produced not only drawings and sketches, but also a large number of essays on art history and aesthetics.

Even in his main courses, he would sometimes happily forget his note-taking and occupy himself with sketching portraits of the professor who was lecturing at the front or of fellow students who were sitting near him. In those strict days, it surely was better not to get caught pursuing such distractions; to do so would undoubtedly have resulted in a reprimand.

But finally he had to let his dream of becoming an artist fade. He felt responsible for his family and considered it his duty to help preserve the wealth and material security his father had worked so hard for. So, complying with the wishes of his parents, he devoted himself to the task of following in his father's footsteps and becoming his successor in the factory for fine-cardboard manufacture. He could not imagine what a burden this would turn out to be and what hostility he would later face from the partners in the company.

CHAPTER 4

ANNA HARTMUTH

As part of his professional training, Hermann Grossmann undertook a period of practical work experience in a factory belonging to one of his father's customers, the shoe manufacturer Wilhelm Hartmuth in Pirmasens. In those days, shoes were fitted with toe-caps and ankle reinforcements made of cardboard, which were supplied by his father's firm.

Wilhelm Hartmuth and his wife Anna had three daughters, of whom the eldest, who shared her mother's first name, had just turned sixteen at this time. Anna, or Annel as she was called by family and friends, was born in Pirmasens on 16 August 1905. The family was long established in the town and enjoyed a comfortable degree of prosperity that allowed them to live in a state of simple elegance. Her father was an upright and reserved man who was scrupulously correct in all his business dealings. Her mother was characterized by qualities of love, empathy and compassion, so that she frequently arranged assistance for needy people. She was the family mediator who always calmed the waves whenever, for instance, Anna's younger sisters had been playing tricks and had provoked the anger of their rather strict father. Anna's maternal uncles lived on large estates in Argentina and traded in cattle and timber. As convinced republicans and democrats, they had had to leave their Palatinate homeland in south-west Germany and had emigrated to South America. The development of a leather-tanning process using the bark of the quebracho tree had earned them a considerable fortune. The uncles frequently visited Germany with their families, so that Anna's family had a strong attachment to Argentina. To Anna's great delight, her great-aunt Lina Harteneck, her grandmother's sister, accepted the Bahá'í Faith towards the end of her life – the only member of the family to do so.

At sixteen, Anna Hartmuth was both pretty and charming, and even at this early stage her character was 'angelic', as it was later described by the Universal House of Justice in the message it sent following her passing. It was not surprising that she would attract the attention of the young man from the cosmopolitan city of Hamburg. He dedicated poems and drawings to her, which naturally impressed her. They fell in love, and Hermann Grossmann asked his employer, Wilhelm Hartmuth, for the hand of his eldest daughter in marriage.

Anna Hartmuth often had to take on the role of mother to her two younger sisters. The hardships of the war had left her mother with tuberculosis of the lung, which obliged her to pay repeated visits to a sanatorium at Ebersteinburg, near Baden-Baden, for the beneficial effects of the pure air of the Black Forest. At that time no other treatment was available. Despite her gentle character Anna Hartmuth was an energetic and independent person. Nevertheless, she was also an obedient daughter and so she bowed to the wishes of her parents who, after much consideration, consented to the marriage on condition that she waited until after her eighteenth birthday. Her parents' reservation was understandable, for she came from a staunchly Protestant family, and although her future husband also came from a Protestant family, he had turned his back on the church and, in their eyes, now belonged to a sect. This understandably caused Anna's parents some misgivings – after all, the soul of their beloved eldest daughter was at stake. It was also quickly evident that she would soon adopt her husband's religion. It was thanks to Hermann Grossmann's charm and persuasive manner, and especially his love for their daughter, that they eventually granted their consent.

Anna Hartmuth successfully completed the tenth grade at the Pirmasens High School for Girls in 1922. To mark the occasion, her fiancé composed a farewell magazine that delighted the girls – of course less so the teachers. It included the following comic strip:

ANNA HARTMUTH

Nächtliche Ballade vom furchtsamen Mädel.

Vom Turme mahnt die Uhr halb acht,
Herr Max zieht einsam durch die Nacht.

Der Regen aber fällt so dicht:
Na, gottseidank, er sieht sie nicht.

Auch Röschen Nolte geht allda,
Die sehr besorgt, ob er sie sah.

Indes- der Zweifel quält oft sehr ;
Dann seufzt man: wenns doch Morgen wär!

Und bricht der Morgen endlich an
Klopft wohl das Herz vor dem, was dann,
Doch diesmal bleibt der Himmel schön:
Gottlob, er hat sie nicht gesehn!

Die Seele aber, hochbeglückt,
Ein Dankgebet zum Himmel schickt. —

The Ballad of the Timorous Girl

The tower clock is striking eight,
Herr Max is walking out so late.

Rosie Nolte, too, is there:
To show her face she cannot dare.

The rain, however, falls so fast
That, Lord be praised, he walks straight past.

Yet gnawing doubts disturb the night –
She sighs and longs for morning light.

And when the sun at last appears
Her heart still beats with cares and fears.
But, this time, thanks to Heaven's grace
He really didn't see her face.

Her soul, though, with relief unchecked
A prayer of thanks to Heaven directs.

There were no opportunities for girls to continue their education in Pirmasens, so Annel Hartmuth travelled to Stuttgart to round off her education at a girls' boarding school. Above all, however, she paid regular visits to Annemarie Schweizer in Zuffenhausen near Stuttgart. 'Mariele', as she was called, was together with her husband Albert one of the pillars of the Bahá'í community. She introduced Anna Hartmuth to the teachings of Bahá'u'lláh at the request of her future husband.

Anna Hartmuth and Hermann Grossmann were married in Pirmasens on the deliberately chosen date of Friday the thirteenth – namely, on Friday, 13 September 1924. After their marriage they settled in Wandsbek, near Hamburg, where the young husband had recently joined his father's firm. His father had by this time retired. In 1928, they were blessed with a daughter whom they named Susanne Anna Bahíyyih. They had asked the Greatest Holy Leaf, the sister of the Master, 'Abdu'l-Bahá, to give a name to the as-yet-unborn child. Bahíyyih Khánum replied that the first child should be called after herself if it was a girl, and should be called Fuad if it was a boy. It turned out to be a girl.

Anna Grossmann started to work for the Bahá'í Faith immediately after her marriage. She supported her husband, giving him the strength he needed for his work, but she was also active in the Faith and her name began to appear more and more frequently in publications and at various events.

CHAPTER 5

FIRST ENDEAVOURS ON BEHALF OF THE BELOVED CAUSE

Shortly after becoming a Bahá'í, Hermann Grossmann wrote an enthusiastic letter to 'Abdu'l-Bahá in Haifa, to which he received the following highly significant Tablet in Persian, together with an English translation provided by 'Abdu'l-Bahá's secretary:

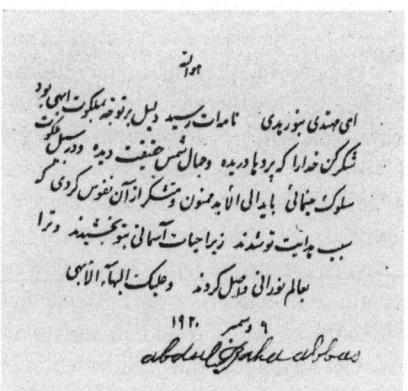

He is God.
O thou who hast been guided by the light of divine guidance:
Thy letter hath been received. It indicated that thou hast turned thy face toward the Abhá Kingdom. Yield thee thanks unto God that thou hast been enabled to rend the veils asunder, to gaze on the beauty of the Sun of Reality, and to walk in the path of the Kingdom. Thou shouldst be eternally obliged and thankful to those who were the cause of thy guidance, inasmuch as they conferred heavenly life upon thee and enabled thee to be admitted into this resplendent Kingdom.

Upon thee rest the Glory of the Most Glorious.
abdulBaha abbas Dec. 9, 1920[9]

Immediately after first encountering the Bahá'í Faith in 1920, Hermann Grossmann placed himself at the service of this new Revelation. He and his sister Elsa Maria sought ways to spread the Bahá'í teachings in Hamburg. As they were young and had many young friends, they mainly worked with other youth. They held regular firesides and soon experienced the joy of a young girl accepting the Faith and helping them to build up the community.

In a letter to the Bahá'ís in the United States written in August 1923, Hermann Grossmann describes the difficulties they faced in their work because the people, already impoverished as a result of the war, were now confronted with utter destitution and misery owing to hyperinflation.

> Until two months ago there were just separate little groups, meeting regularly in their homes. But now we have a general meeting for all, once a week, on Mondays. There is much to do ... The hearts of men are open, because they must endure much privation and many trials ... Although our circle is small, yet the friends are very active in spreading His Teachings. It is a great joy to us when letters or, better still, friends, from other cities come to us. We heartily beg therefore that when any of you come to Europe and to Germany you will not forget our little group. It gives us much strength and will make it easier for us to overcome the difficulties which every new day brings. There are many difficulties, especially in such a large city as Hamburg, because the friends must ride a long way to meetings and the fare is very expensive with our present resources. It is possible that the trams will soon cease running because there is no money to keep them going. Also the expenses for a hall and advertising and postage are so great that we can no longer hold public meetings in a large hall, and the teachers find it difficult, on account of the high fares, to go about with the Message. Then too, all the friends, owing to the difficulties of supplying their daily needs, must spend most of their time in earning the means of living and so can give but little time to spreading the Heavenly Teachings. But none of this robs us of courage and we are full of joy that in our city the Cause has begun to grow after being so long without apparent result.[10]

In the mid-1920s the revered and much-loved American Bahá'í teacher Martha Root paid a visit to northern Germany. She reported about the activities of the Bahá'ís in Berlin, Rostock, Warnemünde, Schwerin and Hamburg.[11] Martha Root had been the first to respond to 'Abdu'l-Bahá's call and spent twenty years travelling around the world under the most difficult of conditions. She talked to kings and queens, princes and princesses, presidents and ministers, reporters and professors, religious representatives and countless ordinary people. In his major work on early Bahá'í history *God Passes By* the Guardian gave her the title of 'Leading Ambassadress of His Faith and Pride of Bahá'í Teachers, whether men or women, in both the East and the West'.[12] In recognition of her invaluable services, he raised her posthumously to the rank of Hand of the Cause of God.

As an Esperantist, Martha Root addressed the Esperanto society in Hamburg, and she also reported about a large meeting at the home of the Grossmann family which was attended by Bahá'ís and people interested in the Faith. Music contributed to the festive atmosphere of the meeting, at which Martha Root gave a talk about the holy places in Palestine. The event was rounded off by the children performing a short play written by Adelbert Mühlschlegel, 'a wonderful Bahá'í poet from Stuttgart'. Martha Root praised the work done with the children by Anna, Elsa Maria and Hermann Grossmann. She mentioned that these three, in association with Friedrich Gerstner, published three magazines: *La Nova Tago* in Esperanto, a magazine for children, and another for youth. Hermann Grossmann was already beginning to start a Bahá'í archive. Most importantly, he recorded the history of the Bahá'í Faith in Hamburg from its very inception.[13]

While travelling in southern Germany, Hermann Grossmann made contact with the Bahá'ís there. In 1925 he met Dr Esslemont, who was recuperating from severe pleurisy at the home of Viktoria von Sigsfeld in the Black Forest.[14] John E. Esslemont had been summoned to Haifa by 'Abdu'l-Bahá, and had served both Him and later His grandson Shoghi Effendi with deep devotion. He wrote the standard work on the Bahá'í Faith *Bahá'u'lláh and the New Era*; it was the first comprehensive work about the new religion and has since been translated into countless languages. Dr Esslemont died that same year, 1925, in Haifa and was laid to rest in the Bahá'í cemetery at the foot of Mount Carmel. A few days after his death, the Guardian honoured him by appointing him a Hand of the Cause of God.

Hermann Grossmann reported on a very well-attended public talk on 29 October 1922 at which Wilhelm Herrigel from Stuttgart had spoken and had expressed great hopes for the Bahá'ís of Hamburg. Several families lent their support. They were subsequently joined by two ladies who had formerly belonged to the 'Bahá'í Association' established by Pastor Heydorn.

Wilhelm Heydorn was a minister in a working-class district of

Hamburg and a very troublesome figure for the church authorities. He had heard of the Bahá'í Faith and in 1917 had contacted Wilhelm Herrigel and the believers in Stuttgart, because he intended to establish a Bahá'í publishing house for the northern region of Germany in Hamburg. The founding of the publishing house was followed at the beginning of 1918 by the creation of a society which Heydorn named the 'Bahá'í-Vereinigung' (Bahá'í Association). From the outset, both of these institutions were merely a mouthpiece for Pastor Heydorn himself, who published not only writings about 'Bahaism' but also pamphlets directed against his church. The Stuttgart Bahá'ís, who were in close contact with 'Abdu'l-Bahá, told Heydorn in no uncertain terms that his actions were contrary to the spirit of the Bahá'í Faith, and the pastor – not wanting to submit to any authority or regulation – turned his attention to other interest groups. The society was dissolved in 1921, after its founder had taken the logical step by distancing himself from the Faith.[15] In 1926 he offered the Hamburg friends the documents relating to the Bahá'í-Vereinigung and the remaining copies of his publication about the Bahá'í Faith. The Hamburg community was pleased thus to become the 'successor' to the Bahá'í-Vereinigung and to take over from this non-Bahá'í publishing house the texts that gave a false impression of the Cause, thus preventing their further dissemination.[16]

In the early 1920s, regular meetings and talks took place in Hamburg at the home of a Bahá'í family and in a meeting place belonging to the Protestant church. They were frequently attended by more than fifteen people. The Bahá'ís were able to develop valuable relations with the Theosophical Society. This society included people who were open-minded with regard to all religions. They tried to unite the fundamental esoteric and mystic truths of all religions in order to attain their own salvation. One of the trends popular at the time was spiritism. Some of the Bahá'ís occasionally took part in spiritualistic meetings and, as Hermann Grossmann lamented in a letter to Shoghi Effendi in 1923, 'believed the words of the medium more than the words of His Divine Holiness'.[17] Again and again he had to remind the friends of 'Abdu'l-Bahá's words on this matter. Even at this early stage, he fought like a lion to preserve the purity of the Faith. Every four weeks he made a weekend trip to visit the friends in Mecklenburg – in Schwerin, Rostock and Warnemünde – in order to speak at meetings. Up to sixty people came to his public talks and the newspapers reported on the Bahá'í Movement.

Every nineteen days the Hamburg group sent out a circular containing the words of Bahá'u'lláh and 'Abdu'l-Bahá. It reached 42 groups in Germany and other German-speaking countries. As a contributor to the *Bahá'í World* yearbook published by the Bahá'ís in North America, Hermann Grossmann wrote reports about the work of the Bahá'ís in Germany and also published several essays.

When 'Abdu'l-Bahá had visited Stuttgart and Esslingen in 1913, He was constantly surrounded by numerous children and, inspired by this example, the Bahá'ís attached great importance to the teaching of children. In the early 1920s several children's groups were set up. The children met regularly and were taught by adult Bahá'ís. The groups were known as the 'Little Rose Garden', 'Garden of Cheerfulness' or 'Little Garden of Light'. On 3 February 1924 the Little Rose Garden called 'Children of the Sun' ('Sonnenkinder') was established in Wandsbek.

From March 1924 until the end of 1928, a children's magazine entitled *Das Rosengärtlein* (The Little Rose Garden) was published at irregular intervals in Hamburg. It was edited by Hermann and Anna Grossmann, and had a circulation of 500 copies. The editor's announcement stated, 'It is to children that the new Kingdom of Love and Light belongs! Everywhere we must dedicate our best efforts and our sincerest love to our work with children.'[18]

In a total of twenty issues, children could read stories about 'Abdu'l-Bahá, poems and moral tales, in addition to taking part in children's classes. A very popular feature of the magazine was the 'Letters to the Editor', in which children could write to the editor of *Das Rosengärtlein*, 'Uncle Hermann', and make contact with one another.

Das Rosengärtlein.

Eine Neunteljahrsschrift für die Baháíjugend und ihre Freunde.

Jahrgang 1. Nr. 1.
1. Bahá (Herrlichkeit) 80.
21. März 1924.

Der wahre Bahái liebt die Kinder, weil Jesus sagt, daß das Himmelreich ihr ist. Ein aufrichtiges reines Herz ist Gott nahe - ein Kind hat keinen weltlichen Ehrgeiz.
('Abdu'l-Bahá. London Talks, S. 52).

The first issue was introduced by a song, 'Das Rosengärtleinlied', by Elsa Maria and Hermann Grossmann set to the tune of 'Joseph, lieber Joseph mein':

Rosengärtleinlied

Rosen blühn in dem Gärtlein,
Tausend süße Blümelein.
Horch des Herren Ruf erschalln
Voll Wohlgefalln:
Erwacht, erwacht ihr Schläfer mein!
Alle die Köpfchen zart und fein,
    ja zart und fein
Erblühn zum Licht,
Das mit leuchtendem Morgenschein
Die Nacht durchbricht.
Rosen! Rosen! Süßer Duft
Erfüllet leicht die linde Luft.
In der Kinder Lockengold,
    ja Lockengold
Voll Fröhlichkeit
Spielt der Sonne Strahl so hold
In Ewigkeit.

Aus den Kehlchen leis hervor
Klingt ein wunderfeiner Chor,
Frühlingsfeines Singen schwebt
Vom Licht belebt
Vieltausendfach zu Gott empor.
Sei gesegnet Morgenstund,
    ja Morgenstund
Weil Nacht entwich!
Dessen jauchzet der Blumen Mund
Wir preisen Dich!
Rosen! Rosen! Süßer Duft
Erfüllet leicht die linde Luft.
In der Kinder Lockengold,
    ja Lockengold
Voll Fröhlichkeit
Spielt der Sonne Strahl so hold
In Ewigkeit.

Little Rose Garden Song

Roses in the garden bloom,
Filling the world with sweet perfume,
Hear the calling of the Lord
With one accord:
Arise, arise now from your gloom!
Little heads so tender and fine,
    Yes, tender and fine,

FIRST ENDEAVOURS ON BEHALF OF THE BELOVED CAUSE

Blossom in the light
That in the morning sunshine
Breaks the night.
Roses! Roses! Your scent so fair
Lightly fills the balmy air.
How the children's locks of gold,
    Yes, locks of gold,
With felicity
The sun doth in his rays enfold
To all eternity.

Softly from the chalice ring
Voices sweet as the children sing.
Vernal tones many thousand-fold,
In light untold,
To God their way do wing.
Blessed be the morning hour
    Yes, morning hour
For night doth flee!
Thus rejoiceth many a flower
In praise of Thee!
Roses! Roses! Your scent so fair
Lightly fills the balmy air.
How the children's locks of gold,
    Yes, locks of gold,
With felicity
The sun doth in his rays enfold
To all eternity.

In another issue we can read Hermann Grossmann's poem 'Bitte' (Request), written in 1924:

Hab ein Herz voll Licht und Sonne,
Augen hell voll Freudigkeit,
Dass sich wahres Glück und Wonne
Wie ein Leuchten um euch breit.

Gottes Engel sollt ihr werden,
Gebt Ihm euer Herz zu eigen.
Ihm zu dienen heißt, auf Erden
Allen Menschen Liebe zeigen.

Lieben heißt zu allen Zeiten
Wachen um den Armen, Kranken
Freudig Hilfe zu bereiten,
Und Sein Segen wird euch danken.

HERMANN GROSSMANN

Euer Vorsatz sei am Morgen,
Stets zu helfen und zu lieben,
Und am Abend sollt ihr denken,
Ob ihr Ihm auch treu geblieben.

Und ihr werdet täglich besser
Lernen Gottes Weg zu wandeln
Und als Heilige hienieden
Treu nach Seinem Willen wandeln.

Fill your heart with love and sunlight,
Eyes that shine with cheer unbound,
That bright joy and true delight
May embrace you all around.

Angels of God you all shall be,
Lift up your hearts to Him above.
For to serve Him means to see
That you treat all mankind with love.

Love means always being there
To provide for those in need,
Joyfully to give and care,
As thanks His blessing for your deed.

Let it be your morn's desire
Constantly to love and serve,
And when at evening you retire,
Consider whether you did not swerve.

Thus will you learn from day to day
Along the path of God to stroll,
As holy ones on earth to stay
And act with His Will as your goal.

The second issue contains a fairy-tale by Hermann Grossmann:

The House without Windows

Once upon a time, there was a big city where many people lived. They were all very rich and thought themselves cleverer than all other people. One day, the most highly respected of them came together and said, 'Let us build a big house to show the people how rich and clever we are.' So they did, and then they took all their treasures to make it a very splendid house indeed. Inside, they hung the most magnificent paintings and lined the halls with huge mirrors. When they had finished and were about to hold the opening ceremony, they suddenly realized that they had forgotten the windows. It was too dark inside, because no sunshine could enter the building.

'We will have to provide light,' said the cleverest of the people in the city, 'so that we can see.' But they could not agree on what kind of light they should use and what light fittings there should be. Many people came and recommended their own lighting, so that in the end everyone was carrying his own light and using it to try and illuminate the paintings and mirrors in the halls. But because there were so many little lights, each person was only able to see what was immediately around him. Eventually, the people got used to this and thought the sun no longer existed, because it did not shine into the house. Each person called his own light 'the sun'.

But one day a spark from one of the lights set fire to the roof and it went up in flames. Suddenly, the people saw the sun again and noticed the wonderful paintings on the walls and their reflection in the mirrors. 'Indeed', they all said, 'we wanted to show off with the magnificence of our treasures, but their splendour was hidden because the sun did not shine on them. We thought we were more clever than other people, but we forgot to construct windows in our house for the sun to fill the rooms with light.'

And they thanked God that he had let them see the sun again; they stopped showing off about their cleverness and remembered that their riches were only valuable by virtue of the sunshine.

* * *

The annual report of the Hamburg group for the Bahá'í fiscal year 1928/29 includes activities in places all around the city. Many regular meetings took place, attended by a total of nearly 1,000 people. A Spiritual Assembly had also been elected by this time. It issued a newsletter entitled *Mitteilungen der Bahá'í-Bewegung Hamburg* (News of the Hamburg Bahá'í Movement), which was distributed to 90 addresses in Hamburg. Hundreds of information leaflets were produced, as well as publications presenting Bahá'í views on various topics such as the transmigration of souls, reincarnation and resurrection. Hermann Grossmann spoke at a large number of public events. His articles appeared in local papers such as the *Nützliche Blätter*, *Hamburger 8 Uhr Abendblatt*, *Wandsbeker Bote* and *Hamburgischer Correspondent*. There were also publications in Esperanto. The Bahá'ís in Hamburg made efforts to reach the German-speaking friends in the Balkans and the rest of Europe. The Hamburg community also welcomed ten friends from elsewhere.[19] One of these was once again Martha Root. She and Dr Grossmann visited Professor Strohtmann, an orientalist at Hamburg University.[20]

In 1929 Hermann Grossmann reported that in Wandsbek a reading room had been opened in connection with a lending library containing more than 300 books, and an archive. Next to it was also a room for the accommodation of travel teachers, 'thus realizing the idea of a special Bahá'í Centre'.[21]

Bahá'ís lived scattered throughout northern Germany and the friends tried actively to contact one another and to cultivate friendships. Mrs Schwedler and Emil Jörn worked for the Cause in Warnemünde, mother and daughter Walcker in Rostock, the Klitzing family in Schwerin and the family of Kurt Döring in Gera.

In Warnemünde Emil Jörn, who was a teacher, established a school for disabled children on behalf of the education authority. He was given a free hand, and so he set up a model school on the basis of Bahá'í principles. The school had 13 pupils, boys and girls. In a letter to the Guardian, Hermann Grossmann described the rooms as bright, decorated with flowers, pictures, 'white painted furniture, every pupil having his own table and chair. Among the pictures on the walls is one of Jesus Christ and another of our beloved Master ... Four weeks ago I was in Warnemünde visiting this school and was surprised at the good results Mr Jörn has obtained with these children. I gave them a lecture [sic] ... They chanted Bahá'í songs and recited Bahá'í verses and I must say that I was never touched more by any song ... The success of his [Mr Jörn's] efforts is due especially to the idea of parallellysing [sic] material and spiritual training ... The superior authorities are evidently contented with the work of Mr Jörn and therefore, though in general they do not like the Cause they do not prevent him in his manner of teaching.'[22]

In the year 1922 there were Assemblies in Stuttgart, Esslingen, Heilbronn, Zuffenhausen, Göppingen, Fellbach, Karlsruhe, Leipzig, Gera and Vienna. In September of that year the Assemblies held elections on a national level for the first time. They sent 57 delegates to the Convention in Stuttgart, and in turn these delegates recommended 23 individuals from among them, the delegates then voted for nine Assembly members in a secret election. At Riḍván 1923 this Assembly was confirmed by Shoghi Effendi; it was one of the first National Spiritual Assemblies in the world.[23] Thus, an extremely important institution for Germany had been created. It was the point of contact for the Guardian and gave the friends the necessary backing and support that they would need later during the difficult period of the Faith's prohibition under the National Socialist regime. In 1924 the German Bahá'ís elected a new Assembly, of which Hermann Grossmann was a member, as he was

FIRST ENDEAVOURS ON BEHALF OF THE BELOVED CAUSE

also of the next Assembly, elected in 1926. No election took place in 1925. He remained a member of the National Spiritual Assembly until August 1936, when ill-health forced him to resign.

In addition to the work of the National Spiritual Assembly, there was a 'World Fellowship Organization' which also had a German branch called the 'World Fellowship German Branch, German National Education Committee'. This brought together the committees for children's education, Esperanto, the advancement of women and the youth association. The work of these committees was directed by Anna Köstlin from Esslingen, Annemarie Schweizer from Zuffenhausen, and Hermann and Anna Grossmann. In the spring of 1926 Shoghi Effendi thought it timely to place these committees under the authority of the National Spiritual Assembly. Accordingly, the Assembly replaced the German branch of 'World Fellowship' with a national committee headed by Dr Grossmann.[24]

During the 1920s and in the early 1930s the character of the Bahá'í community and its view of itself changed from one of an idealistic and often enthusiastic spiritual movement with a diffuse set of ideas that was still embedded in the prevalent social traditions, to that of a religious community with a clear identity, its members regarding themselves as the 'people of the new Covenant' that God had entered into with humanity through Bahá'u'lláh. There were those who had originally been attracted to the Faith as something exotic. They were fascinated by the strange-sounding names. Now, however, they were confronted with requirements that shocked them and required sacrifices that they were not prepared to make. Consequently, they left the Cause of Bahá'u'lláh. This self-purifying process brought some ostensible set-backs for the community, with all the work falling to the hands of just a few dedicated believers. In association with the Guardian, Shoghi Effendi, they developed the administrative order of the community in Germany. They also evolved 'a clear understanding, based on the secure foundations of historical and religious scholarship, of the Covenant of Bahá'u'lláh with mankind,' as Anna Grossmann described it in her reminiscences concerning this period – a concept that is self-evident for us today.

> Through the publication of many new books and translations, a number of canonical texts – the words of the Báb, Bahá'u'lláh, 'Abdu'l-Bahá and Shoghi Effendi – were spread around the world. These eventually exceeded by far all the original texts revealed by the Founders of all the

great religions of the past taken together. The themes from the abundance of our Teachings that most moved Hermann Grossmann were Bahá'u'lláh's demands for the unity of religion and science and for unity in diversity. These two topics also set the pattern for his work in teaching the younger generation. With endless perseverance over a period of decades, he built up a collection of materials having in mind a future Bahá'í university, or the 'Institute of Religion and Science' that had been approved by Shoghi Effendi in the Five Year Plan. He consistently used these materials as the basis for his publications. The Bahá'ís only gradually became aware during those years that the Will and Testament of 'Abdu'l-Bahá, who had left the visible world in 1921, is the charter of an important administrative order for the Bahá'í world community. This administrative order is something quite new, a synthesis of monarchy, aristocracy, democracy and theocracy, as the Guardian explained it to us. Finally, it is the beginning, the embryo and model, of a completely new future world order, of which the chaotic human race is in need, just as the Jews fleeing Egypt long ago were in need of their many new, God-given laws, in order to become a 'chosen people'.[25]

Dr Hermann Grossmann.

CHAPTER 6

ESPERANTO

Towards the end of the 19th century, the Polish physician Dr Ludwig L. Zamenhof created the Esperanto language. He intended it to be easy for everybody to learn as a second language, so that it could function as a means for international communication. In this way, he hoped to overcome the language barriers that divided the peoples of the world. Within just a few years he found many adherents in Eastern Europe and soon afterwards in Western European countries too.

'Abdu'l-Bahá repeatedly emphasized how important it was to introduce an international auxiliary language, and the rapid spread of Esperanto raised justifiably high hopes. International Esperanto Congresses took place every year in different countries and cities, bringing together Esperantists from all over the world. The Bahá'ís also regularly found an open-minded audience at these meetings. At the beginning of the 1920s, a young teacher called Friedrich Gerstner moved to Hamburg. He was a Bahá'í and had followed 'Abdu'l-Bahá's advice and learned Esperanto. Friedrich Gerstner passed on his knowledge of Esperanto to the Hamburg friends. Enthusiastic and hopeful cooperation with the Esperantists began throughout the world.

Martha Root too was an active Esperantist. In her worldwide travels to teach the Bahá'í Faith she was much assisted by the friendship of the Esperantists. Lidia Zamenhof, the youngest daughter of Dr Zamenhof, was guided into the Faith by Martha Root. Lidia Zamenhof was extremely prominent in the Esperanto movement, not only as a teacher of the language but also as a result of her many articles published in Esperanto magazines. She also translated the novel *Quo Vadis* and a small number of novellas by Henryk Sienkiewicz into Esperanto. After becoming a believer, she was probably the most important personality among the Bahá'í Esperantists. She was a mainstay of activities at the Esperanto Congresses. In her talks, and also in some of the essays she wrote, she presented the Revelation of Bahá'u'lláh in an open, eloquent and powerful manner. In addition, she provided many contributions to the Bahá'í magazine *La Nova Tago* (The New Day), a quarterly Bahá'í magazine written entirely in Esperanto, and translated Dr Esslemont's book *Bahá'u'lláh and the New Era*, published in 1930, and 'Abdu'l-Bahá's *Paris Talks*, published in 1932. Unfortunately, she did not manage to complete the translations of Bahá'u'lláh's Kitáb-i-Íqán and *Some Answered Questions* by 'Abdu'l-Bahá, as well as some other shorter works that she had started.

Dr Esslemont corresponded worldwide in Esperanto, of which he had excellent mastery. He published his treatise *What is the Bahá'í Movement?* for the Universal Esperanto Congress in Geneva in 1925.

Lidia Zamenhof was a friend of Elsa Maria Grossmann, and at the Guardian's recommendation the two women corresponded with each other frequently until the National Socialists put an end to the correspondence. The daughter of Dr Zamenhof died in the Treblinka concentration camp in Poland at the hands of the SS, the brutal henchmen of the National Socialist regime.[26]

In 1925 Friedrich Gerstner and Hermann Grossmann established the above-mentioned Esperanto magazine *La Nova Tago*. The Guardian was very pleased with the publication of this international magazine and in 1926 he translated extracts from 'Abdu'l-Bahá's *The Secret of Divine Civilization* into English especially so that they could be further translated into Esperanto and published in *La Nova Tago*. The content of *La Nova Tago* consisted primarily of translations of Bahá'í texts – most of them from the words of 'Abdu'l-Bahá – and articles about specific Bahá'í themes and teachings, as well as news about Bahá'í activities around the world. This made it possible to reach Esperantists throughout the globe and introduce them to the Faith. At the same time, the magazine served as a means of communication and information between the believers in the east and the west. In a letter dated 26 October 1925, Shoghi Effendi encouraged the editors in their efforts to publish 'the one medium of international Bahá'í intercourse' and emphasized that for this purpose it was essential 'to devise ways and means for the establishment and maintenance of regular and frequent communications with the various Bahá'í National Spiritual Assemblies, that in time this promising Magazine may faithfully portray with force and beauty the diverse achievements of Bahá'í communities throughout the world'.[27]

La Nova Tago appeared from June 1925 until March 1936, that is until the prohibition of Esperanto activities by the National Socialists, the Bahá'ís sacrificing a great deal of time and financial resources in order to ensure its publication. The magazine's first editor-in-chief, up to the end of the third year of publication, was Friedrich Gerstner, and the last – from issue vol. X, no. 1 – was Adolf Lorey. In between, from issue vol. IV, no. 1 (March 1928) until issue vol. IX, no. 4 (March 1934), the editor-in-chief is cited as being Hermann Grossmann. Thus, for a period of seven years – until the burden of other national Bahá'í work became too heavy – the fate of the first international Bahá'í magazine, for which the Guardian had cherished so many hopes, was in the hands of Dr Grossmann. Shoghi Effendi repeatedly urged the German Bahá'í Esperantists to continue their work and to carry on publishing the magazine that was of such great importance. In 1934, publication had to be discontinued 'owing to lack of time and private resources', as stated in a report to the 1935 National Convention. When *La Nova Tago* started to appear again in 1935 after a year's interruption, the report of the National Spiritual Assembly for 1935/36 pointed out that, in reviving the magazine, 'the National Spiritual Assembly had responded to the repeated, urgent wishes of the Guardian, who attaches great significance to this Bahá'í magazine in the universal auxiliary language, Esperanto'.[28] In a letter to Adolf Lorey written in August 1935, the Guardian expressed the hope that *La Nova Tago* would ' ... gradually develop into a leading Esperanto magazine and thus into an effective means for the world-wide dissemination of the Teachings in Esperantist circles'.

Dr Grossmann wrote no fewer than 18 major essays published in *La Nova Tago*, some in serial form. Thus, an extensive article of his appeared in at least every second edition out of a total of ten volumes and forty issues. The topics touched upon were extremely diverse, covering introductions to the Bahá'í Faith, peace, the relationship between religion and science, the concept of God and knowledge of Him, as well as other important religious questions and social issues, interpretations of the Bible, Bahá'í martyrs in Persia, and finally a travel report. Hermann Grossmann also did most of the editorial work, especially when he held the position of editor-in-chief.

The first issues of *La Nova Tago* were printed by the company that produced the major Esperanto journal *Heraldo de Esperanto* in Horrem, near Cologne. As of issue vol. II, no. 3 it was printed in Wandsbek

Susanna Mongsfeld, beloved 'Coca', grandmother of Hermann Grossmann

Johanna and Curt Grossmann, Hermann Grossmann's parents, in 1935

Elsa Maria Grossmann with her brother Hermann, in Argentina

Hermann Grossmann, a soldier in World War I, 1918

The young Hermann Grossmann in Hamburg, 1924

Anna and Hermann Grossmann, wedding photograph, 1924

Martha Root visiting Anna and Hermann Grossmann in February 1927. Left to right: Anna Grossmann, Martha Root, Hermann Grossmann, Elspeth Klitzing from Schwerin

At Wandsbek, about 1928. Left to right: unidentified, Doris Lohse, Elsa Maria Grossmann, Clara Sieg, Anna Grossmann, Hermann Grossmann

Bahá'ís of northern Germany meeting in Wandsbek, 7-8 December 1929. Anna and Hermann Grossmann are 5th and 7th from right

Dr Youness Khan (Afroukhteh) and Dr Hermann Grossmann (front row, 4th and 5th from left) visiting the friends in Berlin, December 1929

Dr Youness Khan (3rd from left) visiting the Grossmann family in Wandsbek

and from this issue onwards the publishing details mention the 'Bahaa Esperanto-Eldonejo', a Bahá'í Esperanto publishing company that published several small volumes about the Faith in Esperanto in the years that followed. These included Hermann Grossmann's *Historio, instruoj kaj valoro de Baha'i-Movado* (History, teachings and significance of the Bahá'í Movement) and *La esenco de l'Bahaismo* (The essence of the Bahá'í Faith). Other works issued by this publishing house were the Persian section of Bahá'u'lláh's Hidden Words, as translated by Lotfullah Hakim and Dr Esslemont, the book *Bahá'u'lláh and the New Era* by Dr Esslemont, and 'Abdu'l-Bahá's *Paris Talks* – the latter two works having been translated by Lidia Zamenhof.

Thus, *La Nova Tago* expanded through the addition of this small publishing house, creating a great deal of work, most of which fell upon the shoulders of Hermann Grossmann. The magazine and the publishing house moved, along with the Grossmann family, to Weinheim and later, in June 1933, to Neckargemünd. In 1935 Dr Grossmann's role as editor was taken over by Adolf Lorey, but the headquarters of the publishing house and *La Nova Tago* remained in Neckargemünd. Adolf Lorey was a Bahá'í and a devoted Esperantist. At Hermann Grossmann's request, he had taken a position as a bookkeeper at his company in Waldmichelbach. During this period, Martha Root, Lidia Zamenhof, Professor Auguste Forel and Professor Christaller were regular contributors to *La Nova Tago*.

Hermann and Anna Grossmann also gave Esperanto classes for children. The 'Children of the Sun' from Wandsbek reported in their magazine *The Little Rose Garden* in 1926 that they had regular Esperanto lessons. The international auxiliary language was also taught in other children's groups. A little girl called Elisabeth from the 'Little Garden of the Future' in Leipzig wrote a letter in Esperanto that was published in *The Little Rose Garden*.

In association with Dr Mühlschlegel, Hermann Grossmann organized a special Bahá'í event to be held at the Universal Esperanto Congress in Cologne in August 1933.

In the late summer of 1936 the National Socialist government dissolved all Esperanto societies in Germany and prohibited the promotion or teaching of the language. For this reason, the National Spiritual Assembly decided that publication of *La Nova Tago* should cease, although they expressed the hope 'that its continuation might be possible for friends in other countries'. According to a letter to Adolf

Lorey from the 'Spiritual Working Group of the Bahá'ís in Stuttgart', dated 6 December 1936, the Guardian himself had stated that it was 'advisable to stop publishing this magazine for the time being'. His secretary added on his behalf that, 'the Guardian hopes, however, that conditions will sooner or later permit the friends to restart publication of this magazine, whose importance as a means of teaching in Esperanto circles cannot be overestimated'.[29]

After the end of the war and the fall of the National Socialist regime, the few Bahá'ís in Germany were faced with the task of quickly trying to draw the attention of the despairing people to the message of Bahá'u'lláh. Literature was urgently required, but even this was an almost insuperable task in the war-ravaged country, and it was equally urgent to start the process of rebuilding the communities. It is therefore not surprising that the work connected with Esperanto never fully recovered from the blow dealt to it by the National Socialists. Nevertheless, some friends did soon seek to restart this work, and the National Spiritual Assembly appointed an Esperanto Committee, which tried to revive *La Nova Tago*. As early as May 1946, Roan Orloff, one of the subsequent founders of the Bahaa Esperanto-Ligo, expressed her enthusiasm over the imminent revival of *La Nova Tago* in a letter to Hermann Grossmann on behalf of the World Language Committee of the United States and Canada. However, circumstances made this impossible. In the spring of 1948, Adolf Lorey requested permission from the American military government in Darmstadt to restart publication – but in vain. Only individual permits were issued for the printing of leaflets and small booklets, e.g. for the first German Esperanto Congress in Munich in 1948. On 'Zamenhof Day', 15 December of the same year, to mark the occasion of the 89th birthday of Dr Ludwig Zamenhof, Hermann Grossmann spoke to the Esperanto Group in Heidelberg on 'The Spirit of Esperanto'.

In addition to the attempt to restart publication of *La Nova Tago*, there were also regular Bahá'í activities at the Esperanto World Congresses. One such event took place in Mainz in 1958, where the 'Esperanto-sekcio de la Nacia Spirita Konsilan-taro de Bahaoj' – the Esperanto section of the National Spiritual Assembly of the Bahá'ís in Germany – held a meeting on the subject: 'The Bahá'í Faith. Why do we need it?' Attempts to establish an international society of Bahá'í Esperantists, such as that initiated by Waldemar von der Ley in connection with the Esperanto World Congress in Brussels in 1960, and that of Adelbert

Mühlschlegel at the Budapest Congress in 1966, unfortunately met with no success. Much later, in 1973, the international Bahaa Esperanto-Ligo (Bahá'í Esperanto League) was founded, authorized by the Universal House of Justice.

CHAPTER 7

THE YEARS UP TO 1937

In 1930 Hermann and Anna Grossmann, along with their young daughter, moved to Weinheim an der Bergstraße, since the Wandsbek branch of the company had closed down. Hermann travelled every day by train to his work at the company headquarters in Waldmichelbach in the Odenwald.

Dr Grossmann was soon a well-known personality in the small town of Waldmichelbach. One day he happened to be travelling home in the company car. Not knowing this, the stationmaster made the train wait for the missing passenger until, after a while, he telephoned the company and asked where 'the doctor' was, since he had seen him arrive in the morning. 'The doctor' never drove home by car again without informing the stationmaster.

The Grossmanns had left behind a strong community in Hamburg, and they began their work afresh in their new hometown. They soon came across souls who were open to the Faith in both Weinheim and Heidelberg, and so the groups started to grow.

Two years later, Hermann and Anna Grossmann fulfilled their wish to have a house of their own. They built it in the middle of a meadow, with a view over the valley and the woods in Neckargemünd near Heidelberg. Their home was to become a centre of hospitality and friendship, and a teaching centre for all their friends as well as the Bahá'ís. They moved into the still rather modest home in 1933. Dr Grossmann had drawn up the building plans himself. Later, two extensions became necessary, eventually making it quite large and spacious. As a result, during the Second World War it served as a refuge for members of Anna Grossmann's large family who had become refugees or whose homes had been destroyed by bombs. A chauffeur now brought Hermann Grossmann from Neckargemünd to his work in Waldmichelbach and back.

Their son Hartmut Hermann Harlan was born in Neckargemünd in

1933. He was given the name Harlan in memory of Harlan Ober, the believer through whom Hermann Grossmann had become acquainted with the teachings of Bahá'u'lláh.

The administrative boundaries of the Bahá'í community were still very wide at that time and did not coincide with the civic limits of the locality. Hence, the Grossmann family belonged to the Heidelberg group, which was able to elect a Local Spiritual Assembly at Riḍván in 1936.

The German Bahá'ís soon began to hold summer schools based on the American model. With their own hands they erected a residential centre for this purpose, a small house known as the 'Häusle' (Little House) in Esslingen near Stuttgart. It was officially opened during the National Convention in 1931. Friends from all over Germany met there on weekends and for week-long teaching events. The 'Häusle' became a very important centre, where the friends listened to talks, discussed burning questions and also enjoyed unforgettable evenings of fun together. Here they could experience a few days of release from the stress of everyday life and take time to appreciate nature, since the house was surrounded by a large garden and meadows. At the same time they could seek truth, deepen their knowledge of the teachings, and develop deep and sincere friendships with like-minded souls. Persian and American Bahá'ís who came to Esslingen provided important personal contacts extending beyond the national boundaries. People got to know and understand one another and found others who, despite differences of nationality, thought and acted like themselves and spoke the same Bahá'í 'language'.

A frequent guest was Mary Maxwell, who later became the wife of the Guardian. At his request, she spent the years 1935 to 1937, with a few interruptions, in Germany in order to support the teaching work there. During this time, she developed an almost perfect command of the German language. With her mother May Maxwell or her cousin Jeanne Bolles, she travelled around the country and, above all, never missed a summer school. Wearing the traditional regional costume, the 'Dirndl', the two young women raised the spirits of the Bahá'ís, and there was always much fun and laughter in their company.

A Munich newspaper light-heartedly observed:

> Two American women are visiting the beautiful and artistic German city of Munich. Seeing here the picturesque folk costume of the Bavarian mountain women they decide to let themselves be admired in it too. Hardly

having set foot on the streets in their new outfits, they were addressed by a gentleman – an American – and asked to pose for a photograph. He – the said gentleman – undoubtedly thought this photo one of the best of his holiday snapshots. From the way this gentleman mistreated the German language, the two young women recognized him immediately as a fellow countryman. A quick glance of agreement and a gracious nod of consent – and so it happened that an American man portrayed two American women in authentic Bavarian dirndls and presumably showed them off [as Bavarian girls] back home.[30]

The pioneering activities of German believers were constantly expanding, as shown in the 1930 edition of *The Bahá'í World*. They spread the Faith in Scandinavia, Austria and Bulgaria:

> The efforts of Dr Hermann Grossmann and of Herr [Adam] Benke have been greatly appreciated by the German believers ... A strong foundation for a future flourishing Bahá'í community has, for example, been laid by Herr Benke in the city of Sofia.[31]

A few years later Dr Grossmann was able to report that during his business trips to Czechoslovakia he had come into close contact with Vuk Echtner in Prague and the work of the Bahá'ís there.[32]

In his doctoral thesis submitted in 1922, Hermann Grossmann had already been able to include Bahá'í ideas concerning social problems. A year later, he gave expression to these thoughts in the booklet entitled *The Social Question and its Solution According to the Spirit of the Bahá'í Teachings*.[33] The social tensions that arose in the aftermath of the First World War had had serious repercussions in Germany: inflation had impoverished the mass of the people, whereas there were immensely wealthy individuals who had profited from the war. In Russia, Communism was attempting to realize the ancient and repeatedly shattered dream of social equality. Hermann Grossmann explained in his booklet that the idea of the equal distribution of the means of production among all was bound to fail. Total equality is impossible, as he showed with reference to the Writings of Bahá'u'lláh and 'Abdu'l-Bahá, and he attempted to 'indicate the short path directed by the Bahá'í teachings for the solution of today's burning social issue ... and [to show] that ... a change in conditions can only be achieved when people change ... Therefore, the Bahá'í Faith places the main emphasis – even concerning the solution of the social question – on the spiritual education of mankind.' This was the first publication by a Bahá'í in Germany that presented the position of the Faith on a specific issue.

It was followed in 1932 by the book *Am Morgen einer neuen Zeit* (At the Dawn of a New Age) with the subtitle 'Collapse or Rearrangement? A Cultural Diagnosis of the Exigencies of the Present Time', which was published by Strecker and Schröder in Stuttgart. Dr Eugen Schmidt stated in the foreword that the book offered a new spiritual orientation on the basis of the Bahá'í teachings. It was well received and enjoyed wide distribution but later fell victim to the book-burning campaigns of the Gestapo, the secret police in Hitler's Germany.

Hermann Grossmann tirelessly gave public talks in order to make the Faith known. He frequently visited Frankfurt am Main, Karlsruhe, Heilbronn, Göppingen, Esslingen, Friedberg, Mannheim, Bamberg, Würzburg, Weinheim and, of course, Heidelberg, and he also spoke in the northern German cities of Hamburg, Schwerin, Rostock, Warnemünde, Berlin and Leipzig.

In 1935, after Hermann Grossmann had informed Shoghi Effendi that he had translated Bahá'u'lláh's Seven Valleys and prepared the text for publication, the Guardian's secretary wrote to him on his behalf:

Dear Dr Grossmann,

... He wishes me to congratulate you most heartily for this great service you have been able to render the Cause, and which no doubt will serve to enrich the record of the manifold contributions you have, during the last few years, so brilliantly made towards the spread of the Faith throughout Germany. He is praying to Bahá'u'lláh that He may continue to guide and inspire you, and assist you in accomplishing still more outstanding works for the Cause in your country.

The Guardian added in his own hand,

Dear and valued co-worker:

I am so eager to learn that your health is fully restored, for I believe your services are a most valuable asset to the Faith you serve in these troublous days. I welcome your efficient and unrelaxing co-operation, in spite of the obstacles which face you, in so many fields of Bahá'í activity. I am confident that as a result of your strenuous endeavours the administrative institutions in your land will be further consolidated and extended and the cause of teaching receive an added impulse. Your true brother, Shoghi.[34]

In a letter to the friends in Switzerland in 1931, Hermann Grossmann praised the zeal and fresh vigour displayed by the Bahá'ís and stated that the Cause in Germany had evidently reached a new stage of development. He unceasingly reminded the friends, even in small gatherings, that it was upon their shoulders that the burden of erecting a new world order was laid. The Bahá'ís had not only recognized the problems of society; they could and should offer a solution in the form of the teachings of Bahá'u'lláh. There was as yet little literature in German for the Bahá'ís to refer to, and so Dr Grossmann, who was never tired of collecting and studying the Writings of Bahá'u'lláh, 'Abdu'l-Bahá and Shoghi Effendi, developed into an excellent teacher and speaker who had the ability to captivate his audience and awaken their deepest feelings and emotions. He once told his daughter, 'You have to speak in such a way that your audience lean forward in their chairs when you lean forward and lean back when you lean back. Then they are captivated by your words.' And he was truly successful in doing exactly that. The audience listened attentively for forty minutes. His talks were characterized by simplicity, clarity and logical thinking. He wanted everyone to be able to follow what he was saying and to understand the particular teaching of Bahá'u'lláh that he was trying to put across. He made a conscious effort to reach the less sophisticated sections of the population, those who had not had the benefit of secondary education. Such people sought simple and clear answers to their questions. Hermann Grossmann knew how to talk to them and answer their queries. However, he was also able to talk to professors and other intellectuals. There was probably no field of which he did not have well founded knowledge. His broad education and his excellent memory meant that he left no inquirer unsatisfied.

'Nevertheless, he developed the greatest spiritual strength in the more intimate atmosphere of his home and his study,' wrote René Steiner, a good friend of the family, 'for he was an exacting scholar who took a methodical approach to the teachings and systematically dealt with a great number of academic fields ... Some of us called Adelbert Mühlschlegel the mystic Hand of the Cause of God. Hermann Grossmann, on the other hand, was a lion, the faithful champion of the Faith, firm as a rock in his will and intention.'

Dr Grossmann always exerted himself to the utmost in the service of Bahá'u'lláh – and did so in addition to his stressful professional career. Inevitably, he was often utterly exhausted, and even when still young he suffered from health problems and breakdowns that repeatedly compelled him to interrupt his activities. He was very sensitive, and differences of opinion and disharmony among the friends caused him great distress.

He found relaxation in the company of his family. In 1935 his parents and his sister Elsa Maria moved from Hamburg to Neckargemünd and built their 'Little Red House' in the immediate vicinity. Thus, he had the closest members of his family around him and he experienced the joy of seeing his father coming ever nearer to the Bahá'í Cause. Only his brother Rudolf in Hamburg remained distant, not only in a geographical sense.

When his parents moved to Germany in 1910, Rudolf Grossmann was eighteen years old. He enrolled at the University of Marburg to study English, Romance and Germanic languages and literature, but then moved to Munich and subsequently to Leipzig to attend university. There, he was awarded a doctorate for his thesis on a theme concerning Spanish literary history. Like his brother and sister, he considered Argentina as his homeland and so it is not surprising that he chose to work first on the academic staff and later (from 1926) as the Director of the Institute for Ibero-American Research in Hamburg, where he specialized in Latin American literature. The Institute was integrated into the newly founded University of Hamburg in 1919. Rudolf Grossmann qualified as a university lecturer on the basis of a post-doctoral thesis in 1924 and was then appointed associate professor before being appointed a tenured professor in 1946. In 1960 he was granted emeritus status. Like all the children of the Grossmann family, he was talented in the arts; this was evident in his research and teaching activities. He was fascinated by culture, in particular the literary history of Spain and South America. His publications made him famous throughout the Spanish-speaking world. Notable among his countless works are the following: the *Dictionary of the Spanish and German Languages*, known as the 'Slabý-Grossmann', many editions of which have been published; the summary of his life's work, *History and Problems of Latin American Literature* and *Poems of the Spaniards*, as well as *Spanish Poems from Eight Centuries*, which includes his wonderful renderings of the poems into German. Rudolf Grossmann was much appreciated by his students and colleagues for his calm and friendly manner, and for his typically South American warm-heartedness. He was a mediator between the two cultures.[35]

Hermann Grossmann found relaxation working in his garden.

He drew up plans, selected plants and built a rockery that flowered constantly throughout the summer. He took responsibility for the flower garden, while his wife Anna looked after the vegetable garden. The latter provided the family with fresh fruit and vegetables and was practically a necessity, because disputes in the firm in which the Grossmanns were shareholders led to a significant decline in the family's financial fortunes. During the war and especially during the years of famine in the post-war period, Anna Grossmann's garden was the main source of food for the family and she often worked until she was physically exhausted, with only a little assistance from a gardener employed on an hourly basis.

In the evenings, whenever time permitted, Hermann Grossmann would sit in an armchair, his children perched on the sides, and tell serial stories that he invented as he went along. The nicest story was that of Dwarf Flowerpot, who was walking along a street one day when a careless woman dropped a flowerpot on his head. The flowerpot stuck so tightly that from then on he had constantly to wear it on his head. Every evening Dwarf Flowerpot experienced a new adventure, to which we children always looked forward to with great anticipation.

He also frequently made up nonsense rhymes, which sometimes had an unexpected moral at the end, such as the poem about the double-shoe-sole-chewing rhinoceros ('*doppelsohlenkauendes Nashorn*', a pun on the German word for sodium bicarbonate, '*doppelkohlensaures Natron*'):

Ein Nashorn, das im Urwald war,
Vermutete recht sehr Gefahr,
Da es am oberen Kongostrand
Zwei gut geputzte Stiefel fand.

Doch war es sichtlich ausgesöhnt,
Als es sich an den Glanz gewöhnt,
Und dachte, ob nicht so ein Schuh
Sich auch zum Fressen eignen tu.

So war er wohlgepflegt und rundlich,
Denn in der Tat auch ziemlich mundlich,
Und was ein rechtes Nashorn ist,
Schnell gutes Leder runterfrisst.

Nun war in dem besondren Fall
Das Bodenmaterial fatal,
Denn Gummi hält sich ganz enorm,
Zumal in Doppelsohlenform.

THE YEARS UP TO 1937

Nun kaut das Tier und kaut und kaut
Bis andern Tags der Morgen graut,
Und in des dritten Tages Schein
Fings einer als Reklame ein.

Sei achtsam, dass nicht mit der Zeit
Auch deine Ahnungslosigkeit
Wie es für dieses Tier hier gilt,
Benutzt wird als Reklameschild.

* * *

A jungle-born rhinoceros
Thought it seemed rather dangerous
When on the upper Congo shore
A pair of polished boots he saw.

But soon he clearly felt quite fine
Once grown accustomed to the shine,
And wondered if this leather shoe
Might be something good to chew.

For round he was, and quite well-fed,
His mouth filled most of his great head,
And doing as a rhino will
He quickly gobbled up his fill.

But now in this particular case
He had some problems with the base,
For rubber really is quite coarse
Especially when reinforced.

He chewed and chewed it all night long
Until the dawn birds sang their song,
Then next day he was caught and sent
For use in an advertisement.

So be prudent, lest one day
You have a similar price to pay,
When finding something appetizing
You end up used in advertising.

These are surely the happiest memories of his children, who otherwise only too often had to vie for the attention of their parents in view of their innumerable activities. This was a fate they probably shared with many other children of parents who were active Bahá'ís.

CHAPTER 8

PILGRIMAGE TO HAIFA

A special highlight in Hermann Grossmann's life was his pilgrimage to Haifa in 1937. He stayed in the Holy Land, along with his wife Anna, sister Elsa Maria and daughter Susanne from 29 March to 20 April.

An Italian ship took them from Trieste to Haifa, a journey that lasted five days. Elsa Maria Grossmann described the first day after their arrival as follows:

> At lunch-time Shoghi Effendi came to the Pilgrim House. Our hearts now started pounding, since it was the fulfilment of our longing when he suddenly stood before us. I think we were very quiet for a long time. So many impressions rushed upon us and we were deeply moved, so that it took us a while to compose ourselves. But our Guardian was very understanding and demonstrated his love and kindness. The longer one is permitted to remain in the presence of Shoghi Effendi, the more intensely one senses the calm with which he fills his surroundings, the spiritual power that emanates from him. To sit opposite him at the table, to see his clear-cut features and feel the penetrating depth of his eyes is – I felt – to step into another world, a world in which we realize that it alone is spiritual reality and everything else is insignificant. It is a world in which matter is not eliminated but in which spirit has overcome matter. And in this world one remains in his presence, whether his conversation, through which he is teaching us, is concerned with the most difficult and most spiritual problems or is about the down-to-earth questions and issues of everyday life ...

'On the evening of this first day,' Elsa Maria Grossmann continues,

> Shoghi Effendi again delighted us with his presence in the Pilgrim House, this time in the company of his young wife. Since her extended stay among the Bahá'ís in Germany, Rúḥíyyih Khánum – Mary Maxwell – was like a close friend, and while working there she had, in particular, succeeded in penetrating the German mentality ... When we congratulated the Guardian and Rúḥíyyih Khánum on their marriage [on 24 March] Shoghi Effendi

said that he had wished to unite East and West through his marriage and that he hoped that through Rúḥíyyih Khánum the bond with the German Bahá'ís would grow especially strong, because she could speak German and was acquainted with Germany. He then asked whether we believed that the German friends would be pleased to hear this news. However, I do not think our assurances could have intensified much more the radiant smile on his face. We were the first pilgrims to be permitted to take such a close and personal part in this event and we felt a deep sense of gratitude that the Guardian had allowed us to undertake our pilgrimage to the holy places at this particular time.

The pilgrims spent several days in intensive conversations with Shoghi Effendi, primarily concerning the Bahá'í Administrative Order. In 1937, the friends in Europe were mostly unaware that this is the core and the model for the World Order of Bahá'u'lláh. The Guardian described teaching the Cause as the inner kernel and the Administrative Order as the outer shell of the seed, which is not rigid but constantly developing. It is a bulwark for the Faith and is intended to protect the friends against attacks from their enemies. He instructed the pilgrims to develop their fellow believers' understanding of these issues through talks and lectures.

The following paragraph paraphrases his words in personal notes that Anna and Elsa Maria Grossmann made during table talks:

> Concerning the significance of the Revelation of Bahá'u'lláh, the Guardian said that His advent marked the culmination of a developmental cycle on our planet. There is no higher stage of development than unity. It is conceivable – and Shoghi Effendi expressly pointed out that this was a personal opinion – that a later Manifestation, coming some 500,000 years hence, might bring about the unity of several planets. Since one of the fundamental principles of our Faith is progressive revelation, we must accept the possibility of an even greater divine revelation. Under the shadow of Bahá'u'lláh, however, a new Divine Messenger with the power to change His laws will not appear before a minimum of one thousand years has elapsed. Within the said 500,000 years, many other such teachers will come who will confirm the laws of their predecessors and reveal new laws. They will all be subject to attack, but the persecution they suffer will no longer be so severe and there will not be as many martyrs as at the start of this Dispensation. Humanity as a whole cannot achieve absolute perfection any more than an individual can. Hatred and jealousy will remain, but the evils will diminish and the worst of all evils – war – will disappear. He said that in the Bahá'í teaching, America is the arm and Germany is the

head. The arm is extremely important, as it must sometimes bear heavy burdens, and the American Bahá'ís had already opened many doors. Shoghi Effendi declared that he was very proud of the German Bahá'ís. Germany possessed great vitality and would experience a great cultural, political and spiritual upswing. Just as the United States of America had opened up the whole continent to the teachings, Germany would become the focal point for the whole of Europe and open the Balkans in the south, the Nordic countries, Russia and France to the Cause of God.

The Guardian customarily took his evening meal together with the Grossmanns, who were the only Western pilgrims in Haifa at the time. He entered the Pilgrim House through a side door and they ate at a large table on the ground floor. The delicious Persian food was brought from the house of the Master on the other side of the road. Since the time of 'Abdu'l-Bahá Fujita was the helpful soul who had been caring for the friends staying in the house. He brought oranges and other exotic fruits, which in those days were an amazing luxury to a child from Germany.

Saichiro Fujita was born in Japan in 1886 and had become a Bahá'í in North America in 1905. When 'Abdu'l-Bahá was travelling in the United States of America in 1912, he invited Fujita to accompany Him. In 1919 Fujita followed his beloved Master to the Holy Land and was thenceforth permitted to remain in Haifa. After the passing of 'Abdu'l-Bahá, he transferred his loving services to the Master's grandson, the Guardian, Shoghi Effendi. He died in Haifa in 1976 at the great age of 91, honoured and mourned by many generations of pilgrims.[36]

In 1937 the Shrine of the Báb did not yet have the wonderful superstructure and dome that were erected in later years under the supervision of the Guardian, and the gardens around it were not yet as developed and spacious as today, but even then the cypresses that had given shade to Bahá'u'lláh towered above the building. The spotless white marble of the mausoleum of Bahíyyih Khánum, the Greatest Holy Leaf, shone in the evening light.

The pilgrims spent many hours in prayer at the Shrine of the Báb and 'Abdu'l-Bahá. 'The Shrine', Elsa Maria Grossmann in her notes quoted the Guardian as saying, 'is at the focal point of Mount Carmel, and Haifa is at the focal point of the world, geographically, spiritually and through the Universal House of Justice, which will have its permanent seat in Haifa, also administratively. The Shrine of Bahá'u'lláh [in Bahjí] is both consciously and subconsciously the spiritual power-source for the world.'

One afternoon the pilgrims were permitted to visit the International Bahá'í Archives with its precious mementos of the Báb, Bahá'u'lláh and 'Abdu'l-Bahá, including the original manuscripts, documents, and literature in 33 languages.

Anna Grossmann recounts in her notes that Hermann had taken with him the original Tablet that he had received from 'Abdu'l-Bahá in order to give it as a gift to Shoghi Effendi. The Guardian took it with him, but he brought it back again the next day and asked Dr Grossmann if he knew that it was a significant Tablet. Hesitating briefly, the latter said that he had always felt the passage to be important that stated: 'Thou shouldst be eternally obliged and thankful to those who were the cause of thy guidance ...' Shoghi Effendi responded in the negative, saying that the words of 'Abdu'l-Bahá stating that the addressee had 'been enabled to rend the veils asunder, to gaze on the beauty of the Sun of Reality, and to walk in the path of the Kingdom' was the most significant part.[37]

One day the pilgrims were driven to 'Akká in the Guardian's car. Following a visit to the House of 'Abbúd, where Bahá'u'lláh and His family lived in 'Akká, they proceeded to the resting place of Bahá'u'lláh – the Spot that is most revered by Bahá'ís and to which they turn in prayer. After passing a night in the Mansion where Bahá'u'lláh spent the final years of His imprisonment, which were also the last years of His earthly life, they were permitted to visit the Shrine of Bahá'u'lláh the next morning.

Elsa Maria Grossmann writes in her memoirs:

> Whereas in the resting place of the Báb the impression of loveliness and tenderness dominated all other feelings, in the Shrine of Bahá'u'lláh there was a sense of unwavering power, unspeakable glory and majesty, and then – like a victory call permeating everything and drowning out all other sound – the consciousness of a Faith that no power on earth could possibly destroy. To kneel at the threshold of the inner Shrine in Bahjí and to immerse one's face in the flowers is like sensing the proximity of the countenance of the Lord of the Universe, and our prayers will continue to be but stammers until in the storm of our innermost feelings we find rest in being close to Him.

At that time it was possible for the friends to enter the room itself where Bahá'u'lláh is buried and pray at the side of His grave.

This was followed by a visit to the wonderful green and blooming

Riḍván Garden near 'Akká, which 'Abdu'l-Bahá had lovingly created for His father. Five Persian brothers laid out the gardens according to the plans of Shoghi Effendi and under his supervision, and were caring for them with devotion. After this, the pilgrims returned to Haifa.

Shoghi Effendi, who knew and appreciated Hermann Grossmann's scientific interests, arranged a visit to the newly-founded Hebrew University in Jerusalem, where Dr Grossmann was able to hold instructive conversations with a number of professors. The Grossmanns also visited the old city of Jerusalem and the Church of the Holy Sepulchre, where the Arab tourist guides quarrelled loudly as they competed for business, not even ceasing their disputes at the grave-site of Jesus Christ. This church is a striking illustration of the divisions among the Christian churches, each of which controls one part of the building. At that time, the dome was in danger of collapse but could not be repaired because the room through which the construction workers would have had to walk to get to it belonged to a different Christian community who refused them access.

After a visit to Tiberias and Nazareth, the Grossmanns returned to Haifa. With sad hearts, they now had to take leave of the Shrine. One last time, the female pilgrims were invited to tea with the women of the Guardian's family. On the occasion of the last meal in the Pilgrim House, the Guardian brought the originals of the Testament of Bahá'u'lláh and the Will and Testament of 'Abdu'l-Bahá, so that they could see them with their own eyes.[38]

Anna Grossmann wrote in her memoirs:

> The Guardian's clear, superior wisdom, his answers to many a question, his encouragement and ideas, served to reinforce and expand the future activities of the pilgrims, inspiring them for the coming years in the service of this great Revelation. The deep reverence and appreciation that the pilgrims constantly felt towards Shoghi Effendi was even more strongly rooted when they left Haifa. For Hermann Grossmann, Shoghi Effendi as the leading figure of the Bahá'í Faith became the focal point of his being, and the unexpectedly early passing of Shoghi Effendi in 1957 was therefore the most painful loss in Hermann Grossmann's life.

Mr and Mrs Maxwell, the parents of Rúḥíyyih Khánum, who had come to Haifa for the wedding of their daughter to the Guardian, accompanied the Grossmanns to their ship, along with the Guardian's secretary Ḥusayn Rabbání and Fujita. The pilgrims wistfully bade farewell to the Holy Places. Their luggage contained a carpet as a gift

View of the balcony outside the room of Bahá'u'lláh in the Mansion of Bahjí, aquarelle by Hermann Grossmann, 8 April 1937. The original was placed by Shoghi Effendi in the entrance hall of the House of 'Abbúd in 'Akká

'Bahá'í Garden in Haifa and Shrine of the Báb', aquarelle by Hermann Grossmann, 1 April 1937. The original was placed by Shoghi Effendi in the entrance hall of the Mansion of Mazra'ih

The garden at the House of 'Abdu'l-Bahá in Haifa, aquarelle by Hermann Grossmann, 1 April 1937

'Bahjí: Looking towards 'Akká', aquarelle by Hermann Grossmann, 9 April 1937. The original was placed by Shoghi Effendi in the entrance hall of the Mansion of Mazra'ih

from the Guardian to the National Spiritual Assembly of Germany and Austria. It was carefully wrapped in a travel blanket and safely reached its destination. By the time they reached Neckargemünd, a parcel of books that Shoghi Effendi had presented to Hermann Grossmann for his library had already arrived.

CHAPTER 9

INTERDICTION UNDER THE NATIONAL SOCIALISTS[39]

The spiritual energies that the pilgrims had been privileged to experience in Haifa and Bahjí, and the intensive instruction granted to them by Shoghi Effendi, soon turned out to be desperately needed spiritual armour. They knew that a dark and threatening period lay ahead, but they were also confident of being included in the prayers offered at the Holy Places.

In a letter to Anna and Elsa Maria Grossmann, Rúḥíyyih Khánum wrote in German, '*Eben habe ich im Zimmer Bahá'u'lláhs für Sie alle, für Deutschland und sein Volk gebetet. Gott möge Sie alle in Seiner Heiligkeit segnen*' and she also adds, '*es kommt mir wie ein Vorrecht vor, wenn ich die Gebete für Sie – für uns – in Deutsch aussprechen kann* [I have just prayed for you all, for Germany and its people, in Bahá'u'lláh's room. May God in His Holiness bless you all. It seems like a privilege to me to be able to say the prayers in German for you – for us!]'.[40]

After the National Socialists took power in 1933, the gradual suppression of freedom of opinion in Germany began. It was only a question of time before the Bahá'í institutions would be prohibited, too. Nevertheless, or perhaps for that reason, the Bahá'ís tirelessly continued their work. They organized courses, welcomed visiting friends from other countries and held public talks, at which, however, representatives of the secret police (Gestapo) were sometimes present. On the 24th and 25th of April 1937, the National Convention took place in Heidelberg. It was a brilliant climax to all the work that had gone before, and demonstrated the vitality and progress of the Faith in Germany. At a public meeting Mrs Alice Schwarz from Stuttgart gave a remarkable speech. It was part of a programme that included prayers and stirring songs beautifully sung by Herma Mühlschlegel in her deep full voice. Friends from all over the country had come. They listened attentively to the encouraging report by the Grossmann family about their pilgrimage and to the instructions that the Guardian had given them for the German Bahá'ís, along with his words of appreciation, his love and his hopes for Germany. Three Bahá'ís from other countries were able to participate in the Convention: Mrs Schopflocher, Mrs Matthiesen and the American artist Mark Tobey.[41] He is famous for the soft, fragile lines of his drawings, known as 'white writing'.

The indications of an imminent interdiction were already evident at the beginning of 1937, after the Esperanto movement had been prohibited in the late summer of 1936 and the Esperanto magazine *La Nova Tago* had had to cease publication. For the time being, it was still possible for the Bahá'í magazine *Sonne der Wahrheit* (Sun of Truth) to appear and to report to the friends about the National Convention in Heidelberg.

Between the 7th and 11th of June 1937 the daily newspapers published a brief announcement that the 'Bahá'í association' had been prohibited on 21 May 1937 by the Reichsführer SS and Chief of the German Police in the Ministry of the Interior, Heinrich Himmler. The 'dissolution' of the 'Bahai sect' was carried out with immediate effect on the basis of paragraph 1 of the Presidential Decree for the Protection of the People and the State, 1933. The continuation or re-establishment of the organization was forbidden and its assets liquidated. The decree was signed on Himmler's behalf by a Mr Müller, with the request 'to do what is necessary'. The information was passed on to the Gestapo office.[42]

On 9 June 1937 Anna Grossmann sent a message to the Guardian notifying him of the interdiction and at the same time affirming her devotion to the Cause:

> Dearly beloved Guardian, I want to put on the threshold of the Beloved and before you my perfect readiness to become a sacrifice for the fortune and development of the Faith of God. I am ready at any time. With deep love from all, your devoted servant Anna Grossmann.[43]

In a letter to Annel Grossmann, the Guardian wrote:

> May the Almighty Protector sustain you in these days of stress and trial, and enable you and your dear and unforgettable co-workers to bear heroically the tests that confront you and to surmount the obstacles which face you. Your true and grateful brother, Shoghi.[44]

Just one day after the announcement of the interdiction, officials of the Gestapo confiscated all pamphlets and books of the Bahá'í Publishing Trust in Stuttgart, founded in 1919, and those of some friends.

In 1934 the Guardian had responded to a question posed by Dr Adelbert Mühlschlegel and given clear instructions concerning the behaviour of the Bahá'ís towards the National Socialist government. Here are some extracts from this important message:

> ... At the outset it should be made indubitably clear that the Bahá'í Cause being essentially a religious movement of a spiritual character stands above every political party or group, and thus cannot and should not act in contravention to the principles, laws, and doctrines of any government. Obedience to the regulations and orders of the state is indeed, the sacred obligation of every true and loyal Bahá'í ... For whereas the friends should obey the government under which they live, even at the risk of sacrificing all their administrative affairs and interests, they should under no circumstances suffer their inner religious beliefs and convictions to be violated and transgressed by any authority whatever. A distinction of a fundamental importance must, therefore, be made between *spiritual* and *administrative* matters. Whereas the former are sacred and inviolable, and hence cannot be subject to compromise, the latter are secondary and can consequently be given up and even sacrificed for the sake of obedience to the laws and regulations of the government ... But, as already pointed out, such an allegiance is confined merely to administrative matters which if checked can only retard the progress of the Faith for some time. In matters of belief, however, no compromise whatever should be allowed, even though the outcome of it be death or expulsion ... The actual trend in the political world is, indeed, far from being in the direction of the Bahá'í teachings. The world is drawing nearer and nearer to a universal catastrophe which will mark the end of a bankrupt and of a fundamentally defective civilization.[45]

At a meeting with Shoghi Effendi in Haifa in 1934 Max Greeven, a devoted American believer who had moved from New York to Bremen in 1930 as a partner in an American firm, had met members of the German National Spiritual Assembly. The Guardian asked the friends to involve Max Greeven in their Bahá'í work. He became a member of the National Spiritual Assembly and was of inestimable value to the German believers. Since the Guardian wished the summer schools in Esslingen to become a permanent institution, he urged Max Greeven to work towards this goal. Max Greeven was asked to try to attract an increasing number of Bahá'í visitors from other countries to the teaching events. When the Bahá'í institutions were prohibited in 1937 and the difficulties began, the Guardian asked him – as an American citizen – to lodge a request at the Ministry of Church Affairs that the interdiction be lifted and the books and archive materials returned. This he did in the autumn of 1937 and again in the summer of 1938. Both times he was assured that the confiscated material would be returned and both times the officials concerned conceded that they were powerless against the Gestapo. At the Guardian's instruction Max Greeven, who was now living in Holland, finally gave up his difficult and delicate efforts. Soon afterwards, all doors were closed due to the outbreak of the Second World War. It was not until after the collapse of the National Socialist regime that the German Bahá'ís learned that the Guardian had tried to help them through the intervention of Max Greeven.[46]

In Stuttgart, Göppingen and Esslingen the homes of many believers were searched and books, magazines and letters confiscated. The way the officials of the political police acted in each case was very different. It ranged from rude threats to polite apology and even to the return of a prayer book for personal use. A Bahá'í couple, Klärle and Hugo Bender, moved into the 'Häusle' in Esslingen in order to prevent it being confiscated. The criminal investigation department of the Heidelberg police initially only confiscated the Esperanto magazines from the Grossmanns' home and assured the family specifically that the private ownership of Bahá'í books and visits between the friends were not prohibited. Hence, as late as November 1938 Bahá'ís from Stuttgart, Esslingen, Karlsruhe, Heilbronn, Heppenheim and Frankfurt am Main met in Heidelberg.[47] Public activities and the proclamation of the Word of Bahá'u'lláh were no longer possible, and the administrative structures of the community had been dismantled.

About two years later came the next wave of attacks. It was initiated by the renewed vigour of the political police in Karlsruhe.

In October 1939, a request by Marta Brauns-Forel from Karlsruhe for her Swiss passport to be extended attracted the attention of the Gestapo. Her Bahá'í books, her Jewish books, all her manuscripts, her letters and her address book were confiscated. Marta Brauns was the daughter of Professor Auguste Forel, the famous Swiss psychiatrist and researcher into the behaviour of ants, to whom 'Abdu'l-Bahá had addressed an important Tablet. The letters and the address book were inspected closely and used as the basis for a virulent cross-examination.

She was treated like a traitor or a criminal, she said later. She was given strict instructions not to talk about the interrogation.

It was probably the same official, a certain Mr Gerst, who shortly afterwards summoned Anna Grossmann to the criminal investigation department of the Heidelberg police, after a number of police officers had appeared at the yellow house in Neckargemünd demanding her correspondence. Writing later about Gerst's interrogation, she stated that for the first time she had vividly sensed the spirit of darkness that was to intensify more and more and cause countless people both to live and to die in excruciating agony. Just as quickly, she realized the extent of the threats to the Faith and to the friends that emanated from this source. However, she felt secure in the certainty that here, as everywhere, the best weapon the friends could wield was a heart filled with the spirit of Bahá'u'lláh and divinely-inspired love.

During the interrogation, it turned out that Gerst, like Anna Grossmann, was a native of the town of Pirmasens, which – curiously enough – caused him to adopt a milder, less stringent manner. He even accepted her observation that 'if this Cause is from God, it will surely prevail'. For the time being she was released with a reprimand. Anna Grossmann was a very courageous person. Lurking in the background there was, after all, the ever-present threat of deportation to a concentration camp.

Among the personal belongings of Marta Brauns-Forel, a letter was found from Paul Köhler in Dresden. He had sent her a copy of the long obligatory prayer after the interdiction had come into force. After the interrogations, Anna Grossmann and Marta Brauns realized that he would undoubtedly be in major trouble. It was not possible to warn him, and any warning would, in any case, have come too late. For the Köhler family a period of bitter trials began, during which Rosel and Theo Lehne – a Bahá'í couple from Berlin – stood faithfully by their side. After the collapse of Hitler's regime, the Lehnes provided the following report:

> It was in the year 1940 that a Gestapo agent managed to worm her way into the confidence of our friends, the Köhlers. After several visits, during which she pretended to be interested in the children, she came one evening and asked them to put her up for the night, as she had missed her train. Despite their limited living space, our friends took pity on her and offered her accommodation. The agent took this opportunity to spy everything out. A few days later, Gestapo officers came and, without having to search

long, they removed the Bahá'í books from the cupboard and declared them confiscated. A long interrogation followed, during which our friend Köhler was reproached for having continued his activities in the forbidden sect, contrary to Himmler's decree, by passing on writings. They then cut the picture of 'Abdu'l-Bahá out of its frame, remarking that as a German he had no need to run after a foreigner now that we had the Führer [Adolf Hitler]. Finally, Paul Köhler was escorted away by the officers and put in prison. Further interrogations followed, in which it turned out that his illegal activity consisted in our friend Köhler having given the above-mentioned agent, upon her repeated request, a copy of the long 'daily prayer' of Bahá'u'lláh. The great calm and dignity that Paul Köhler retained throughout all the interrogations did not fail to make an impression. Instead of being removed at once to a concentration camp, he was handed over to the court and eventually sentenced to nine months' imprisonment. The work he was forced to do there was very difficult for him, because he had a serious eye condition resulting from a detached retina and could not see clearly. Here in the prison he now found the opportunity to talk about the Faith to his cellmates, who changed several times. Fellow inmates became friends, and bonds of friendship developed between the families that continued after his release. This came about quite unexpectedly for Paul Köhler after a term of imprisonment lasting 99 days.

Henceforth, the Köhlers lived in conditions of severe poverty and privation. Yet Paul Köhler's faith was deep and unbroken, and he had infinite confidence in the Cause of Bahá'u'lláh. He died in a tram accident in 1943, his little daughter Angelika having died in a diphtheria epidemic the same year. His wife Katharina Köhler and the remaining three children were all killed in the inferno that engulfed Dresden in the aerial bombardment of February 1945. Thus, the Köhler family was completely wiped out.

After the war, when the Guardian was informed by Mrs Walcker of Rostock that the Köhler family had all died, his secretary wrote on his behalf in July 1946, 'I need not try and convey to you in words how the Guardian has deplored, and suffered over, all the tragic happenings of the last few years! He was particularly sorry to hear such a dear Bahá'í as Paul Köhler, of Dresden, had died, as well as his wife and children ...'[48]

In Mecklenburg the more rigorous approach of the Gestapo was focused, in particular, on Emil Jörn in Warnemünde. He had become acquainted with the teachings of Bahá'u'lláh in 1921 or 1922 and had invited Wilhelm Herrigel from Stuttgart to give a talk in Rostock.

This was to be the first of many meetings. Travelling Bahá'í teachers helped him to build up the group: Mrs Schopflocher, Martha Root, Mrs Distelhorst, Anna Grossmann and 'Uncle Hermann' Grossmann with the 'Little Rose Garden'. In 1937, an anonymous person reported Emil Jörn to the Gestapo. Two officers interrogated him for five hours, and miraculously he managed to convince them both of his innocence. Although they had come to arrest him, they left as his friends. Since Emil Jörn was a teacher, the matter was passed on to the school authorities in Schwerin. He was interrogated several more times, but the course of the war brought that to an end, as he was now urgently needed. He was eventually even given a post as headmaster of a school. After the occupation by Soviet troops in 1945, the Russian commander of Warnemünde, Novikov, charged him with the task of reopening the school. This he did, making an opening speech in the schoolyard, in the presence of Novikov, in which he said, 'We are all brothers and sisters of *one* world and *one* homeland.' The commander responded, 'The *peoples*, too, should be brothers.' After the Cause was once again prohibited by the Soviet regime, the school authorities dismissed Emil Jörn in 1953 because he refused to recant his faith.[49]

In Schwerin, Karl Klitzing – who had become interested in the Bahá'í Cause in 1922 – had built up a flourishing community with the assistance of friends from elsewhere: Mary Maxwell, Emil Jörn and Hermann Grossmann had frequently visited Schwerin. The Gestapo suppressed these efforts too. The friends were forbidden to contact one another in any way. After the Second World War, Schwerin was occupied in 1945 first by American and then by British troops. An active community re-emerged. Then, however, the British handed over control of the city to the Soviets, and once again all Bahá'í work was forbidden and all traces of Karl Klitzing's efforts were lost. He died in 1958.[50]

As the war progressed, with the National Socialists coming under mounting pressure, the Bahá'ís were increasingly subject to observation and persecution by the authorities. The third wave of persecution began in 1943. It became clear that the Gestapo well knew who the leading members were.

In the early autumn of 1943, Anna and Hermann Grossmann were again subjected to harassment. Several officials appeared at their home in Neckargemünd in order to search the house. By chance, the husband of Annel Grossmann's sister Karla Gerber was in the house, on short-term leave from the front. The officials saw his officer's uniform hanging in the entrance hall. Evidently, the officials were too embarrassed to carry out a thorough search in the presence of a soldier from the front, so they only made a superficial inspection of the rooms. Karla Gerber and her two young sons lived with the Grossmanns throughout the final years of the war, because she had lost everything she possessed in an air raid on Cologne. Her husband's incidental leave turned out to be a great blessing. If they had conducted a thorough search, the Gestapo would certainly have found the large amounts of Bahá'í material, which were poorly hidden in the coal-cellar. What was also certain was that they would return. Anna and Hermann waited together with Karla Gerber until nightfall and then burned in a heating stove everything that might serve as a pretext for their arrest. They were concerned not only for their own safety, but also of the Bahá'ís who were associated with them.[51]

In December 1943, Hermann, Anna and Elsa Maria Grossmann were again visited by the Gestapo, who this time conducted a thorough search of the house. As a result of all the material having been burned, no incriminating evidence was found. Nevertheless, Anna and Hermann were summoned to the criminal investigation department at Heidelberg police station. Whereas Hermann was left in peace for the time being, Anna's case was pursued further.

On 21 February 1944, at the request of the public prosecutor, a six-month prison sentence was imposed by a special court in Mannheim on Carla Macco, a member of the Heidelberg Bahá'í community. It was forbidden to contact her in prison. Even her defence counsel was unable to find out what charge had been made against her. Only when Hermann and Anna Grossmann were themselves charged several months later were they able to find out where Carla Macco was and what she had been accused of. This gave her son, Fritz Macco, the opportunity to visit his mother, and he succeeded in preventing her removal to a concentration camp.

Fritz Macco was a soldier in the German army, the Wehrmacht. He was one of the seven young Bahá'ís who were forced to join the armed forces and who lost their lives in the Second World War. The law made no provision for conscientious objectors, and so Shoghi Effendi instructed the Bahá'ís that it was not possible to avoid military service. Anyone refusing to serve would have faced proceedings in a special court and would have been sent to a concentration camp. Even a request to serve in a medical unit was usually not granted. Fritz Macco knew of the atrocities being committed and was in a state of despair. Hartmut

Grossmann remembers how, during a short period of leave, Fritz Macco visited the Grossmanns in Neckargemünd and wept bitterly, because he thought he could no longer bear the cruelty of the war. But it was precisely his being a soldier that gave him the opportunity to protect his mother and to attempt to rescue Lidia Zamenhof.

Anna Grossmann reports in her diaries that the Grossmanns had not heard from Lidia Zamenhof for some time. They guessed, however, that owing to her Jewish background she was confined in the Warsaw ghetto, and so they asked Fritz Macco, who was in action in Poland, to find out about her. With the help of a Polish family, he succeeded in finding her. As an ambulance driver, he was able to enter the ghetto, which was otherwise completely cut off. Despite the risk to his own life – contact with the inhabitants of the ghetto was, of course, strictly prohibited – he managed to find Lidia Zamenhof. He offered to help her escape from the ghetto, but although she faced certain death, she rejected his offer. She did not wish to leave her friends, preferring to share their fate. This was the last that Lidia Zamenhof's friends in Germany heard of her.[52]

On 18 January 1947 the Guardian wrote to Elsa Maria Grossmann,

> It now appears absolutely certain that our dear Bahá'í sister Lidia Zamenhof lost her life in a gas chamber during the war! This is a great loss, since she was able to render so many services to the Faith in the pre-war days! However, her service for the Cause and the memory of her are incomparably great!

Fritz Macco fell shortly afterwards in September 1944 on the eastern front near Suleyov-Tarlov. The six other young Bahá'ís who fell as soldiers in the war were:

Jörg Brauns from Karlsruhe in 1942 near Leningrad (today St Petersburg)
Wilhelm Gollmer from Stuttgart in 1944
Hansjörg Kohler from Stuttgart in Vlodova in 1944
Theodor Leidinger from Stuttgart in 1944
Alfred Schweizer from Stuttgart-Zuffenhausen near Staraya Rossiya in 1944
Klaus Weber from Karlsruhe near Tutes in Latvia in 1944

Mrs Köhler and her children were not the only friends to have died in air raids. In 1943 Else Gericke and her daughters Margot and Rita were killed in Leipzig, as was Fritz Winkler in Karlsruhe just a few days before the war ended in 1945.

Five dear Bahá'ís of Jewish background were deported in 1941/42 and can be presumed with certainty to have been killed. They were: Sophie Rothschild; the sisters Berta, Thekla and Thea Wertheimer, last resident in Frankfurt am Main; and a Bahá'í from Stuttgart who formerly lived in Göppingen. It is with a bitter sense of melancholy that we commemorate the lives of those who died during those years of darkness.

Wenn du nicht stirbst, kannst du nicht leben,
Und wenn du lebst ist alles tot.
Es gehn, die sich Ihm ergeben,
Hindurch zu neuem Morgenrot.

Ins Nichtsein sinkt, was Form besessen,
Was gestern wahr schien, muss vergehn,
Dann wird aus heilendem Vergessen
Die neue Wirklichkeit erstehn.

Denn wirklich ist, was uranfänglich
Im Schöpfungsschoß und Ewigkeit,
Und nur ein Schatten und vergänglich
Sein stofflich Bild in Raum und Zeit.

So wird fortan ein ander Leben
Und ander Sein und andres Licht
Dich auf dem neuen Weg umgeben,
Die weder Tod noch Ende ficht.

(Hermann Grossmann)

If you do not die, you cannot live,
And if you live, all else is dead.
Those who to Him devotion give
Pass on to a new dawn, so red.

What once had form is nothingness,
What once seemed real meets its demise,
Restorative forgetfulness
Lets new reality arise.

For real is that which from creation
Exists in all eternity
And as but a transitory reflection
Takes on temporality.

> Henceforth a different life surrounds you,
> A new existence, different light
> Illuminates the path you pass through,
> Nor death nor end seeking to fight!

During the third wave of persecution, the approach taken by the police was much more severe. Elsa Maria Grossmann and Frieda Eichler, a member of the Heidelberg community, were threatened during interrogation and held at gun-point. Their books and letters – even those that had nothing to do with the Bahá'í Cause – were confiscated. Hermann Grossmann had already destroyed his valuable archives. Irreplaceable documents that testified to the development of the Faith in Germany and that had been painstakingly collected over a period of twenty years were lost forever. However, when the Grossmanns' house was searched, Hermann Grossmann succeeded in diverting the attention of the officers away from a large proportion of the books. He took the audacious step of asking the Director of the University Library in Heidelberg, Professor Preisendanz, to take the books for the library in order to prevent them falling into the hands of the Gestapo. Professor Preisendanz immediately sent a reliable man to pick up the books, thus effecting their rescue. In this way, Heidelberg's University Library became the first major library in Germany to have an important collection of materials concerning the Bahá'í Faith. Also, a small number of books were hidden by a friend who was not a Bahá'í and whose home was therefore not liable to be searched.

Later, in 1958, Hermann Grossmann applied to the relevant official body to claim financial compensation for his losses. He tried to draw up from memory a list of the books, magazines, yearbooks and author's proof copies that he had lost and pointed out that

> my Bahá'í library had been assembled according to academic criteria and, as far as western publications are concerned, it was unique in its completeness, at least in Europe. Apart from published books, it also contained a large number of newspaper cuttings relating to the Bahá'í Cause, a collection of leaflets, programmes of events and illustrative material.

He also notes,

> The list does not include the literature written in oriental languages, since I am not familiar with their titles. Most of them were probably valuable, sometimes hand-written works, amounting to about 30 volumes ...

This was followed by a long list of valuable books in German and English that were no longer available.[53]

Elsa Maria Grossmann was arrested on 22 September 1944 and was held in Heidelberg prison, in cell 19, for nine days without any charges being brought against her. One ray of hope for her was that there she met Carla Macco, who was still in detention. She also had the opportunity of talking to her cellmate about the Bahá'í Cause and holding long conversations with her. Owing to the vigorous intervention of her brother Hermann, Elsa Maria Grossmann was released. Instead of a one-month prison sentence, she was charged a fine.

On 2 May 1944 the first public trial of seven Bahá'ís was held before a Special Court in Darmstadt. The seven believers were August and Mariechen Ehlers from Hambach/Bergstraße, Anna Grossmann, Marie Schenk from Darmstadt-Trautheim, Gaius and Margarete Schmidt from Heppenheim and Mariele Schweizer from Stuttgart. They were accused of having continued in 'the dissolved and prohibited Bahá'í sect'. The Special Court proceedings in Darmstadt were based on 'a violation of the Decree by the Reichspräsident [Hindenburg] for the Protection of the People and the State promulgated in February, 1933'. The trial was chaired by Regional Court Director Rode, with the assistance of Senior Judge D. Doerr and Regional Court Advisor Dr Friedrich. Counsel for the prosecution was a Mr Mayer. Two lawyers, Carl Neuschäffer from Darmstadt and Edwin Leonhard from Heidelberg, defended the seven believers with admirable courage and a warm and sympathetic attitude towards the Bahá'í Faith. The friends were all ordered to pay a fine – all, that is, except for Mariele Schweizer. She was sentenced to three months' imprisonment. Thus, she was taken to the women's prison in Stuttgart, where three metal doors slammed shut behind her. It was by virtue of her upright eloquence that she was soon released from prison, something that the Gestapo themselves said had never happened before, to which Mrs Schweizer responded by pointing to the omnipotence of God.

Edith Horn, an outstanding believer from Frankfurt, also had serious charges raised against her at this trial. She was accused of having given a talk at the home of the Schmidt family in Heppenheim about her visit to Haifa and about Shoghi Effendi, despite the interdiction. She had to flee Frankfurt under cover of darkness. A cousin of Anna Grossmann's hid her for six months in her house near Colmar in Alsace, a part of France that had been occupied by German troops during the war. Since she was absent, her case before the Special Court was adjourned.[54]

In a commemorative contribution on Edith Horn's services to the Faith, Anna Grossmann writes that she was a strong and devoted believer. When in 1929 Ruth White's attacks on the Covenant of Bahá'u'lláh caused many German Bahá'ís to waver in their faith, Edith Horn stood firm and worked untiringly to bring the doubting believers back to the Faith. In the years 1935 and 1936 she had the honour of living in Haifa. When she returned to Germany, the Guardian asked her to leave her former hometown of Stuttgart and move to Frankfurt am Main, because the future Mother Temple of Europe was to be constructed in the wooded Taunus hills close to Frankfurt. Thus, her life was intimately associated with the construction of the Temple. During the Third Reich, she fearlessly assisted the Bahá'ís of Jewish background from Frankfurt. She did all she could to support the three Wertheimer sisters, but these loving and modest souls were, as Anna Grossmann put it, simply swept away. Edith Horn also frequently entered the Frankfurt ghetto in order to take food to Sophie Rothschild, another dear friend from a Jewish family from Weinheim. Edith Horn tried to convey to her friend that only through the power of her faith could a person benefit from facing certain death. Sophie Rothschild was among those deported to Poland. Edith Horn was with her when she was taken away, and she herself only just managed to escape without being seen by the Gestapo.[55]

In June 1944, Frieda Eichler from Heidelberg and, in a separate trial, 20-year-old Ruth Espenlaub-Schnizler from Beuren were prosecuted in the Heidelberg local court for an offence against the 'Decree for the Protection of the People and the State'. Ruth Espenlaub had first encountered the Bahá'í Faith during her apprenticeship as a seamstress in Göppingen, as she reports in her memoirs. She opened the door to two men who had come to see her employer, Mrs Schoch-Häcker. The employer later explained to her that the two men had been Gestapo officers, that she herself belonged to the Bahá'í Faith, and her Bahá'í literature had now been confiscated. This aroused the curiosity of young Ruth. She also reports in her memoirs that at night they sewed clothes for a Jewish family named Ott who wished to emigrate to the United States. Mrs Ott was a Bahá'í. Ruth Espenlaub came to know other Bahá'ís and when she returned a book about Muhammad that she had borrowed from Carla Macco, she enclosed a note. This note was found in the home of Carla Macco when it was searched, and that was how the Secret Service found Ruth's address. In 1944 she was summoned to Saarbrücken for interrogation. At this time she was living in the Palatinate, where she had been seconded to help on a farm. The National Socialist state demanded that young women spend a year in the '*Reichsarbeitsdienst*' (community service). Ruth Espenlaub's parental home was searched and she was prosecuted and summoned to a hearing at Heidelberg.[56]

In contrast to the court in Darmstadt, this court held public proceedings. The courtroom was full of spectators. Carla Macco had been brought there from prison, and Ruth Espenlaub-Schnizler remembers her standing at the back between two men during the hearing. The counsel for the prosecution gave a detailed explanation of the history and doctrines of the Faith and clearly set out the claim of Bahá'u'lláh. This took place at a time when the Bahá'ís were forbidden to present the Faith in public in any way, and was truly a form of proclamation in such a dark period! Hermann Grossmann was able to act as a witness on behalf of Ruth Espenlaub. She was sentenced to six months imprisonment, but the sentence was suspended because she was still a minor.[57]

Strangely, the persecution of the Bahá'ís was not yet directed against Hermann Grossmann. This enabled him, as in the case against Ruth Espenlaub, to appear as a witness before various courts and to present the Cause of Bahá'u'lláh whilst standing up in defence of the friends. Above all, he attested to the absolutely non-political nature of the Bahá'í Faith and the loyalty of the Bahá'ís towards the government of the country where they reside, and he was successful insofar as the accusation of disloyalty to the government was dropped. However, there still remained the charge of violating the order that had imposed the interdiction. The express aim of the judges at the proceedings before the Special Court in Darmstadt was to eliminate the Bahá'í Faith in Germany – but the almighty arm of Bahá'u'lláh was stronger than the power of His enemies. Nevertheless, on 22 September 1944 Hermann Grossmann was in the end prosecuted and ordered to pay a sizeable fine or face six months' imprisonment.

After the collapse of the Third Reich, the driving force behind the persecution, detective Gerst, was sentenced in a sensational court case to a period of ten years behind bars. He was charged with the horrific torture of prisoners and was designated the most brutal Gestapo officer in the Baden region.[58]

Only when the law rescinding unjust National Socialist verdicts

HERMANN GROSSMANN

was passed on 25 August 1998 was it possible to have the convictions repealed, although the victims had all died by then. On 10 November 1998, the public prosecutor's office in Heidelberg informed the Grossmann family that their application for revocation of the sentences imposed on Hermann and Elsa Maria Grossmann had been approved, and on 22 November 2000 the public prosecutor's office in Darmstadt similarly revoked the verdict on Anna Grossmann.

The letter from the Heidelberg Public Prosecutor's Office reads:

Staatsanwaltschaft Heidelberg
Kurfürstenanlage 23, 69115 Heidelberg
Telefon: 06221/59-0
Telefax: 06221/59-1822

Staatsanwaltschaft Postfach 105308 69043 Heidelberg

Bescheinigung

1. Gegen Herrn Dr. Hermann Großmann, geboren am 16.02.1899 in Rosario/Argentinien wurde durch Strafbefehl des Amtsgerichts Heidelberg vom 22.09.1944 - C 1 Cs 109/44 - wegen Vergehens nach § 4 der Verordnung des Reichspräsidenten zum Schutz von Volk und Staat vom 28.02.1933 i. V. m. dem Runderlaß des RFSS und Chef der deutschen Polizei im Reichsministerium der Justiz vom 21.05.1937 (S-PP II B 1430/37) die Geldstrafe von 1.500,00 RM, im Unbeibringlichkeitsfalle eine Gefängnisstraße von sechs Monaten festgesetzt.

   Es ist davon auszugehen, daß die Entscheidung Rechtskraft erlangt hat.

2. Es wird festgestellt, daß die vorgenannte strafgerichtliche Entscheidung durch das Gesetz zur Aufhebung nationalsozialistischer Unrechtsurteile in der Strafrechtspflege (NS-AufhG) vom 25.08.1998 aufgehoben ist.

(Glette)
Oberstaatsanwalt

Bankverbindung: Landesoberkasse Karlsruhe: Baden-Württembergische Bank Karlsruhe (BLZ 660 200 20) Konto-Nr. 400 606 0000
Sprechzeiten: Mo. Mi. Do. Fr. von 9.00 Uhr bis 11.30 Uhr; Di. von 13.30 Uhr bis 15.30 Uhr u. nach Vereinbarung

INTERDICTION UNDER THE NATIONAL SOCIALISTS

Attestation

1. In an order of summary punishment issued by Heidelberg Local Court on 22nd September 1944 under registration number C 1 Cs 109/44, a fine of 1,500.00 Reichsmarks or a six-month term of imprisonment was imposed on Dr. Hermann Großmann, born on 16 February 1899 in Rosario, Argentina, for an offence in accordance with paragraph 4 of the Presidential Decree for the Protection of the People and State issued on 28 February 1933 in association with the Decree of the Ministry for State Security and the Chief of the German Police in the Ministry of Justice issued on 21 May 1937 (S-PP II B 1430/37).

It is to be presumed that the court order had been passed into law.

2. It is hereby confirmed that, in accordance with the Law on the Repeal of Unjust Criminal Verdicts under the National Socialist regime (NS-AufhG), the said court order has been annulled.

[signature]
(Glette)   [stamp]
Senior Public Prosecutor

Anna and Hermann Grossmann end a report written for Shoghi Effendi about the persecution and deaths of Bahá'ís during the National Socialist period with the words:

> May the sacrifice of their lives, and the fact that none of the living believers, as far as we know, hesitated or swayed for a single moment in the profession of their faith, be the foundation for the development of a new era of the Bahá'í Cause in Germany and, together with the brilliant achievements of the believers all over the world, particularly of our American friends, lead to the ultimate establishment of the World Order of Bahá'u'lláh.[59]

It was not only because he was a Bahá'í that Hermann Grossmann had difficulties during Hitler's regime. He was viewed with suspicion by the authorities and, in particular, was placed under pressure in his professional life, because he was not a member of the National Socialist German Workers' Party – the NSDAP. At some point he had received a letter calling upon him to join the Party and to sign the enclosed form. Everyone in the home who knew about this prayed that he would be spared this step, and under the guidance of Bahá'u'lláh he did the right thing: he burned the letter and acted as if he had never received it. Miraculously, nobody ever asked about the letter. For the time being, Hermann Grossmann was able to escape from danger.

HERMANN GROSSMANN

Almost as soon as he joined the Koch & Co. fine-cardboard factory in 1920, Hermann Grossmann had had problems with his partners. He was subjected to constant personal attacks and intrigues. As well as this hostility, several NSDAP party leaders plotted to remove Hermann Grossmann and Adolf Koch, the two partners who were also managing directors, so as to be able to take over the company themselves. From 1934 to 1938 they were successful, insofar as an interim managing director was appointed in their stead. In 1938 Dr Grossmann succeeded in having this coercive measure removed, and the two managing directors were reinstated. Now the party leadership started to pressure him to join the NSDAP. When he refused to conform, his rights as managing director were again infringed. These hostile acts undermined his health. In addition, a scarlet fever infection had left him with a serious heart condition which prevented him from working for several months. The next step taken by his opponents was to attempt to use his former activities as a Bahá'í against him, and when this did not succeed, they initiated in 1944 'penal proceedings for damaging the war economy' against both managing directors. During the Second World War this charge covered, among other things, the illegal distribution of food or other goods that were only permitted to be given in exchange for ration tickets. The court in Darmstadt, where the trial took place, only admitted witnesses whose false statements supported the case against the defendants, whereas witnesses who wished to testify in their defence were forbidden to speak. Thus, the Party leadership finally managed to achieve its goal. However, by then the economic situation in Germany was so bad – after five years the war now being all but lost – that every productive individual was urgently needed, and so Hermann Grossmann did not have to go to prison after all, his six-month sentence being commuted. Although it was clearly a political trial, it was not until December 1951 that a lawyer succeeded in having the penalty removed from the register.[60]

Since, on the one hand, the difficulties within the company continued and, on the other hand, Hermann Grossmann wished to devote himself fully to activities promoting the teachings of Bahá'u'lláh, he withdrew from his position as managing director of and partner in Koch & Co. in 1953, selling his shares in exchange for the registration of a land claim.

In 1968, he saw the company sink into bankruptcy.

CHAPTER 10

THE RENEWAL OF BAHÁ'Í ACTIVITIES, 1945–1948

In the spring of 1945, German military resistance in the west fell apart. In the final days of the war, the Grossmann family had to leave their home and seek refuge with neighbours. The building was taken over as a command centre and as accommodation for German army officers as they retreated from the approaching American troops. However, after a few days the German soldiers left the house in a hurry – a clear sign that the American army was already very near. The German units pulled back but continued to fight, and machine-gun fire was heard at close range. Everyone was thankful when this extremely critical phase of the war finally came to an end without any members of the family being hurt. Shortly before the front had reached Neckargemünd, Hermann Grossmann had managed to borrow an old bicycle and ride all the way home from Waldmichelbach so as to be with his family during the hours of the greatest danger.

Whilst the thunder of gunfire was still rumbling in the distance, the family was alarmed to see an American jeep stop in front of the house. They were greatly relieved when the officer who emerged identified himself as an old acquaintance from the Weinheim days. As a young Jew, he had managed to emigrate to North America in the 1930s, in time to avoid the worst excesses of the National Socialist regime. Captain Brown, as he was known, asked about the family's experiences over the past few years and gave the Grossmanns a hastily written letter of safe-conduct, which was a very valuable document at that time. It read,

> Dr Hermann Grossmann has long been a personal friend of mine. He is a vigorous opponent of National Socialism and has never belonged to the Party or any other organization. It is recommended that Dr Grossmann and his family be treated with goodwill and courtesy.

Germany was occupied by American, British, French and, in the east, Soviet troops. Hessen and North Baden, where the persecution of the Faith in the past years had been initiated, were the first areas to be liberated. The American troops entered Neckargemünd on 1 April 1945. For the Bahá'ís, this meant that freedom of worship was at last restored.

However, life continued to be very difficult. There was no electricity for several weeks and people were thankful if they at least had candles as a source of light in the evenings. Since the water supply had broken down, the inhabitants of Neckargemünd had to collect drinking water from distant springs where there were, of course, long queues. Anyone who still had a little food stored at home could count himself lucky. It was several days before the American forces arranged for the supply of a limited amount of flour, allowing each family to receive a loaf of bread in exchange for ration cards. There was no public transport, and neither postal services nor telephone lines were to be restored for a long time. All this meant that Bahá'í activities were restricted to the immediate vicinity.

The friends in Neckargemünd and Heidelberg re-established the contacts that had been interrupted for so long and tried to gain an overview of the whereabouts of the believers in other places and of the little remaining Bahá'í literature that had survived. Hermann and Anna Grossmann tried to arouse the interest of acquaintances old and new in the Cause of Bahá'u'lláh. As had been the case after the First World War, the people who had suffered the horrors of the conflict – this time including the civilian population, old people, women, and children, who had experienced the air raids in the cities and the collapse of law and order – were open and ready, as never before or since, to discuss religious topics and give consideration to the teachings of Bahá'u'lláh.

At first there was a partial curfew imposed by the military authorities to prevent unrest and looting. In addition, owing to the division of Germany into zones, movement from the American to the French, British or Soviet zones was impossible. Bahá'í activities could expand only gradually, partly through the invaluable support of two young Bahá'ís who were members of the US military forces, Robert Bruce Davison and John C. Eichenauer. On 19 June 1945 the American military government of the Bergstraße region of Hessen confirmed that it had no objections to the holding of Bahá'í meetings. Furthermore, it issued a permit for the production of duplicated copies of Bahá'í literature. The shortage of paper meant that printed publications would not become available for a long time yet.

Hermann Grossmann arranged for a former employee who had been dismissed from the firm on account of his Party membership to type out his compilations of texts with as many carbon copies as possible. The Grossmann family stapled the sheets together by hand and placed them in a somewhat harder cover, then distributed the booklets among the friends under the overall title *Bahá'í Texte* (Bahá'í Texts). Thus, the Bahá'ís had the literature they needed for teaching the Faith. The individual compilations were entitled: *A New Day*, *Knowledge*, *Man in the Image of God*, *Community Spirit*, *Foundations of Civilization*, *Divine World Order*, *Being a Bahá'í*, *The Mashriqu'l-Adhkár*, *Muhammad*, *'Abdu'l-Bahá's Will and Testament* and *The Administrative Order of the Faith of Bahá'u'lláh* by Shoghi Effendi.[61]

Hermann Grossmann travelled about tirelessly, and the more life returned to normal, the further afield his journeys took him – although travelling was still very difficult. Now at last he was able to put his profound knowledge of the Bahá'í teachings to use again.

Young Bahá'ís and guests from near and far came together in Esslingen in September 1945 for the first youth gathering. At this event and at the weekly meetings that followed, they began an intensive training process to increase their knowledge of the Faith. There was an atmosphere of great enthusiasm, and the young people immersed themselves in the Writings, seeking to deepen their faith and their knowledge of the teachings. They hungered after the Word of Bahá'u'lláh that had for so long been withheld from them. The Esslingen gathering also inspired Bahá'í youth in other towns, and regular meetings and public events were being held in Neckargemünd, Stuttgart, Trautheim (near Darmstadt) and Heppenheim.

Martin Aiff, who later worked along with his wife Gerda at the National Centre in Westendstraße, Frankfurt am Main, and who afterwards was a self-sacrificing pioneer to Southern Africa, vividly describes the immediate post-war situation:[62]

> I cannot help recalling that first evening ... it was in October 1945. Hunger and deprivation were our lot in Germany at that time. There was virtually no social or cultural life ... One evening I went out with a piece of wood in my pocket, because we wanted it to be warm in the house where we were meeting. It was called 'Haus Schenk'. There was an open fire in the house and we sat around the fireplace. Mr Schenk, a fine gentleman, stood up and

said that he wished to fulfil his wife's heartfelt desire and had therefore invited Dr Grossmann from Neckargemünd to talk about the Bahá'í Faith. This man, Dr Hermann Grossmann, was standing there – a tall, slightly corpulent man – and started talking about the oneness of mankind and world peace, and he kept using strange-sounding names – Bahá'u'lláh, 'Abdu'l-Bahá, and the Báb. It all rushed through my head in a mixture of impressions. Somehow my heart was touched, yet on the other hand I could not but protest – what was this man talking about, what could he possibly know of what we had been through in the war years as young soldiers in France, Poland, Africa, Russia, Poland again, and finally in Germany? When the discussion started, I put up my hand and said, 'What planet are you living on, talking to us about world peace when even the people here in the village are not at peace with one another.' And I must admit that I, myself, did not have peace in my heart. I had returned from the war exhausted and drained ... In my final-year class at school, at the start of the war, there had been twenty-five young men, full of youthful hopes – only three returned home, two seriously wounded and myself with slight wounds ... Then there was the second evening in November. I again went with a piece of wood in my coat pocket and listened, waiting only for the discussion and the chance to offer defiant counter-arguments to that man who painted such idyllic images of angelic conditions on earth ... He looked at me kindly with his gentle eyes when I said that I couldn't understand what he was talking about. He said, 'Give yourself time, let what you have heard sink in, and voice the things that trouble you.' And later, when doubts arose inside me, he again said, 'Martin, give yourself time. If you wish to declare yourself a Bahá'í, you must realize that, by doing so, you are entering into a Covenant with God. That means you must obey God; it means that, in declaring, you make a promise that you will spread His Teachings and obey His commandments and laws.' I will never forget how he explained to us, 'You must imagine the Bahá'í Cause like this: God has spread out a table before you full of the world's tastiest and best dishes and invited you to feast upon it. Be careful not to upset your stomach – take small portions and choose what appeals to your appetite; and if there is something that you don't fancy yet and which you perhaps don't fully understand or you don't know what it is, leave it be. The time will come, and if it is important for you it will come to you and you will learn to understand and to love it.' Hermann Grossmann was a very special person for us. You could ask him whatever you felt like, we were fascinated by his knowledge in every field, whether religion or atomic physics, music or painting – he always had an answer, and we were very impressed.

Sometimes I went to the study class in Neckargemünd by motorcycle. At that time you had to be off the streets after dark [owing to the curfew by the Military Government] and Hermann Grossmann begged me not to go, saying, 'Martin, don't go, don't go, they'll catch you.' But they never caught me and we managed to drive back to Trautheim in the dark in spite of everything.

In 1946 and 1947, several youth conventions and summer schools took place in Heppenheim, Esslingen and Rainbach near Neckargemünd. Hermann Grossmann attended them all, motivating and enthusing the young people. Working with the youth was very important for him and a matter of heart.

Massoud and Hermine Berdjis recount how 'Uncle Hermann' made a great impression on them at the youth gatherings.

> He didn't hold long, boring talks but just gave an introduction to the topic and then moved on to questions. Through his gentle encouragement, he managed to make everyone feel involved, so that many people participated in the exchange of ideas. He directed the conversation precisely to the point he had intended, without us realizing it and without adopting a schoolmasterly tone. His personality created a wonderfully harmonious, relaxed atmosphere. The secret of his effect on us young people was undoubtedly his great calmness and the genuine, even tangible love that radiated from him. We could be with him for hours and were never tired of his company. He could also be very cheerful and witty. So it was no wonder that we young people revered and loved him as a spiritual father.[63]

The youth gathering in Heppenheim from 8–10 June 1946 was attended by youth from all over Baden, Württemberg and Hessen. These days were an unforgettable experience for all.

The following description by a young participant gives a vivid impression of the atmosphere permeating those few precious days:[64]

> At our feet is the plain of the River Rhine. In the distance, the towers of Worms and Mannheim rise up above the haze, and far away, almost at the end of the world, the mountains are just visible, like a delicate layer of mist. Above all this is the radiant sun and the fluffy clouds, looking like balls of cotton wool ... Half way up a slope on the edge of the Odenwald, high above the houses of the little town, is our host's house with its large patio. From there, it is only two kilometres to our campsite and the barn that is to serve as sleeping quarters for the youth. In the evening we stand around the campfire. Holding hands in a circle, we cast oversize shadows on the tents. Then we sing ... a prayer ... We lie down, feeling secure and happy, each of us part of the community.

Then it is morning again, in the house with the patio. A piece of music plays – gentle yet powerful. We are filled with a sense of sublimity and warmth. Then the tender voice of a girl is heard reciting the words of Bahá'u'lláh: 'The divine spring-time is come ...' Outside the wind rustles in the tree-tops and in the murmuring sounds of nature Dr Grossmann talks to us young people: 'Friends! We are living in a strange time, a time of change. And this change has taken on forms whose ultimate extent we cannot predict. We may often be plagued by doubts, believing ourselves to be chasing utopias. Why is the world deviating from the old paths? – It is simply in the nature of change that it initially appears disruptive. Once the change has happened, it appears to be self-evident. People had retired into themselves, because there was no daylight. When we are in darkness, we do not perceive our neighbour. A few people huddle together around a small lamp, any little source of light. But the night lasted too long. Many things were forgotten, even the short path to the neighbour. But now the night is over. All the rays of the sun are filled with the desire to unite, to merge into one light, the light of unity. And we desire to become a community embracing the entire globe. Outside, the day has already dawned, yet many people are still huddled round their little lamp. Manifold thoughts are directed towards unity. Talking about unity is nice, but that is not enough. Unity is something that must be grasped profoundly. The issue of the oneness of people cannot be solved through materialistic ways of thinking. Mankind has spent too long thinking and working in materialistic ways. The result is ruins. Do we wish to start in this materialistic way again, to repeat the same mistakes? – No, we must learn new ways, learn instead to comprehend and apply the spiritual laws. The storms of materialism have destroyed matter. But a new picture is emerging out of the spiritual cosmos of religious faith. We must learn to tread both paths, to stand on both feet. We cannot manage without trust in God. The key to that has been given to us by the Manifestation. We must learn to recognize new material and spiritual truths. As when constructing a house, we stand in need of collaboration with others. It is unspeakably difficult to start again from scratch. But recognizing truths sometimes entails having to start again from scratch. For Bahá'í youth, it is necessary to go forward. We must try to perfect ourselves, but not as hermits, for then it would be very easy to regard ourselves as perfect, because no one would be there to measure ourselves against. The era we live in requires strong trees – not plants from a hot-house. To be an example to others – that is our sacred duty!'

When Hermann Grossmann had finished there was silence – all the faces showed great detachment. Then music began to play, a slow and stately composition vividly recalling the depth of the talk we had just heard ...

It reinforced our belief in our power to fulfil a great task and caused our hearts to long for the world to listen to us, so that peace and calm might reign at last ...

The final day was again devoted to discussion ... Towards evening, the participants started to depart ... We bade one another goodbye with heavy hearts but in the certainty of coming together again very soon for another such beautiful meeting.

The participants at the gathering had written to Shoghi Effendi. A reply dated 1 July 1946 was received from Rúḥíyyih Khánum:

Dear Bahá'í friends,

Our beloved Guardian was overjoyed and particularly happy to see that so many youth were gathered together. Your generation will be called upon in the difficult years that lie ahead of the peoples of Europe, not only to live for the Cause and build it up, but also to serve it, to unfold its institutions and to spread its teachings in the future. You must prepare yourselves now for these great deeds of service by exhaustively studying and mastering the teachings, by learning always to demonstrate the kind of behaviour that is worthy of Bahá'ís, and by giving to the other young people who live in this corrupt world an example of high moral rectitude.[65]

The hopes of the youth for another gathering in the near future were fulfilled just two months later in the first German Bahá'í summer school, which took place in the same 'house on the hill' in Heppenheim from 3–10 August 1946. The National Spiritual Assembly had given its approval and hoped the youth summer schools would become a permanent and ongoing institution.

At this event, again, Hermann Grossmann gave his time to the youth, and although, as far as possible, the young people themselves made all the necessary arrangements, his spiritual influence and guidance was constantly evident.

As is clear from Hermann Grossmann's reminiscences about this event, the meeting went extremely well, even though opportunities were still very restricted so soon following the end of the war. He writes:

Forty-two participants had come together. Almost all the participants – both male and female – had seen active service at the front and in anti-aircraft units or they had been deployed in an auxiliary service at the front. There was hardly anyone among them that had even so much as heard the word Bahá'í or the name Bahá'u'lláh nine months before. But, in the meantime, they had studied hard, had discussed spiritual duties and consulted on how to spread the Faith among young people ... This new generation was critical [we read in the notes], not for the sake of criticism but because they took the state of spiritual despair in the world seriously and because they did not wish to stop half way but to recognize and tread the path of Bahá'u'lláh with all its consequences for the sake of the distress of the world. And they knew that time was short. After ten years of involuntary isolation, the older believers, who had shaped the Bahá'í activities before that time, took a while to comprehend the spirit of this generation hungry for knowledge, faith and a sense of community, shaken by so many storms ... they had to find their way out of the pre-war mentality they had known in their previous activities to that of a youth robbed of its ideals ... Before the war, we had met almost exclusively satiated people, who thought they could do without the world of Bahá'u'lláh. Now their world lay in ruins and their satiation had been replaced by utter disillusionment. Now we met people who hungered after spiritual satisfaction that would not be followed by disillusionment and who longed for that world that cannot collapse in ruins.[66]

That the first summer school for Bahá'í youth, indeed the first summer school in Germany altogether, took place in the 'house on the hill' in Heppenheim was symbolic of a new beginning. In the last two years of the war, the enemies of the Faith had selected this house and its residents as the site from which one of the hardest blows to the Bahá'ís was to be dealt. In the Darmstadt court case, the prosecution deemed this house a centre of the Faith, which in fact it had never been. Seven Bahá'ís were accused of holding prohibited meetings there and conducting activities to promote the Bahá'í Cause. However, just a few weeks after the final verdict was pronounced, the opponents were swept out of office and the house really did become a centre, where so many young people were united in the Cause of Bahá'u'lláh.

Between Christmas and New Year 1946, the Heidelberg-Neckargemünd youth group invited their friends for a three-day meeting at the 'Zum Neckartal' restaurant in Rainbach, near Neckargemünd. The innkeepers Waibel were courageous enough to take on the task of feeding so many young people with large appetites. It is close to miraculous that they managed to obtain sufficient food, despite the requirement that each participant bring ration cards for 200 grams of meat, 20 grams of fat, and 750 grams of potatoes, as well as a loaf of bread. Possessing ration cards by no means guaranteed that the food products would actually be available.

The days spent there were truly an experience. There were talks with plenty of time for discussion, as well as an introduction to and training in the Administrative Order of the Bahá'í community, given by Hermann Grossmann, which promoted the spiritual progress of the participants. In addition they enjoyed relaxing walks, dancing, singing folksongs, as well as artistic presentations that provided much-needed recreation. A total of 53 young people from 13 locations came, and it was incredible that a solution was found to the difficult problem of accommodation.

The second German Bahá'í youth summer school was held from 27 July to 2 August 1947, again in Rainbach. This time, seventy young people from all three western occupied zones were able to come together. American soldiers assisted with accommodation, lending the participants tents to put up on the meadows alongside the River Neckar.

The magazine *Sonne der Wahrheit* (Sun of Truth) then reported:

> Rainbach, a picturesque village at the foot of the Dilsberg between Neckargemünd and Neckarsteinach, which nestles delightfully between hills and forests along the banks of the River Neckar, was our meeting place for seven wonderful days. Everything here is harmonious and beautiful: the hills of the Odenwald, the bend in the Neckar down below, castles and walls dating from the times of the knights, farming villages and symbols of modern civilization such as railway lines and motorboats – despite their difference they all fuse into a single image that, with the radiant sun pouring its light over everything, could not have been a better setting for our days of inner striving after unity and the knowledge of God.
>
> Far away were all the ruins, far away thoughts of hunger. Yet in the hours of our working together we did not selfishly shut our eyes to the great needs. A deep understanding and experience of the eternal Divine Laws was the fruit of our talks and discussions. 'Religio' – reconnection with God – came to life within us and revealed to us the deeper causes of all human failure. We did not remain on the surface of trivial observations. By independently seeking the truth, we tried to recognize God's love and goodness at all times. We explored the realms of poetry, music, painting and architecture and recognized wherever eternal values were evidently the divine keynote, without which true culture cannot exist.[67]

The themes covered a wide range of topics: from economic and legal issues, the Administrative Order and the Guardianship, to very personal problems such as morality, bringing up children, and the body and the soul. Hermann Grossmann was always present. He shaped the discussion by means of his wealth of knowledge, he created the spirit and he provided the motivation. He sat and spoke in a large meeting, he sat in a small circle of friends, he walked to and fro while talking to individual boys and girls. He seemed never too tired and was the inexhaustible source of information and advice, being constantly aware that the present opportunity for teaching the Faith was unique and irretrievable, and that the Bahá'ís had not a minute to lose or to waste. The thought that this was an opportunity to teach the Faith to open-minded, hungry people urged the believers on, but again and again they were also driven forward by those who wished to hear about Bahá'u'lláh.

In February 1947 Rúḥíyyih Khánum wrote on behalf of the Guardian to Anna Grossmann:

> He realizes that every effort the friends make in Germany these days is made in the face of great obstacles and at the cost of real sacrifice. But they must ever keep their goals in sight, and persevere for the sake of the Cause and for the sake of their fellow-countrymen who now, in their greatest hour of need, have the right to hear of Bahá'u'lláh Who alone can save the world and lead it to peace and happiness ...[68]

The youth were very active from the start. Having grown up during the Hitler era and been indoctrinated by its ideology, they found the collapse of the regime and the lost war to be, at the same time, the destruction of all their values. That, in turn, made them receptive and caused them to become seekers. They were also simply grateful for the chance to be with like-minded people. There was much laughter and exchange of amusing anecdotes, and in the evenings everyone sat outside on the grass and sang folksongs. Bahá'í songs had not yet been written or put to music – that was a task for future generations – but the old folksongs were beautiful and full of sentiment, and everyone knew and loved them.

Martin Aiff recounts from this summer school:

> There was a small incident to which we didn't really attach any importance. Someone came up to me and said, 'Hey, Martin, there's a young man out there having difficulties with his bike – it broke down.' 'OK,' I said, 'we'll see what we can do.' And there stood a young man, with his bike: the chain had broken. We repaired it and by then it was lunch time. I invited the young man to eat with us. He sat next to me and we talked. Then we said goodbye.[69]

In 1986, a delegation of Bahá'ís visited the German Federal Chancellor, Helmut Kohl, in Bonn in order to present him with the Peace Message

THE RENEWAL OF BAHÁ'Í ACTIVITIES, 1945-1948

from the Universal House of Justice. Christopher Sprung, then Secretary of the National Spiritual Assembly and a member of the delegation, reports:

> Helmut Kohl asked us how we thought he had first heard of the Bahá'í Faith. 'Because of the persecution of the Bahá'ís in Iran, perhaps?' we suggested. 'No, no, much earlier!' he replied. He then proceeded to tell the story: When he was a young man, shortly after the war, he was riding his bicycle along the banks of the River Neckar and on the way home he came across a group of campers. He was given a very friendly reception, and it turned out that it was a Bahá'í youth camp. Christopher Sprung joked, 'If we had known then that you would later be Federal Chancellor, we would have given you an extra piece of cake' ... at which he laughed heartily.[70]

Here was that young man whose bike the Bahá'ís had repaired, the future German Federal Chancellor!

The Bahá'ís of Frankfurt and Karlsruhe had been driven out of the cities by the events of the war and had been scattered to various regions. That made it difficult to start Bahá'í activities afresh. In Frankfurt, Bruce Davison helped by placing a small advertisement in the *Frankfurter Rundschau* newspaper to bring together the circle of friends around Edith Horn. From September 1945, regular meetings took place with the assistance of the Frankfurt Esperantists. As early as 19 October 1945, Hermann Grossmann held the first public lecture after the lifting of the interdiction. His talk was entitled, 'What Religious Unity Can Bring to Mankind'. In early December he delivered a second lecture on 'The Spirit that Gives Strength'. Despite many difficulties and adverse conditions, Bahá'ís and other people interested in the Faith came from even quite distant locations. Bruce Davison helped to print several hundred leaflets with the words of Bahá'u'lláh and 'Abdu'l-Bahá. These were distributed and given away upon request. Over the next few years, Hermann Grossmann continued to speak regularly in Frankfurt and his talks were always very well attended. During the same period, introductory talks were held in Darmstadt, Heppenheim and the university town of Giessen, all of which are located in Hessen. In March 1946, Hermann Grossmann gave two public talks in Weinheim, and in May and June of the same year he spoke in Wiesbaden. The friends in Karlsruhe organized their first public events in July and September. The local Bahá'ís joyfully took on the task of providing regular deepening sessions.[71] 'Islam and Bahá'í' was the title of the first talk in Mannheim in October 1948. This was the first public mention of the new Revelation in that major city.

Anna and Hermann Grossmann's efforts were concentrated particularly, of course, 'at their own front door' in Heidelberg and Neckargemünd. Despite the difficulties caused in this very region by the interdiction, contact among the friends there had never been interrupted, and although there were neither tram nor railway services in the summer of 1945, the Bahá'ís in both towns managed to make a new start and begin proclamation activities. The atmosphere of the old University of Heidelberg, which had been spared from the terror of bombing – the Ruperto Carola is the oldest university on German territory – was a most fitting venue for morning devotional meetings. Invited guests met at the beautiful 'Alte Aula', the old assembly hall, which was full to capacity.

They listened to music and recitations before hearing a talk by Dr Grossmann. This was also the site of the first public meeting by Bahá'ís after the end of the National Socialist regime. The believers and their friends who were interested in the Faith met every week for a lecture, discussion or feast. Since Heidelberg had not been destroyed by bombs, it was possible for the meetings to be held in very attractive public venues. Sometimes the room would be too small and people had to stand. Many outstanding individuals came into the Faith as a result of these meetings.

In Neckargemünd, the Grossmann family invited friends and acquaintances to their home. In the autumn of 1948 the Bahá'í 'youth home' was ceremonially opened. It was a large, solidly built wooden structure that had been erected at the same time as the yellow house. Its location was ideal, since the person who served as both teacher and discussion partner lived right next door. However, it soon turned out to be too small for youth courses and could thereafter only be used for local meetings.

During the first days of Riḍván 1945, the Bahá'í communities in Württemberg were also able start to work freely again. On the very night of the entry of American troops into Stuttgart, the Bahá'ís met to thank Bahá'u'lláh for His guidance and protection, though heavy gunfire still resounded across the city. Owing to the severe damage in the city, the first public lecture could not be held until January 1946. Hede Schubert spoke to a packed audience on 'The Bahá'í Faith as the Way to a New

THE RENEWAL OF BAHÁ'Í ACTIVITIES, 1945–1948

World Order'. An introductory leaflet entitled *The Bahá'í Faith* helped to satisfy the most urgent need for literature.[72]

In nearby Esslingen, Bahá'ís and interested friends met for the first time on 23 May 1945. Problems with the authorities delayed the start of public activities, but these problems were eliminated when the Bahá'í Faith was granted official recognition on 30 October 1945. The permit reads as follows:

> Stuttgart APO 758, 30 October 1945
> To whom it may concern:
> Permission is hereby given to Tec 4 John C. Eichenauer, 398 577 99, to contact groups belonging to the Bahá'í Faith in Baden-Württemberg in order to assist in the rebuilding of these groups.
> The Bahá'í Faith is a recognized religion and may be freely practiced in Germany.
> Signed: John P. Steiner, Major,
> Education and Religion Officer[73]

On 1 December 1945 a series of talks began, the first being delivered by Heide Koller-Jäger entitled 'And the Light Shineth in Darkness'. The second on 'Unity in Faith' followed in May 1946 – the speaker this time Hermann Grossmann. Here, as in the nearby towns of Plochingen, Göppingen and Ludwigsburg, all the meetings attracted a large audience. There was still a severe lack of reading material. The Esslingen friends tried to meet the demand by producing typewritten booklets.

In his memoirs, Martin Aiff tells an amusing story:

> We used to meet regularly at our home (in Trautheim). We didn't have much Bahá'í literature. Mariele Schweizer from Stuttgart-Zuffenhausen produced some translations of passages in *Gleanings* – terrible translations, I have to say, type written on an ancient typewriter that had no 'e' and where the letter 'q' kept jumping in somehow. We therefore called her Madame Q – and yet we would sit for whole Sunday mornings over such a typewritten page and heatedly discuss its meaning, and we were privileged to inhale the spirit of Bahá'u'lláh that spoke to us out of these translations, however unpolished they were.[74]

In the late autumn of 1945 the Bahá'ís of Mecklenburg, Saxony, Berlin, Hamburg and Bavaria made contact. Bavaria was in the American zone, Hamburg in the British, and Mecklenburg and Saxony in the Soviet zone. Berlin was divided between the four victorious powers, the USA,

Britain, France and the Soviet Union. In these areas the Bahá'ís initially met in small groups.

On the occasion of the first meeting in Frankfurt, those present sent a cable to Shoghi Effendi via John Eichenauer and Bruce Davison, and the Guardian replied via the same route on 15 October 1945. It was the first message the German Bahá'ís had received from him in eight years:

> ... ASSURE EICHENAUER DAVISON DELIGHT NEWS, CONVEY FRIENDS ALL CENTRES MENTIONED HEARTFELT GRATITUDE SAFETY, ARDENT PRAYERS SUCCESS, LOVING REMEMBRANCE, ADMIRATION CONSTANCY. SHOGHI RABBANI.[75]

The work done in the immediate aftermath of the war would have been unthinkable without the American Bahá'í soldiers John C. Eichenauer and Robert Bruce Davison, and a little later Henry Jarvis. In close cooperation with the German Bahá'ís in the American zone of occupation, they made every effort to re-establish the Faith in Germany and to procure its recognition by the American military authorities. An independent German administration no longer existed. Americans in Germany were forbidden to fraternize with Germans, so associating with the German believers was not without risk. On 15 June 1945, American soldiers were granted permission to talk to Germans in public places, and from 1 October they were allowed to enter German homes.[76] These American Bahá'ís provided the first opportunity for the high, tight wall that surrounded Germany after the war to be breached and for cautious contacts to be re-established with friends around the world. The German believers had a lot to catch up on and needed to recognize and understand what enormous developments had meanwhile taken place in the Bahá'í community under the guidance of Shoghi Effendi.

In December 1945 the Bahá'ís received a letter from the Guardian. He spoke of the great ordeal they had endured and successfully overcome, assuring them that they had been constantly in his prayers throughout this time of danger. Now he urged them to speedily re-establish the communities and their institutions.

On 31 December 1945, the National Spiritual Assembly of the Bahá'ís of the United States and Canada received this cable from Shoghi Effendi:

> The German Bahá'í community, dearly beloved, highly honoured by 'Abdu'l-Bahá, and destined to play an outstanding role in the spiritual revival of an oppressed continent, has abundantly demonstrated in the

course of ten years of severest tribulations, dire peril and complete suppression, the high character of its indomitable faith. I appeal to the entire community of the greatly blessed, highly privileged American believers, to arise unitedly and contribute generously through dispatch of funds and literature designed to alleviate the distress and rehabilitate the institutions with which the future prosecutors of the second stage of the Divine Plan must be closely associated.[77]

By this time, four Local Spiritual Assemblies had been formed – those of Esslingen, Frankfurt am Main, Heidelberg and Stuttgart. After solving legal problems with the military government, a task undertaken primarily by Paul Gollmer of Stuttgart and John Eichenauer, a total of 150 Bahá'ís assembled in Stuttgart on 6 and 7 April 1946 for the first National Convention after the Second World War. Hermann Grossmann chaired the meeting of delegates. He reviewed the nine-year period of interdiction. In his final speech, which deeply moved everyone of those present, he pointed to the

> extraordinary obligation and responsibility borne by every single believer for the spiritual formation of the New World Order of unity and peace that has been so clearly and unambiguously prophesied by Bahá'u'lláh, an inevitable development the first signs of which are starting to appear upon the horizon of the world. But the path towards the full achievement of the great unity, whose durability can ultimately be assured only through unswerving faith, demands from the Bahá'ís – as the champions of this spirit – unprecedented efforts whereby each individual surpasses himself for the sake of finally redeeming mankind from the chaos of prejudice, hatred and war. Being a Bahá'í cannot be limited to merely seeking religious edification; rather, it means doing one's utmost to serve and to struggle and, in concert with all those who wrestle for the redeeming great unity, to guide humanity to the path of light.[78]

In a solemn and responsible atmosphere, the delegates elected the nine members of the National Spiritual Assembly on 7 April 1946. The chairman was Dr Hermann Grossmann, the vice-chairman Hede Schubert of Stuttgart, the secretary Alfred Kohler of Stuttgart and the treasurer Paul Gollmer, also of Stuttgart.

The National Assembly formed a number of committees that reflected the priority of teaching. The necessary literature and the re-establishment of the monthly journal *Sonne der Wahrheit* (Sun of Truth) were to assist this work.

The joyful news of the formation of the National Spiritual Assembly of the Bahá'ís of Germany and Austria was sent to Shoghi Effendi and all the National Spiritual Assemblies in the world. The press and radio also carried the news. On 24 April 1946 the Guardian responded to the delegates' message and announced that a considerable sum was to be donated in support of the teaching activities. Above all, he urged the Bahá'ís to establish a National Centre in Frankfurt am Main.

The sixth general German Bahá'í summer school, the first after the long involuntary break, took place, as in the past, in the 'Häusle' in Esslingen-Krummenacker from the 8th to the 14th of August 1946. 'It was a daring challenge ... in the middle of all the difficulties with travel, occupation zones, accommodation and food,' wrote Hermann Grossmann in his notes:

> The house, which had been already too small at the last summer school in 1936, would have needed to be twice the size to provide for the much greater numbers this time, but the mysterious, magic words 'love', 'harmony' and 'goodwill' resulted in the miracle that allowed 150 people to live together in such a small space for a week – dedicating themselves, despite rain and stormy weather, in complete harmony and absolute devotion, to the tasks of the week, to learn, to replenish their energies and prepare themselves for further service on behalf of the Sacred Cause. In view of the life-giving spirit and ample and inviting meals, the work of those same magicians sometimes seemed reminiscent of that ancient miracle of the Feeding of the Five Thousand.

At the opening ceremony in the packed assembly hall of the Teacher-Training Institute in Esslingen, Dr Grossmann, in his capacity as chairman of the National Spiritual Assembly welcomed friends and guests from the government and administrative authorities with a review:

> Despite being a relatively young institution, the German Bahá'í summer schools have wellnigh developed into a tradition, winning the appreciation and the hearts of large circles, and although we have to miss nearly all guests and Bahá'í speakers from various continents and numerous countries of the Bahá'í world, we still feel most intimately associated with them in spirit and affection, in keeping with the Bahá'í principle which is, to us, much more than a mere motto: 'This handful of dust, the earth, is *one* home, let it be in unity.'
>
> The eight years during which the Bahá'ís had to keep silent and suffer deprivation and persecution did nothing to affect their courage and

intrepid confidence in the coming of the Great Age of all-embracing unity prophesied by Bahá'u'lláh, nor to reduce the readiness of the German Bahá'ís to devote their energies fully to the implementation of the high ideals for mankind. When the hour of tribulation began in 1933, the Bahá'ís, having been brought up in a spirit of unswerving pioneering to the whole world, were able to look on the countless examples of heroism and the difficult tests endured throughout a century by their fellow believers in the birthplace of their religion, those faithful souls whose only reliable solace was so often the power of this Faith and the exalted Source from which it came. At this hour we are even more grateful to those insightful personalities and governments that, sometimes risking their reputation and good standing, have lent their assistance over the past century to this young religion whose efforts are directed towards the benefit not of itself but of the world, and this includes those in Germany who have helped and are helping to smooth the way.

During the time we Bahá'ís, whose faith commands us to refrain from rebellion and unauthorized interference in state matters, were obliged to keep silent during the eight years when our administrative order and the Bahá'í Faith itself were prohibited, we were aware that this was the time when – as Bahá'u'lláh and 'Abdu'l-Bahá had predicted – mankind would experience unspeakable sufferings as a result of religious, racial, national and social prejudice, before being subjected to seemingly unbearable birth pangs that would ultimately usher in a new age in which unity and peace would at last be achieved throughout the world. With almost frightening precision, that which Bahá'u'lláh and 'Abdu'l-Bahá predicted in urgent warnings from the middle of the last century onwards is now becoming reality before the very eyes of the world, and beyond the disruption, we can already discern the sublime beauty of that new age. In view of the current processes, does anyone whose eyes are open require further proof of the need for and truth of the Cause of Bahá'u'lláh, a religion of which Sir Herbert Samuel, former High Commissioner of Palestine, once said at a Religious Conference of the British Empire, 'Other religions and denominations have to consider how they might contribute to the idea of world unity. The Bahá'í Faith, however, exists almost entirely for the purpose of contributing to the friendship and unification of humankind.'

Thus, we Bahá'ís in Germany used the years leading up to the inevitable collapse of the regime to deepen ourselves in the Faith, to mature and grow, so as to be ready, whenever and wherever we might be called upon, to carry the light of clarity to a more mature humanity, drawing upon the abundant source that is the Faith of Bahá'u'lláh to guide people to the only path that, engaging all their efforts, can lead them out of their suffering. May the 6th German Bahá'í summer school, 1946, be a further link in the chain and a contribution to the German Bahá'í community as it re-establishes itself, as well as to the salvation of mankind and the fulfilment of humanity's great dream of a time when there will be 'one flock and one shepherd and peace on earth and goodwill to all men'.[79]

Most of the friends who were able to take part in the summer school came from the American or British zones of occupation. Crossing the border from the French and Soviet zones was still difficult. The many friends from other countries, who had enriched the summer schools before the interdiction, were missed – only John Eichenauer and Manutschehr Zabih, the first Persian believer that the German Bahá'ís had seen after ten years of isolation, were able to attend. A year later, in the summer of 1947, the summer school was so much in demand that two schools had to be held. The difficulties that were still associated with such an event are evident from a remark on the invitation stating that

> Participants are required to bring the following with them: cutlery, plate, cup and a woollen blanket, also ration cards for one week. Participants must provide their own bread for the week. Potatoes can be sent to the Bahá'í 'Häusle' prior to the start of the summer school.[80]

The wonderful atmosphere of a new start is also evident in the memoirs of Jean Sévin, who – like all male French citizens – had to do a year of military service after the Second World War in 1946. He was an officer cadet in the French occupation troops and was stationed in Idar Oberstein. One weekend when he was on leave he travelled to Neckargemünd to visit the Grossmann family. 'Entirely forgetful of political circumstances (namely the military occupation of Germany),' wrote Jean Sévin looking back more than fifty years later,

> I remained, all during this first meeting with the [later] Hand of the Cause, enchanted by his harmonious, vibrant and extremely warm voice. Despite several years' study of the German language at school, I did not understand all his words, but to tell the truth, this was not necessary, since he was so radiant with faith, enthusiasm and love ... No doubt it was necessary at that time, to overcome so much hatred and prejudices among belligerents, through these flames of love ... When I happen to look at photos of that period of time, I smile at seeing myself, during a Bahá'í summer school in Esslingen, dressed in uniform and surrounded by dozens of young Germans who, like me, had faith in a united, just and peaceful world: what might the others actually have thought on seeing our warm and obvious friendship, while I was supposed to be in an 'occupied enemy territory'?!

I have had the privilege afterwards to meet Hermann Grossmann again on several occasions and it was always a renewed joy. He appeared to me like a catalyst of love, constantly dispersing 'the divine fragrances'. What luck to have known such individuals ... It was mostly thanks to the influence of that vibrant Hand of the Cause of God that I was inspired to leave afterwards as a pioneer to the South Seas ... I am proud to be one of his friends.[81]

Jean Sévin became the Knight of Bahá'u'lláh to the Tuamoto Archipelago.

From the summer of 1946 and throughout 1947, the German Bahá'ís put all their efforts into a proclamation campaign. In countless public talks announced by means of posters and newspaper advertisements, they reached thousands of people with the Word of Bahá'u'lláh. All the available friends, whether they had been Bahá'ís for decades or only for a year, were tirelessly engaged in these activities. Teachers who were much in demand and constantly travelled throughout the country were Dr Adelbert Mühlschlegel, later to be appointed a Hand of the Cause of God by the Guardian, Dr Eugen Schmidt, Hede Schubert, Dr Heide Jäger, Dr Hermann Grossmann and Anna Grossmann.[82]

From January 1946 Hermann Grossmann was able to revive the publication of the *Bahá'í-Nachrichten* (Bahá'í News) that had been published by the National Spiritual Assembly prior to the interdiction in 1937. It was typed using a stencil, duplicated by hand with a machine, and then sent to all the believers to provide them with information about the most important events in the Bahá'í world. Everyone looked forward to it with excitement and it became an urgently needed link between the communities and groups, restoring a degree of normality to Bahá'í activities.[83] This publication has remained the internal organ of the Bahá'í community in Germany, a newsletter concerning all matters within the sphere of the National Spiritual Assembly and beyond, in the whole Bahá'í world. Via this regular newsletter, communications from the Guardian and – after his death – from the Hands of the Cause of God in the Holy Land and later from the Universal House of Justice could be distributed rapidly among the believers. Today the *Bahá'í-Nachrichten* comes in a modern form with plenty of pictures, printed on high gloss paper and overflowing with the latest news. When one compares today's newsletter with the issues produced in the years immediately after the Second World War written on a wax stencil and duplicated by hand, one cannot but be amazed. It was Hermann

Grossmann who restarted this publication and who remained its editor, producer, distributor and financier for many years, with the support of his wife and a few friends.

During this period he was also assisted by Martin Aiff, who remembers an episode that made a great impression on him and was to affect his future.

> I used to help Hermann with the duplication using wax stencil machines. He always gave me advice and he once gave me a severe scolding – and quite rightly so – because he had put a lot of work and effort into typing out study texts and making carbon copies and then we got this old manual wax stencil machine on which we could duplicate even more. I had not worked carefully enough – I had turned the handle too fast, so that the print was insufficient. That rightly annoyed our dear Hermann and he gave me a real roasting. Thus I gradually learned that if you are doing something on behalf of the Bahá'í Cause, or if you are doing anything at all as a Bahá'í, you must do it as well as you possibly can.[84]

In addition to the *Bahá'í-Nachrichten*, the American military government granted a licence for the publication of the *Jugendbrief* (Youth Letter), the new magazine for Bahá'í youth, and some small booklets. The printing of books and permission to restart publication of the magazine *Sonne der Wahrheit* – through which, until 1937, the friends had been supplied, in particular, with translations of the words of Bahá'u'lláh, 'Abdu'l-Bahá and sometimes with news from the Bahá'í world – was not possible owing to the paper shortage. It was not until August 1947 that restrictions were lifted and *Sonne der Wahrheit* could again be printed, albeit on poor quality paper. It continued to appear until March 1953, in its 22nd year of publication.

By the end of 1948 the typewritten study material produced in Neckargemünd amounted to 18 booklets with a total of almost 700 pages, of which about 2,100 copies were made – in all, approximately 73,900 individual sheets. This material, along with the 'Declaration of Trust' printed in the *Bahá'í-Nachrichten*, constituted the spiritual and administrative basis for instructing the believers and for teaching the Faith.[85]

At the end of 1946 work for the Cause nearly came to a standstill, because the health and working capacity of those engaged in teaching, especially the travelling teachers, were under serious threat due to shortage of food and over-exertion. The Guardian responded by requesting assistance for the German Bahá'ís, and thereupon it was possible to overcome this crisis through the many parcels of food and clothing sent by American and Persian believers. These parcels enabled the German Bahá'ís to continue the work and constituted a priceless gift of service to the Cause in Germany.

By April 1948 the number of communities had risen to 14 – one of which was Vienna in Austria. Bahá'ís also lived in 11 groups and 59 further localities. The isolation of Austria from Germany was implemented very strictly by the military governments, so that even correspondence between Bahá'ís in the two countries had to be sent indirectly via Switzerland. Nevertheless, the friends still succeeded in re-establishing the Local Spiritual Assembly of Vienna.

The Guardian's desire for a Ḥaẓíratu'l-Quds to be established in Frankfurt was difficult to fulfil because of the severe war damage suffered by the city. What living accommodation remained was rent-controlled, which meant that the Bahá'ís could neither rent nor purchase any property. The only alternative was to rebuild a building that had been partially or completely destroyed, but building materials could only be obtained on the 'black market', something that was incompatible with Bahá'í principles. The 'grey market' – a form of exchange that arose because of the devaluation of the German currency – would have required bartering food or valuables for building materials or the cost of labour, which the Bahá'ís could not afford to do. Therefore, the negotiations had to be shelved for the time being.[86]

The rebuilding of the Bahá'í community was more or less complete by April 1948, and on 10 June 1948 Rúḥíyyih Khánum wrote to Anna Grossmann on behalf of the Guardian:

> The progress being made by the Faith in Germany is excellent. It is as if at last the Cause were let out of the cage and can spread its wings there and fly – and the hearts of the German people are a very rich field in which to sow the Divine Seeds. He [the Guardian] has always foreseen for Germany a great future in the Bahá'í world ...[87]

A letter from Amatu'l-Bahá Rúḥíyyih Khánum to Anna Grossmann written in April 1948 reads: '... It is wonderful to see how fast our Movement is spreading in Germany ... What a pity it is that people have to go through such disappointment before they give up the worship of political ideals ...' And in another letter to Anna Grossmann dated March 1947 we read her words of warning: 'I think now is the time to teach the Cause ... later it may be too late to achieve the same success.'[88]

That development happened only too soon. By 1948 the people of Germany were slowly starting to recover from the disaster of the Second World War. The country began to rise up from the ashes, and the currency reform of June 1948 – the reorganization of the financial system which had been shattered by the war economy – caused the black and grey markets to disappear. The impoverished people could once again obtain material goods. Hard work was worthwhile again because it was possible to buy things with the money one earned – and Germany experienced what became known as the *Wirtschaftswunder*, the 'economic miracle'. However, this economic miracle was accompanied by materialistic thinking. The hearts of the people were no longer open to spiritual matters; they increasingly turned a deaf ear to the Cause of Bahá'u'lláh. After suffering deprivation and hunger for so many years, people wished to eat their fill, indeed to feast if they could afford it. Building a house and achieving prosperity became more pressing desires – as if this generation had not just experienced the futility of all material values and the loss they engender. At the same time, however, a necessary cleansing process took place in the Bahá'í community: those who had only wanted to have a share of the food and clothing parcels from the United States and Iran withdrew from the Faith.

The Guardian expressed some concern about the state of the German Bahá'í community and admonished them that:

> The process that has been set in motion after so long a period of forced inactivity ... must, in no wise be arrested or even retarded ... I appeal to them, with all my heart, to close their ranks, purge their hearts, broaden their vision, renew their determination, rededicate themselves to their glorious task, march resolutely forward ... until their goal is attained, and the first stage in the evolution of their collective task is brought to a victorious conclusion ...[89]

The currency reform, which constituted the basis for the rebuilding of the devastated country, could only be implemented in the American, British and French occupation zones. The Soviet Union did not permit the part of Germany under its occupation to participate in this reform and introduced a separate currency reform in its own zone. Hence, there were now two currencies in Germany, and whereas the Western zones were given a democratic form of government with all the concomitant liberties, the Eastern, Soviet-controlled zone was increasingly cut off.

THE RENEWAL OF BAHÁ'Í ACTIVITIES, 1945–1948

In 1949, the Soviet-occupied zone became the German Democratic Republic (GDR). The three Western zones of occupation were united to form the Federal Republic of Germany (FRG), and henceforth the two states took a different path of development. The world divided into two camps, the 'Cold War' began, and the border between the two camps ran right through the middle of Germany. Under pressure from the occupying powers, the two German states re-armed and, only three years after the military and economic collapse, they looked upon each other as enemies.

The utterly different and irreconcilable ideologies also caused a different development of the Bahá'í community in Germany. Whereas in the American zone the efforts to obtain permission for Bahá'í activities bore fruit as early as the summer of 1945, all attempts to do the same in the Soviet zone were in vain. A written interdiction on activities was issued on 17 November 1948. It read:

> In response to your letter, I hereby inform you that the activities of the Bahá'í community are not permitted in the Soviet occupied zone. Signed: (name) Hauptmann.[90]

According to the report issued at the 1950 National Convention, the Spiritual Assemblies of Schwerin and Leipzig were still able to function, whilst the friends in Rostock and Warnemünde 'are not only struggling with material privations, but are also in grave danger'.

The friends in the Federal Republic tried to maintain contact through correspondence and, by sending coded messages, to inform the Bahá'ís cut off in the east about the progress being made in the western part of Germany and in the world at large. The renewed isolation and repression imposed by the new regime – one which every Bahá'í had hoped would bring liberation – was hard to bear for the believers in the east. A letter to Anna Grossmann from a believer in Rostock reads,

> ... How I miss exchanging spiritual thoughts. There are some things I can't stop thinking about day and night. Who can imagine how someone feels who knows that the clouds are only an obstacle before the sun but who nevertheless suffers for lack of sunshine? And in these difficult times one searches for a possible way to express what one is feeling inside ...[91]

In July 1950, freedom of religious worship was suppressed throughout the GDR. Thereupon, the National Spiritual Assembly dissolved the community structures in that sector, hoping to prevent any persecution of the friends there. Activities in the Soviet-occupied zone came to a standstill. Only five years after the repeal of the interdiction imposed by the National Socialists, the Bahá'í community in eastern Germany was again proscribed. The Social Committee of the National Spiritual Assembly continued to support the friends by sending food parcels for as long as possible, but eventually even this became too dangerous. The GDR hermetically sealed off its 17 million citizens from the western part of Germany by means of walls, fences, and a 'death strip' in which border guards were ordered to shoot at anyone trying to 'flee the republic'.

In a message from the Guardian about the Ten Year Crusade we find the prophetic words:

> Collateral with this ominous laxity in morals, and this progressive stress laid on man's material pursuits and well-being, is the darkening of the political horizon, as witnessed by the widening of the gulf separating the protagonists of two antagonistic schools of thought which, however divergent in their ideologies, are to be commonly condemned by the upholders of the standard of the Faith of Bahá'u'lláh for their materialistic philosophies and their neglect of those spiritual values and eternal verities on which alone a stable and flourishing civilization can be ultimately established.[92]

In the years that followed, peoples suffered deprivation and despair or were driven to death or perpetual poverty as a result of localized 'proxy wars' fought around the world on behalf of the two power blocs. Some tribes were completely wiped out, since the basis of their livelihood was destroyed through certain individuals' hunger for profit.

CHAPTER 11

THE FIVE YEAR PLAN 1948–1953

In 1948, the Guardian considered the time right for the German Bahá'ís to draw up a Five Year Plan, so as to have clearly outlined goals for their work. In October 1948 the National Spiritual Assembly issued the Plan. Its general objective was, on the one hand, to consolidate the Administrative Order and expand the teaching work and, on the other, to penetrate more deeply into the teachings and to establish a National Bahá'í Centre in Frankfurt am Main. A whole series of primary works by Bahá'u'lláh, 'Abdu'l-Bahá and Shoghi Effendi were to be published – initially in the journal *Sonne der Wahrheit* and later in book form. These included *Gleanings from the Writings of Bahá'u'lláh* and *The Dispensation of Bahá'u'lláh*, which Elsa Maria Grossmann had translated. The Assembly planned the printing of compilations that had so far existed only as typewritten manuscripts produced by Dr Grossmann. In addition to a new edition of Dr Esslemont's *Bahá'u'lláh and the New Era*, the Five Year Plan also envisaged the republication of Hermann Grossmann's book *Am Morgen einer neuen Zeit* (At the Dawn of a New Age) and his book *Umbruch zur Einheit* (Breakthrough to Unity). The number of communities was to be increased from fourteen to twenty-eight and a large number of centres were to be established. Work with the youth was to be intensified and the youth magazine *Jugendbrief* was to be made more attractive. Training centres for pioneers were to be established in Esslingen and Neckargemünd.[93]

After the currency reform it finally became possible to purchase a location for a Bahá'í Centre in Frankfurt. The Bahá'ís managed to acquire a severely damaged house at Westendstraße 24. It was in a very convenient location, close to the railway station of this aspiring city that was soon to become a major European metropolis. The raised ground floor of the building was in fairly good condition. The rubble from the upper floors of this once attractive late nineteenth-century house was piled up in the garden. The elderly couple who owned the house retained their right of residence in the undamaged basement apartment. Young Bahá'ís from all over Germany came and cleared the rubble, which was taken away in large trucks. The National Spiritual Assembly called for donations so that at least the raised ground floor could be protected by a temporary roof, and measures could be undertaken to secure the fire gable, corner tower and a bearing wall. The response to the call was modest, since the Bahá'ís – like everyone in the Federal Republic of Germany – were still very poor at that time. To make matters worse, a sum of 80,000 *reichsmark*, which had been donated before the currency reform, was lost because it could no longer be exchanged for the new, hard currency. The Guardian had promised to send money, which was now transferred via Switzerland and sent in the form of food vouchers. The Bahá'ís in Germany then bought these, because there was still a shortage of food. This method ensured that the losses incurred through the transfer were minimized. The resulting money enabled the reconstruction work – planned and supervised by the architect Bruno Bauer of Stuttgart – to begin, and as soon as each room was finished the Bahá'ís immediately took possession of it and put it to use.

The Hand of the Cause of God Dr 'Alí Muḥammad Varqá visited the Ḥaẓíratu'l-Quds as early as 1949, when only the ground floor had been completed. In 1995 he wrote to Counsellor Hartmut Grossmann:

> [My] first encounter [with Hermann Grossmann] was in 1949 when I travelled for the first time to Germany and had the privilege of visiting a group of German Bahá'ís in Frankfurt assembled for a meeting in the basement of an old building which served as the Bahá'í Centre. The gathering was chaired by your dear father who offered me a seat beside himself to facilitate the translation of the discussion for me. In the gathering I was attracted by his strong personality and his capability in administering the Bahá'í meeting. Two days later, in Heidelberg, I had the bounty of visiting your dear mother in a larger gathering in which she was the chairperson and a speaker.[94]

In April 1950 it was possible for the first time to hold the National Convention in the Bahá'í Centre in Westendstraße. The Secretary of the National Spiritual Assembly now resided in the building, thus fulfilling Shoghi Effendi's urgent request that the seat of the National Spiritual Assembly be transferred from Stuttgart to Frankfurt am Main.

THE FIVE YEAR PLAN 1948–1953

During the 1951 National Convention the architect handed the keys over ceremonially to Dr Eugen Schmidt, the chairman of the National Spiritual Assembly.

At this conference Anna Grossmann gave a talk on teaching as the cornerstone of the Faith. The words of 'Abdu'l-Bahá, that God will support all those who arise to serve Him ... and that nothing is impossible for them as long as they have faith, Anna Grossmann said, are not only words of comfort or edification but are a fact, and this fact has been proven a thousand times. At the same time, however, the Bahá'ís should remember that they constitute a unified, living body consisting of many cells, each of which has to be healthy. Our unity and unanimity is our protection in this world, which is so very different in outlook. The stronger our faith, the easier will be our path.[95]

The Ḥaẓíratu'l-Quds was the venue for a great many events before it was eventually sold in 1970. In addition to the annual National Conventions there were conferences and even summer schools, such as one held in May 1950 led by Anna Grossmann. The house in Westendstraße was not only a material asset, it was *the* focal point of the German Bahá'í community. It was the backbone for public appearances, for representation of the Faith in relation to the State and the Church, and its existence marked an extremely important stage in the process of the Faith's emergence from obscurity, as the secretary of the National Spiritual Assembly pointed out in his 1952 report. In 1952 'Westendstraße 24 had been raised, but it was not yet complete', and – above all – it was still under mortgage. A primary goal was therefore to pay off the mortgage.

Work with the youth was still carried on intensively. As well as working to remove the rubble at the Ḥaẓíratu'l-Quds in Frankfurt, the Bahá'í youth held a camp at Gross-Heubach am Main, just below the Church of Pilgrimage at Engelberg, from 20–30 August 1948. It was led by Hermann Grossmann. The youth made contact with young people from the local area, and even the monks from the Engelberg Monastery occasionally came down to the camp.[96]

In the summer of 1950 Ian Semple, later to become a member of the Universal House of Justice, came to Germany for the first time. He was a young man and he came to participate in the summer school at Breuberg castle. He later wrote about this visit:

The south of Germany was at that time the American zone of occupation and, for some obscure reason, all I had to do was to show my [British] passport on the buses to be allowed to travel free ... I saw my first Autobahn and was greatly astonished by it. In the afternoon we took the train to Breuberg, an old castle, now used as a youth hostel, where the Youth Summer Week took place. We slept in bunk beds in dormitories, and the only washing facility for the boys was a horse-trough in the courtyard ... Beatrice Ashton came to give a course on the Lesser Covenant. Dr Grossmann was also there for part of the time. In those days the German Bahá'í youth used to sing a lot – not Bahá'í songs, there weren't any – but old German songs. It was a most wonderful experience and tremendously confirming, and I gained a profound love and admiration for Hermann and Anna Grossmann.[97]

In an interview with Anke Grossmann, in which she asked Ian Semple whether Hermann Grossmann was a quiet person or very energetic, he described him as follows:

It is difficult to say. He was not boisterous. He was not a dominating figure. He was quiet in that sense. But he had quite a presence. And so he did not have to push, he was simply there. At the summer school for example I don't remember him taking a prominent part. But he was there and just influencing.[98]

The German Bahá'í youth soon regarded Ian Semple as one of their own. He spoke excellent German and took part in everything.

In the 1949/1950 winter semester, the Federal Republic of Germany opened its universities and polytechnic High Schools to students from abroad. Young Persians came, including some young Persian Bahá'ís, mainly to study medicine and mechanical engineering in Heidelberg, Freiburg, Stuttgart and Frankfurt am Main. They were an important stimulus to the work of the Bahá'ís in Germany and brought with them something that the German believers often lacked: spontaneous warmth and openness, expressing their affection and their innermost feelings without formality or reservation.

Dr Mokhtar Afscharian, later a successful radiologist in Cologne and a popular Bahá'í teacher, humorously describes the situation of young Persians at that time:

None of us could speak a word of German. The language of communication was our imperfect English. The place where we sought refuge from our worries, answers to our questions, consolation and comfort, was with the families of Dr Schmidt, Dr Grossmann and Dr Mühlschlegel, whose doors were open day and night for us. Some of us were still very young and some had never before been out of their homeland, or even their home town. For many of us, German manners and habits seemed very strange, such as not cutting potatoes with a knife, or sometimes having to balance peas on the back of one's fork, or that during meals it wasn't permissible to express one's emotions loudly or use additional hand movements or gestures. This made it difficult for some of us to fit in.

A few were enticed by the freedoms available. I myself came from a pious Muslim family and had only had the bounty of learning about the Bahá'í Faith at the age of 16, not through reading about it, but through contact with very loving people in Persia. In Heidelberg I often forgot the dates of Nineteen Day Feasts and Bahá'í Holy Days. A somewhat older student with a funny name (Udo Schaefer) occasionally reminded us in the canteen that there had been a Nineteen Day Feast the night before, and I could not understand why that was a reason to miss out on going dancing when it was Carnival time.

Thank God, the Grossmann family in Neckargemünd showed great patience and understanding in the face of our lack of punctuality and our laxity in such matters. It was through the patience of Anna Grossmann, in particular, that we eventually came to appreciate the importance of the Bahá'í summer schools. But when Dr Grossmann once spoke to us about the importance of the National Convention and called upon our sense of duty, I tried to explain to him – in my poor German – about the dangers of nationalism. Thanks to Anna's patience, the family eventually managed to help me understand the difference.

When one day a Spiritual Assembly was to be formed in North Rhine-Westphalia and Dr Grossmann asked me and another Bahá'í student in Heidelberg if we could move to Cologne to continue our studies, my understanding was at an end. Was I supposed to give up my place at the university in beautiful Heidelberg and go to Cologne, an industrial city? That was asking too much! And what about my large circle of friends! His face full of hope, Dr Grossmann said, 'I will pray for you.' However, it was very difficult for me to make a decision, especially because I had lost my heart in Heidelberg. Until, that is, I was coming home from the cinema at 10 o'clock in the evening two days before Riḍván, when by chance I bumped into the girl who had captured my heart in the company of another young countryman. With that, the fetters tying me to Heidelberg were removed. I immediately called the Grossmann family and informed them that I was ready to move to Bonn the next day to help form the Spiritual Assembly, since the Guardian wished an Assembly to be formed there first. Dr Grossmann did not ask what had brought about my change of heart, but he calmed me on the telephone, saying, 'Mokhtar, I don't know what has happened, but what has happened is God's Will and is important for your future.' For years, whenever I met him I referred to this incident and he always stressed that, 'We are all children of God and gain strength from our prayers. Our efforts are important, but ultimately we should let God decide.'[99]

Hermann Grossmann knew that the young Persians were at risk when living in a western culture that they had not learned to adapt to. He tried to let them sense his deep love for them, and for some of them he became a spiritual father. Shoghi Effendi requested reports about the Persian students, and he was very concerned about some of them abusing their newly-found personal freedom.

Hermann Grossmann also met the young friends in their very simple living quarters, often student dormitories. 'We spread a newspaper as a tablecloth over a box,' remembers Dr Parviz Eschraghi, 'and I prepared some Persian dish in a frying pan, which we then ate with various bits of cutlery straight from the pan. Then we went for a walk. He told me a lot, and although I only understood five words, a sense of love, association and friendship developed. Dr Grossmann was deeply fond of the Persian friends and reacted extremely sensitively to any criticism of them.'[100] Some German Bahá'ís found it difficult to understand the young Persians and thought they ought unhesitatingly to adopt western ways of behaviour and thinking.

From 5–7 August 1949, Hermann Grossmann participated in the annual conference of the European Teaching Committee in Brussels. After the forced isolation and the catastrophic war that had caused so much damage to people's minds, this was the first time that a believer from Germany had participated as a representative in an international Bahá'í conference.

Eunice Braun, an American believer, remembers that Edna True, then chairman of the European Teaching Committee in Geneva and member of the U.S. National Spiritual Assembly, once told the following story:

> A German believer appeared unexpectedly at the conference in 1949 while the horror of the war was still keen in the minds of the people. These newly declared Bahá'ís, whose experience and knowledge of the teachings was still quite limited, were disturbed and upset by the appearance of the

Hermann and Anna Grossmann on the land in Neckargemünd on which their house was to be built, with friends from Heidelberg and Neckargemünd, 1931

The 'yellow house' in Neckargemünd, home of the Grossmann family. Hermann Grossmann drew up the building plans himself

Neckargemünd, 1939. Left to right, standing: Hermann Grossmann, Irmgard Macco, Fritz Macco, Martha Macco, Lina Bracht, Carla Macco, Anna Grossmann. Sitting: Elsa Maria Grossmann, Johanna Grossmann, Susanne Grossmann, Fritz Strauß, Eduard Bracht

Saichiro Fujita and Susanne Grossmann, 1937

The young Elsa Maria Grossmann

Pilgrimage, Haifa, 1937. Front row from left: Anna, Susanne and Elsa Maria Grossmann, Javidukht Khadem and her children, with May Maxwell seated behind. Back row: Hermann Grossmann, Fujita and Zikrullah Khadem. Hussein Rabbani is seated in the centre behind Elsa Maria Grossmann

Summer school at the 'Häusle' ('little house') in Esslingen near Stuttgart, c. 1935

First Bahá'í youth summer school after the Second World War, Heppenheim an der Bergstraße, 3–10 August 1946. From left: unidentified, Herta Böhmer, Susanne Grossmann, Erich Clauer, Bernhard Krekel, Hermann Grossmann, unidentified

Participants at the youth summer school, 1946, in their tent

Anna and Hermann Grossmann

Poster announcing the first public lecture on the Bahá'í Faith after World War II, Heidelberg, 1947

A visit from Johnny Eichenauer, Neckargemünd, c. 1946. From left: Elsa Maria Grossmann, Peter Gerber, Carla Macco, Lina Benke, Anna Grossmann, Johnny Eichenauer, Susanne Grossmann, Hartmut Grossmann

Bahá'í World Youth Day in Heidelberg, 12 February 1949

Hermann Grossmann with his son Hartmut, and Lina Benke

German visitor. Then Edna True spoke with the assembled believers and explained to them what the Bahá'í principles were in this regard. As a result the understanding of the believers was greatly expanded and changed completely. They welcomed the new friend – Hermann Grossmann – with love and open arms, a deeply moving experience for those present at the conference. Then the new visitor spoke to the Bahá'ís and won their hearts as many heartfelt tears were shed. These were wonderful days as the new friends from various countries began their great work for the Faith.[101]

Still enthused from this wonderful conference, Hermann Grossmann travelled on to the summer school in Esslingen and reported about the friends he had met in Brussels and about the teaching activities going on in the rest of Europe.

In preparation for a training course for pioneers, the National Teaching and Liaison Committee in Neckargemünd headed by Hermann Grossmann held a Whitsuntide conference in 1949 which was dedicated exclusively to the concept of the Covenant. Accommodation was provided in the Bahá'í hostel next to the yellow house, and the participants were asked to bring blankets and 'breadspread' (butter, cheese, jam, etc.) The hosts also asked each participant to study a certain text in advance, which would form the basis of discussion. In the *Bahá'í-Nachrichten* one of the participants wrote,

> It is hard to say which factors combined particularly well to cause this meeting to make such an unforgettable impression that is still vivid in the hearts of the participants. Perhaps it was the fact that what was done there complied with that which our Guardian regards as the most urgent necessity for the progress of the Faith ...[102]

By 1950 the Guardian was of the opinion that the pioneering activities should be expanded. He pointed out that the mortal remains of the first martyr of the European Bahá'í community, Adam Benke, had been laid to rest in the soil of Bulgaria in 1932 and declared,

> No more adequate and better field can be imagined ... than the neighbouring territories situated in the Balkan Peninsula, the Baltic States and further afield the vast stretches now enveloped in darkness ...[103]

The life of Adam Benke was evidently blessed by divine guidance. He was born in 1878 to German parents on a farm in southern Russia. Like many other Germans, his ancestors had responded to the call of the Czar and settled as farmers in the south of Russia. At the age of nine, Adam Benke contracted smallpox and did not recover from the illness for four years. His pious mother vowed that if God saved him, he would become a missionary. Eventually a woman skilled in the preparation of herbal remedies managed to cure him using Sarsaparilla grass and unleavened bread. When Adam Benke was old enough and his parents wished to fulfil the promise they had made, there were several bad harvests and a severe famine in southern Russia. Their livestock died and the family had only the bare minimum needed to survive. The idea of undergoing the expensive course of training to become a priest had to be dropped. Instead, Adam Benke trained as a teacher and taught the children of an aristocratic family. In Kiev he married Lina Wolf, who had been born in Karlsruhe in southern Germany and who, likewise, now worked as a governess for members of the Russian landed gentry.

During the First World War the German army penetrated deep into Russia and when the German soldiers were forced to retreat, along with the White Army, the Benkes went with them to Germany and settled in Leipzig. Their experiences had turned them into seekers after spiritual truth, and their souls were prepared, so that Lina Benke immediately accepted the new teachings when she first heard about the Bahá'í Faith from Mr and Mrs Ober in 1920. When her husband returned from a journey, she greeted him with the words, 'I've found what we've always been looking for.' Like his wife, Adam Benke embraced the Cause of Bahá'u'lláh and from then on both of them dedicated their lives to it. One of the places where they served the Faith was in Sofia, Bulgaria, responding to the call of Marion Jack, 'the radiant example for all pioneers', as Shoghi Effendi called her. During his travels in Bulgaria, Adam Benke's knowledge of Russian and Esperanto were of great value. This enabled him to bring the message of Bahá'u'lláh to many people. He worked day and night to serve the Cause and did not pay attention to his poor health. He died unexpectedly in Sofia in 1932 with the 'Remover of Difficulties' on his lips. The Guardian honoured him with the title 'the first martyr of Europe'. His grave in the cemetery in Sofia is still cared for by the Bahá'ís. Did he not indeed become a missionary of God as his mother had once pledged?[104]

Lina Benke, who had accompanied her husband to Bulgaria, now returned to Leipzig and worked actively there for the propagation of the Bahá'í Faith until she was prevented from doing so by the National Socialist interdiction. When her home was destroyed by a bomb in the Second World War, causing the loss of all her possessions, she came to Neckargemünd and lived from 1944 to 1966 in gratitude and contentment with the Grossmann family. She died in her 97th year in a nursing home in Nussloch near Heidelberg.

In the spring of 1950 Anna Grossmann led a pioneer-training course in Frankfurt, in which believers were prepared for their teaching work by Hermann Grossmann. The central theme was the Covenant of God as the basis for all Bahá'í activities.

On 17 and 18 November the second All-Swiss Conference took place in Zurich. Several German Bahá'ís were able to take part. Hermann Grossmann used this journey to the conference for intensive teaching activities, and on his way back he visited all the centres in Switzerland.

The conflict between the world's two dominant political power blocs intensified during the following years, and the idea of travelling to the countries of Eastern Europe, which were in the sphere of influence of the Soviet Union, was no longer viable. The friends living in the eastern part of Germany, behind the 'iron curtain', were in great danger.

'The progress achieved in recent months ... is highly exhilarating,' Shoghi Effendi wrote to the German friends on 2 March 1951. 'The one dark cloud on an otherwise bright horizon has been the disabilities suffered by their brethren and compatriots in the Eastern zone of their divided land and their virtual separation from them at a time when their close association and collaboration would have greatly reinforced the foundations of their common Faith and redounded to its fame and glory.'[105]

The first Bahá'í conference in Berlin after the Second World War took place in July 1951. The city had been divided by the Allied Forces into American, British, French and Soviet sectors. It was surrounded by the Soviet-occupied zone. As a result of the Cold War, the part of Berlin occupied by the Western powers soon took on the character of an island of democratic freedoms in a sea controlled by a hostile regime. American, British and French citizens could generally travel through the Soviet zone to Berlin without hindrance. For many years, Germans could not. They had to fly in, which was very expensive. Therefore, Hermann Grossmann was the only speaker from the Western part of Germany to attend the conference, so that he became an important point of contact with the communities there. He delivered two well-attended public lectures and was moved when, on the second evening, a woman he did not know handed him a bouquet of flowers, thanking him for the evenings that had given her so much. For the Bahá'ís, the climax of the conference was when Hermann Grossmann explained the New Covenant and its significance for the Faith. This was followed by explanations about the Administrative Order and its spiritual consequences. The successful meeting ended with a promise from the National Spiritual Assembly that it would support the young Berlin community.[106]

In a letter dated 30 October 1951, the Guardian urged the Bahá'ís to arise and pioneer despite the restrictions:

> The most important thing of all ... is to make the friends pioneer conscious; they must learn to venture forth ... and go to new cities and towns ... This will mark an entirely new phase in the history of the Cause in Germany ... When they see how, after years of persecution, of war, occupation, financial chaos and instability, they have built their Ḥaẓíra and moved their National Headquarters to it, they must feel both astonished at their victory and immensely proud.[107]

The Guardian saw the consolidation and expansion of the administrative base and the reproduction of literature as a precondition for the German community to

> spread out into Eastern and Southern Europe, and beyond these spheres into the heart of Northern Asia, as far as the China Sea ... Then and only then, will this community be empowered to launch befittingly its first campaign across the borders of its native land, and manifest ... the potencies with which its Divine Founder, the Centre of the Covenant, endowed it in the course of the last decade of His Ministry.[108]

Shoghi Effendi once said during a table talk that not only the German Bahá'ís, but also the German nation had an important task to fulfil in Russia. The German, and also the Chinese communities, were to take the Faith to Russia.[109]

In a letter to the German believers at the end of the Five Year Plan, Shoghi Effendi wrote,

> They, no doubt, stand, emerging as they have done, from two successive world ordeals that have served to purify, vitalize, and weld them together, on the threshold of an era of glorious achievements, both at home and abroad. Their present Plan is but the initial chapter in the history of their collective achievements in the service of the Faith of Bahá'u'lláh ...[110]

CHAPTER 12

APPOINTMENT AS A HAND OF THE CAUSE OF GOD

In His Will and Testament, 'Abdu'l-Bahá provided for the establishment by the Guardian of an institution called 'Hands of the Cause of God' to support both Shoghi Effendi and the future Universal House of Justice:

> O friends! The Hands of the Cause of God must be nominated and appointed by the guardian of the Cause of God. All must be under his shadow and obey his command ... The obligations of the Hands of the Cause of God are to diffuse the Divine Fragrances, to edify the souls of men, to promote learning, to improve the character of all men and to be, at all times and under all conditions, sanctified and detached from earthly things. They must manifest the fear of God by their conduct, their manners, their deeds and their words.
>
> This body of the Hands of the Cause of God is under the direction of the guardian of the Cause of God. He must continually urge them to strive and endeavour to the utmost of their ability to diffuse the sweet savours of God, and to guide all the peoples of the world, for it is the light of Divine Guidance that causeth all the universe to be illuminated. To disregard, though it be for a moment, this absolute command which is binding upon everyone, is in no wise permitted, that the existent world may become even as the Abhá Paradise, that the surface of the earth may become heavenly, that contention and conflict amidst peoples, kindreds, nations and governments may disappear, that all the dwellers on earth may become one people and one race, that the world may become even as one home ...[111]

In her book *The Priceless Pearl*[112] Amatu'l-Bahá Rúḥíyyih Khánum, the Guardian's wife, describes the steps taken by the Guardian in response to 'Abdu'l-Bahá's instructions. In November 1950 he sent the first invitations to seven Bahá'ís to come to Haifa in order to establish an International Bahá'í Council consisting of these seven friends. On 9 January 1951 he sent a cable informing the Bahá'í world about this important step. In March 1952 and again in May 1955, he expanded the Council to a membership of nine. The Council functioned as a secretariat and received its instructions directly from the Guardian. All members were occupied with the tasks entrusted to them, some of these being discharged outside the Holy Land. This international body was the liaison with the Israeli government and the city authorities of Haifa when administrative matters were concerned. It was intended as a preliminary institution in preparation for the establishment of the Universal House of Justice.

On 30 November 1951 the Guardian announced a 'Great Jubilee' commemorating the centenary of the birth of Bahá'u'lláh's revelation in the Síyáh-Chál prison. The celebration was to begin in October 1952 with the opening of a Holy Year.

Just over three weeks later, in a cable to the Bahá'ís of the world on 24 December 1951, Shoghi Effendi announced that he had taken the next 'fundamental step in the development of the World Centre of the Faith' by appointing the first contingent of Hands of the Cause of God. In accordance with the instructions given by 'Abdu'l-Bahá in His Will and Testament, the twelve Bahá'ís appointed were entrusted with the dual obligation of propagating the Faith and preserving its unity. The twelve friends were distributed equally between the Holy Land and the continents of Asia, America and Europe. Among the three European Hands to be appointed was Hermann Grossmann.

On 23 December 1951, the Guardian had sent the following cable to Hermann Grossmann:

> GUARDIAN CABLES MOVED CONVEY GLAD TIDINGS YOUR ELEVATION RANK HAND CAUSE. APPOINTMENT OFFICIALLY ANNOUNCED PUBLIC MESSAGE ADDRESSED ALL NATIONAL ASSEMBLIES. MAY SACRED FUNCTION ENABLE YOU ENRICH RECORD SERVICES ALREADY RENDERED FAITH BAHÁ'U'LLÁH, SHOGHI.[113]

For Hermann Grossmann, this message from the Guardian was completely unexpected, and it was something for which he was not at all prepared. Thus, his initial reaction was one of perplexity. Full of humility towards the Cause of Bahá'u'lláh and with sincere love for Shoghi Effendi, who was bringing to fruition the task entrusted to him by 'Abdu'l-Bahá, he replied to the Guardian on 28 December 1951:

APPOINTMENT AS A HAND OF THE CAUSE OF GOD

SHOGHI RABBANI HAIFA ISRAEL, DEEPLY IMPRESSED ASSURE LOVING OBEDIENCE. DR HERMANN GROSSMANN.

The Guardian's cable had been sent via the International Bahá'í Bureau in Geneva. On 28 December Anne Lynch, secretary of the Bahá'í Bureau, wrote an accompanying letter which reads as follows:

> Dear Hermann,
> During my absence the Guardian's cable arrived with the wonderful news for you. As far as I know, no such honour has been bestowed on a Bahá'í before, at least during his lifetime, and I can well imagine how happy this blessing has made you. Every day of your life, it will bring you new blessings and new strength. I should like to congratulate you most sincerely, although I do not know how to find the right words to express my joy for you. And I should like to say one more thing: how very happy I am that this gracious favour, this blessing ... has been bestowed upon a German. That is really something great that will also bring blessings upon your country.

Congratulations poured in from all over the Bahá'í world. The secretary of the National Spiritual Assembly of the Bahá'ís in Germany and Austria wrote to Hermann Grossmann saying,

> the appointment of the Hands by the Guardian is vivid evidence that the New Age is dawning ... Your appointment ... is a blessing for the Bahá'í community in our country, and one for which we may be immensely grateful ... We see in your appointment the careful guidance of the Guardian, the blessings of which we hope to benefit from in our work ...[114]

The Iranian Committee of the National Spiritual Assembly also offered its congratulations and blessings on behalf of all Iranian Bahá'ís – at this time almost exclusively students – residing in Germany.

In a beautiful letter, the National Spiritual Assembly of India, Pakistan and Burma assured Hermann Grossmann of its great joy on hearing of his appointment:

> Oh! We are happy, so happy at this historic step of the Sovereign of our hearts and souls that we feel like flying in the air. The vision of coming triumphs of the Faith of Bahá'u'lláh and of the termination of misery and afflictions in the world of being make our spirits to dance with glee and sing the songs of praise of our beloved Guardian through whom the Great God is achieving this most significant victory of His Cause. We are looking forward with pleasure to the days when we shall have blessings of sitting

at your feet and learn the lessons of devotion and servitude to the First Guardian of the Great Faith embracing the whole Planet.[115]

The Bahá'ís of Iran wrote via the secretary of their National Spiritual Assembly:

> Indeed your elevation to so noble a rank will render your name as well as your brilliant services imperishable in the annals of the Faith. It is a matter of heartfelt delight for all the suffering friends in this country to witness the beloved Guardian taking so significant a step towards the creation of yet another mighty institution as provided in the Will and Testament of the Master.[116]

The National Spiritual Assembly of the British Isles sent its loving greetings on behalf of the British friends and expressed the hope of meeting Hermann Grossmann during the forthcoming African and European conferences already announced by the Guardian as part of the Holy Year.[117]

The Africa Committee in London and the Bahá'ís of Kampala, Uganda wrote of their joyful anticipation of seeing him at the Conference in Uganda as the Guardian's personal representative:

> Oh what joy we feel and with what eagerness we look forward to your coming. The very hills of Kampala rejoice at the thought, and we, the few humble souls working here in His Name, have the great privilege of preparing for that wonderful day.[118]

The Bahá'ís of the United States of America and the friends from Egypt and the Sudan all sent their good wishes. The National Spiritual Assembly of the Bahá'ís of Canada wrote:

> These services which you have, over a long period of time, tirelessly rendered to the Cause stand as an example which all of us, to the degree of our capacity, may attempt to emulate. Your appointment brings to all of us the new and tangible evidence of that 'Celestial Strength' which lies at the very heart of the Faith, and which is now making itself felt with ever increasing momentum. We recognize and rejoice in the fact that your appointment to this station, representing as it does the fruits of long years of dedicated service, is a new outpouring of Divine bounty which has been bestowed upon our community.[119]

The friends in Luxembourg were particularly happy that six of the

APPOINTMENT AS A HAND OF THE CAUSE OF GOD

newly appointed Hands had in the past visited their community, and they hoped that this would have a significant influence on their teaching activities.[120]

Many Bahá'ís from far and near – both friends who were already well known for their work on behalf of the Cause of Bahá'u'lláh and others who worked quietly in the background – sent their greetings and congratulations. One of the most moving letters came from Ben Levy, who had been of great assistance to the Bahá'ís in Germany after the Second World War. He wrote as follows:

> In the forests near Brückenau, August 18, 1952 – Monday.
>
> Beloved Hand of the Cause – Dr Grossmann,
> It is with deep humility and loving gratitude that I write you as I sit in the shaded forests on maneuvers, for now, as it has been since I left Esslingen, my thoughts turn to the Bahá'í Sommerschule and the wonderful time I had there. Meeting so many beautiful and radiant Bahá'ís filled me to the brim with happiness.
>
> Most outstanding in the events that I witnessed was on a Wednesday evening outside the entrance of the Sommerschule as the sun was about to set, when there gathered about a figure a number of loving friends. And as he was about to take his leave from them there arose a most melodious hymn – chanted by a Persian Bahá'í named Heschmat, singing *The Promised One is Come*; and the assembled believers joined in the refrain singing Alláh-u-Abhá. As the song progressed there emerged a spirit that stirred one's very soul, and the figure seemed as if to cry out with a deep and compassionate gratitude for being a Bahá'í and knowing so many radiant souls. That figure, Dr Grossmann, was you. I could not but help being overcome by so touching a sight, and it was but a climax to a lasting impression I got of you.
>
> There is so much I do not know about our great Cause, but I am able to recognize great spiritual stature. To my mind you are a very great man, my dear Dr Grossmann, and it is therefore with the love of the Faith and gratitude too that comes from being one of its exponents that I pay this, my humble tribute to you.
>
> And I thank you for the love and kindness you showered upon me, as you did with all the friends; and may the blessings of the Most Great Spirit never cease to flow from the chambers of your heart. I am most proud to know you.
>
> A loving friend, Ben Levy

Agnes Alexander wrote from Tokyo,

> How thrilled I have been knowing that you have attained to that great station mentioned in our Master's Will! The days spent in Neckargemünd are never to be forgotten. They always live in my heart ...[121]

Agnes Alexander became a Bahá'í in 1900. At 'Abdu'l-Bahá's request, she moved from Rome, where she had first learned of the Faith, back to the land of her birth, Hawaii, in order to teach the Faith there and later also in Japan. In March 1957 Shoghi Effendi elevated her to the rank of a Hand of the Cause of God. On the occasion of her passing in Honolulu on 1 January 1971, at the age of 96, the Universal House of Justice referred to her as a long-standing pillar of the Cause in the Far East and recalled the imperishable honour she shared with May Maxwell of being mentioned by 'Abdu'l-Bahá in the Tablets of the Divine Plan.[122]

A joyful letter reached Anna and Hermann Grossmann from Beatrice Ashton, whose services to the Bahá'í Faith in post-war Germany are unforgettable. Beatrice Ashton spoke German and came to Germany at biannual intervals in order to help with teaching activities. She wrote,

> What tremendous and joyous news has come in our beloved Guardian's latest Message! I can imagine how overwhelmed you are. I am so happy for you both! And that Germany is represented in this historic step – my heart is singing with gratefulness that our Beloved Guardian has felt it is the time to take this step, and to be alive to see this day![123]

Ian Semple from England, a frequent guest who was always welcomed very warmly by the German Bahá'í youth and who participated in the 1950 and 1951 youth summer schools, and who was later to become a member of the Universal House of Justice, sent congratulations in German saying: *'Lieber Herr Doktor! ... Mein Herz fließt vor Freude über, und ich bitte, Sie werden meine kleine Achtungsbezeigung der Liebe ... annehmen* (Dear Doctor! ... My heart is overflowing with joy and I hope you will accept my little token of love).'[124]

Ian Semple later said, in his memoirs for his son Michael:

> The real bombshell of the Conference [on 5th and 6th January 1952 in Birmingham], however, was the Guardian's cable announcing the appointment of the first contingent of Hands of the Cause of God. I don't know if you can conceive of what this meant to the Bahá'ís of that time. We knew about Hands, of course, from the Will and Testament of 'Abdu'l-Bahá and we had known of outstanding believers, like Martha Root and

APPOINTMENT AS A HAND OF THE CAUSE OF GOD

John Esslemont, raised to the rank of Hands after their passing. However, to actually have the possibility of knowing and meeting such precious souls had been beyond our wildest dreams. Now, suddenly, this had become a reality. For me personally the greatest joy and confirmation was to know that Hermann Grossmann was among these Hands, for him I had known and he had aroused my intense admiration and esteem and love.[125]

In 1946, Manutschehr Zabih had come from Tehran to a Germany still devastated by the war. At a time when universities were only just being rebuilt, and wood, coal and potatoes – or even rice – were exchanged as forms of payment, he studied and completed a doctoral degree at the University of Tübingen. His doctoral thesis was entitled *Solving the Social Issue* and was one of the first books to be printed after the Second World War. In his letter of congratulation he wrote:

> A cable from our beloved Guardian has filled my heart with gladness. Not only because the world has come closer to the goal established by Bahá'u'lláh, the foundation of the Universal House of Justice, but because you, my dearly beloved, have proved yourself worthy, through your spiritual qualities, of being appointed a Hand of the Cause of God by our Guardian.
>
> Since I have always regarded myself as a most devoted servant of our beloved Bahá'ís in Germany and my soul is very closely associated with our dear friends who have suffered so much in that land of promise, it is my innermost desire to celebrate quietly with you. I am very proud that someone from Germany has been appointed a Hand of the Cause of God. May Bahá'u'lláh grant you strength and health so that, with His grace, you can conduct your difficult and wide-ranging duties in faithful accordance with His Teachings. May Bahá'u'lláh bless you for your loyal services.
>
> My dear Hermann, my soul is so occupied with thinking about you that my pen can hardly write anything to you. There is therefore nothing else for me to do but pray for you and let your heart perceive what I feel for you in my heart. So I will not spoil the paper with any more ink nor disturb the deep spiritual language of my heart by trying to find the right words.
>
> I embrace you and wish you God's blessings, strength and success in service to our Sacred Cause.[126]

When he heard that Shoghi Effendi had appointed twelve Hands of the Cause of God, Bozorg Hemmati said to his friends, 'Surely our dear Dr Grossmann of Germany will have been appointed – and yesterday', he wrote in his report, 'I was told that it was true ...' At this time, Bozorg

Hemmati was a student in Tübingen. As one of the top-scoring pupils in the nation-wide graduate examinations, he had been sent to Germany by the Persian government in order to study there. Although he only reached the age of forty, he spent his whole life tirelessly working for the Cause of Bahá'u'lláh in his adopted country. His warm-hearted and loving manner united the friends and increased their love for one another whenever he was among them.

From Warnemünde in the Soviet-occupied zone of Germany, a coded message of 'ardent congratulations' was sent by Emil Jörn.

In June 1999 Martin Aiff, then 80 years old and in his fortieth year as a pioneer in southern Africa, recorded his memories of Hermann Grossmann and sent them to Susanne Pfaff-Grossmann. He said:

> Your father had been appointed a Hand of the Cause by the Guardian. The jubilation in my heart when this news reached Germany is unforgettable. Only today do I properly understand, or rather, do I think I understand, what motivated Shoghi Effendi to bestow this high station on your father.[127]

Martin Aiff went on to point out Hermann Grossmann's unswerving steadfastness in the Faith after the passing of the Guardian.

On 29 February 1952, Shoghi Effendi announced further appointments, increasing the number of the Hands serving him to nineteen. Now Adelbert Mühlschlegel, Hermann Grossmann's close friend and companion, was also elevated to this noble rank.

Four Hands of the Cause, Ugo Giachery, Hermann Grossmann, Zikrullah Khadem and Adelbert Mühlschlegel, took part in the European Teaching Conference and in the subsequent summer school in Luxembourg from 30 August to 7 September 1952. In a cable to the Conference, the Guardian had earnestly appealed to the participants to rise up and

> EXTEND REGENERATING INFLUENCE SAME ORDER EASTERN SOUTHEASTERN TERRITORIES SAME CONTINENT EVENTUALLY BEYOND ITS CONFINES, ACROSS URAL MOUNTAINS NORTH, WEST ULTIMATELY HEART ASIATIC CONTINENT.

'Mentally we were packing bags, making plans,' said an American participant. 'The Channel Isles, Orkney Isles, Siberia, Tibet – would one need a horse or mule for Tibet! This was a group who knew what action and sacrifice meant and their hearts flew ahead to the tasks to come ... Then came the Roll Call. Do you know what a Roll Call means here in Europe? Six years ago not a handful would have responded ... [Now there were] twenty-one countries represented, one hundred and thirty-two believers present.' The conference was devoted to studying and consultation on the Covenant, the Administrative Order, teaching, and the history of the Faith, as well as to preparation for the forthcoming conference in Stockholm. The discussions following the talks were enriched by the contributions of the Hands of the Cause of God. This Conference was the last of the European Teaching Conferences organized by the European Teaching Committee (ETC) in Geneva, and deep gratitude was expressed for the help from America. The following year, everyone was to meet in Stockholm and after that only Regional Conferences were to be held. The report closed by saying, 'How great had been the gifts of the week together. We wanted to linger but there were tasks ahead. "Goodbye! See you in Stockholm," were our last words.'[128]

CHAPTER 13

ANNA GROSSMANN

In the period prior to the Second World War, Amatu'l-Bahá Rúḥíyyih Khánum and Anna Grossmann became good friends and they corresponded frequently despite the daily burden of their work for the Bahá'í Faith. Their deep relationship did not require a great many words. 'My dearest,' wrote Rúḥíyyih Khánum in August 1939, in her last letter before the war prevented them from hearing from each other for several years, *'Ich bin in Gedanken immer bei Dir – das weißt Du – und werde es immer sein – ... unser Leben, unsere Liebe wird Gott behüten'* (I am always with you in my thoughts – you know that – and I always will be – ... God will protect our lives, our love).

'*Jetzt möchte ich Dir etwas von Shoghi Effendi sagen* (Now I would like to send you a message from Shoghi Effendi). He says you are a pillar of God's Faith and you have a great privilege and responsibility that your hours be full of the love of God and a source of help to others. God will surely reward you greatly. He is very close to you and yours and your friends and no matter what happens God will protect His own children ...'[129]

In 1984 Rúḥíyyih Khánum wrote to Hartmut Grossmann from Western Samoa, saying: 'As you know, I was extremely close to your mother from the days I was in Germany ... always Annel and I had a special bond ... Annel was a very wonderful woman, exemplary in every way, and a most distinguished Bahá'í.'[130]

When Hermann Grossmann had the honour of being appointed a Hand of the Cause of God, those who knew him well and were aware of his poor state of health wished him, above all, strength and good health so as to be able to carry out the duties of his high office. They also thought of his wife Anna, who had now been his faithful companion and helpmate for nigh on thirty years. She not only managed her large household and educated her two children, she also took care of her husband, who was frequently ill, as well as cultivating the large garden and carrying out all her tasks in the Bahá'í institutions and in teaching activities. In 1954 she was elected secretary of the National Spiritual Assembly. She was able to do most of the work from her home in Neckargemünd. However, the abundance of tasks multiplied and when the Guardian, Shoghi Effendi, requested that the secretary be resident at the National Centre in Frankfurt am Main she had to refuse the request, since she could not leave her husband alone in Neckargemünd. Anneliese Bopp took her place in the Ḥaẓíratu'l-Quds as assistant secretary and initially helped her with the secretarial work before taking over as secretary in 1958.

In a cable dated 6 April 1954 the Guardian called into being the institution of the Auxiliary Board. In this cable he addressed all the Hands of the Cause and all National Assemblies of the Bahá'í World and specified that the members of this Board 'acting as deputies, assistants and advisers of the Hands, must increasingly lend their assistance for the promotion of the interests of the Ten Year Crusade'. He also instructed that the Hands in each continent must convene in Tehran, Wilmette, Frankfurt, Kampala and Sydney and he wrote: 'The Auxiliary Boards of the American, European and African Continents must consist of nine members each, of the Asiatic and Australian Continents of seven and two respectively.' What was 'left to the discretion of the Hands' was 'the allocation of areas in each continent to the members of the Auxiliary Boards, as well a subsidiary matters regarding the development of the activities of the newly appointed bodies, and the manner of collaboration with the National Spiritual Assemblies in their respective Continents.' It was also stated: 'All Boards must report and be responsible to the Hands charged with their appointment.' The Hands of the Cause in Europe met during Riḍván at the National Centre in Frankfurt am Main in order to appoint a total of nine Auxiliary Board members; one was Anna Grossmann.

Thus, because she held both this office and that of secretary of the National Spiritual Assembly for Germany and Austria, it could happen that, in her capacity as secretary, she had to write a letter to her husband as a Hand of the Cause of God in order to request that she, in her capacity as an Auxiliary Board member, be authorized to visit a particular community. With some amusement, she told Ian Semple of this state of affairs when they met in Haifa in 1957, when they were both on pilgrimage.[131]

In 1957 the Auxiliary Board was expanded by another six members who were to be responsible for the protection of the Faith. At the request of the Hands of the Cause of God, Anna Grossmann transferred to this Auxiliary Board. One tribute to her work reads:

> She was appointed ... as one of the first Auxiliary Board members for Protection, and again she met all the demands with exemplary zeal: she enjoyed the love and confidence of all the believers, and she advised, encouraged and inspired institutions and individuals. Tirelessly she helped to raise the good reputation of the Faith, she deepened and strengthened the believers, invigorated the institutions and spread the call of God in many European countries.[132]

In addition to the large amount of correspondence connected with her role as an Auxiliary Board member, she still found time for writing personal letters. When she was no longer able to use a pen owing to trembling in her hands, she used a typewriter instead. Nevertheless, the flood of incoming and outgoing letters by no means abated. She had the gift of finding just the right words to provide solace, assistance and strength to those to whom she wrote.

To a friend whose husband had left her she wrote:

> All tests come upon us, I believe, for the sole purpose of bringing us closer to God. In order to come closer to Him, one must detach oneself from all but Him. Of course, we humans do not do that voluntarily, but only through suffering. So we have to learn the lesson of detachment in many different ways. The Indian religions, Jesus Christ, and now also Bahá'u'lláh teach us that lesson very intensely. 'He who loves his father or mother, sisters or brothers more than Me is unworthy of Me' and 'Turn thy face to Me and detach thyself from all else but Me.' My dearest, if such a lesson is destined for us, we cannot escape it, and then God gives us the strength to learn what is necessary, so that in the end, perhaps only years later, we can recognize that the test was 'outwardly fire but inwardly light and mercy'. I hope you can understand me.

And she adds:

> Of course, no human being is a standard or some kind of authority for another. In our Cause it is the institutions and, as far as our inner lives are concerned or, rather, also our outward lives, it is the Word of God as revealed through Bahá'u'lláh.

She reports on a deepening with young people:

> It has again demonstrated to me that there is only *one* true and everlasting happiness – to immerse oneself in the ocean of His Truth. He is immeasurable, there is no need to fear that His ocean might one day be fathomed, suddenly leaving us exposed to the unexpected. Such things belong only to this world ... We began with the first Arabic Hidden Word and then turned our attention to Bahá'u'lláh's words in the Epistle to the Son of the Wolf: 'Be generous in prosperity and thankful in adversity.' One of the youth talked about how we should not take a narrow view of God's mercy and goodness, and how life continues in another world and solutions are to be found there to problems we have failed to solve here. Almost all of us have someone we love who is not prepared to see the truth in Bahá'u'lláh. However things are, these words are valid for all situations: 'Be thankful in adversity.' For us, this means taking this path and living the life.

An iron constitution, strong will and robust health assisted this rather delicately built personality. Anna Grossmann often had no rest and, in particular, little sleep owing to her many diverse duties. However, one had the constant feeling that she saw her primary duty as supporting her husband – a Hand of the Cause of God – and providing him with an atmosphere in which he could work without disturbance. She never ceased to serve.

'My memories of Hermann Grossmann are totally entwined with those of his life's companion, Anna Grossmann,' writes Harry Liedtke from Canada:

> I never remember one without remembering the other. They were a blessed team, as were so many other devoted Bahá'í couples. I suspect that Hermann Grossmann sought and found immense strength and comfort in dear Annel. [He was] never particularly robust physically, despite of his size, Annel was always concerned about his well-being. She made sure he got his rest when his boundless enthusiasm threatened to overwhelm him with fatigue. She also tried to shield him from petty situations that would have unnecessarily consumed his precious energy.[133]

René Steiner, who often stayed at the Grossmann home in Neckargemünd during the second half of the 1950s, pays tribute to Anna Grossmann:

> ... my memories of Hermann Grossmann can never be separated from his dear wife Anna. Anna to me was the Angel of Germany, she was alert, observant, caring, but uncompromising in principle and in matters concerning the protection of the Faith. In that she was the perfect extension

of the function of her dear husband, the Hand of the Cause of God. Together with Herma Mühlschlegel they were as twin shining stars in the firmament of the German Bahá'í community. Of course, there were many others who shone with a supernal and brilliant light, but none matched the brilliance of these twin shining stars who in a very real sense intensified the light the Guardian had shed on their husbands. This is perhaps why memories of Hermann Grossmann come to mind best when also thinking [of] and remembering Anna Grossmann. The two in my Bahá'í experience were inseparable.[134]

'For me, Anna Grossmann was always the ideal image of a real Bahá'í woman,' writes Hermine Berdjis, who worked with her for many years:

> Her modesty and love were accompanied by a very special degree of refinement, a nobility of spirit that was expressed as much in her posture and the clothes she wore as in her characteristic choice of words. I particularly liked the fact that she never said, 'I don't believe that' or 'That can't be true'. She always said, 'Do you think so? I have another opinion on that.' Then she went on to explain the matter from her point of view in words that made her opinion clear but did not hurt anyone's feelings. Or if there were people in a community who were very obstinate and constantly in conflict with one another, she didn't say, 'The friends are arguing,' but rather, 'There are some very strong characters' – so nobody felt insulted or underestimated.
>
> She had a household that was like a swarm of bees. Anyone who came to the area paid a visit to Neckargemünd. And she cared for them all! I learned from her how to quickly bake a cake when surprise visitors arrive or a fireside is arranged at short notice.[135]

(This refers to the famous 'gateau Hélène', the recipe which has been passed on from mother to daughter in the family over several generations!)

Anna Grossmann's grandchildren have loving memories of their grandmother and her gentle ways of educating them. Katharina says:

> When I was about ten I had a significant experience: Whilst staying with my beloved grandmother in Neckargemünd, I helped one evening to dry the dishes after she had washed them. Since that job takes children somewhat longer, she had gone away briefly to do something else. I accidentally dropped a glass, which shattered on the floor. I was horrified. So as not to be found out I put the pieces of broken glass in the cupboard, presumably in the childish belief that they would not be found there. Grandmother

came in and put away the dishes in the cupboard. Not surprisingly, she immediately discovered what had happened. I stood there hanging my head in shame, certain that a scolding was to come. However, she just said in her usual gentle voice: 'Why did you put the broken glass in the cupboard instead of throwing it away? You didn't break it on purpose.' That taught me that one must live up to one's mistakes and if accidents occur without any ill-will there should not be any fuss and certainly no punishment. A piece of wisdom for which I am eternally grateful to my grandmother.

'The house in Neckargemünd was surrounded by a large garden,' recalls Anna Grossmann's granddaughter Andrea:

There were two huts, many big trees, spruces, a weeping willow, hazelnut and fruit trees, bushes, berry shrubs, meadows and flowers. The plants, paths, steps, walls and terraces divided the garden into different areas, each with its own character; different short or long paths led to the same destination. It was like a park, and it took a lot of work to keep it tidy. When my sisters and I noticed that the weeds were again taking over in a section of the garden, it took us the whole afternoon to pull them out. After finishing our work, we would pick a bunch of flowers for grandma before going back indoors. This was made not of flowers but of the many flowering wild herbs and grasses. I was happy to see the love and warmth with which grandma accepted our gift, placing the bouquet in a vase until the flowers wilted. We sensed that her joy at receiving it was genuine; it was just as valuable to her as a 'proper' bouquet of flowers.

Badieh Poostchi remembers being with Anna Grossmann:

I had the great honour to go with her on a one-week teaching trip to Vorarlberg, the western-most federal state in Austria. During this time we attended many events with Bahá'í friends, who of course wanted to ask Anna lots of questions. She always answered with great humility, an infectious humility that ... engendered humility in others, too. Her answers were very clear and went straight to the heart. At the end of her explanations she always said: 'But, my dear, I would ask the House [the Universal House of Justice], too.' The most striking memory from this trip is that although we had a lot to do, met many Bahá'í friends and enquirers, and went to bed very late, Anna always got up at 5.30 a.m., performed her ablutions and said her obligatory prayer with great devotion. Then she went back to bed. Her example has accompanied me throughout my life. Although I am an owl, rather than a lark, and like to sleep longer in the mornings, I always say my obligatory prayer before leaving the house in the morning. I am very grateful for having had the privilege of experiencing so intimately the company of this personality who is such an important figure in Bahá'í history.

Badieh Poostchi then adds the following words of her mother-in-law about Hermann Grossmann, which demonstrate the contrasting characters of husband and wife: 'We all regarded Dr Grossmann as an authority. When he said something, we knew it was so and not otherwise, and we had to act on it.'[136]

In the 1950s, Anna Grossmann often accompanied visitors on the long walk to the station in Neckargemünd, balancing their suitcases on her bicycle. Mindful of their welfare, she would slip a sandwich for the journey into their bag as they left. One pioneer remembers that enclosed in the official letter she received from the secretary of the National Spiritual Assembly, Anna Grossmann, there was some money and a personal note stating that the money was to buy provisions for the journey.

At the end of the 1950s, the Polish Bahá'í and Knight of Bahá'u'lláh Ola Pawlowska returned to Poland from her pioneering post in St Pierre and Miquelon in order to cautiously make contacts. The country was within the sphere of responsibility of the German National Spiritual Assembly and Anna Grossmann was charged with the task of carefully preparing the visit, since Poland was cut off behind the Iron Curtain. Ola Pawlowska stayed for several days in Neckargemünd. Reminiscing about this time, she recalls the impression that Anna and Hermann Grossmann made on her:

> Anna impressed me as a warm, loving, mature lady of great social culture and deep spirituality ... Dr Grossmann was very tall but seemed frail in spite of his large frame, thinning blond hair and gentle blue eyes. I was aware of his dignity, as an integral part of him, which inspired respect ... I was struck ... by his great gentle love that encompassed everybody and by his inner peace and detachment ...
>
> Anna Grossmann was in charge of his well-being, health and protection ... At lunch the Hand was seated at the head of the table, Anna on his right and myself at his left ... The table talk and the activities of everybody turned around the progress and interests of the Faith ... Those days spent in Neckargemünd allowed me to establish deep bonds of understanding with Anna who helped me greatly with her experience and advice during my stay in Poland. I recall even now, with love and gratitude, the glimpse I had in Dr Grossmann's home of a family life as it should be lived – dedicated to the service of the Cause, and the guidance of Bahá'ís.[137]

'She was also a good speaker, who could speak freely without clinging to her manuscript,' recalls Hermine Berdjis, 'and as an Auxiliary Board member I often sought her advice. Of all of us, she had the most experience with every section of the Bahá'í community. She was certainly one of the women who had the greatest influence on the development of the Bahá'í community after the Second World War.'[138]

In all the communities and groups in which Hermann Grossmann spoke, we also find his wife Anna. Whereas Dr Grossmann developed his thoughts on the subject at hand during the course of his lecture, speaking freely and without any previous planning, Anna Grossmann made a few notes on a small file card. And whereas his audience was struck by his clear, logical thoughts, she appealed to her listeners' feelings and emotions. Thus, their talks complemented each other perfectly.

'What I liked about Dr Grossmann's lecture was his logical clarity,' writes Ursula von Brunn in her memoirs,

> his lovely character, his smile, but not the discussion that followed. It was with students from the faculty of natural sciences, and I found it too dry. I didn't know what that had to do with religion, immature as I was. Annel Grossmann's talk was so warm, so sincere, I was immediately enraptured by her whole being. And that led to real friendship. These two people dedicated their whole lives to the Faith and to love, and they built up, as we should also, trust, friendship, love, and helpfulness, especially in relation to people's spiritual needs.[139]

In 1995, the Hand of the Cause of God 'Alí-Akbar Furútan recounted,

> I ... had the opportunity of meeting Mrs Anna Grossmann in Germany. I saw her at Bahá'í summer schools and at a number of other occasions, and was a guest in their home one evening. Her spirituality and enthusiasm for teaching are known to German believers.[140]

Anna Grossmann undoubtedly influenced the lives of many people, if not always in such a dramatic way as that of Gisela Zonneveld-von Brunn and Arnold Zonneveld, who, newly married and expecting their first baby, had no thoughts of pioneering when they attended the summer school in Gauting in 1965.

Arnold Zonneveld had been a pioneer on Spitzbergen from 1961 to 1964. During the first year, he was a hunting companion to the Knight of Bahá'u'lláh Paul Adams, who had opened Spitzbergen to the Faith, and later he had been an assistant to a Norwegian hunter and then a miner in an opencast mine.

In Gauting, Anna Grossmann gave a slide show about her trips to South America with her husband Hermann.

> She spoke with great love and respect for the native peoples of that continent [recalls Gisela Zonneveld-von Brunn]. We were so fascinated by her talk that we immediately knew we must go to South America. We could not tell the different countries apart. So we looked in an encyclopedia to find out which country had the highest percentage of indigenous people. That was Bolivia. And so from that moment on it was clear to us that we would go to Bolivia ...

They sought some additional advice at the 'yellow house' in Neckargemünd and then emigrated to that country at the heart of South America, where their children and grandchildren have grown up both in the highlands of the Andes and in the low-lying rainforest – and 'along with the people there are contributing to a new race of men'.[141]

Whenever possible, Anna Grossmann accompanied her husband and relieved him of the burden of planning and solving the inevitable difficulties associated with a journey, such as their three voyages to South America from 1960 to 1962. The friends in South America spoke of the strong bond between the couple and remarked how obvious was the care and concern of each for the other. 'They were a delightful couple,' says Fred Schechter, 'and it was a pleasure to be in their company. There was an atmosphere of friendliness and calmness between them. You could sense the love between them even if they were not sitting next to each other.'[142]

When Hermann Grossmann died in 1968, Anneliese Bopp was the secretary of the National Spiritual Assembly at the National Centre in Frankfurt am Main. On the day after the passing of the Hand of the Cause, expressions of grief flooded in and many Bahá'ís came to Westendstraße 24 to express their sympathies. Among the many telegrams received was one that was initially communicated by the telegraph office via telephone. It was a cable from the World Centre and it surprised Anneliese Bopp because it contained a request to contact the National Spiritual Assembly of Italy immediately in connection with arrangements for a conference in Palermo. Surely, she thought, the Universal House of Justice knows that Hermann Grossmann has just died – how could it be asking him to attend this conference? She therefore made efforts to obtain the cable in written form as soon as possible, and then she realized that it was addressed to her. She was now faced with a dilemma. There was no deputy secretary to stand in for her, and it was impossible to find one at such short notice. After Hermann Grossmann's funeral she talked to the members of the National Spiritual Assembly who were present, and also with Anna Grossmann. Despite her grief and her physical exhaustion after nursing her husband, Anna Grossmann immediately volunteered to come to Frankfurt for eight to ten weeks and take over the secretarial duties.[143] What she regarded as her duty towards the Faith was always her first priority.

A Bahá'í remembers that when he and his wife enrolled in the Faith his mother stated her opinion that at the age of 64 she was too old to do so. When she later met Anna Grossmann, she remarked to her: 'But yesterday you were in Münster, today you are in Duisburg and tomorrow you are travelling on to Bonn. Isn't it too much for you? I mean, you aren't the youngest of people after all.'

Anna Grossmann replied: 'No, no, no! Age is not a limitation; rather, it offers lots of opportunities.'

This must have impressed her a great deal, for when, to everyone's surprise, she became a Bahá'í at 73, she repeatedly referred to that evening with Anna Grossmann and said: 'Since that unique lady visited me, we don't speak of age any longer, do we? That evening I knew I had to become a Bahá'í regardless of my old age.'[144]

Looking back when advanced in years, Anna Grossmann once wrote:

> In the end, life does not actually seem to have been so successful, but I think one must be satisfied with having done one's best. One should not be ungrateful, and one might easily appear so if one were not happy and glad, despite some hardships in this life.
>
> I pray that I will always remain faithful to the Cause. Great storms are still to come and many leaves will be blown off the tree. I pray that we will never fall off, but always stay faithful to the Cause.[145]

Little else could better characterize Anna Grossmann.

CHAPTER 14

THE TIRELESS SCHOLAR

From his earliest days as a Bahá'í it was Hermann Grossmann's intention to establish a library which would present the Faith as a modern 'world religion', through Bahá'í writings, documents, newspaper articles, statements, commentaries and illustrations. In a letter to Shoghi Effendi dated 11 November 1927 he states that his Bahá'í library contained 260 titles – a high number of Bahá'í books indeed for that time.

There were the following subdivisions:

1) Writings of the Báb, Bahá'u'lláh, and 'Abdu'l-Bahá
2) Books about the Bahá'í Faith
3) *Bahá'í News*
4) Works mentioning the Cause of Bahá'u'lláh
5) Small Bahá'í pamphlets and booklets
6) Newspaper articles and remarks about the Faith
7) Photographs presenting the Cause of God

Hermann Grossmann was thus able to offer to universities, libraries and academics a comprehensive presentation of the Faith. He opened his private library in a catalogue and as a lending library to the University of Hamburg and to its Faculty for Oriental Languages. These institutions, in turn, advised him how to catalogue his library in a way that would match theirs. In 1929 his public lending library in Wandsbek comprised 300 volumes of and about the Faith. There was also an archive and a reading room.

Hermann Grossmann persistently promoted the Bahá'í teachings, not only among intellectually and spiritually receptive people but, especially, in deepening and training the believers themselves. The list of his publications serving this purpose is long: the periodicals *Star of the West*, *World Order* and the United States *Bahá'í News* specify 12 articles and reports between 1923 and 1936, and more than 30 publications between 1950 and 1968 (see Appendix 2 for a complete list).

THE TIRELESS SCHOLAR

After the Second World War Hermann Grossmann tried to confront in his discussions with intellectuals, academics and spiritually receptive seekers the decline of values and ethics with the standards of the Faith as a modern religion. His systematic approach and his scientifically trained mind assisted him greatly in this attempt.

In 1948 a new, revised edition was published of his book *Am Morgen einer neuen Zeit* (The Dawn of a New Age), which had originally appeared in 1932. It included a foreword by Hanna Guckeisen, a friend of the Grossmann family, in which she wrote:

> The author wrote this book nine years before the outbreak of the last great war. Developments since then have confirmed his thesis. Today, the ground is more prepared than ever for the ideas contained in the book to take root.[146]

Shortly before, in 1947, Hermann Grossmann's new book entitled *Umbruch zur Einheit – Gott, Mensch und Welt an der Schwelle einer neuen Ordnung* (A Changeover to Unity – God, Man and the World on the Threshold of a New Order) had been published on extremely poor quality post-war paper under permit number US-W-1084 issued by the news control body of the American military government.

In his introduction, the author wrote:

> Spengler was right when he prophesied the decline of the Occident. But this decline turns out not to be its destruction, rather its transformation and opening up for a new era ... that, filled with a fresh impulse, is leading it towards further new opportunities for growth ... Bahá'u'lláh's teaching concerning the spiritual cycles shows the way to a deeper understanding of this transformation, probably the greatest change in mankind's spiritual history, which signifies the birth of a new order in which we are at once spectators and actors and which demands the greatest possible degree of participation by both individuals and the human race as a whole. What Bahá'u'lláh teaches is in fact the conception of a future world founded on the Law of a Will that is independent of space and time and that is now in the process of taking on an organic form in the striving of the peoples of the world.[147]

In 1950, Hermann Grossmann's new translation of Bahá'u'lláh's *The Seven Valleys* was published after being proof-read by Dr Aminulláh Ahmedzadeh.

In 1956, the German Bahá'í Publishing Trust, Bahá'í-Verlag, issued his book *Das Bündnis Gottes in der Offenbarungsreligion* (God's

Covenant in Revealed Religion), followed by an introduction to the Kitáb-i-Iqán, Bahá'u'lláh's Book of Certitude, in 1959. In 1962, an introductory work, *Was ist die Bahá'í-Religion* (What the Bahá'í Faith Is) was published, and in 1966 a compilation of texts entitled *Der Bahá'í-Gläubige und die Bahá'í-Gemeinschaft* (The Bahá'í Teachings and the Bahá'í Community) appeared. A third, revised edition of the last-mentioned publication was issued by the Bahá'í-Verlag in 1994 under the title *Der Bahá'í und die Bahá'í-Gemeinde*, and this book is regarded by many as Hermann Grossmann's most important and valuable work.

Among his many other writings, mention should be made of his contributions to the regular yearbook *The Bahá'í World*, which were interrupted by the interdiction of the Bahá'í Faith in Germany. For many years, he took responsibility for reports about German Bahá'í activities. In addition, he published essays in these yearbooks both in German and in English. In an essay (vol. 4, 1930–1932) about the Swiss scientist Professor Forel, who received a well-known Tablet from 'Abdu'l-Bahá, Hermann Grossmann discusses the works of this famous personality. In his article entitled 'Der Sinn unserer Zeit' (The Meaning of the Age in Which We Live) (vol. 5, 1932–1934), he discerns a turning point in the spiritual development of humanity. 'Ein junger Glaube wird bekannt' (A Young Faith Gains Recognition) (vol. 6, 1934–1936) is a historical study dealing with publications about the Bábí and Bahá'í Faiths written by outsiders, mainly 19th and early 20th century travellers and researchers, which helped to a considerable degree to make the Faith known.

After the defeat of the Third Reich in the Second World War, vol. 10 (1944-1946) included a contribution entitled 'Neue Arbeit' (New Work), a review of

> nine years of suppression and persecution, during which the work of the communities was destroyed, individual freedom of religion was taken away and literature destroyed ... Yet none of this was able to hold back the living waters of solidarity or destroy our sense of the unbreakable bonds of fellowship. Throughout all the interrogations, prison sentences and special court hearings, the firmness and steadfastness of the friends concerned only grew yet stronger ... Now, after years of forced isolation, the world that we German Bahá'ís look upon in our new-found freedom is a changed one ... The time of inner tests has suddenly been replaced by one of outer tests ... Only through extremely hard work and effort will it be possible to find solutions to the huge problems.

Hermann Grossmann closes this essay by saying that writing about the past is not meant as a condemnation of past events, 'for the future alone must be our goal. Before us is the light and behind us the darkness sinks into the oblivion of yesterday.'

In 'Die kleine Welt und der Große Friede' (The Small World and the Great Peace) (vol. 11, 1946–1950) he considers how the world has been made smaller by technical developments and discusses the Lesser Peace, a political arrangement that

> would not be able to bring a permanent solution were it not to be followed by the 'Most Great Peace', the true fulfilment of the ancient dream, a peace ... that draws its power from the essence of true religion and has its foundations in the recognition of the all-embracing, prejudice-free unity in diversity taught by Bahá'u'lláh.

In 1958, an essay was published in the *Zeitschrift für Religions- und Geistesgeschichte* (Journal of the History of Religion and Ideas) edited by Professor Benz of Marburg. It outlines the historical development of the Bahá'í Faith.

Hermann Grossmann's archives include a number of folders containing invitations to lectures he gave in the immediate post-war years. They demonstrate how he gradually managed to expand the sphere of his activities promoting the Faith. Starting out from the region around Neckargemünd and Heidelberg, Weinheim, Heppenheim, and Bensheim, he initially travelled as far as Frankfurt; and then, from as early as 1946, there are invitations to be found from the Bahá'ís of Esslingen, Wiesbaden, Karlsruhe and Stuttgart. In the early 1950s the localities of Ulm, Tübingen, Freiburg, Munich, Berlin, Bonn, Ebingen, Giessen, Reutlingen and Hamburg were added to the list.

Some of the earliest of these invitations preserved in the archive were written by hand, others were typed, which allowed carbon copies to be made. Even some time later, the invitations were still written on very poor-quality paper. The gradual return to normality after the war is reflected here, too.

The first lectures were intended to make the Bahá'í teachings known: 'What is the Aim of the Bahá'í Faith?', 'Why the Bahá'í Faith?', 'A New Religion', and 'The Bahá'í World Faith' were just some of the titles.

Soon, however, the selected themes show that Hermann Grossmann again and again responded to the Guardian's request that the new Covenant of God be emphasized: 'The Covenant of God with Mankind in the Present Day', 'Progressive Revelation', 'The Concept of the Covenant in the Course of History', 'God's Covenant with Man, Past and Present', and so on. He tried to make the friends aware that, through Bahá'u'lláh, God has entered into a new Covenant with humanity, that this is what is so completely new about the Bahá'í teachings and that recognizing this is the focal point and essential foundation for the life of every believer.

In the booklet entitled *Das Bündnis Gottes in der Offenbarungsreligion* (God's Covenant in Revealed Religion), to which reference has already been made, he summarized this message. The text was finished in 1949 and published in a series of typewritten outlines before being printed by the Bahá'í-Verlag in 1956. It was the fruit of years of systematic work, methodical research and deep thought. This little book was of exceptional importance for anyone who wanted to penetrate more deeply into the teachings of the Faith. In his foreword, he quoted the words that Rúḥíyyih Khánum had conveyed to Anna Grossmann on behalf of Shoghi Effendi: '[The] knowledge and appreciation of the Covenants of both Bahá'u'lláh and 'Abdu'l-Bahá ... is the stronghold of the Faith of every Bahá'í, and that which enables him to withstand every test and the attacks of the enemies outside the Faith ...'[148]

In the introduction he states:

> The following outline deals with one of the most serious problems of revealed religion, on the correct or incorrect understanding of which ultimately depends the value or worthlessness of the religiosity of both an individual and a whole people or age. It is the question of man's relationship to the divine, how we approach divinity, how we wish to allow it to touch our lives and let it work in us and through us. Our age, which is so distant from God and which, through an all-pervading rationalistic and materialistic way of thinking and drawing conclusions, has lost its roots, causing us to lose the ability to sense the mysteries of the great creative Will, gaining instead a mere intellectual grasp of a mechanistic law of nature. Likewise, the specialization of scientific investigation and the division of humanity into innumerable separate individuals have obscured our awareness of the inter-dependence of all forms of existence, without which life is impossible ... Anyone who is prepared to grasp with honesty the hand of the new Faith of God will understand that, facing it, only all that counts is: perception, service and attraction.

Hermann Grossmann goes on to discuss man's need of salvation, which he may perhaps seek to achieve through renunciation of the world or through social reforms to improve living conditions. According to the revealed religions, however, man's salvation emanates from the mercy of God. However, we are obliged to do something ourselves, 'so that [divine mercy] can come to us and work in and through us. Thus, in the revealed religions, salvation becomes a Covenant between the Creator and His creatures, which is passed on as a "Testament" through the ages and vicissitudes of the world with increasing power and authority, and this Covenant is the essence of all revealed religions.'

After explaining the term 'Covenant', he discusses the 'inevitable significance of the Manifestation of God as a mediator for the Covenant of God':

> Submission to the Covenant means that the individual has to constantly reconsider the relationship between his own self and God ... a process rewarded by eternal happiness and victory in redemption on the Path of God ... However, the willingness of the believer to submit to the authority of the Covenant should be born of his own free will to decide ...
>
> The authority vested in the Manifestation in the Covenant of God follows ... from the essential characteristics that distinguish Him for us as a Manifestation of God. We recognize this authority both as an expression of the power and might that are evident in and through Him and which exceed all human concepts ... and through His unequalled and unerring knowledge and understanding.

After an extensive discussion of the origins of the infallibility of the Manifestation and the consequent unfailing guidance He provides for mankind, Hermann Grossmann comes to the concept of the 'Law as the core of the Covenant'. He points out the 'assistance provided by mercy in the Covenant of God' which

> desires the preservation of every creature of God and therefore does not demand of anyone more than he is able to bear ...
>
> Throughout the chain of the Manifestations of God, the fundamental purpose of the Covenant is evident, an eternal legacy promoting mankind's ongoing development and increasing perfection. We can see in this the concept of 'Progressive Revelation'...

After a detailed presentation of the Revelations of the Báb and Bahá'u'lláh, he goes on to explain the order of the Bahá'í community as a continuation of the Covenant.

> The cycle of Bahá'u'lláh will extend over a period of at least five hundred thousand years ... Other Manifestations will come as often as ages and circumstances require ...

Unceasing study was Hermann Grossmann's great strength. He would sit at the large table in his study, surrounded by countless books and with a sharp pencil in his hand, and page by page he would gradually fill the sheets of paper in front of him with his small handwriting. He had used the period of the interdiction of the Bahá'í community to study scientific themes from the point of view of the Faith. He was always acutely aware that study of the holy texts must be accompanied by education and knowledge in all spheres of learning. His knowledge was wide-ranging and enabled him to talk to theologians and religious scholars about the Cause of Bahá'u'lláh in such a way that they could not dismiss it and had to recognize that it is not a sect of narrow-minded fanatics or dreamers. The Guardian, Shoghi Effendi, often encouraged him in taking this approach.

Dr Udo Schaefer, a critical analyst who constantly reflects on fundamental issues concerning the Faith and who has been a leading figure in providing an intellectual framework for the theological analysis of the Bahá'í Faith, is the author and co-author of a great many books, such as *Der Bahá'í in der modernen Welt* (published in English as *The Light Shineth in Darkness*) and *Desinformation als Methode* (published in English as *Making the Crooked Straight*), a rebuttal of a diatribe which had gained currency as a source of information for those wishing to know about the Faith. For many years, he lived in the same community as Hermann and Anna Grossmann. He recalls:

> Dr Hermann Grossmann was a brilliant man with a high degree of scholarship in a great many fields. In addition to his own special field and his artistic interests – he painted beautiful water-colours and could have made a successful career as a painter – he was impressively well-versed in the field of comparative religious studies, religious history and philosophy. Far from being dogmatically narrow-minded, he opened wide the gate of free research and in his discourses he drew on all the colourful diversity of the world's religions. He was probably the first person who tried to provide a methodical and systematic presentation of the message of Bahá'u'lláh in the context of religious history. The first attempts in the German-speaking world at the scientific analysis of the revealed content of the Faith are to be found in his works. The fact that I – who was an atheist when I first encountered Bahá'ís and averse to any kind of sectarianism

– joined the Bahá'í community in 1948 was primarily thanks to him, his competence and his quality as an intellectual. He opened my eyes to the truth. He never evaded my endless critical questions but answered them with sensitivity and patience. Our critical dialogue, which continued for many years afterwards, gave me an abundance of food for thought, ideas that were of decisive importance for my own life and for my view of the Bahá'í Faith ...

His wife, Anna Grossmann, was also a deeply religious soul who was very talented in teaching the Cause of Bahá'u'lláh. Her wide-ranging contributions and public talks were always well-founded and full of substance. Protecting the Cause of God was her top priority.

In their teaching work, they both always concentrated on the essential. They focused on the central theological principles enunciated by Bahá'u'lláh: the doctrines of the Covenant, of the sovereignty of God and the infallibility of the Manifestations, their laws and ethics. In this way, they laid a sound foundation in the hearts of many believers and rendered invaluable services to the development of the German Bahá'í community. For many years, both of them, along with Dr Adelbert Mühlschlegel and Dr Eugen Schmidt, were the outstanding figures in the German Bahá'í community. I also remember with special affection Hermann Grossmann's sister Elsa Maria ...

Dr Schaefer dedicated his first book to be published in English to Dr Hermann Grossmann in recognition of the fact that many of his own insights as a Bahá'í were attributable to ideas that had been discussed in the dialogues between them.[149]

During the years when Hermann Grossmann was not permitted to speak publicly about the Bahá'í Faith, he began writing a book about the history of the revealed religions, which he was, unfortunately, unable to complete later owing to lack of time.[150]

In the preface we read:

> For the Bahá'í, the essence of religion is the Revelation of God as the announcement of the divine purpose for the individual and for mankind. Its development takes place under the commandments of the divine Covenant in interaction between the Creator and His creatures, so that religious history, too, takes on a meaning in accordance with a regular pattern and at its deepest level becomes a history of the Revelation of God in His creatures. The leaders in this process are the Manifestations of the divine Will, the 'Men of God', prophets and seers; Their main purpose is the guidance of man towards the ultimate goal set by the Creator and Their course in history is a constantly rising series of pendulum swings

between what should be and what is desired, until at last, at the highest swing of the Universal Manifestation of God, the greatest height, the Mountain of God, is attained.

The first chapter, 'Religion and Science', discusses 'Religion as the constantly moving expression of the Divine', 'The changeable and the Eternal', 'Religious history under the Covenant of God', 'Independent and dependent prophets', 'Time periods in religious history', 'The true spirit of religious history', 'The historiography of the Holy Books is not an end in itself', and 'Symbolic forms of expression', ending with an 'Overview of time periods', i.e. a chronology of the revealed religions.

A complete manuscript exists for the period 'From Adam to Joseph' with a chronological table and illustrative map. This shows clearly how Hermann Grossmann drew on Old Testament, Islamic, Mesopotamian and Egyptian sources for the book.

The chapter concerning the period immediately following this is complete as well. It deals with the Mosaic religious cycle and analyses the religious development of India, Iran and China. Chapters were planned, but never written, on 'Jesus of Nazareth and the Development of the Churches', 'Islam', and 'The Dispensation of Bahá'u'lláh'. The chapter on 'The Dispensation of the Báb' exists as an unfinished manuscript.[151]

Another of Hermann Grossmann's frequent topics for lectures and discussions was the reconciliation of religion and science; 'Borderline Issues in Physics from a Religious Point of View', 'Spirit and Matter', 'The Oneness of Faith and Knowledge', 'Knowledge and Revelation', and 'From Materialism to God' were just some of the titles.

One of these lectures, entitled 'Religion and Science', held in Frankfurt am Main in 1957 was recorded on cassette by Mr Ben Levy. It is included verbatim in Appendix 1.

After his appointment as a Hand of the Cause of God by Shoghi Effendi in 1951, Hermann Grossmann analysed the significance and role of this institution in Bahá'í scripture. In a great many conversations, he explained the significance of the institution to the friends.

The speeches given on this subject by Hermann Grossmann and his friend and fellow Hand of the Cause of God, Adelbert Mühlschlegel, during the 1954 Benelux Conference near Arnhem in the Netherlands have been preserved. They bring back to life the wonderful poetic language of Adelbert Mühlschlegel and the clear approach, making ample use of quotations, of Hermann Grossmann, thus reflecting the different characters of these two German Hands of the Cause.[152]

Plans for a Bahá'í Institute of Religion and Science

One of the aims of the Five Year Plan was

> The development, by March 1953, of the existing foundations in Neckargemünd into an Institute for Religion and Science with the dual task of contributing Bahá'í ideas to science and of studying general scientific developments from the point of view of the Bahá'í teachings.[153]

Hermann Grossmann's extensive and carefully selected library and his archives, whose documents reached back to the earliest days of German Bahá'í history, had been intended to serve as the basis for a Bahá'í Institute, for which he wished to have a building erected in Neckargemünd. However, many of his books were now lost. As soon as the war was over, in spring 1945, he tried to obtain books and archive materials again. In both cases, this proved to be practically impossible. His archives from the period before 1937, which were bequeathed to the National Spiritual Assembly of Germany, contain only sparse remnants; the early history of the Bahá'ís in Germany can still not be fully reconstructed.

The three-storey building planned for the Institute in Neckargemünd was to house the archives and a 100,000-volume library, along with a reading room, conference hall and residential accommodation for those who came there to learn. The 'yellow house' was to be linked to the Institute building, so that its rooms could be used, too. The neighbouring 'red house' belonging to Hermann's parents was also included in the plans. The Guardian granted permission for the construction of the Institute and provided long-term support for it, donating a large number of books in 1937, when Hermann Grossmann was in the presence of the Guardian for the first time.[154]

At Riḍván 1953 he presented the final blueprint, which he dedicated to Mirzá Abu'l-Faḍl, Nabíl, Professor Forel, Dr Esslemont, Martha Root and Lidia Zamenhof. The plans contained the following foreword:

> The need for religion to permeate science, their fusion into a single whole, requires an ever-higher degree of precision and perfection, and the

builders must be careful to avoid leaving behind dangerous substances that might inadvertently endanger the new. This applies in particular where the manifestation of the new creation provides the standard measure and purpose, the size and design of the structure, but entrusts all else to the judgment and care of the builders. Thus, the path is already mapped out for science, too. We know that in the days of the early Manifestations it was science that mixed the poison of superstition and turning away from God into the pure wine of true knowledge, thus laming the uplifting power of religious life. Hence, the false doctrines of the Babylonian priesthood have continued to fascinate mankind right up to the present day, irrespective of all rational thought and advanced knowledge, and heathen thinking has damaged the fruits of Islamic and Christian thought at their innermost core. Today, Bahá'u'lláh has raised science to a level of importance higher than in any previous cycle by describing it, along with religion, as one of the two wings required for humanity's advancement. This, however, places immense responsibility on the shoulders of those who represent His Faith in this New Day. They are obliged to watch over the development of both science and religion. They are able to do so by fixing their eyes firmly on the guidance provided by the creative Word and by observing the development of the sciences, drawing from both in order to gain new knowledge and new wisdom and retrospectively promoting and expanding the understanding of both science and religion. For the individual, the means for doing this are available through study, Bahá'í courses and summer schools, and for science as a whole the Bahá'í Academy wishes to serve these objectives in association with the Bahá'í Institute for Religion and Science and the two Bahá'í institutions of higher education for the study of religion and science.[155]

The dream of establishing this Academy occupied Hermann Grossmann's mind for decades. It sometimes helped him overcome difficulties and hours of hardship. Yet, in the end, circumstances forced him to give up these plans, and he withdrew the request for building permission that had already been approved by the authorities. His daily work in teaching the Faith, his professional career and responsibility as Managing Director of his company – as well as his less than perfect state of health – left him with no strength to implement his plans. In the final analysis, the time was probably not yet ripe for the establishment of a Bahá'í Institute.

CHAPTER 15

LAUNCHING THE TEN YEAR CRUSADE

In a cable sent on 8 October 1952, Shoghi Effendi informed the Bahá'í world of the launching of a Ten Year Plan, a world-embracing spiritual crusade. The start of this plan was to be marked by the Holy Year.

> HAIL, FEELINGS HUMBLE THANKFULNESS UNBOUNDED JOY, OPENING HOLY YEAR COMMEMORATING CENTENARY RISE ORB BAHÁ'U'LLÁH'S MOST SUBLIME REVELATION MARKING CONSUMMATION SIX THOUSAND YEAR CYCLE USHERED IN ADAM, GLORIFIED ALL PAST PROPHETS SEALED BLOOD AUTHOR BÁBÍ DISPENSATION.[156]

The Holy Year was to feature four major international conferences during 1953. In February a conference was planned for Africa in Kampala, Uganda; in May another was to be held for the Americas in Wilmette, Illinois; a third – for Europe – was to take place in July in Stockholm, Sweden; and the final conference, for Asia, was arranged for October in New Delhi, India.

As explained in the *Bahá'í News*, the Guardian cited the four objectives of the new plan as:

> FIRST, DEVELOPMENT INSTITUTIONS WORLD CENTRE FAITH HOLY LAND. SECOND, CONSOLIDATION, THROUGH CAREFULLY DEVISED MEASURES HOME FRONT TWELVE TERRITORIES DESTINED SERVE ADMINISTRATIVE BASES OPERATIONS TWELVE NATIONAL PLANS. THIRD, CONSOLIDATION ALL TERRITORIES ALREADY OPENED FAITH. FOURTH, OPENING REMAINING CHIEF VIRGIN TERRITORIES PLANET THROUGH SPECIFIC ALLOTMENTS EACH NATIONAL ASSEMBLY FUNCTIONING BAHÁ'Í WORLD.[157]

In a message addressed to the Inter-American conference, Shoghi Effendi added:

> Let there be no mistake. The avowed, the primary aim of this Spiritual Crusade is none other than the conquest of the citadels of men's hearts. The theatre of its operation is the entire planet. Its duration a whole decade.[158]

At a colloquium on the occasion of a Bahá'í teaching conference at the National Centre in Frankfurt am Main, Hermann Grossmann explained the principles of the Ten Year Crusade: The plan drawn up by the Guardian was based, to its smallest details, on the outlines laid down by the Blessed Beauty and by the Master in three documents that form the real backbone of the development of the Bahá'í Cause: Bahá'u'lláh's Tablet of Carmel (Lawḥ-i-Karmil), 'Abdu'l-Bahá's Tablets of the Divine Plan, and His Will and Testament.

Dr Grossmann explained the following:

> In connection with the Shrine already begun by 'Abdu'l-Bahá on Mount Carmel, it is stated in the Tablet of Carmel that the kings and heads of state will come and circumambulate it, a custom that is common in Islam, that we find reflected in the processions of Catholic Christians, and that we can assume to be an ancient religious ritual. This is the context of the steps leading directly up to the Shrine. Although not generally accessible today, they will be the path along which, on special occasions, such as the visits of kings and rulers, people will make their ascent to the Shrine.

Dr Grossmann also alluded to the prophecy in the Tablet:

> Ere long will God sail His Ark upon thee, and will manifest the people of Bahá who have been mentioned in the Book of Names.

And he continued:

> The Ark is the symbol of the Covenant of God, thus expressing the significance of the Bahá'í World Centre both for the Cause and for the security of the world. As the World Centre of the Bahá'í Faith, Carmel is, for all believers, at once the centre of security, order, law, inspiration and teaching. In 'Abdu'l-Bahá's Will and Testament we find a clear indication that a Universal House of Justice is to be elected by the National Spiritual Assemblies, an institution that ... is to decide upon all laws and regulations that are not expressly recorded in the sacred texts. Through this body, all difficult problems are to be solved.[159]

On the subject of teaching in virgin territories, Hermann Grossmann explained:

> A further source for the Ten Year Plan is the 'Divine Plan'. It consists of a series of Tablets by 'Abdu'l-Bahá addressed to America and Canada in the years 1916 and 1917. One of these Tablets sets out in detail the conditions that pioneers should fulfil. The first thing that 'Abdu'l-Bahá expects

from a pioneer is firmness in the Covenant, the second is the unity of the believers, and the third is travelling. And in one of the Tablets Germany is mentioned, too ...[160]

When on 24 December 1951 the Guardian had appointed the twelve Hands to support him, he called upon three of the Hands – Sutherland Maxwell, Mason Remey and Amelia Collins – to come to Haifa as members of the International Bahá'í Council. The remaining nine Hands were to stay at their posts and continue to carry out their administrative duties and teaching work, until the necessity arose to provide them with other instructions.

That necessity had evidently now arisen, for the Guardian asked them to participate in the four Intercontinental Conferences of the Holy Year as his representatives.

Hermann Grossmann was to attend the first conference held in Kampala, Uganda, in 1953 and deliver a lecture on the Bahá'í Administrative Order. Much to his chagrin, he was forced to cancel his participation at short notice due to ill health.

Hand of the Cause of God Leroy Ioas participated in the Kampala conference as the Guardian's representative, and a total of ten Hands as well as people from no fewer than 30 ethnic groups and 19 countries were in attendance. The vast majority of the participants were representatives of the indigenous peoples of Africa. The climax of the conference was the unveiling by Leroy Ioas, on behalf of Shoghi Effendi, of a portrait of the Báb, in front of which each participant was able to spend a short time in prayer. The main task of the conference was to prepare for the expansion of the Faith into those countries and islands of the African continent that had not yet been opened.

At Riḍván 1953 the believers were summoned to Chicago for the All-American Conference. Amatu'l-Bahá Rúḥíyyih Khánum represented the Guardian at the dedication of the House of Worship, the Mother Temple of the West. On behalf of Shoghi Effendi, she unveiled a portrait of the Báb, and the Bahá'ís filed past it in silent procession. The conference was enhanced by the presence of twelve Hands among the 2,300 participants from 33 nations. Here, too, one of the purposes of the gathering was to call upon the Bahá'ís to carry the Faith to virgin areas of the continent and to the as yet unopened neighbouring islands in the Atlantic and Pacific oceans.

The venue for the third Intercontinental Conference was Stockholm, the capital of Sweden, from 21st to 26th July 1953. The European Teaching Committee in Geneva had summoned the believers to attend. Shoghi Effendi asked the Hand of the Cause of God Ugo Giachery to convey his greetings to the participants. Thirteen other Hands of the Cause participated, along with representatives of the National Spiritual Assemblies of the United States, the British Isles, and of the regional National Assemblies of Germany and Austria, Italy and Switzerland, Iran and Iraq, as well as Bahá'ís from 30 different countries. One believer remarked that she now understood why Europe was called the pulse of the world. If this pulse could be strengthened, we could conquer the world. At a dignified public event, 700 visitors listened to a talk by Professor Zeine N. Zeine from Beirut. Dr Giachery unveiled a portrait of the Báb sent by the Guardian, and the friends had the opportunity of reverently filing past it in prayer. Dr Giachery appealed to the nearly 400 Bahá'ís at the conference to donate funds for the purchase of the land required for the construction of the Houses of Worship in Frankfurt am Main and Stockholm, and to rise up as pioneers to countries in Europe and islands in the Mediterranean, the Atlantic and the North Sea that had not yet been opened to the Faith. Sixty-three believers spontaneously offered to pioneer, among them Ursula von Brunn and Elsa Maria Grossmann for the Frisian Islands of Föhr and Westerland, and Rolf Haug for Crete.

One participant observed:

> The dominant language of that conference was English. Several of the Hands of the Cause addressed the friends. I remember Dr Grossmann walking to the podium; his very walk, his bearing reflected his personality, his humility and love for every one of us. And then Dr Grossmann addressed the friends. He did not speak in English. Dr Grossmann spoke in Spanish. He addressed the minority among us, touching the hearts of the Spanish friends and every heart in the gathering, as his voice rang through the auditorium. Although I did not speak Spanish, I understood the language of his heart. Dr Grossmann's loving heart knew the needs and longings of every soul he encountered.[161]

He spoke about the part of the Ten Year Plan that fell within Europe's sphere of responsibility.

The last of these historic gatherings was the Asian Intercontinental Conference held in New Delhi in October 1953, which was attended by 400 people from 31 countries. It was here that the colourful mixture of races and peoples unified under the banner of Bahá'u'lláh was most strongly in evidence. Many believers volunteered to move to areas that had not yet been opened to the Faith. The sum donated for the purchase of Temple sites and for the maintenance of existing schools as well as the establishment of new ones was overwhelming.

CHAPTER 16

ELSA MARIA GROSSMANN

Under the Ten Year Plan launched in 1953, the Guardian charged the German Bahá'í community with responsibility for the opening of the Frisian Islands to the Faith, and when the Bahá'ís were called upon at the Stockholm conference to pioneer to virgin territories, Elsa Maria Grossmann walked onto the stage to join the line of pioneers. She had lived in northern Germany for many years and sensed a special bond with the Frisian Islands because of family connections.

Elsa Maria Sofia Grossmann was born on 19 July 1896 in Rosario de Santa Fé, Argentina. She was two years old when her brother Hermann – Germán – was born, the brother with whom she was later to be particularly close, particularly because of their work together promoting the Bahá'í Faith. Her maternal aunt and uncle were nominated as godparents when she was baptized into the Protestant congregation of Esperanza in Santa Fé province. She was a hard-working and successful pupil and, like her brother, she attended the German school in Rosario de Santa Fé, the Colegio Aleman at Calle España 150. After the family moved to Germany, she attended the Paulsen Foundation High School for Girls in Hamburg, graduating (*Lyzeumreife*) in 1913. Her marks there were good right from the start, indicating that she had less difficulty adapting to school life in Germany than her brother Hermann. The following year, she travelled with a friend from Hamburg to Lausanne in order to improve her knowledge of French at an all-girls boarding school. But her father soon had to bring the girls back to Hamburg because of the outbreak of the First World War. Elsa Maria now devoted her time intensively to the study of languages – she attained high proficiency in her two native tongues, German and Spanish, as well as in English and French, and later Esperanto. She not only spoke these languages fluently but was also able to translate very complicated texts.

In 1920, Elsa Maria Grossmann became a Bahá'í. In her memoirs she records how on that day in August 1920 when she first heard of the Faith from her brother Hermann she was in a state of utter desolation:[162]

> Our souls had lost all that had been dear and precious to them without getting anything in return. I remember imploring the Almighty on more than one night during that period, crying out thus from the inmost depths of my being, 'Let me find a point, O God, only *one* point to which I might cling!'

According to her memoirs, she already learned from the first excited words of her brother about his encounter with the Bahá'í Faith in Leipzig, that

> Christ had come back to this world in Bahá'u'lláh, the Manifestation of God for our days, and that His son, 'Abdu'l-Bahá, was still living in the Holy Land and we could address and write to Him whenever we liked. The only question I asked was, whether this Prophet taught that there was a life beyond death, for this problem above all troubled me at that time. And after my brother said yes, I accepted the Cause from the bottom of my heart.

On that momentous day in 1920, when Hermann and Elsa Maria Grossmann arrived home to their mother so full of excitement, they told her about the Cause of Bahá'u'lláh, which they had so eagerly sought and had now found. Johanna Grossmann recognized the depth of her children's conviction that this was indeed the right path, and she was moved to see how in such a short time their former despair had been transformed into happiness. Deeply impressed, and herself convinced, she only asked her children not to talk about it to their father just yet.

For their father, Curt Grossmann, the struggle for survival had started early in life and had made him tough and somewhat hard-hearted. He had become serious and stern on his way to success. He was highly educated and multi-lingual, and he was free of prejudice and full of love for the whole of humanity, but he was strongly attached to the church of his forefathers and wished his family to be so too. He made not the slightest attempt to study the Bahá'í writings, and so it was not possible to convince him of the teachings of Bahá'u'lláh. Hermann and Elsa Maria's mother supported them whenever she could, and as relations within the family gradually became unbearable, she tried to create an atmosphere of reconciliation between traditional religious observance and the new light. Again and again she carefully explained to her husband what it was that motivated his children's activities on behalf of the Bahá'í Faith.

Working together, brother and sister achieved quite a bit first in Hamburg and then in the whole of northern Germany. Many teaching activities were held and there was lively exchange between the various groups in the North of Germany.

Elsa Maria Grossmann was tirelessly engaged in teaching activities in the Bahá'í communities and at summer schools. Her proficiency in foreign languages enabled her to draw on English and French literature for her talks, since there was still very little Bahá'í literature in German. She assisted with the magazine of the 'Deutsche Bahá'í-Bund' (German Bahá'í Association) *Sonne der Wahrheit*, as well as the children's magazine *Rosengärtlein*. She represented the Bahá'ís at the Esperanto Congresses in Oxford, Cologne and London. She corresponded frequently with Lidia Zamenhof and Martha Root. In 1948, at the Esperanto Congress in Munich, she delivered a talk entitled 'At the Start of a New Era', and she so improved her knowledge of Esperanto that in 1950 she was able to pass an examination qualifying her as an Esperanto course leader.

One day, after Hermann Grossmann had moved to Neckargemünd with his wife and child in 1933, he sent his father a copy of his book *Am Morgen einer neuen Zeit* (The Dawn of a New Age). Elsa Maria Grossmann reported that her father studied the book intensively and then said, 'So you Bahá'ís believe that Bahá'u'lláh is a Manifestation of God?'

> I was so fully amazed at this unexpected question [she wrote in her memoirs] that I really did not know what surprised me more, whether the question itself or the fact that father uttered, with such assurance and fluency, this name, which – as far as I remember – never before had passed his lips. But in the next moment like a flash of lightning this idea crossed my mind: 'If I say yes I perhaps must leave home, as I already had to do so some years ago because of the Cause, and this time it may be for ever!' So I picked up all my courage and said very calmly 'Indeed.' But nothing special happened.
>
> Some time after this a new regime had taken hold in Germany, and publicly broadcast the announcement of its drastic programme. One evening after such a disturbing proclamation, father turned off the radio and said most thoughtfully: 'I am very much afraid they will some day interdict your noble movement which only wants the good of the nations and the best for humanity.' And again some time later he said to me: 'I no longer have anything against your working for the Bahá'í Cause.'

In November 1927 Elsa Maria Grossmann had had to leave her parents' home. She intended to help out at the International Bahá'í Bureau in Geneva. At that time there were only two or three believers in Switzerland. Unable to find work in the city, she was forced to return to her parental home after ten months.

In 1935, Elsa Maria Grossmann and her parents all moved to Neckargemünd, where they lived next door to Hermann and Anna. Johanna Grossmann, with her husband's consent, now became a declared adherent of the Faith of Bahá'u'lláh. Several months later, Curt Grossmann died unexpectedly after an operation in a Heidelberg hospital. His daughter recalls in her memoirs that his face showed the peace of a person who had passed out of this earthly life in harmony with his Maker. In 1936, Elsa Maria Grossmann and her mother Johanna formally withdrew from the church, which was not yet a requirement for Bahá'ís at that time. They were to have a further three calm and happy years living in their house in Neckargemünd. In the evenings they studied the Writings together and reflected on the Faith.

In June 1940 Johanna Grossmann unexpectedly passed away at the age of 72. Despite the war and the interdiction of the Faith, many friends and acquaintances came to lay her to rest beside her husband in the cemetery at Neckargemünd.

In the 1930s, Elsa Maria Grossmann translated *The Dispensation of Bahá'u'lláh* by Shoghi Effendi as well as *Gleanings from the Writings of Bahá'u'lláh* from English into German. The manuscript of *The Dispensation of Bahá'u'lláh* was taken by friends to Switzerland during the period of the interdiction, when it appeared too dangerous to keep it in Germany. Together with her brother Hermann, she revised the translation of 'Abdu'l-Bahá's *Paris Talks*. Apart from *Gleanings*, the most important task was the translation and compilation of a prayer book, again together with her brother. The prayer book was published by George Ronald in Oxford, England in 1948 and was eagerly awaited by the German Bahá'ís, especially those who had lost all their books to the Gestapo, not even being permitted to keep a single prayer book, as well as by those who had only recently joined the Cause.

Elsa Maria Grossmann corresponded frequently with the Guardian, Shoghi Effendi, concerning translation and other matters. For her, as for all the Grossmann family, he had become the admired and much-loved head of the Bahá'í Faith after the passing of the Master, 'Abdu'l-Bahá, in 1921. Her pilgrimage in 1937 was therefore a long-awaited and major event in her life. Elsa Maria Grossmann had suffered from ill-health for some time, and so the pilgrimage had to be postponed by more than a year. This, however, gave them the opportunity to speak to the Guardian and receive instructions from him once more shortly before the expected interdiction on the Bahá'í Faith imposed by the National Socialists.

In a poetry album, she wrote the following lines:

Das Land ist heilig, darauf wir gehn
Und Blumen uns duftend umbreiten,
An Bahji's Tore leis verwehn,
Verdämmern der Erde Zeiten.

Die Schwelle beugt sich noch lichterfüllt
Der Herrlichkeit, die sie geborgen,
Da drinnen aber, da Schlaf Ihn hüllt,
Umfängt uns der strahlende Morgen.

Das Herz schlägt leiser und Wunder erblühn
Wohl hier an der Welten Mitte,
Da Erd und Himmel in Einheit glühn
Und schreiten in göttlichem Schritte.

Verrinnen fühlst du des Daseins Flut,
Verhalten die Flammen noch ragen,
Und beugst dich still vor der stärksten Glut,
Die jemals die Erde getragen.

Dein Selbst vergeht und es wächst im Raum
Die Kraft, die dem Ursprung verbunden,
Da, Welt, du hier an des Lebens Baum
Den Atem der Gottheit gefunden.[163]

The land is holy beneath our feet
And fragrant the flowers around us,
Soft breezes stir at Bahji's gate
As worldly time fades into paleness.

The threshold bows still, light-enshrined
To the Glory held within that place,
And though in sleepful rest now veiled
We sense the brilliant dawn's embrace.

The heartbeat softens and miracles flow
Here at the centre of this planet, our home,
For earth and heaven in unity glow
And with divine steps through the universe roam.

The flood of existence ebbs away,
Still the gentle flame burns bright,
You silently bow your head to pray
Before the everlasting light.

Your self drifts away and you sense in that place
The power from the Source on high,
For here, world, the Tree of Life is embraced
And the Breath of God wafts nearby.

This strength later enabled her to act fearlessly when confronted by the National Socialist Secret Police, the Gestapo, when being imprisoned without charge in 1944. She later told of how a man had searched her home for suspicious literature, but had not found anything. When he asked if she was a Bahá'í, she said yes. She was arrested and forced into a car that had been waiting in front of the house. In the car, she had to sit next to the driver. The man who had arrested her sat down on the seat behind her and took out his pistol. Her remark: 'If you think you have to shoot me, go on and pull the trigger,' annoyed him, because she evidently showed no fear. In prison she was interrogated every day. The authorities wished, above all, to force her to reveal the names of other Bahá'ís, but she named only those who were already known to the Gestapo and said that she did not even know how many Bahá'ís there were in Germany.

On one occasion, a female prison warden found her crying in her cell. The warden comforted her, saying that the criminals were not those 'inside' but those who were 'outside'. This remark came just at the right moment and restored her courage and confidence.[164]

Elsa Maria Grossmann spent the days of her imprisonment in Heidelberg in a state of uncertainty, unable to contact her family and unaware of the efforts being made by her brother. After nine days he managed to secure her release. She was now ordered to pay a large fine for 'breaching the Decree for the Protection of the People and State ... of 1933'. As has been stated in a earlier chapter, this punishment was eventually revoked by the Heidelberg Public Prosecutor's Office in 1998, many years after her death, upon application by her family.

Her courage and independence are again revealed in the following episode. In the final days of the Second World War in Spring 1945, the house of the Grossmann family in Neckargemünd was the headquarters of a German army unit. When she found out that a court martial was taking place in the house and a straggling soldier was to be sentenced to death for desertion, she strode into the courtroom full of indignation. Such interference in the proceedings of a court martial was unthinkable and not without risk, especially as her previous conviction meant that she was regarded as politically unreliable. She demanded that the death sentence be commuted to a milder form of punishment. The harsh verdict against the soldier was particularly senseless, since by this time nothing could stop the collapse of the German army. The officers of the court martial, surprised at her intervention, calmed her and agreed to pass a lighter sentence. But they broke their promise: the convicted soldier was taken out and later his body was found in a nearby forest – he had been shot.[165]

At the Stockholm conference, Elsa Maria Grossmann had volunteered to pioneer to Westerland on Sylt, an island of the Frisian chain in the North Sea off the coast of Germany. She arrived there on 24 September 1953 and was named a Knight of Bahá'u'lláh. A few days later, on 30 September 1953, she received a cable from the Guardian via the National Spiritual Assembly of Germany. It read: 'ASSURE ELSE GROSSMANN DEEPEST LOVING APPRECIATION. SHOGHI.' Her health was by this time quite poor – her eyesight had deteriorated and she had a liver and heart condition. The constant and frequently strong winds, combined with the cold – Shoghi Effendi had described the Frisian Islands as 'inhospitable and windswept' – caused her great suffering. She gave English lessons to children, both in order to help them reach the standard required at school and in order to make contact with the local population. She was referred to as 'Saint Johanna' but she found that the Frisians were but little receptive to the Bahá'í message, and it was very difficult to get to know people and develop friendships with them.[166] Eventually, however, an elderly lady, Martha Petersen, opened her heart to the Faith, and Elsa Maria Grossmann gained another companion in Berta Grünewald from Giessen, who also came to live on the island.

In a letter to the American *Bahá'í News*, written after five years as a pioneer, she wrote:

> The story of the opening of the Frisian Islands to the Cause of God is, as yet experienced, not a very crimson-coloured one when compared with many others from more radiant pioneer places. This was for a long time a heavy load on us here, but only the fact that our beloved Guardian was fully aware of the situation, and often transmitted to us his inspiration and loving comfort, lightened its weight. We think of the little white lighthouses everywhere on these islands, looking over the sea calmly and firmly, and

fully indifferent to the storms and tempests around them, just showing the seeking sailor the right route. This exactly is our way: to be like lighthouses of His Cause for whosoever seeks His Path. And this finally, God willing, may lead to His spiritual victory.[167]

In March 1958, after the passing of Shoghi Effendi, the Bahá'ís of Westerland on Sylt received a letter from the Hand of the Cause of God Rúḥíyyih Khánum, in which she wrote:

> As you well know the work in the Frisian Islands was a source of great satisfaction to the beloved Guardian, and he eagerly looked forward to the day when you would have your own spiritual assembly. I hope that day is not too far distant ...[168]

The importance attached by the Guardian to the opening of these North Sea islands is also evident from Rúḥíyyih Khánum's letter to Elsa Maria Grossmann of 16 February 1958:

> He was so proud of the Center established there [in the Frisian Islands], and you must be glad that you rejoiced his heart during his lifetime. So many of the friends are now going to arise and carry out his wishes, but it will never be quite the same as if they had done so while he was alive and could have been made directly happy by their self-sacrificing acts.[169]

After eleven years, when Elsa Maria Grossmann was 68 years old, her poor state of health compelled her to return to the mainland. She settled in Neckargemünd again and died in her eighty-second year on 6 August 1977 in Plankstadt, near Heidelberg.

She had once told a dear Bahá'í friend that she did not wish to be alone when her end drew near. Her wish was fulfilled: she died in the presence of a doctor who had just examined her and whom she was just telling about the Cause of Bahá'u'lláh.[170] She now rests alongside her brother, Hand of the Cause of God Dr Hermann Grossmann, in the cemetery in Neckargemünd.

At Riḍván 1997, forty-four years after the Knight of Bahá'u'lláh Elsa Maria Grossmann had first set foot on the Island of Sylt and twenty years after her death, a Spiritual Assembly was formed in Westerland on Sylt. The work she had begun now came to fruition.

In the course of her life, Elsa Maria Grossmann wrote a great many sonnets and poems which she set to music and sang, accompanying herself on the guitar. At the age of 20, filled with longing for her childhood in her South American homeland, she wrote the following poem:[171]

HERMANN GROSSMANN

Der Maldreseva Balsamduft
Weht leise durch den Abend hin
Moskitosummen füllt die Luft,
Berauschend duftet der Jasmin.

Die Mutter will zur Ruh mich singen
Und schläfern mich zur Nacht.
Die Palmenblätter leise schwingen,
Das Kreuz des Südens hält die Wacht.

The Maldreseva's balmy scent
Drifts through the evening air,
Mosquitoes buzz without relent
Heady the jasmine fair.

Mother sings a song to calm
Me gently off to sleep.
The breeze disturbs the rustling palm,
As the Southern Cross watch does keep.

She wrote the following poem two years before she first encountered the Bahá'í Faith:

Das ist die Stille,
Die große Stille
Die Deinem Namen vorangeht.
Ich liege auf den Knien und warte.
Ich fühl Dein Kommen, Herr,
Und Deine Flügel rauschen.
Dunkel ist die Nacht,
Und die Wünsche schweigen.
Das Ewige schwingt über der Erde,
Zeitlos,– raumlos,– groß, verheißend ...
Herr! ...
Das bist Du, Herr! –
Und ich bete.

This is the silence,
The great silence
That precedes Thy name.
I go down on my knees and wait.
I sense Thy coming, Lord,
And Thy wings susurrate.
Dark is the night,
And wishes hold their tongues.
The Eternal lingers over the earth,

*Conversation in the 'Häusle', c. 1950: Hermann Grossmann with
Professor Hans Peter of the University of Tübingen*

*Dr Hermann Grossmann
in his study
(photo by René Steiner)*

*Anneliese Bopp and Hermann
Grossmann, with Anneliese's dog
Assa at her feet*

*Hands of the Cause of God Dr Adelbert
Mühlschlegel and Dr Hermann Grossmann,
with Dr Eugen Schmidt (right)*

Friends with Hermann Grossmann at National Convention, 1951, outside the National Ḥaẓíratu'l-Quds, Westendstraße 24, Frankfurt. The building had been severely damaged in the War (see pages 95-7)

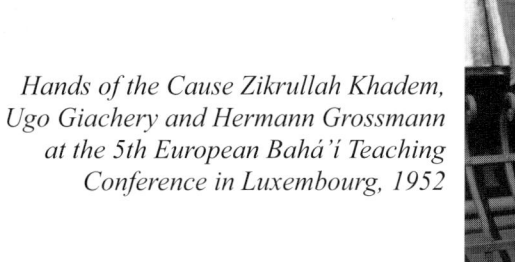

Hands of the Cause Zikrullah Khadem, Ugo Giachery and Hermann Grossmann at the 5th European Bahá'í Teaching Conference in Luxembourg, 1952

Hand of the Cause Hermann Grossmann at the International Bahá'í Conference in Stockholm, 1953 (photo by Hermine Berdjis)

Hermann Grossmann with friends at the 5th European Bahá'í Teaching Conference in Luxembourg, 1952

At the British Bahá'í summer school, Exeter, 25 July 1954. From left: Charles Dunning, Knight of Bahá'u'lláh to Orkney; Brigitte Hasselblatt, Knight of Bahá'u'lláh to Shetland; Philip Hainsworth, pioneer to Uganda; Hand of the Cause Hermann Grossmann; Ḍíyá'u'lláh Aṣgharzádih, pioneer to Jersey; Dorothy Ferraby, Auxiliary Board; Ruth Moffett, visitor from the USA

At the dedication of the National Ḥaẓíratu'l-Quds of the Bahá'ís of the British Isles, 1955. From left: Hasan Balyuzi, unidentified, unidentified, Hands of the Cause Leroy Ioas and Hermann Grossmann

Two married couples at the Bahá'í summer school, Esslingen, 1956: left, Adelbert and Herma Mühlschlegel; right, Anna and Hermann Grossmann

Dr Hermann Grossmann in Ireland, 1957

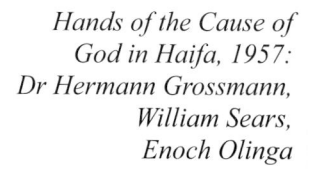

Hands of the Cause of God in Haifa, 1957: Dr Hermann Grossmann, William Sears, Enoch Olinga

Beyond the realms of time and space, great, promising ...
Lord! ...
Thou art here, Lord! –
And I pray.

The following lines were penned on the inside cover of a volume of poetry:

Nicht schon im Kampf
Der mir im Innern lebt,
Liegt wohl ein Handeln, Herr,
Das ich begehe.
Doch ob mein Selbst dabei
Zur Höhe oder Tiefe strebt,
Ist meine Wahl,
Aus ihr entspringt,
Wie ich bestehe.

Not in the struggle
That is waged within me
Is the action, Lord,
That I do make.
Yet whether my Self
Strives heav'nward or is worldly
Is my own choice;
From it is shaped
The course I take.

A few years after Elsa Maria Grossmann had recognized the new Revelation, a few lines entitled *The New Day* were to be found in her collection of poems:

Die Sonne schreitet ihre Bahn,
Da noch die Menschen dunkel träumen,
Das Land liegt still, doch in des Himmels Räumen
Bricht schon der junge Morgen an.

Auch Du, mein Herz, vom Schlummer schreite
Zum neuen Licht, das dich erhellt,
Und sende in des Himmels Weite
Dein frohes Dankgebet dem Herrn der Welt

The sun pursues its daily flight
As still mankind in darkness slumbers,
The earth is quiet, yet in the heavenly chambers
Is breaking a new morning light.

HERMANN GROSSMANN

Thou too, my heart, from slumber now arise
To greet the light that such brightness doth afford
And send into the lofty skies
Thy happy prayer of thanks unto the Lord!

CHAPTER 17

THE FIRST FIVE YEARS OF THE TEN YEAR CRUSADE, 1953–1957

After his retirement in 1953, Hermann Grossmann was able to travel freely and independently in order to fulfil his duties as a Hand of the Cause of God. Only his persistently poor health set limits to his activities. On the other hand, it was not in his nature to live a more restful life. He constantly drove himself to exhaustion in serving Bahá'u'lláh.

At Riḍván 1954, a conference of the four European Hands of the Cause of God – Ugo Giachery, Hermann Grossmann, Adelbert Mühlschlegel and George Townshend – was held at the National Centre in Frankfurt am Main at which they appointed the members of the newly founded Auxiliary Board. Dr Giachery, Dr Grossmann and Dr Mühlschlegel were present, but sickness prevented George Townshend from attending.[172]

The 24th National Convention which took place in Frankfurt am Main immediately afterwards ended with speeches to the delegates by the two German Hands. They were characterized by confidence that the aims set out in the Ten Year Plan would be achieved.[173]

The third Benelux Conference and a subsequent summer school from 5–25 June 1954 in Arnhem were opened by the two German Hands. They encouraged the friends to take up with joy the goals set by the Guardian, Shoghi Effendi, which envisaged a large increase in the number of communities, groups and isolated centres.[174]

In July, Hermann Grossmann attended the British summer school in Exeter. The National Spiritual Assembly of the British Isles wrote to the conference of the Hands of the Cause in Frankfurt:

> On the last evening of Summer School, Exeter, the friends gathered together to review the two weeks of joy which were just ending. It was then resolved to ask the British National Spiritual Assembly to forward to the Conference of the Hands a note expressing our deep, overwhelmingly

> deep, gratitude to Dr Hermann Grossmann for the wonderful contributions he made. His presence, his talks, his consultations, his abounding love and sympathy, his understanding and his scholarship combined to make his stay at Summer School the largest single factor which contributed to its great success. Through him we learned of the function of the Hands and their Boards; we witnessed the confirmations a Hand can attract and we learned much by actually seeing a Hand of the Cause in action. For all these things, we thank him, and beg you to facilitate his speedy return.[175]

In September 1954 the first summer school took place at the National Centre in Frankfurt am Main. Every evening, Hermann Grossmann was available to answer questions from believers and enquirers alike.

The four European Hands called a conference for the first three days of October. It was held in the heart of Europe, in the Ḥaẓíratu'l-Quds in Frankfurt am Main. It was the first meeting of the Hands with their Auxiliary Board members and the first opportunity for consultation between the National Spiritual Assemblies of Europe and the European Teaching Committee (ETC) in Geneva. Marion Hofman, Auxiliary Board member, reports on the conference as follows:

> It was indeed a thrilling moment in Bahá'í history which set all our hearts 'singing and swinging', to borrow the delightful phrase of Dr Mühlschlegel. And he reminded us in his opening remarks before our work began that 'we are placed by Providence in this age, this day, this continent, this Conference. So, overwhelmed by thankfulness for the bounty of Bahá'u'lláh, we shall take up our tools and work like masons, obedient, thankful, humble, and filled with the love of mankind.'

The main theme of the conference was the question as to how the Hands and their Auxiliary Board could best co-operate with the National Assemblies.

> The Conference realized that the Board is in fact a new reservoir of energy and encouragement for local communities and individual believers, and everything possible was done to clarify the members' tasks and invite their activity. Experiences shared by Dr Grossmann from his recent travels in Britain pointed a way for Board members in their relations with the friends.

The consultations took place in a spirit of harmony, unity and joy. On the last day, Ugo Giachery said: 'It is really a time for rejoicing ... for these last few days have made possible the most wonderful understanding of our common problems.'[176]

THE FIRST FIVE YEARS OF THE TEN YEAR CRUSADE, 1953–1957

Between this journey to Frankfurt and a visit to Switzerland that lasted several days, Hermann Grossmann gave a number of talks in Germany.

At the beginning of 1955, he again spent some time in Ireland and Britain. In Ireland he visited Dublin and Belfast, and in Britain he travelled from Glasgow via Edinburgh, Newcastle, Bradford, Manchester, Norwich, Brighton and Northampton to London. He went to twelve places and delivered nineteen talks, as he wrote to the pioneer in Texel, one of the West Frisian Islands belonging to the Netherlands. In London he attended the dedication of the new National Centre along with Hand of the Cause Leroy Ioas. Afterwards, the friends asked him to speak at a public meeting. There, he met many old acquaintances and pioneers, embracing them, as was his wont. He later recalled how wonderful it was. He closes his letter to the pioneer with the encouraging words:

> It is late and tomorrow I have to go to Giessen and the day after to Frankfurt. Write soon! Always be as happy as I saw you in Holland. In my memory you will always remain the jolly Geertrui [Knight of Bahá'u'lláh Geertrui Ankersmit, later Mrs Bates], who loves to laugh. Retain your joyfulness, for it assists in opening people's hearts, and we need open hearts so that the love of Bahá'u'lláh can enter them.[177]

In London he received a cable from the Hand of the Cause George Townshend, who was ill and living a secluded life in a home in Kilbarron, Ireland. The two Hands were able to spend a day together. They took a walk in the garden so as to be able to talk together undisturbed, and Hermann Grossmann encouraged George Townshend to finish his book *Christ and Bahá'u'lláh*. Much to the regret of both men, Dr Grossmann had to travel back the next day, immediately before the arrival of the Hand of the Cause Leroy Ioas.[178]

The believers in Switzerland were able to hold the official dedication of their National Centre in Bern on 1 May 1955. Hermann Grossmann conveyed a message of congratulations from the Bahá'í community of Germany and Austria. He took the opportunity of this visit to Switzerland to continue teaching the Cause, giving public talks in Bern and Zurich.[179]

The Guardian had appointed Hermann Grossmann to be a member of an Appeals Committee that in late July 1955 submitted a written appeal to the United Nations in Geneva and conducted talks with the individual UN delegations in order to seek justice and protection for the persecuted Bahá'ís in Iran. The international committee headed by Dr Giachery was able to hand over the document to the General Secretary of the United Nations, Dag Hammarskjöld, personally on 1 August 1955. The appeal called upon the UN and its member states to prevent further persecution of the Bahá'ís in Iran:

> The Bahá'ís are the anvil on which Providence is forging a future for the world in unity and human dignity. The Bahá'ís represent the new universal principles needed by humanity.[180]

Hermann Grossmann knew that the Bahá'ís in the British Isles were urgently in need of encouragement at the time, and so he spent another two and a half weeks in Ireland and Great Britain in the autumn of that year. During this sojourn, which had been carefully organized by the friends, he visited fourteen towns and cities. Reporting on the trip, he pointed out that the British Bahá'í community had been seriously weakened by so many pioneers leaving to fulfil goals on other continents, primarily in Africa. He also wrote that he had visited the Hand of the Cause of God George Townshend again and that he was saddened to see that this precious soul was in such a poor state of health. Although George Townshend tried to encourage the friends through written messages, a tangible void was felt as a result of his absence due to ill health and physical weakness.[181]

A teaching conference and summer school at the 'Häusle' in Esslingen in autumn 1955 was followed by another teaching conference and summer school in Frankfurt am Main, both of which were chaired by Dr Grossmann. They aimed to prepare the friends for teaching the Faith.

In November, Hermann Grossmann set off on a fourth trip to Britain. He attended a weekend course in Edinburgh. After his return he thanked the friends for the brilliant organization of his travels, expressing his confidence and hope for the progress of the Faith in the near future.

Prior to this trip to Britain, he had spent three weeks with his sister Elsa Maria in Westerland on Sylt, hoping to find a little relaxation there. She had now been alone on the island for two years and was very glad of his company.

On the neighbouring island of Föhr was the Knight of Bahá'u'lláh Ursula von Brunn with her little daughter Gisela. She later recalled:

THE FIRST FIVE YEARS OF THE TEN YEAR CRUSADE, 1953–1957

> On Föhr we were, of course, very lonely. Nobody was interested in what I had to say. We were never invited into people's homes, although I myself always tried to ask people to come and visit us. It was therefore a joyful piece of news when Hermann Grossmann came to visit his sister on Westerland and they both came over to see us. We stood at the quay and wished we could pull the ship in faster. And then at last they arrived! Hermann Grossmann with his kind, warm-hearted manner and his sister, Elsa Maria, who was so modest and so rich in spirituality! I had invited relatives who ran a children's home on Föhr. They were very impressed by him, but they had no desire to know more about the Faith afterwards.[182]

For a variety of reasons, the von Brunns had to return to Tübingen. It was not until Gisela von Brunn was grown up that the whole family was able to fulfil their longing to pioneer by emigrating to Bolivia.

The Bahá'ís made careful preparations for a visit by Dr Grossmann to Munich. He delivered two talks to an attentive audience at the German Museum and another to a smaller group of enquirers. Whilst travelling onward to Vienna, he paid a brief visit to Salzburg and spoke at a number of firesides. In Vienna he was very pleased to see how active and enthusiastic the Austrian Bahá'ís were and he interrupted his return journey to visit Ulm and spend some time with the friends there. In 1955, Hermann Grossmann spent a total of 149 days teaching and travelling.[183]

In 1955 the Bahá'ís of Heidelberg successfully completed the difficult process of having the Spiritual Assembly of that city included in the Register of Associations. It was the first Spiritual Assembly in Germany to achieve this. The process meant adapting the 'Declaration of Trust' of the Spiritual Assemblies of the Bahá'ís of the United States to the German law on associations. It involved countless visits to various authorities and much negotiating skill. The registration of as many Local Spiritual Assemblies as possible was one of the goals of the Ten Year Plan. The National Spiritual Assembly had charged the Heidelberg community with the task of spearheading this process.[184]

Many communities celebrated World Religion Day in January 1956. Stuttgart publicized the event, which included a number of musical contributions, by holding a press conference with the Hand of the Cause of God Leroy Ioas. The audience, numbering about four hundred, was impressed by the talks given by seven representatives of different religions and denominations.

A similar event was organized by the Viennese community. The five renowned representatives of various Christian denominations and of Buddhism emphasized the common features shared by all religions. Last to speak was Dr Grossmann. He finished his talk by saying, 'It is not that we need to change the truth in the religions, but people's understanding of that truth needs to grow.'[185]

He had a conversation with Professor Thiring, a physicist at Vienna University, which he was able to continue over subsequent years. Their discussions were inspiring and fruitful and always a source of joy to Dr Grossmann.

He spent two weeks in France during the second half of January 1956. As was always the case for journeys abroad, he required an entry visa, which entailed further travels, usually to the consulate in Stuttgart. His Argentine passport was often an advantage in this connection.

Many pioneers had come to France from the United States of America, so that Bahá'í activities there had experienced an upswing. His journey had been well prepared by the believers. He visited Paris, Orleans, Chateauroux, Poitiers, Chatellerault, Bordeaux, Marseilles, Nice and Lyon. In all nine of these places he noted that many French people were now attracted to the Cause. In Monaco he had the opportunity to hold deepenings with newly-declared Bahá'ís.[186]

Hermann Grossmann was overjoyed to meet Laura Dreyfus-Barney at a meeting she hosted in Paris on 24 January 1956. She had had the bounty of staying in 'Akká, in the presence of 'Abdu'l-Bahá, in 1900 and again in 1905. Her conversations with Him are recorded in the book *Some Answered Questions*. She married Hippolyte Dreyfus, the first French believer, who rendered invaluable services to the Bahá'í Faith. In an appreciation written in 1928, Shoghi Effendi called him his trusted friend. In recognition of her humanitarian services, Madame Clifford-Barney was appointed an 'Officier de la Légion d'Honneur' by the French government in 1937. She died a highly esteemed personage in 1974 in Paris, at the age of 95.[187]

Interesting conversations took place between Dr Grossmann and Professor Massé, an orientalist at the University of Paris, and the famous Catholic writer M. Christofleur. The journey to France was thus 'a great joy, full of hope'.

In mid-February Dr Grossmann obtained visas for the Benelux countries – Belgium, the Netherlands and Luxembourg – in Stuttgart and Frankfurt. He stayed in these three countries for two weeks, speaking at various large and small-scale events in Luxembourg, Liège, Charleroi, Brussels, Antwerp, The Hague and Amsterdam.[188]

THE FIRST FIVE YEARS OF THE TEN YEAR CRUSADE, 1953–1957

In Brussels the friends were able, on 1 April, to celebrate the opening of the Belgian Ḥaẓíratu'l-Quds. The Hand of the Cause Hermann Grossmann conveyed greetings and a gift to the Belgian friends from Shoghi Effendi. This opening ceremony was the first Bahá'í event to be broadcast on a European television channel. The speaker was Professor Zeine N. Zeine of Beirut.[189]

On 20 and 21 May, Hermann Grossmann was again in The Hague, this time to take part in the dedication of the National Centre for the Netherlands. The rooms were abundantly decorated with fragrant flowers. After the ceremony and the welcoming of the guests, 'Dr Grossmann arose', a Bahá'í friend reported later,

> and with his face beaming with love, spoke of the great significance of this building. He said that these Ḥaẓíratu'l-Quds are buildings made of brick, made by man, but nevertheless they are different. They are institutions given by God through the mouth of the Manifestation. That is why they are different from other buildings. But the Spirit can only come into this building if we are ready to accept the fact that these Ḥaẓíratu'l-Quds are different from other buildings ... and it is our responsibility to see that they are different. There are few Bahá'ís in the world compared to other groups. But these few are known throughout the world to be different. If Bahá'ís do something, it is different than if others do ... for the shortcomings of others are taken as natural, but the public expects Bahá'ís to be perfect. This gives a tremendous responsibility to every believer. In this same way, even Ḥaẓíratu'l-Quds are different from other buildings. The non-Bahá'í world expects the Bahá'ís to make it a real Bahá'í Centre ... We shall enter this house in the proper spirit and dedicate our knowledge and love for the sake of humanity, because God wishes this ... Professor Zeine N. Zeine followed Dr Grossmann to the speaker's table. He apologized in his charming way for presuming to add 'his footnote talk to the inspirational one of Dr Grossmann.'[190]

The dedication ceremony was followed by the Benelux Teaching Conference attended by 60 friends from four continents. Hermann Grossmann reported that the conference was reminiscent of the brilliant teaching conferences held there by the Geneva-based European Teaching Committee during the period when pioneers were first sent to the Benelux countries. Nature also contributed to the atmosphere: 'The warm spring sun shone down at that time on the vernal countryside, festively adorned with blossom, and over the beach and sea at Scheveningen.'[191]

As always, he interrupted his journeys with visits to intermediate localities. This time he visited Bonn, Cologne and Düsseldorf to deliver talks or to meet and encourage the Bahá'ís.

Hermann Grossmann had found his first stay in Westerland beneficial, so in June 1956 he spent another period of nearly three weeks with his sister on the island of Sylt.

After many talks, meetings and the summer school in Esslingen, he travelled once again to Brussels. In the second half of October, he spent some time in Vienna, Graz, Salzburg and Innsbruck. As part of the Ten Year Plan, Austria was to form its own National Spiritual Assembly, and the friends needed assistance. Hermann Grossmann was pleased with their degree of consolidation and deepening, but he urgently called upon the German friends to move to the goal areas in Austria in order to fulfil the Guardian's request. On the way to Austria he visited Nuremberg, and on the way back he stopped in Munich and Ulm to reinforce the 'new spiritual impulse' of the Bahá'ís in those cities. In Munich he gave a well-attended talk at the German Museum.

Alex Käfer, an Austrian Bahá'í, writes about his visit to Graz:

> Unfortunately, I cannot remember specifically what Dr Grossmann talked about. But what is still clear in my memory is the wonderful radiance that emanated from Dr Grossmann. He exuded such confidence and certainty that they were in themselves proof that what he was talking about, the Message of Bahá'u'lláh, must be a source of spiritual joy and strength. Even today, it fills my heart with joy to recall that precious meeting with Dr Grossmann.[192]

Hermine and Massoud Berdjis recall that

> when we were pioneers in Austria during the Ten Year Plan, he was a very loving and understanding source of support. He encouraged us and advised the institutions. Everyone was happy when he came. When we lamented the slow pace of teaching success, he comforted us and said that the breakthrough would not come until the children of the pioneers started to marry the locals. How right he was![193]

'During one of his visits to Linz', reports Nahid Aschari,

> Hermann Grossmann once laid his hand upon mine whilst we were talking. He said, 'You know, Nahid, we Europeans have closed up our hearts in an iron closet to which there is no door. One must kindle a fire of love and break open the closet in order to reach people's hearts and souls.' This

image has never left my mind. Throughout my life, in my relations to Bahá'ís and non-Bahá'ís, I have always thought of this love that is needed in order to break open the symbolic closet.[194]

In January 1957 the Hand of the Cause was in the Rhineland, visiting Cologne, Düsseldorf, Bonn and Altena. At the beginning of February, Hermann Grossmann held a public talk in Frankfurt am Main, and in the second half of the month he paid visits to Hanover, Braunschweig and Hamburg. In mid-March he returned to the goal towns in Austria and in April he went to the Rhineland cities once again.[195]

During Riḍván the believers from the Benelux countries came together for their first National Convention in order to elect their National Spiritual Assembly. On this occasion 'our thoughts went back over the past years', reported participants in the Convention:

> ... It was a little over ten years ago that our beloved Guardian entrusted the American believers with the tremendous task of spreading the Faith in the European countries, and having pioneers settle in Belgium, the Netherlands, and Luxembourg ... With the never-failing help and assistance of our American friends, in the course of the following years the seed grew up, till a small but strong young tree was rooted in the soil of three neighbouring countries. An overwhelming feeling of joy and gratitude came over us all when we learned that our beloved Guardian found the young Benelux tree strong enough to serve as a new pillar for the future International House of Justice in the row of National Spiritual Assemblies ... Our ranks were reinforced by our reliable friend, Dr Hermann Grossmann, Hand of the Cause of God, whose presence on various occasions in the past had become so very dear to us, and who came with a special message from our Guardian ... containing the specific tasks and goals for the Benelux countries.

Via Dr Grossmann, the Guardian had sent attar of roses with which to anoint the friends and 'With that lovely aroma of the attar of roses around us ... we all went back to our own places enriched again by that very strange power that we drew from our first Convention.'[196]

From Brussels, Hermann Grossmann travelled on to the National Convention in Frankfurt am Main, Germany's 27th National Convention. In May Anna and Hermann Grossmann spent nine days in the presence of the Guardian in Haifa and 'Akká. They then travelled throughout Germany and Austria until the end of June, reporting to the various communities about their pilgrimage.

HERMANN GROSSMANN

On 15 July Hermann Grossmann flew via Amsterdam and London to Edinburgh and Aberdeen. His destination was the Shetlands, Faroes and Orkneys, as well as the Hebrides, where he intended to visit pioneers and offer them support and encouragement. They lived a solitary life, isolated from the Bahá'í community, among indifferent and even hostile people; and the inhospitable climate made life even more difficult for them.

We are indebted to Brigitte Lundblade for her account of some brief episodes concerning Hermann Grossmann's stay on the Shetlands in October 1957. She was the Knight of Bahá'u'lláh to these lonely, rugged islands:

> I felt honoured to have the Hand of the Cause visit me, but at the same time unworthy of such attention. The question of worthiness came up in our conversation; of who is worthy to serve the Cause. Dr Grossmann became very serious and with an upward movement of his arm, flicking his hand from the wrist he said in a tone of voice that startled me: 'None of us is worthy, never are we to think or say that we are.'
>
> Being in the presence of the Hand of the Cause was like bathing in the bright, warm sunshine of the love of God. The very air seemed purified and warm. One had a feeling of safety and security. At the same time one wanted to absorb every word, every gesture, every action, in order to learn more and draw closer to God.
>
> Every pioneer misses the occasional small personal attention, which only someone close to us knows how and when to give. One afternoon Dr Grossmann and I walked along North Road, close to the sea, on our way to visit Lilian [the only other Bahá'í living on the island] and her family. Without any apparent reason Dr Grossmann asked me if I liked chocolate. Oh yes, I liked chocolate very much. Then he asked what kind of chocolate I liked. My favourite was Nestle's milk chocolate. We stopped at a candy store and Dr Grossmann bought the biggest Nestle's milk chocolate bar for me. This chocolate bar meant very much to me, because it had made me feel special. It had made me happy in a very personal way by a very dear person. It was so precious that I saved it for two years, taking it out from time to time (without any desire to eat it) and recalling the moment of receiving it. Eventually I shared it at a very special occasion with some dear friends.
>
> One of the people I introduced to Dr Grossmann was the veterinary surgeon of the islands ... I had stayed several weeks with his family as a companion and housekeeper while his wife ... was expecting their third child ... The vet had to look after the entire four-legged animal population of the islands. This kept him very busy, and for long days away from

home ... At the time of Dr Grossmann's visit to the islands, his wife and the children were away on the mainland and he invited Dr Grossmann and myself to the house ... I made tea for us and we sat chatting for a while. Shortly afterwards the vet had to leave on a long drive to visit one of his four-legged patients. As there was room for only one person in his car, he invited Dr Grossmann to accompany him. This had been his way of showing hospitality to visitors to the islands, taking them on his long trips over the barren peat-covered treeless hills to some faraway crofts. When Dr Grossmann returned from this long trip he said to me: 'There are many things we have to do for the Faith. Sometimes we might even have to visit a cow.'

Dr Grossmann knew of the loneliness a pioneer has to experience, to be away from family and friends, in a new environment, among people with different customs and habits. The presence of Dr Grossmann removed all the loneliness and feelings of being among strangers. He radiated love, tranquillity, understanding and warmth. On the day of Dr Grossmann's departure I became sad and insecure again. I was afraid of being alone, feeling empty, his support and love gone. Dr Grossmann left the Lerwick harbour with the S.S. St. Claire for Aberdeen. It was a hazy morning. We said good-bye on the pier and Dr Grossmann boarded the ship. Then I saw him standing on the boat deck waving to me, looking at me. I know that he was praying for me. I felt a powerful stream flowing from Dr Grossmann to me. His strength, his faith and certitude was transferred to me, removing my fears of being alone, and all my insecurities. It all changed into happiness and joy. Later I received a letter from Dr Grossmann with a tablet translated by Zeine N. Zeine: 'Alone is he who does not know God ...'[197]

After eighteen days Hermann Grossmann left the Scottish islands. He travelled on to Belfast, where he participated in the Northern Irish summer school, and then via Dublin to London, reaching Neckargemünd in mid-August after an absence of more than four weeks.

In September he attended the French summer school in Sanary-sur-Mer and the European Conference in Bex-les-Bains. On 1 November he travelled to Luxembourg for the dedication of the Ḥaẓíratu'l-Quds. In his speech there he recalled his first visit to Luxembourg in 1952, when the Bahá'ís had been busy painting furniture and decorating their first National Centre, which had been located in a rented apartment. Now they had their own wonderful home, and he wished them every success and expressed the hope that they would always remember the words of 'Abdu'l-Bahá selected for the dedication: 'The best way to thank God is to love one another.' The Hand of the Cause of God Zikrullah Khadem also expressed joy at the dedication of the new Centre and reminded the friends of the letter from the Guardian addressed to the Persian Bahá'ís after the destruction of their Ḥaẓíratu'l-Quds by the enemies of the Faith. In place of the one in Tehran, forty-eight had sprung up all over the world.[198]

During the night of 3-4 November, Hermann Grossmann arrived back in Neckargemünd, and on 4 November the devastating news was received that the beloved Guardian had unexpectedly passed away early that morning.

CHAPTER 18

SECOND PILGRIMAGE 1957

In the spring of 1957, Anna and Hermann Grossmann had set off on their second pilgrimage. This was in response to an urgent request by the Guardian sent to the German believers via Martin and Gerda Aiff, to which he had added the words, 'You must come now, otherwise it will be too late.'[199]

On 4 May they flew from Munich to Athens, in order to spend two days visiting friends there. 'Hermann Grossmann came to coffee with a large scroll under his arm,' recalls a pioneer, much impressed. 'It contained the plans for the House of Worship in the Taunus hills, which he allowed us to see.'[200] Deeply moved by the purity of heart and courage of the friends, who were living in an environment of rejection, almost hostility, the Grossmanns then left Athens.

Whilst waiting in the transit lounge for their onward flight, they met a pioneer from Africa who, like them, intended to board the plane to go to Haifa. He later reported, 'I saw Dr Grossmann and Mrs Grossmann in the transit waiting room. He recognized me immediately after five years since we had met, and embraced me (as the Persians do). The joy of having found a friend and another pilgrim with whom I travelled to the Holy Land was immense. He asked me question after question ...'[201]

On 7 May the Grossmanns touched down in the Holy Land at Lydda (later Ben Gurion) Airport, near Tel Aviv. They travelled up the coast to Haifa by car. How the city had changed since their last pilgrimage twenty years earlier, in 1937! It had developed into a modern city, with brightly coloured blocks of flats along the streets and up the slopes of the Carmel. What had changed most, however, was the Shrine of the Báb. In a report to *Bahá'í-Nachrichten*,[202] Anna Grossmann expressed her amazement:

At last, after a final bend around a promontory, the 'Queen of Carmel' came into view, robed in white and crowned with gold. Pictures, even colour photographs, cannot reproduce anything like the beauty of this building. With its gardens, it is the perfect complement to this mountainside, to this city, to the blue sea – it is as if it could never have been otherwise. During my frequent visits there, I sometimes stopped and raised my eyes to the elegant octagon crowned by the dome, trying to take in the beauty of the structure. I had a deep sense of how needful man is of beauty as a remedy for the soul, and how this sense of beauty can be felt nowhere more deeply than when it is associated with the glorification of God.

After staying in Haifa for three days, the pilgrims were informed by the Guardian that he had prepared everything for them to be able to stay in Bahjí for two days. In the early afternoon, the five pilgrims, who had come from Britain, France and Germany, boarded the large car to make the journey around the bay.

First, we drove past 'Akká and Bahjí, travelling further north towards the Syrian border, to Mazra'ih, the place where Bahá'u'lláh had lived for a time before moving to Bahjí. It is a dreamy, romantic place with flowers and a small pond, in close proximity to a Roman aqueduct. Entering the high-ceilinged hallway is like being transported back to the time when Bahá'u'lláh lived there.

One is greeted by a picture of a Turkish officer hanging on the wall. He ... became first a friend of the prisoners and later a Bahá'í. Now he looks down upon his son, the caretaker of Mazra'ih, and upon the photos of his grandchildren, now pioneers in Tripoli.

After a visit to Bahá'u'lláh's room and a delicious snack provided by the hospitable couple, our car turned around and drove us to Bahjí. Who could describe the mood of this place – its noble and yet warm and comforting silence, its atmosphere of enchanting joy? Praying at Bahá'u'lláh's resting place cannot fail to touch one's heart. The uplifting sense of peace imparted by this room is underlined by the plants and flowers in the adjoining room. Climbing plants wend their way up to the glass ceiling and pink-flowering bougainvilleas hang down.

When one has not seen Bahjí for twenty years, one finds its essential character unchanged, but the area has been enriched by large gardens extending around part of the building complex.

The next day, the pilgrims visited the cell in the Most Great Prison in which Bahá'u'lláh had spent two years under conditions of strict confinement. In 1957 the prison was being used as an infirmary. The visitors looked through the two windows and were moved to think of the Persian pilgrims who used to stand outside the city moat gazing up at the prison in the hope of perhaps catching a glimpse of Bahá'u'lláh's hand waving to them. They had travelled thousands of miles on foot all the way from Persia.

> After that, we entered the ancient city of 'Akká, wandering through its narrow winding lanes [continues Anna Grossmann], of which M. H. Phelps in his book *The Life and Teachings of Abbas Effendi* rightly says that 'a hard-working person could clean them with a single stroke of a broom'. You expect to see, just as Phelps describes, 'Abdu'l-Bahá in spotless flowing robes and with a small white turban crowning His silver head, stepping out of one of the nearby houses to distribute gifts among the poor.

Next, the pilgrims visited the places of remembrance in 'Akká and

> then rested in a café by the ancient fishing harbour. We were conscious of the fact that this was the place where the ship carrying the prisoners had docked, and that somewhere here they had been brought ashore into the fortress city.

During those days in May 1957, Ian Semple was also on pilgrimage in the Holy Land. He describes his visit to Bahjí as follows:

> Of the visit to the Shrine I can say little, it was beautiful and so moving ... then we each read a prayer and Rúḥíyyih Khánum chanted the Tablet of Visitation. It was now quite dark. So we went and walked in the Harám-i-Aqdas, up the Guardian's hill. It was magnificent and crickets were chirping in the background.[203]

After supper, everyone was tired and went to bed. Rúḥíyyih Khánum had accompanied the group to Bahjí on account of her friendship with Anna and Hermann Grossmann. She and Anna Grossmann slept in one of the rooms in Bahá'u'lláh's Mansion. Ian Semple shared a room with Hermann Grossmann which was dominated by a portrait of the Purest Branch and which was located next to the room of Mírzá Abu'l-Faḍl, where Mason Remey slept.

After two nights in Bahjí everyone rose early in the morning, prayed in the Shrine of Bahá'u'lláh and then bade farewell to the rooms in the Mansion. They recited another prayer in Bahá'u'lláh's chamber. Then they left the Most Holy Spot of the Bahá'í Faith and paid another short visit to the Garden of Riḍván. 'Abdu'l-Bahá had acquired this small garden for His father as a place where He could rest after the conditions of His imprisonment had been somewhat relaxed.

At supper in Haifa they met Shoghi Effendi. Anna Grossmann wrote of this meeting:

> We found our Guardian fresher, more energetic and more joyful than he had been during our last pilgrimage twenty years earlier. The unexpected successes of the Ten Year Plan, especially in Africa and in the Pacific Ocean, made him happy. 'The so-called backward peoples are more receptive than the so-called civilized peoples,' he said with a gentle smile.

At the dinner table he told the story of the gardens around the Shrine of Bahá'u'lláh in Bahjí. They had formerly belonged to a Christian who, on his deathbed, had insisted that his son promise not to sell the land to the Bahá'ís under any circumstances. The son fell into financial difficulties and sold the land to a Muslim family who demanded that the grave of his father be removed. This family was friendly with the Covenant-breakers and the garden remained in their possession until they were forced to flee during the Palestine War in 1948/49. The government of Israel took possession of the estate and then sold it to the Guardian.[204]

In 1957 the duration of a pilgrimage was already limited to nine days, but the pilgrims did not all arrive on the same day. At supper in the Western Pilgrim House Shoghi Effendi sat facing the door, Mason Remey to his left, Rúḥíyyih Khánum to his right, followed by the other members of the International Bahá'í Council. The pilgrims took their seats opposite the Guardian, those arriving last always sitting closest to him.[205] Anna Grossmann recalls:

> The main theme of the evening conversations were the major phases in the development of humanity and of our Faith ... leading up to the World Order of Bahá'u'lláh, which will come to fruition in the global civilization of a spiritualized mankind. The stages in this astonishing development of the human race arose before us in the Guardian's explanations ... We wished we could preserve these explanations, record every word our Guardian uttered. Everything is so clear, so self-evident, and the distinction between what is important and what is unimportant, even in one's own life, is obvious. After these evenings with our Guardian, one knows why one is, and must be, a Bahá'í and one loves the Faith more than ever before.[206]

At the dinner table Shoghi Effendi also talked about day-to-day events, as in the moving story of an elderly Persian pilgrim told by her granddaughter Nahid Aschari:

> At Riḍván 1956 I was on pilgrimage in Haifa along with my parents and

my brother. The family wished to go pioneering for the second time. The Guardian named several countries as possible new pioneer goals, the first of which was Austria. Thereupon, the family – with their five children aged between two and twenty years – immediately set about making arrangements. They wound up their affairs in Iran and by autumn 1956 they were already in Austria. At Riḍván 1957, shortly after my twenty-first birthday, I was elected, along with my parents Naim and Sabete Reyhani, to the first and thus newly formed Local Spiritual Assembly of Graz. A few days later my mother Sabete died. Her youngest son was three years old at the time. My grandmother, Javahir Madzjoub, was in Haifa when her daughter died in Austria. Shoghi Effendi himself conveyed the sad news to her and she had the privilege of listening to his words of comfort. When she returned to her group, she told a fellow pilgrim: 'The beloved Guardian spoke about the passing of my daughter in such a way that I felt no grief. He carried me to the heavenly realm of God and showed me Sabete in the presence of Bahá'u'lláh.' Shoghi Effendi told her that he had sent a telegram to Austria, requesting that a gravestone for Sabete be erected on his behalf. In response to this great honour, however, the humble woman replied, 'that is unnecessary. Her [Sabete's] husband is not without means.' The next day, the Guardian talked about the reaction of this devoted pilgrim to a group of western pilgrims, among whom were Anna and Hermann Grossmann, who later told her family about it.

In her memoirs, Nahid Aschari continues:

> Hand of the Cause of God Hermann Grossmann had visited my mother in hospital during the few months of her life as a pioneer in Austria, and I well remember the tulips at the window of her ward, which he had brought her. His visits left a deep impression in Austria due to his manner and the spirit of faith that emanated from his dear face and which was also personified in his wife.[207]

Hermann and Anna Grossmann, acting on behalf of the National Spiritual Assembly of Germany, discussed at length with the Guardian the architectural designs for the House of Worship near Frankfurt. Shoghi Effendi preferred the design submitted by the architect Rocholl, which was later the one that was indeed used in Hofheim.[208] In his pilgrim's notes, Ian Semple describes how Shoghi Effendi asked Anna Grossmann to show him the revised designs for the Temple.

> Then Rúḥíyyih Khánum sent for some of the other drawings submitted for Germany and Persia. They were monstrosities. Shoghi Effendi said one looked like a frog, at which Anna broke into uncontrollable laughter,

tears streaming from her eyes. This set Shoghi Effendi off. He chuckled deep down and tucked his chin into his collar. I have never seen him laugh so. It was delightful.[209]

'Bidding farewell to Haifa must always be difficult,' wrote Anna Grossmann at the end of her article in *Bahá'í-Nachrichten*:

> saying goodbye to the sites of divine loftiness, goodbye to so much beauty and light, goodbye to the community of spiritual, selfless, loving people in the cosy atmosphere of the Pilgrim House, saying goodbye to the Guardian of the Faith! These farewells are difficult for many people and, for me, it was most painful twenty years ago. This time I could not grieve, for we were leaving with such bounty having been showered upon us. Looking back, our life may not be sufficient to fully appreciate all these gifts, even less to be worthy of them and to repay our debt of gratitude in service to the Faith.[210]

Shortly afterwards, on 4 November 1957, Shoghi Effendi unexpectedly passed away in England. Therefore, the only German Bahá'ís who were able to see the Guardian after the war and the long period of being unable to travel were Gerda and Martin Aiff and Anna and Hermann Grossmann. Waldtraut Weber also had the privilege of travelling from Iraklion, where she was living as a pioneer, to visit the beloved Guardian. However, Shoghi Effendi said that she was now a 'Greek Bahá'í'.[211]

CHAPTER 19

THE PASSING OF THE GUARDIAN SHOGHI EFFENDI

Since returning from pilgrimage, Hermann Grossmann had been constantly travelling, and had only just arrived home when he heard of the Guardian's sudden death. Nonetheless, the following day, Tuesday 5 November 1957, the two German Hands of the Cause of God arrived in London. Rúḥíyyih Khánum had asked the Hand of the Cause Dr Adelbert Mühlschlegel to wash the Guardian's body, anoint it with attar of roses and prepare it for the funeral, which was to take place on Saturday 9 November. In her report on the passing of Shoghi Effendi, Rúḥíyyih Khánum writes that she asked him to perform this final act of service for the beloved Guardian, however painful, not only because he was a physician, one of the Hands appointed by the Guardian, and a man who was known for his spirituality, but also because he was capable of doing it in a spirit of consecration and prayer.[212]

Numbed and broken-hearted from the loss of the dearly beloved head of the Faith, Adelbert Mühlschlegel and Hermann Grossmann met with their fellow Hands of the Cause of God Hasan Balyuzi, John Ferraby and Ugo Giachery, who were already in London. That same evening, the Hand of the Cause of God Amelia Collins arrived to provide her loving support to Rúḥíyyih Khánum. By Friday evening thirteen Hands of the Cause had come together.

On Saturday, the day of the funeral, hundreds of Bahá'ís joined the funeral procession, accompanied by an official representative of the Israeli government. Countless believers were already assembled in front of the cemetery chapel. After the funeral they filed past the coffin and all were able to pay their last respects.

After the funeral Rúḥíyyih Khánum sent a cable in which she said:

BELOVED GUARDIAN LAID REST LONDON ACCORDING LAWS AQDAS BEAUTIFUL BEFITTING SPOT AFTER IMPRESSIVE CEREMONY HELD PRESENCE MULTITUDE BELIEVERS REPRESENTING

OVER TWENTY COUNTRIES EAST WEST. DOCTORS ASSURE SUDDEN PASSING INVOLVED NO SUFFERING. BLESSED COUNTENANCE BORE EXPRESSION INFINITE BEAUTY PEACE MAJESTY. EIGHTEEN HANDS ASSEMBLED FUNERAL URGE NATIONAL BODIES REQUEST ALL BELIEVERS HOLD MEMORIAL MEETINGS EIGHTEENTH NOVEMBER COMMEMORATING DAYSPRING DIVINE GUIDANCE WHO HAS LEFT US AFTER THIRTY-SIX YEARS UTTER SELF-SACRIFICE CEASELESS LABOURS CONSTANT VIGILANCE. RÚḤÍYYIH.[213]

Shoghi Effendi had borne the burden of the Guardianship for thirty-six years. Unceasingly and without consideration for his own self, he had carried out the task entrusted to him by 'Abdu'l-Bahá – that of strengthening the Cause of Bahá'u'lláh and implementing His Divine Plan. He spread His evidences throughout the world and built up the institutions of the Faith in cooperation with the Bahá'ís of the United States and Canada. The Guardian did everything himself. He was painstakingly meticulous and extraordinarily thrifty in administering the believers' donations; he consulted with the engineers working on the building projects on Mount Carmel; he conferred with legal advisors; and he discussed with gardeners every detail of the designs for the gardens in 'Akká and Haifa. Shoghi Effendi was informed about all communications arriving by post and gave instructions on how they should be answered. He always added a few words of his own at the end of letters and signed them 'Your true brother, Shoghi'. In addition to all these tasks, he still found time to meet the pilgrims, often talking and consulting with them for long periods.[214]

At that time the German National Bahá'í Centre was located at Westendstraße 24, close to the railway station in Frankfurt am Main. Martin Aiff, who had visited the Guardian in Haifa along with his wife Gerda in late February 1957 and who loved him and honoured him 'as the greatest man on earth at that time', related these sorrowful events to Susanne Pfaff-Grossmann as follows:

> Then came the day the telegram arrived from Haifa saying that the beloved Guardian had fallen seriously ill ... We immediately typed the Long Healing Prayer onto a wax matrix, intending to send it to the friends with the Nineteen Day Feast letter, but then came the second phone call with the shattering news that Shoghi Effendi was no longer of this world. I called your father and he said, 'Martin, I'm on my way to London and will arrive in Frankfurt at about mid-day.' I said, 'Right, Hermann, I'll pick you up at the station.' And then I saw your father – not just on that day and in the months that followed – as he really was: a man I would describe as an Officer of Bahá'u'lláh, completely disciplined, manly, determined and responsible.'

THE PASSING OF THE GUARDIAN, SHOGHI EFFENDI

Martin Aiff continues:

> We linked arms and marched to the Ḥaẓíratu'l-Quds, which had meanwhile become a place of refuge for a crowd of distraught Bahá'í friends. As we approached we could hear people weeping. In the Ḥaẓíra office, Anneliese Bopp was tirelessly sending out cables and translating incoming ones. We copied them, sent them out and telephoned the friends. Your father set off for London, not as the gentle man that we knew so well but as a soldier discharging his duty.[215]

In the cable informing the Bahá'ís of the passing of the Guardian, Rúḥíyyih Khánum implored the friends 'to remain steadfast and continue to look to the institution of the Hands'. Five days after their return from London, on 16 November, the Guardian's appointed Hands of the Cause of God travelled to Haifa for their first Conclave.[216]

On 4 June 1957 Shoghi Effendi had addressed the Bahá'ís of the world in a letter in which he expanded the range of tasks entrusted to the Hands of the Cause of God. Whereas previously their task had been to protect and propagate the Cause of God, Shoghi Effendi now called upon them, first and foremost, to

> ... WATCH OVER INSURE PROTECTION BAHÁ'Í WORLD COMMUNITY, IN CLOSE COLLABORATION THESE ... NATIONAL ASSEMBLIES ...

He catalogued the latest triumphs of the Cause of God and warned that these would lead to new external hostility in the Muslim and Christian worlds and to constant internal machinations by both old and new Covenant-breakers. He called these, shadows of terrible struggles that the Hands on the five continents would have to confront in close association with the elected representatives of the national Bahá'í communities.[217] Just five months after this message was issued, the Hands of the Cause of God were indeed to become the protectors of the Faith.

The term 'Chief Stewards' used by the Guardian in this letter stimulated Hermann Grossmann to look into the history of the Scottish kings. He discovered that the task of the 'high chief stewards' was to represent the king during periods of absence.

René Steiner relates how, while he was staying with the Grossmann family in Neckargemünd shortly after this letter was published, Dr Grossmann wondered about the term, remarking: "'Is this his [the Guardian's] farewell?" Little did we know how close Dr Grossmann was to the truth,' writes René Steiner, 'and how soon the events that overshadowed that letter were to occur.'[218]

In 1960, Hermann Grossmann spoke in The Hague about the Guardian:

> It was a great bounty for me to have been privileged to meet the Guardian in 1937. He mentioned things then that were to become important after his death. I also had the privilege of being one of the last pilgrims to see the Guardian in 1957. On the second day [of our stay] the Guardian talked about matters that he had also talked about in 1937. So it seemed as if there had not been an interval of many years between the two visits. The Guardian himself said that.

Shoghi Effendi had explained that he had written to the Bahá'ís in Iran, saying that the book *The Dispensation of Bahá'u'lláh* was his spiritual testament. 'This last meeting was a final farewell,' said Hermann Grossmann. 'We didn't know why, but somehow we sensed it.'

In his lecture he spoke again of how the Guardian had described the Hands as the 'Chief Stewards of Bahá'u'lláh's embryonic World Commonwealth'. His research indicated that all power was invested in them during the absence of the 'king', practically making them into rulers. On the other hand, however, they were dependent on the king.

> At present, then, the Chief Stewards of the Faith can act only on the instructions of the Guardian. During this current period of transition, until we have a Universal House of Justice, they are the highest authority in the Bahá'í world. This message of the Guardian in which he spoke of the 'Chief Stewards' is to be regarded as his 'will and testament', that is, it is a legal document set down in the Guardian's own hand.

It was to be valid for a limited period of time. After Shoghi Effendi's death it was recognized by the Israeli government, so that the legal succession was secured against any outside claims.[219]

Hermann Grossmann later told a pioneer to South America that during the Grossmann family's pilgrimage in 1937 the Guardian was asked when the 'Lesser Peace' would be achieved (a state of political peace concluded by the nations in order to end war. Bahá'u'lláh had called upon the world's rulers to declare such a peace). 'In 1957?' suggested Hermann Grossmann. The Guardian answered: 'No, but that will also be an important year.' Had he already had a premonition concerning the year of his death?[220]

The Hand of the Cause of God 'Alí-Akbar Furútan reported on the meeting of the Hands in Haifa:

THE PASSING OF THE GUARDIAN, SHOGHI EFFENDI

I first met the Hand of the Cause of God Dr Hermann Grossmann in November 1957 after the passing of the beloved Guardian, when the Hands of the Cause arrived in the Holy Land at the invitation of Amatu'l-Bahá Rúḥíyyih Khánum. I had the pleasure of riding in the same car with him on a number of occasions as we travelled from Haifa to 'Akká in order to attend the meetings of the Hands which were held in the Mansion of Bahjí. On the way to Bahjí, Dr Grossmann spoke solely about the future of the Cause of God and the preservation of the unity of the people of Bahá throughout the world. For example, I remember that in his conversations he often exclaimed that, although the sudden passing of the beloved Guardian was a traumatic shock to the believers, and the hearts of the friends were truly wounded with the anguish of this tragedy, their unity would be safeguarded through the ceaseless confirmations of the Blessed Abhá Beauty, the infinite exhortations of 'Abdu'l-Bahá, and the splendid achievements of Shoghi Effendi. He also repeatedly expressed his confidence that the goals of the Ten Year Crusade would be successfully fulfilled through the continued guidance and encouragement of the Hands of the Cause, and that the people of Bahá would march victoriously in their arenas of service.

While I was with him I could clearly see how that radiant being endured the grief of the loss of the beloved Guardian with such unshakeable faith, and how convinced he was of the glorious future of this blessed Cause. Dr Grossmann demonstrated this same poise, dignity, and assurance during the consultations in the course of our meetings. I often sought his company during moments of leisure and benefited from his words ...[221]

After his return from this first Conclave of the Hands of the Cause of God, Hermann Grossmann summoned the members of the National Spiritual Assembly of Germany and Austria, and also those of the National Spiritual Assembly of Switzerland and Italy, to his home in Neckargemünd. He 'reported on the state of affairs in Haifa and what was going on there' recalls Martin Aiff, then a member of the National Spiritual Assembly of Germany and Austria,

> since owing to the dangerous threat posed by the Covenant-breakers nothing was sent in writing. The Hands of the Cause went out and spoke to the members of the National Spiritual Assemblies ... And here again Hermann Grossmann was the personification of valour – there was no sentimentality, he was clear and firm, simply setting out the facts, without speculation. This gave us, who were still full of hopes and ideas and thoughts, the line of approach we needed.[222]

During this period, Hermann Grossmann and Martin Aiff taught at the winter school held at the Schauinsland near Freiburg in the Black

Forest. Taking every opportunity to calm the believers, who were in a state of uncertainty, and to call upon them to recognize the Will of God and 'contemplate what Bahá'u'lláh [now] expects from every one of us', Hermann Grossmann also spoke on 12 January 1958 in Frankfurt am Main at a meeting of delegates, which had been organized by the National Spiritual Assembly.[223]

> When our beloved Guardian passed away unexpectedly, the older believers amongst us who remember hearing the equally unexpected news thirty-six years ago of the passing of 'Abdu'l-Bahá will undoubtedly have recalled the heavy burden of uncertainty that shook the Bahá'í world until the Will and Testament of the Master was made known and they began to recognize His loving and wise provisions. 'Abdu'l-Bahá had left us a Plan and a Guardian who was to provide us with unerring guidance for the prosecution of the Plan. Hence, the mists of fear for the young Faith began to lift, but it was to be a long time before we started to recognize Shoghi Effendi, the Guardian, in the position to which he had been appointed in the Will and Testament of the Master. It was not a mere continuation of the time of 'Abdu'l-Bahá, when we had been able to cling like children to the hand of the beloved father, but a time when we were to become independent and learn to stand on our own feet, feel with our own senses and think and perceive with our own minds. Only gradually did we begin to learn the lesson, it took us a long time to comprehend, or even to realize, that there was a Divine Plan from the pen of 'Abdu'l-Bahá and that we – with the exception of a few individuals – had failed to recognize this Plan as something that affected each and every one of us. It was the Guardian who, initially in close collaboration with the 'master builders of the Administrative Order of the Faith of Bahá'u'lláh', the National Spiritual Assembly of the United States and Canada, and later with the other countries in the world, laid the basis for an ever-expanding Bahá'í community throughout all five continents in a series of individual Plans, establishing an Order that in the words of Shoghi Effendi himself was to be the foundation and the model for the future World Order of Bahá'u'lláh. These thirty-six years of the Guardianship were infinitely rich and joyful. They moulded us and forged us together and taught us to recognize and carry out our real tasks. From being belittled and contemptuously referred to as a 'Muslim sect' by its enemies, our Faith has developed into an officially recognized 'independent world religion', as even its most bitter opponents have had to recognize.
>
> And yet now that our Guardian has left us, we wonder whether we learned everything we should have learned and whether we have taken it all in as was intended in 'Abdu'l-Bahá's Will and Testament and in the 'Divine Plan'. Have we not been waiting too eagerly for the green and red lights we expected to guide us? Did we not burden the Guardian too often

THE PASSING OF THE GUARDIAN, SHOGHI EFFENDI

with problems that we could, with some effort, have solved ourselves, as we did in the time of the Master, thus overwhelming him with an even greater burden of work than 'Abdu'l-Bahá's Will and Testament already placed on his shoulders? Did we consider thoroughly enough the words of that very Testament, which called upon us to 'take the greatest care of Shoghi Effendi, the twig that hath branched from and the fruit given forth by the two hallowed and Divine Lote-trees, that no dust of despondency and sorrow may stain his radiant nature, that day by day he may wax greater in happiness, in joy and spirituality, and may grow to become even as a fruitful tree'?[224]

Do we not also ask ourselves what would have happened if we had acted more swiftly in performing all the tasks entrusted to us by the Guardian, if we had understood more quickly and enabled the Cause to progress more rapidly? The Guardian did once consider establishing the Universal House of Justice, that pillar that, according to the Will and Testament of 'Abdu'l-Bahá is destined to uphold the Order of Bahá'u'lláh along with the pillar of the Guardianship, and he evidently regarded this as feasible. Events prevented this from happening at that time, but was it really only the fault of those events and not perhaps also of our failings?

Now our Guardian has unexpectedly departed from our midst, and Destiny has so provided that he did not name a successor; not because he failed to appoint one, but because there was no branch capable of living up to the Will and Testament of the Master ...

Why 'Abdu'l-Bahá made no provision in His Testament for the possibility that the Guardian might pass away without having the opportunity to appoint a successor, even though there are reports from the lifetime of the Master indicating that He spoke of this possibility, is a secret whose meaning is hidden from our eyes ...

Now that the shock of the unexpected passing of our Guardian has given way to calm reflection, we are beginning to understand that he has certainly not left us in a state of obscurity and uncertainty, but rather that every detail that we will need to consider when the time comes to establish the Universal House of Justice has been taken care of. Although Shoghi Effendi is no longer with us physically, his spirit lives on in his books and plans, which culminate in the world-wide Ten Year Plan of teaching and consolidation, the basis for the mighty Bahá'í World Crusade, the climax of which will be the great Bahá'í Congress marking the hundredth anniversary of the Declaration of Bahá'u'lláh. We must identify ourselves fully with this Crusade and make the joys and difficulties arising from it completely our own, and we must not hesitate to take action and implement it ...

An important part of the Ten Year Plan is consolidation. When we saw the Plan for the first time, many of us probably realized that this second part of the Plan, consolidation, would have to be written in bright, illuminated capital letters if the Crusade was to be fulfilled as planned. We have achieved a great deal and can say that a large proportion of the tasks set out in the Ten Year Plan have been accomplished. Consolidation, however, is in an unsatisfactory state in many places, not just in Germany. How often in the past few years, when we turned to the Guardian with our problems relating to consolidation including financial difficulties and the excessive burden of administration on some of the friends – did he reply: 'More believers, more new Bahá'ís!' Here we are: consolidation written in capital letters! If we deal with that point, then we will be in a position to fulfil the Ten Year Plan.

And another point has gained in significance since the passing of the Guardian ... the Universal House of Justice. How will we achieve a real House of Justice? The answer at first seems simple; the National Spiritual Assemblies ... in the various countries are to elect the Universal House. As a preliminary step, the Guardian himself instituted the International Council, which is to prepare the ground for establishing the Universal House of Justice ... This Universal House of Justice has an exalted character. For it is a pillar on which the future World Order of Bahá'u'lláh is to be based. We should bear in mind that this institution, which is perhaps to be established in the not-too-distant future and without the visible assistance of the beloved Guardian, has been – in the words of 'Abdu'l-Bahá – 'ordained by God as the source of all good and freed from all error'.

Dear friends, are we clear in our minds as to what this means? What we have here is infallibility, if only conferred infallibility. But for that very reason, that it is conferred and not innate infallibility as in the case of a Manifestation of God, those who partake of that gift must be worthy of infallibility ... Yet how have believers come to be members of the National Spiritual Assemblies, these subordinate Houses of Justice? Through their election by delegates. Can we then expect that the delegates will make the right choice and that the right individuals will be found who are suitable, if they themselves perhaps do not know what this quality means? And who elects the delegates? All the believers! So where do we have to begin to establish the right prerequisites for members of the Universal House of Justice? In ourselves, in each individual believer, and each believer in himself ... Let us henceforth in all our consultations, Nineteen Day Feasts and other meetings, in the committees and Spiritual Assemblies, not only try to use our rational minds, but also to understand the Will of God ... Let us be constantly aware that something has changed since the departure of our Guardian. It is high time we realized this, and perhaps it is part of a higher wisdom ... so that we might really pay greater attention than ever before to that which Bahá'u'lláh expects from every one of us.

Shoghi Effendi left us suddenly, but he did not leave anything undone or unsaid that we will need on our way to the establishment of the World

Order of Bahá'u'lláh and to the ultimate firm foundation of the Order set out in the Will and Testament of 'Abdu'l-Bahá.

At the end of February 1958 a conference took place in Bern attended by the European Hands of the Cause and the members of the Auxiliary Board to discuss the difficulties that had arisen as a result of the passing of the Guardian, Shoghi Effendi.

On 24 April Hermann Grossmann arrived in Paris in order to represent the Hands of the Cause of God at the first French National Convention. Sixty years had passed since a group of enthusiastic young people had brought the Faith to Paris. The election of the National Spiritual Assembly of France was the fulfilment of one of the Guardian's greatest wishes. It constituted the twenty-seventh pillar upon which the Universal House of Justice was to be erected. Hermann Grossmann spoke words of encouragement to the delegates and set out the position following the passing of Shoghi Effendi, urgently appealing to them to stand together, united in love.[225] Unfortunately, all such appeals fell on deaf ears. The troublemakers led by Mason Remey soon dominated the Assembly. It had to be dissolved and new elections were held.

The drama surrounding the Hand of the Cause Charles Mason Remey, who demanded that he be recognized as Shoghi Effendi's successor, caused worldwide consternation in the Bahá'í community during this period of unrest and uncertainty following the passing of the Guardian. To many people, Mason Remey had been an example of loyalty and devotion to duty. For the Hands of the Cause of God, Remey's claims were particularly bitter and tragic. They had all known and loved him, and he had been so evidently held in high esteem by the Guardian and, earlier, by 'Abdu'l-Bahá. The Hands of the Cause of God declared Mason Remey and his followers Covenant-breakers. In its first message issued on 30 April 1963 the Universal House of Justice praised the Chief Stewards of the Faith of Bahá'u'lláh for their dedication, their work and their brilliant leadership during this critical period in the history of the Faith (see below, page 223).

In the second half of May 1958 Hermann Grossmann undertook an extended travel-teaching trip to Austria, visiting the cities of Salzburg, Linz, Vienna, Graz and Innsbruck. This journey brought him great joy. He praised the good organization of the visits and the enthusiasm of the friends.

In a historical review Helga Ahmedzadeh writes that the group in

Linz at that time consisted only of Mr and Mrs Sazedj and their young son:

> A special experience and a treasured memory for Mr Sazedj was the visit by the Hand of the Cause of God Dr Grossmann. 'On 26th May [1958] Dr Grossmann came and visited the group; this' – and one senses the deep impression made at the time – 'was a great experience and the greatest possible joy. Only we three ... were present.'

Within a year, on 21 April 1959, Linz had its first Local Spiritual Assembly. Seven more friends had responded to the call for pioneers.[226]

On his return journey, Dr Grossmann took part in a regional conference in Munich.

A participant in a regional conference in Nuremberg reports that the friends consulted with Hermann Grossmann on the question of what modern man expects from religion. They answered the question by concluding that religion must be in step with scientific development. At the time of Christ, man was not capable of grasping the idea of development in religion, the principle of progressive revelation. For that reason, the believers had to believe that Christ would return in person. The concept of development is something that could only be taught through science.[227]

The 4th International Bahá'í Conference, which took place in Frankfurt am Main from 25–29 July 1958, was an outstanding event that brought together Bahá'ís from many countries and continents. The conference room in the Congress Hall at Frankfurt's trade-fair centre had been decorated by the hosts, the National Spiritual Assembly of the Bahá'ís of Germany and Austria, and was a befitting setting for the ten participating Hands of the Cause of God, the representatives of 16 National and Regional Assemblies, and 2,259 believers from 57 nations. Before his death, the Guardian had appointed the Hand of the Cause Amelia Collins as his personal representative. Accompanied by Dr Giachery and Dr Grossmann, she entered the great hall. In a moving ceremony, everyone paid their respects to the beloved Guardian. Five years had passed since the launching of the Ten Year Plan. It was time to take stock. Many successes had been achieved but there was still much to be done. The architect Teuto Rocholl showed plans and a model of the Mashriqu'l-Adhkár that was to be built at Langenhain in the Taunus hills. A total of 133 friends registered their willingness to move in order to fulfil the goals. However, the climax of the conference was the unveiling of a portrait of Bahá'u'lláh which the friends then filed past in a procession lasting four hours. Towards the end of the conference, Hermann Grossmann showed the many gifts that had been donated for the planned Mother Temple of Europe. Afterwards, the European Hands assembled in the National Centre in Frankfurt for their third conference.[228]

The fifth Italo-Swiss summer school in Bex-les-Bains was blessed with the presence of the Hands of the Cause Dr Giachery and Dr Grossmann. They held seminars in Italian and German. The Italo-Swiss community had a language problem and its summer schools had to be divided into separate German, French and Italian sections. Dr Giachery gave the Italian courses and Dr Grossmann the German ones. The school was a success and the friends came to know one another better. 'This year we had the best summer school ever,' one report states. 'We all sensed a profound spirit of love and unity and were very sad to have to part.'[229]

Hermann Grossmann travelled back via Munich and visited the friends there before meeting several groups in Austria. In early November he attended a teaching conference in Lyon as a representative of the Hands of the Cause of God, infusing the friends there with renewed vigour and enthusiasm.

From 9 November until 3 December 1958, the second historic Conclave of the Hands of the Cause of God took place in the Mansion at Bahjí near 'Akká. Twenty-five of the twenty-seven Hands appointed by the Guardian were assembled for consultations. In their message of 30 November 1958 they reported on the progress of the Faith since the passing of Shoghi Effendi – the successes achieved in Africa and the Pacific region, the arrival of a pioneer on Spitzbergen, the last of the unopened islands, and the imminent completion of two of the three planned Mother Temples. But in this message to the Bahá'ís in the East and West they also spoke of the difficult years that lay ahead. Work on the Mother Temple for Europe near Frankfurt am Main had not yet commenced, and a large number of local and national Assemblies had not yet been formed. They quoted the words of the Guardian who had said at the start of the Ten Year Crusade: 'How staggering the responsibility that must weigh upon the present generation.' He had appealed to every believer on the planet and, in particular, the elected representatives at local, regional or national levels, for '... an upsurge of enthusiasm and consecration ...' and for them to shoulder the chief responsibility in laying an unassailable foundation for that Universal House of Justice, which, as its title implies, is to be the exponent and guardian of that Divine Justice which can alone ensure the security of, and establish the reign of law and order in, a strangely disordered world. Posterity will regard [the Universal House of Justice] as the last refuge of a tottering civilization.

The Hands of the Cause reminded the believers that the National and Regional Spiritual Assemblies were to elect the Universal House of Justice in 1963. Mindful of their primary function to protect the Faith and promulgate its teachings, they arranged for a number of the Hands to travel extensively during the following year, in particular to areas where a large number of National Spiritual Assemblies were to be erected as pillars for the future House of Justice, especially in South America and in the goal countries of Europe. They offered all possible assistance to long-standing communities such as those of Persia, the United States of America, Canada, India, Australia, Britain and Germany, so that they would be able to fulfil all the tasks facing the Bahá'ís.

'Bahá'u'lláh, 'Abdu'l-Bahá, and the beloved Guardian have repeatedly warned us', the Hands stated in their message, 'that the time is short, that these fast-fleeting hours in which we live will come to us no more, and we shall never again have a similar opportunity.'[230]

In a letter dated 26 December 1958, the Hands of the Cause in the Holy Land announced that after the conference in Frankfurt at the end of December, the European Hands would set out on their important journeys: Ugo Giachery to Central America, Hermann Grossmann to South America and Adelbert Mühlschlegel to Scandinavia.[231]

CHAPTER 20

RETURN TO SOUTH AMERICA 1959[232]

During the Grossmann family's pilgrimage in 1937, the Guardian once unexpectedly turned to Hermann Grossmann and asked if he would like to go back to South America. 'Shoghi Effendi,' Hermann Grossmann replied then, 'it was hard for me to adapt to life in Germany, but now I like being there.' With a strange smile, the Guardian answered, 'Perhaps one day you will gladly go back to South America.'[233]

Twenty-one years had passed since this conversation when, in 1958, the Hands of the Cause of God asked Hermann Grossmann the same question and requested that he visit South America.

In November 1958, the Institution of the Hands of the Cause of God decided to send representatives from amongst their number to every continent. They were to assure the Bahá'ís that the Cause of Bahá'u'lláh was safeguarded and that the nine Hands of the Cause of God designated to serve as Custodians in the Holy Land, together with the other Hands of the Cause of God throughout the world, had taken over the role of guiding and protecting the affairs of the Faith until the election of the first Universal House of Justice. The Ten Year Plan initiated by Shoghi Effendi had already reached its halfway point and it was necessary to explain to the believers that this Plan must be fulfilled as a prerequisite for an election of the Universal House of Justice, which should then take over the leadership.

Hermann (Germán) Grossmann was still fluent, indeed highly proficient, in the language of his childhood, despite having lived in Germany for so long. He also felt at home with the mentality of the people of South America. He remembered the Guardian's words and agreed to the Custodians' request in spite of his poor state of health.

The journey required meticulous planning. The Bahá'ís living in Latin America, many of them pioneers from North America and Iran, supplied the necessary information. On his departure, Hermann

Barranquilla
Cartagena
Maracaibo
Caracas
Valencia
Barquisimeto
Panama
PANAMA
Cúcuta
San Cristóbal
Ciudad Guayana
VENEZUELA
Medellín
GUYANA
GUIANA HIGHLANDS
SURINAME
French Guiana (FRANCE)
Bogotá
ANDES
COLOMBIA
Boa Vista
Cali
Macapá
Quito
ECUADOR
Guayaquil
AMAZON
Manaus
Santarém
Belém
Iquitos
Teresina
Piura
BASIN
Rio Branco
Pôrto Velho
Huánuco
PERU
BRAZIL
Lima
MATO GROSSO PLATEAU
BRAZILIAN
Cusco
ANDES
Trinidad
Cuiabá
Brasília
La Paz
Arequipa
BOLIVIA
Goiânia
Cochabamba
Santa Cruz
HIGHLANDS
Sucre
Potosí
ALTIPLANO
Uberlândia
Belo Horizonte
Campo Grande
Vitória
ATACAMA DESERT
PARAGUAY
Rio de Janeiro
São Paulo
Asunción
Salta
Curitiba
San Miguel de Tucumán
Resistencia
CHILE
Pôrto Alegre
Córdoba
Santa Fe
Salto
PAMPAS
Valparaíso
Mendoza
Rosario
URUGUAY
Santiago
Buenos Aires
La Plata
ANDES
ARGENTINA
Bahía Blanca
San Carlos de Bariloche
Puerto Montt
PATAGONIA
Río Gallegos
Arenas
Ushuaia

RETURN TO SOUTH AMERICA, 1959

Grossmann knew not only his itinerary and the names of his contacts but also the location, population and climate of the places he was to visit, as well as the number of believers there and the approximate potential for growth in each place. He had prepared himself carefully and methodically using every available source of information. His notes, which are still stored in his archives, provide an almost complete overview of the state of the Bahá'í community in South America in 1958/59.

Prior to the journey, a number of vaccinations and medical examinations were required, which Hermann Grossmann duly underwent. A yellow-fever vaccination caused him to develop severe hiccups (singultus), which perplexed his doctors and resulted in his admission to the University Clinic in Heidelberg. It is characteristic of his interest in science and in humanity that he permitted the professor who was treating him to present him to students in a lecture, since his was a rare disorder.

On 19 February 1959 the preparations were at last complete and he was able to commence his journey. After a long flight he landed the next day in Recife, on the eastern coast of Brazil. Since one official form appeared to be missing from his documents, he had to stay there for a day, but was able to spend the day with the only believer in Recife and to be of service to the Cause.

In a letter to his wife he describes a brief episode:

> Here in the hotel a little kindness on my part towards a black member of staff caused him to tell me that he had recently become a Christian. He then listened with a radiant smile when I told him that Christ had returned, but with a different name. He gave me his address and I gave him that of our Persian friend. He is happy that Christ has again come into the world with a new name that he can already pronounce.[234]

Hermann Grossmann taught, as was his wont, both in small groups and in intensive conversations with individual Bahá'ís. Travelling along the Atlantic coast, he went on to visit Salvador, Rio de Janeiro and São Paulo. From São Paulo he made short trips to see the friends and pioneers in nearby towns, such as São Vicente, Santos, Santo André, São Caetano and Santa Clara. After stays in Curitiba and Porto Alegre he then left Brazil. In a letter home he reported that it had been never-ending joy to meet the friends in the Brazilian towns along the Atlantic coast:

> Where shall I start? By telling you that in their enthusiasm and their love,

the friends everywhere have exceeded by far my expectations, that in all the Brazilian cities and their environs that I have seen so far they have to find out before the events, which take place three or four every day, which language will be understood by the majority of participants – Spanish and German ranking ahead of English. Or that from Recife to São Paulo, in all the towns I have visited so far around 30% of the believers and enquirers are of German descent, and that of the most attentive contacts many are Jewish. Or that all three of the leading newspapers have published detailed interviews, or that when I visited a simple elderly Bahá'í in hospital in Bahia, his first question – even before we had greeted each other – was whether there was a new Guardian, and a heart-rending sob followed when we had to reply 'not yet'. All this might serve to illustrate the nature of this reserve of energy. Tomorrow morning new pioneers are moving to the weaker states in the North in order, like others, to take up a factory job or other modest occupation so as to gain a financial foothold and then be able to support the Bahá'í work there. Almost all the pioneers here have had to step forward into an uncertain future and lay a new foundation, often using up all their savings, and – now and again on the verge of despair but ultimately with unwavering trust in Bahá'u'lláh, whose power is stronger than that of fate – have finally triumphed over fate. It makes me think of the large communities in Europe ...[235]

On 8 March 1959 he arrived in Montevideo, Uruguay for a brief visit before travelling on to Buenos Aires, Argentina where he arrived on the 12 March.

In South America there were two Regional National Spiritual Assemblies, one for the northern and the other for the southern part. Each represented five countries, and it was the goal of the Ten Year Plan that by Riḍván 1963 ten independent National Spiritual Assemblies should be established, supported by as many Local Spiritual Assemblies as possible. At a meeting of the Regional Spiritual Assembly shortly after Dr Grossmann's arrival, he became acquainted with the most important representatives of the southern part of South America and with the problems facing the Bahá'ís.

The great majority of the Bahá'ís in South America had never seen a Hand of the Cause of God before and knew little about their important rank and their role in the Bahá'í Faith, as Mas'ud Khamsí, one of the Persian pioneers, reported.

> ... this is why the Secretary of the Regional Assembly of the 5 countries of the south sent a circular letter to the Bahá'ís of these 5 countries

informing about the arrival of Dr Grossmann. In the circular he gave an explanation in his own way that the Hands of the Cause were not different from common Bahá'ís and that in any way we could consult with them administrative issues or issues related with these countries. This lack of knowledge was a great surprise to me. I personally asked Dr Grossmann to talk and explain the rank and functions of the Hands. It arrived the right moment and he stood up and instead of starting to talk he said that Mr Mas'ud Khamsí was going to talk about this theme. This was a great mistake I made, to ask to such a humble person to talk about his important rank and functions.[236]

Next, Hermann Grossmann followed the River Paraná northwards, spending five days in the town of his birth, Rosario, which had now grown into a large city. At the cemetery there he found the graves of members of his family and recalled fond memories of his childhood and of his beloved grandmother. With the help of a friend he even managed to find the house in which he had spent the early years of his life. On 23 March he commemorated the 50th anniversary of his departure from Argentina, being back in his old homeland for the first time. He then flew further inland to Córdoba and then on to Asunción in Paraguay, where he experienced such a terrible plague of mosquitoes that he noted it in his reports.

From Asunción he returned for several days to Buenos Aires, which was repeatedly to be the base from which he undertook further trips. During this stay he found time to visit the grave of May Maxwell.

May Bolles Maxwell, the mother of Rúhíyyih Khánum and the spiritual mother of many outstanding Bahá'ís, whom Shoghi Effendi designated ' 'Abdu'l-Bahá's beloved handmaid, distinguished disciple', had died in Buenos Aires in March 1940 immediately after her arrival in South America, where she had gone at the request of the Guardian in order to teach the Faith. She was laid to rest in the Quilmes cemetery near Buenos Aires.[237]

On 11 April Hermann Grossmann flew to the Chilean city of Punta Arenas on the Straits of Magellan, the most southerly city on the American continent. Severe storms kept him in Rio Gallegos, and after a delay of 72 hours he finally arrived back in Buenos Aires. This delay upset his travel plans and he was not able to fly on to Santiago de Chile on the west coast until several days later than he had intended. In Viña del Mar, north of Santiago, a two-day teaching conference and meetings involving believers from the five southern nations was taking place – an opportunity for the Hand of the Cause to teach the Bahá'ís and exhort them to fulfil their goals in the Plan: to double the number of communities by Riḍván 1960 in order to lay the foundation for the election of the National Spiritual Assemblies.

The Teaching Conference was followed by the National Convention, the third of its kind for the Bahá'ís of Argentina, Bolivia, Chile, Paraguay and Uruguay. 'To the visiting friends the region around Viña elevated the spirits with the Chilean panorama of mountain and ocean, vineyards and flowers everywhere,' wrote one of the friends. 'The presence of the revered Hand of the Cause of God Dr Hermann Grossmann during this period widened our vision of the future of the Cause in this area ... As a result, the Convention was characterized by high resolve and serene faith.' The Hand of the Cause also noted how urgently German-speaking teachers were needed in the region.[238]

'The friends present at the third Annual Convention of the Regional Spiritual Assembly ... enjoyed the presence of Dr Grossmann. During the Convention the Hand presented the gathering with an exciting and broad view of the future of the beloved Cause of God and stirred in the minds of those present a deep appreciation of the great spirit emanating toward all from the Bahá'í World Centre,' recalls Katharine Meyer, Knight of Bahá'u'lláh for the island of Margarita in the Caribbean and long-term pioneer to South America.[239]

The *Noticias Bahá'ís* carried a report about this conference, emphasizing the significance of the decisions made and the spirit of deep faith that characterized it:

> Dr Grossmann greatly encouraged the friends and all felt happy knowing that he is an Argentinian by birth and resonates with the Latin American friends, speaking directly to their hearts – in their own language – while identifying with their longings and their high hopes.
>
> The progress of the Faith in the region was demonstrated during the Convention through the formation of three new Local Assemblies: Rosario in Argentina, Viña del Mar in Chile and Jankullo in Bolivia, which is the second assembly in which all the members are all from among the indigenous population. This progress was also seen through the acquisition of the Temple site in Paraguay and the development and expansion of the Bahá'í Publishing Trust in Buenos Aires. It was likewise very encouraging to know that the number of indigenous believers in Bolivia is constantly growing through the formation of new groups, and that the majority of the population of Juan Fernandez Island, a virgin goal of the area, is now very receptive to the Faith.[240]

RETURN TO SOUTH AMERICA, 1959

Still stirred by the exciting atmosphere of that remarkable conference, one of the participants later recalled in old age: 'I cannot remember what he [Dr Grossmann] said, but I can assure you he was an apostle.'[241]

Another Bahá'í writes that Hermann Grossmann was an entertaining conversationalist '... but at the same time he transmitted his love and wisdom in a simple manner that created an atmosphere of spirituality.'[242]

Travelling northward along the Pacific coast, he reached the cities of Callao, Lima and Chiclayo in Peru. From there, he set out to visit the friends in Bolivia, heading for La Paz, Cochabamba and Oruro. From Oruro he made his way to Villakollo, an indigenous village at an altitude of approximately 4,000 metres, accessible only on foot.

Athos Costas, a member of the five-country Regional Spiritual Assembly of the Bahá'ís of Argentina, Bolivia, Chile, Paraguay and Uruguay, recalls the background to this visit in the following paragraphs:

> Andrés Jachakollo was one of the first indigenous Bahá'ís in Bolivia. During a visit to La Paz he had seen a sign on a building which read 'Fe Bahá'í Mundial' and was reminded of the words of Toribio Mirandas, one of the great prophetic leaders whose spirit was still alive among the indigenous peoples of the mountains. He had prophesied that people would come from other countries to help the campesinos. When he knocked at the door of the Bahá'í Centre, he was greeted by an American pioneer and a Bahá'í from Chile. They outlined the Faith to him and then Andrés Jachakollo asked, 'Do you believe that our ancestors had a religion? Was it a true religion or a false religion?' 'It was a true religion,' was the reply. Now Andrés Jachakollo was eager to know more. For three days he kept coming and going, and on the second day he brought his cousin Carmelo Jachakollo along. What they heard there was very different from what they had been told by Christian missionaries: 'Yes, your ancestors had a nice culture, but they had a false religion. Now, to be saved, you have to convert to the one true religion, Christianity.' They were happy when they heard the Bahá'í teachings. In particular, Andrés and Carmelo explained, the teaching about the oneness of humanity had been foreseen in the prophecies of Toribio Mirandas.
>
> They returned to their village, Villakollo, and talked to friends and relatives. Carmelo Jachakollo then went back to La Paz and the friend from Chile, who had a taxi, set out with him to Villakollo, in order to help him teach the Faith. Most of the village's inhabitants became Bahá'ís and Villakollo became the first Bahá'í village.

Athos Costas continues his account:

> When the teaching work in Bolivia began, that [Regional] National Assembly received a list of 40 new believers, all of them enrolled by the first indigenous believers from Villakollo. This was very surprising since nothing like that had ever happened before. Andrés, Isidro, and Carmelo [Jachakollo] had arisen to travel and teach the Faith without anyone asking them to do so and without any preparation in a course or conference. Then Dr Grossmann traveled to Bolivia and visited Villakollo, with all the difficulties that involved, because of its altitude at 5,000 metres above sea level and because the only way to reach there was on foot. This was an inspiration for me, and shortly afterwards I also travelled from Buenos Aires and visit Villakollo. Dr Grossmann then wrote to the World Centre and to our National Assembly, putting our minds at ease regarding the fact that these first indigenous believers were good Bahá'ís. After that we started to work together. We had three teachers, three travelling teachers. They were natural teachers who hadn't had any instruction from us. They were already prepared. So we started to work together and the people startet to come to the Faith from all around.[243]

Villakollo was the first Spiritual Assembly made up entirely of indigenous Bahá'ís and, as the *Noticias Bahá'ís* noted, Hermann Grossmann was 'the first Hand of the Cause of God to visit an indigenous community in Latin America'.

Sabino Ortega, of Cochabamba, who was one of the first indigenous people to have become a Bahá'í and who accompanied Hermann Grossmann to Villakollo, recalled these events in his memoirs, which he dictated to a friend:

> I made his acquaintance ... when he visited Bolivia and invited me to go into the countryside to help him by working as an interpreter for Quechua [an indigenous language]. We travelled in a hired car that broke down half way to our destination. Despite his age and the fact that he was undoubtedly used to a greater degree of comfort, he showed no worry about the situation in which we found ourselves – in a very cold place at [over] 4,000 metres of altitude. He demonstrated great love for the *campesinos* [rural people] and great patience in difficult situations. His attitude caused me to feel trust, respect and love for white people, even though I had previously been resentful towards them, because I had been a slave and had suffered for a long time at the hands of the whites. Dr Grossmann's attitude gave me back my trust, respect and love for white people. I started to distinguish between good and bad. Perhaps this was the seed that he planted in my

heart as to what kind of person a Bahá'í is and how the divine words turn darkness into light. I therefore feel that he was very important at the start of my Bahá'í life, and I remember him with great admiration ...

Concerning Sabino Ortega, the Bahá'í friend notes that for many years he was an Auxiliary Board member in the Department of Chuquisaca and worked on literacy projects. He was the 'fire extinguisher' with the ability to deal with all sorts of communication difficulties and misunderstandings in the rural areas.[244]

The Bolivian Bahá'ís wrote in a report about Hermann Grossmann's first visit to their country that 'Abdu'l-Bahá had once said the love of the friends had drawn him to America.

> It might well be said that the loving desire of the Indian believers in Bolivia brought to them a visit from a Hand of the Cause ... On 10 May 1959 the revered Hand of the Cause Dr Hermann Grossmann, made the historic visit to the Indian village of Villakollo ... The friends ... offered immediate prayers in Spanish, Aymara and Quechua. The believers were profoundly impressed to have their wish for a visit from a Hand of the Cause granted and his loving and encouraging words made them extremely happy.[245]

Love for the indigenous people caused Dr Grossmann to emphasize again and again to the friends that they should pay more attention to work among the poor and deprived. That the native people sensed his sincere love and even saw him as one of their own is demonstrated by the following little incident. Years later, two indigenous Bahá'ís were paying a brief visit to the Mother Temple of Europe in Langenhain when they suddenly saw a portrait of Dr Grossmann in the Rittersaal (Hall of Knights). Filled with joy and surprise, they called out 'That is *our* Hand of the Cause!'[246]

'I remember', writes Yolanda Claros R. who, along with her two sisters was one of the first Bahá'ís in Cochabamba and was later a member of the National Spiritual Assembly, 'how I was introduced to him.'

> It was at a meeting in Cochabamba. I do not remember the subjects about which he spoke to us on that occasion. It is more than 35 years ago. But I have not forgotten the aura of holiness that emanated from his wonderful personality and the love that came directly from his pure heart to those of us who were present, having gathered to listen to him and get to know him. I saw Dr Grossmann a second and perhaps even a third time, once maybe in Bolivia and the other time in a different country. He was some

distance away and I could only see his sweet smile, but even from afar could sense his enveloping love.[247]

These memories of the Hand of the Cause of God were collected by the German pioneer in Bolivia, Ursula von Brunn, and sent to the Grossmann family in 1995. They are a valuable testimony to Hermann Grossmann's work in South America and to the prevailing conditions at that time.

He stayed in Bolivia for three weeks, and since Mas'ud Khamsí was able to drive him around in his car he was able to visit many indigenous villages where Bahá'ís lived, as well as the cities of La Paz, Cochabamba and Oruro. At the meeting in Cochabamba there was such a wonderful spirit that he remarked that he could not distinguish between the Bahá'ís and non-Bahá'ís present.

The Hands of the Cause later asked Mr Khamsí to move to Bolivia in order to devote himself to working with the indigenous people.

Hermann Grossmann's stay in Bolivia was an outstanding success. It was reported in the *Noticias Bahá'ís* that everyone who had had the honour and privilege of meeting and listening to Dr Grossmann would look back upon this first visit by a Hand of the Cause of God with a feeling of love and respect. The report concludes with the words, 'The Bahá'ís of Bolivia will never forget him!'[248] On 16 May 1959 the Bolivian friends said goodbye to Hermann Grossmann at La Paz airport, the highest airport in the world.

After his visit to Bolivia, Hermann Grossmann returned to Peru and travelled to Arequipa, located in the south of the country, in the Andes, at an altitude of 2,300 metres. On 23 May, after a flight lasting several hours, he landed in the northern extreme of South America, in Caracas, which at that time had the only Local Spiritual Assembly in Venezuela. At a meeting of the Regional Spiritual Assembly of the northern countries of South America – Brazil, Peru, Colombia, Ecuador and Venezuela – the members of the Assembly explained to him the matters that they were concerned about. They thought that Venezuela was urgently in need of pioneers. However, since that country was closed hermetically to further immigration, he advised the friends that this was unrealistic and that they themselves should proceed with enthusiasm and take a positive approach to the task in hand. And this they did with admirable success: by Riḍván 1960, communities had been formed in the Venezuelan localities of Maracay, Valencia, Barquisimeto and Sucre.[249]

RETURN TO SOUTH AMERICA, 1959

Four days later he flew to Barranquilla on the Caribbean coast in Colombia. The following two weeks in Medellín and Cali on the high Andean plain at an altitude of over 1,000 metres were again difficult for him. His health, which had not been good at the start of his journey to South America, was now seriously affected by the thin air that prevails at this altitude. He had to cancel plans to visit Bogotá because of its altitude of over 2,600 metres and so left the Andes, flying instead to Guayaquil in Ecuador, which is at sea level. The city was in a state of siege. Many people died of gunshot wounds as government forces tried to put a stop to the turmoil and looting in the streets. In Ecuador it was not possible for Hermann Grossmann to visit Quito because of its high altitude, and after another stay in Lima he travelled on to Buenos Aires once more. After four months of travelling, a bout of typhus fever forced him to break off his journey, and on 11 June 1959 he returned to Neckargemünd to recover his now seriously undermined health.

During those four months, the Hand of the Cause of God had visited all ten countries of South America which were to establish their own Bahá'í administration by the end of the Ten Year Plan. He visited thirty-four places and spoke to people from a further forty-two places, thus making an important contribution to the fulfilment of the Plan. The media resonance was very broad and free of prejudice throughout this visit and all later visits – something that was unthinkable in old Europe. This openness was undoubtedly a preparation for the successes that were soon to be achieved in this region.

From 19 to 23 June a working conference of the Hands of the Cause and their Auxiliary Board members took place in Copenhagen. To the joy and surprise of all the participants, Rúhíyyih Khánum also took part in this event. In the evening hours the Hands of the Cause Ugo Giachery and Hermann Grossmann, who had recently returned from their visits to Central and South America respectively, talked about their impressions and experiences. It is said that their reports were remarkably similar. They each spoke to the other in their native language – Dr Giachery in Italian and Dr Grossmann in Spanish – and found they were mutually comprehensible. During an unofficial part of the conference, the participants had the special joy of greeting 'the brave Knight of Bahá'u'lláh, Paul Adams, who had been the only person – after numerous failed attempts – to succeed in filling an important goal of the Ten Year Plan (Spitzbergen)'.[250] After that, Hermann Grossmann permitted himself a period of rest before a meeting of the German

National Spiritual Assembly in July, at which Amatu'l-Bahá Rúḥíyyih Khánum was also present. August and September 1959 were taken up with summer schools. At the International Youth Summer School in Echternach in Luxembourg, he led the discussions and 'although still strained from his journey to South America, he truly exerted himself to his limits and was the focus throughout the entire event,' reads a report in the *Bahá'í-Nachrichten*.

Ian Semple told Anke Grossmann:

> I remember that once when we were in Echternach, one of the monks – the priests who were in the seminary – wanted to discuss the Faith and invited your grandfather [Hermann Grossmann] to talk with him and he took a couple of us with him to their talk. I was absolutely fascinated, because so often when you discuss the Faith people ask silly questions and raise silly objections – but here it was quite clear that this priest and your grandfather understood spiritual reality, and they knew the nature of human beings. They went straight from all superficiality into the profound relationship between man and God and the nature of human beings, the function of the soul and so on ...[251]

The summer school made it evident, however, just how important it was for a universal auxiliary language to be introduced, remarked the author of one report: 'A lot of time was wasted because everything had to be translated between German, English and French.'

This event was followed by the first summer school organized by the National Spiritual Assembly of Austria in Srjach. At the subsequent summer school in Beaulieu-sur-Mer in France, the evenings were filled with slide shows and entertainment. One evening François Petit sang *chansons* he had composed himself, and on another occasion Dr Grossmann took his audience on a swift tour of the diverse and beautiful continent of South America in the form of a slide show. Next came the summer schools in Bex-les-Bains in Switzerland and Arolsen in the Waldeck region in Germany. In Bex, the Hand of the Cause Dr Giachery conducted a course in Italian, Dr Grossmann one in German and a Belgian Bahá'í one in French. Being with the friends gave Hermann Grossmann the chance to talk to them about the progress of the Cause in South America. These reports were interspersed with many stories and anecdotes about his own experiences, so as to make them entertaining for the listeners as well as giving them a vivid impression of the activities of the friends in Latin America.[252]

RETURN TO SOUTH AMERICA, 1959

At the end of October 1959 he travelled to Bahjí to participate in a fifteen-day Conclave of all the Hands of the Cause of God. There, the Hands of the Cause who had been working in Latin America – Dr Giachery in Central and Dr Grossmann in South America – gave such encouraging reports that a resolution was passed bringing forward the election of the National Spiritual Assemblies in Latin America by two years, to Riḍván 1961. The two Regional Spiritual Assemblies in South America, as well as the Regional Spiritual Assembly in Central America and that of the Greater Antilles were to undertake every effort to make possible the election at that time of twenty-one new National Spiritual Assemblies.

The message issued on 4 November 1959 reads:

> We have therefore formulated the following plan of action which will enable the Bahá'í world to establish the Universal House of Justice in 1963, and which we now share with our fellow-believers.
>
> We call for the election in Riḍván 1961 of the twenty-one National Spiritual Assemblies of Latin America which will constitute some of the pillars of the Universal House of Justice in that region. This historic decision is based on the fact that we have every reason to hope and believe that the devoted band of the followers of Bahá'u'lláh in those countries will succeed during the Riḍván period of 1960 in forming those Spiritual Assemblies required of them by our beloved Guardian in the specific provisions he laid down for them in the World Crusade. Reports we have received from the Hands of the Cause who have visited those countries during the past year, as well as from the four Regional Assemblies responsible for the work in that area, have convinced us the time is ripe to make this joyous announcement to the Bahá'í world. We therefore urge the two Regional Assemblies of South America and the Regional Assembly of Central America as well as that of the Greater Antilles, in collaboration with the Hands of the Cause in the Western Hemisphere and the National Assembly of the Bahá'ís of the United States, to concentrate their attention, during the remaining months of this Bahá'í year, on ensuring that those Local Assemblies which form the bedrock of these future national bodies may be formed next April.[253]

CHAPTER 21

SOUTH-AMERICAN PILLARS OF THE UNIVERSAL HOUSE OF JUSTICE[254]

The early fulfilment of the Ten Year Plan for Latin America would demand great effort on the part of the friends. The Hands of the Cause therefore asked Hermann Grossmann to return to South America to support them. His wife, Anna, was to accompany him on account of his poor state of health. The Hand of the Cause William Sears also travelled to South America, and Dr Giachery paid a second visit to Central America. Anna Grossmann used the time leading up to their departure to learn Spanish.

Anna and Hermann Grossmann left home on 11 January 1960. Two days later they sailed from Genoa on the MS *Conte Grande*. Anna Grossmann described the voyage in a letter to the friends in Germany as follows:

> The surprises began even on the ship. After we had somewhat recovered from the rather rough voyage through the Mediterranean and had passed through the Straits of Gibraltar, our attention was attracted by a charming young couple in the dining room. We wondered whether they were Spanish or Persian, since those two nationalities are very similar in appearance. Something else stood out, too; they were the only people in the dining room apart from us who did not drink alcohol, even when the shipping company provided free champagne. Might they be Bahá'ís? After a day or two of guessing, we went up to them and asked – of course, they were Bahá'ís, Persian pioneers on the way to Brazil. They told us that a few hours before they had met some other friends, also Persian pioneers. That same afternoon, and daily after that, we held meetings. It was rather cramped and hot, even though we used the biggest cabin available to us, but it was enjoyable and refreshing for all. We heard the story of how the Persian friends were leaving home to pioneer, and the story of a young captain

in the Persian army seems particularly worth relating. It was his heart's desire to go pioneering with his old parents-in-law, his wife and daughters, sister-in-law and brother, but he faced the major problem that the army was hardly likely to grant its approval, that is to release him from service, all the less so because he was a well-known skier and climber who had won many prizes and had even represented his country in sports competitions in Europe. Nevertheless, he handed in his application and his General, busy doing routine work, signed it without any ado and passed it on to the Shah, who also signed it. When the day of his departure arrived, our friend went to his General to say goodbye. The General could not believe that he had signed the application and that the Shah had then granted his release. However, he then warmly bade him farewell. So that is the story of a distinguished captain who is now working hard to learn Spanish in order to pioneer to Paraguay and teach the Faith there. What kind of work will he do there in order to support his family? Well, he doesn't know yet, but he'll find something. One could tell many stories of courage, for the world is full of such heroes.

There were twelve Bahá'ís, including children, on the ship and, when two friends left in Santos, another Bahá'í woman with two children boarded. They were heading for Montevideo. Everywhere the ship docked in South American ports, we kept a look-out for Bahá'ís and everywhere we were met by waving and by smiling faces.[255]

On 26 January 1960 the *Conte Grande* docked in Rio de Janeiro, where the Grossmanns met the friends in the Ḥaẓíratu'l-Quds. They stayed overnight in the home of American pioneers who lived at the highest point of that beautiful city. There was a wonderful view from the garden on the roof of the apartment block and it is reported that Dr Grossmann enjoyed going into this garden, visiting it many times. He also produced a lovely little oil painting there, which he presented as a gift to the hostess, at which she was indescribably overjoyed.[256]

Continuing their voyage, they dropped anchor in Santos and Montevideo and had meetings with small groups of those friends who were able to take some time off work. In Montevideo they were greeted by the Hand of the Cause of God William Sears and were able to spend some time consulting with him on board. On 30 January they reached Buenos Aires, where the friends were awaiting them.

Anna Grossmann recounts what happened:

When we arrived in the harbour at Buenos Aires, our little company of travellers was somewhat concerned because, when examining the oldest member of the group, the immigration doctor thought he found traces of an illness from which our friend had long since recovered. According to an old – but still valid – law, persons suffering from this illness were prohibited from entering Argentina. The friends who were waiting for us thought it would be impossible for him to disembark. For three days, he stayed with some members of his family on the empty ship, while one of the friends, on behalf of the National Spiritual Assembly, tirelessly went from one authority to the next and eventually succeeded in securing a special agreement, so that he did not have to leave and try his luck in another South American country, as he had already decided to do.[257]

They spent twelve days in Buenos Aires. Gilbert Grasselly, at that time a student in Buenos Aires and later a pioneer in Paraguay and Uruguay for many years, recalls that there were regular meetings with the friends of that city: 'It is my understanding that he was sent to Argentina by the body of the Hands to protect, nurture and deepen the Argentine Bahá'ís.' The country was shortly due to elect its own National Spiritual Assembly and at this time, in particular, the enemies of the Faith were very active in Buenos Aires. They were led by a long-term pioneer from the United States who had been influenced by the usurpatory claims of Mason Remey and his supporters.

'Her activity', continues Gilbert Grasselly, 'was a serious threat to the survival of the Faith [in that area] ... she had convinced one or two local families and a few isolated individuals of the "authenticity" of Mr Remey's claim.' Once Mr Grasselly had established that the lady in question was indeed an active Covenant-breaker, he informed Hermann Grossmann and, in agreement with the Hands, all contact with her group was broken off:

> I am unaware of whatever happened to her, but by now she is surely long gone, whereas the Argentine Bahá'í community is strong in spite of her early efforts to dismantle it ... It was clear that the Cause had been well protected as a result of Dr Grossmann's dedicated service to the Faith in that country and the response of the faithful friends there. He was a loving and caring individual who touched the hearts and minds of everyone who came into contact with him. His wife, Anna, was also a loving and cordial person, and she was his irreplaceable companion and friend, looking after his every need ... After the meetings on Peru Street were over, the friends would all walk together down Florida Street with the Hand of the Cause to the subway station, many times spending long intervals on the street just talking and telling both serious and funny stories. There was always plenty of laughter and happiness.[258]

Explaining the Faith to a new Bahá'í, Bahia, Brazil, 21 February 1959

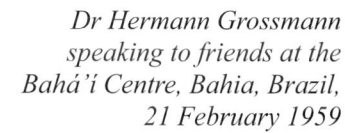

Dr Hermann Grossmann speaking to friends at the Bahá'í Centre, Bahia, Brazil, 21 February 1959

Leaving Brazil from Ipitanga airport, February 1959

Dr Hermann Grossmann on his historic visit to the campesinos in the Andes, Vilakollo, Bolivia, May 1959

With three outstanding travelling teachers. Front row, 3rd from left: Andrés Jachakollo, first Indian believer in Bolivia. Standing, left: Carmelo Jachakollo; 3rd from right: Isidro Jachakollo

Bahá'ís of Llapa-Llapani, Bolivia, in front of their huts built of clay, 1959

Dr Hermann Grossman during his return journey from visiting the indigenenous believers in Villakollo, May 1959

With friends in South America, 1959

Amatu'l-Bahá Rúḥíyyih Khánum during her visit to Frankfurt in July 1959

Departure of Amatu'l-Bahá Rúḥíyyih Khánum following her visit to the site of the Mother Temple of Europe in Langenhain, 11 July 1959

Anna and Hermann Grossmann with Zabih Aschari, on a visit to Graz, Austria, in 1960

A surprise encounter on board the Conte Grande with a group of Persian Bahá'í pioneers on their way to South America, January 1960

Dr Hermann and Anna Grossmann leaving the plane at Ezeiza airport, Buenos Aires, Argentina, 1960

Cali, Colombia, Riḍván 1960: Fourth Regional Convention of the Bahá'ís of northern South America – Brazil, Peru, Colombia, Ecuador and Venezuela

At the first National Convention of the Bahá'ís of Chile, Santiago de Chile, Riḍván 1961. Photograph taken outside the Ḥaẓíratu'l-Quds

Delegates and guests at the first National Convention of the Bahá'ís of Argentina, Buenos Aires, Riḍván 1961

Hermann and Anna Grossmann with Bahá'ís of Punta Arenas, Chile, 7 May 1961. Standing, from left: Santiago Vergara, Helen Willems de Gonzales (her daughter is in the front row), Jamele de Goharris, Cecilia W. de Govacic, Atar'u'llah Goharris (his sons are in the front row). Sitting: Dora B. de Handler, Betty Backer, Hermann and Anna Grossmann, Quendolin Willems

With two Irao Indians at the Bahá'í Centre, Bahia, Brazil, 1961

Hands of the Cause of God outside the Mansion of Bahjí, 1961. Left to right: William Sears, Zikrullah Khadem, 'Alí-Akbar Furútan, Shu'á'u'lláh 'Alá'í, Raḥmatu'lláh Muhájir, Ṭarázu'lláh Samandarí, Collis Featherstone, Abu'l-Qásim Faizi, Dr Hermann Grossmann, Jalál Kházeh

Anna and Hermann Grossman in La Paz, Bolivia, 1962

Visiting the Temple site at Lucke, Paraguay, 1962

While staying in Buenos Aires, the Grossmanns made an enjoyable side visit to Rosario, where they met with the friends on each of four consecutive days. There were important consultations and during the last week of February there was a meeting of the Regional Spiritual Assembly. In addition to the communities in Buenos Aires and Rosario, Argentina had two more communities in 1960 – those of Córdoba and Ezeiza. The summer school in Ezeiza, not far from the capital, provided an opportunity to meet friends from Bolivia, Chile, Paraguay and Uruguay, countries that were still united with Argentina in a Regional Assembly.

Anna Grossmann concludes a letter to the friends in Germany with the confident words:

> It is happy news that as a result of a good number of new declarations, and through the assistance of pioneers in the region served by the National Spiritual Assembly of southern South America, the formation of all the Spiritual Assemblies yet to be established is assured. In the region served by the National Spiritual Assembly of northern South America, which includes Brazil and Peru (which have long since fulfilled their plans), Ecuador, Colombia and Venezuela, the goals seem likely to be achieved soon. That is good news, very good news, and we all must be deeply grateful to those who, with dedication and sacrifice, have laid these foundations for our Faith, for here, too, it takes laborious effort to draw souls to the Faith – except for those who live far away from our much-vaunted civilization and recognize the truth in their hearts.[259]

Here, she was referring to the indigenous people.

At meetings with the Regional Spiritual Assemblies for South America and with the Hand of the Cause of God William Sears, dates were set for the National Conventions of the two Regional Spiritual Assemblies and measures discussed for assisting those groups that lacked experience in Bahá'í administration. They would be in need of support at the local elections on 21 April. Everywhere there was also the problem that some friends were confused by the claim of Mason Remey to be Shoghi Effendi's successor. In order to confront these attacks, the Bahá'ís had to be informed about the Guardian's spiritual testament. Another important matter for discussion was the work with the indigenous population, which was so close to Hermann Grossmann's heart.

The *Bahá'í News* published by the National Spiritual Assembly of the United States reports on the fourth and final election of the joint

Regional National Spiritual Assembly of the Bahá'ís of southern South America, which took place at Riḍván 1960 in Montevideo, Uruguay:

> There are no words to describe the atmosphere of high spirituality, serenity and maturity which prevailed through the entire period. Contributing to this highly victorious and successful Convention was the inspired presence of the revered Hand of the Cause of God, Dr Hermann Grossmann; of the Auxiliary Board member, Sra. Else Cazcarra; of Mrs Grossmann, former Auxiliary Board member in Europe; the devotion of the sacrificial group of Persian pioneers as well as the American contingent who have all rendered such outstanding services this year; the presence of the pure-hearted Indian Bolivian believers; the attendance of the heroic band of native Latin pioneers.[260]

Twenty-nine delegates from Argentina, Bolivia, Chile, Paraguay and Uruguay came together to elect the Assembly that was to assume responsibility for preparing the formation of the five independent National Spiritual Assemblies at Riḍván 1961. The most outstanding victories of the past year had been the mass entry into the Faith among the indigenous population of Bolivia, the fulfilment of all goals with the election of local Assemblies in Chile, Uruguay and Paraguay, and the purchase of land for the construction of a Temple in Bolivia. The Faith was also established on Easter Island without any pioneer travelling there. These islands had been designated a goal by the Guardian shortly before his passing.

On 26 April 1960 the delegates from northern South America met in Cali in Colombia in order to elect their Regional National Spiritual Assembly whose task would be to undertake preparations for the formation of separate National Spiritual Assemblies for Brazil, Ecuador, Colombia, Peru and Venezuela.

'The Hand of the Cause Hermann Grossmann was present at the Convention,' reads a report in *Bahá'í News*, 'and greatly inspired the friends. He praised them for work that had been successfully accomplished during the year, but reminded them that they do not have time to bask in their victories as there is much work to be done.' A message from the Hands of the Western Hemisphere emphasized, in particular, an apparent miracle that had occurred in Venezuela. The country had been shaken by violent unrest and all immigration was prohibited. The friends throughout the region prayed that it would be possible to form the Spiritual Assembly of Barquisimeto, and miraculously on the evening of 20 April not only that Assembly was formed but also four other new ones. This brought the number of local Assemblies in northern South America to thirty. The friends could hardly believe this exciting news.[261]

In his memoirs, Athos Costas emphasizes how important and valuable the consultations with Dr Grossmann were. One of the special qualities of the Hand of the Cause was his serenity, which had a calming effect on others, too. He always radiated confidence, encouraging and motivating those he spoke to, and he also preferred to ascertain things at first hand, as his difficult journey to Villakollo demonstrated.

During the Fast, Hermann and Anna Grossmann travelled around Chile, visiting the various communities. At the end of March the friends arranged an interview and a talk with Dr Grossmann at Radio Valdivia. New declarations reinforced the group in Valdivia and on 20 April 1960 the Grossmanns, as members of the community, were able to join the friends in electing the town's first Local Spiritual Assembly. A friend who was living in Valdivia in 1960 recalls this event:

> There were only two Bahá'ís here, plus one Chilean–North American pioneer. In 1960 the Hand of the Cause Dr Hermann Grossmann and his wife Anna came to Valdivia. It was very moving to welcome them (his strong embrace took my breath away for a moment). Because of his perfect Spanish, there were no problems. We enjoyed their friendship for a few short days and Dr Grossmann delivered two wonderful talks at which several enquirers were present. These were the first firesides in Valdivia and they were held by none other than a Hand of the Cause of God. The pioneer from the United States lived in a rather old three-storey house close to the river. We noticed that the house was on Liberty Street, had the number 9 and was crowned by a dome. We told our guest about that. When he went outside, he had a look for himself and smiled. In this building, on 28 January 1960, five new Bahá'ís declared their faith in Bahá'u'lláh. (This made it possible for another pioneer to move to a different town.) Hence, on the day of the election of the Local Spiritual Assembly there were precisely nine members, and it is an honour to be able to say that Dr Grossmann and his wife were among the names listed on the ballot paper. Bahá'u'lláh had thus enabled this goal of the Plan to be attained. How could we fail to recognize the spiritual influence of a visit by a Hand of the Cause, through which all this was achieved.[262]

In May 1960 Valdivia suffered a terrible earthquake which brought a flood in its wake. Many people, including Bahá'ís, left the town.

HERMANN GROSSMANN

Hermann Grossmann wrote to the community in September 1960:

> Dear brothers and sisters, although I am at present far away from you, I have been thinking of you, dear friends, at every moment and my heart was with you throughout the earthquake. I was deeply grateful to receive all the news concerning your well-being and also your steadfastness in the Faith. We will surely never know why this place was chosen to experience such suffering, a place where Providence has sought out such wonderful believers and where the Bahá'í Assembly was formed in such a short time. As regards the spiritual significance of the disaster, we can take it as a wake-up call to people, which will enable you to make them aware that this is the Day of a new Manifestation of God; and we can also regard it as an honour that this town with its Bahá'í community was chosen to promulgate the revelation of the Plan of God.
>
> The foundations of community life are love and cooperation, understanding and forgiveness, the replacement of imperfections by better qualities, not through criticism and chastisement. I am happy that Enrique, the spiritual father of many of you, is working hard and trying to strengthen your community both spiritually and numerically, so that at Riḍván 1961 you will be both one of the best and strongest communities in Chile and also a strong pillar for the election of your National Spiritual Assembly.
>
> Next month, the annual meeting of the Hands of the Cause will take place in Bahjí, where Bahá'u'lláh spent His last years and passed away. Be assured that they will be thinking of you then and will offer prayers at the Holy Shrines for your country and its communities.
>
> After my return from the Holy Land, I hope to come back to South America and one of the first places I will visit will be Valdivia.
>
> With deepest Bahá'í love and best wishes for each one of you from my wife and myself, in the service of Bahá'u'lláh, Hermann Grossmann.[263]

The friends from Valdivia wrote to the National Spiritual Assembly of Germany, that 'the disaster was truly very great, but the protection of Bahá'u'lláh was even greater. All the believers are safe and in good health. A friend – a radio presenter – even fell from the second floor of a building and miraculously suffered no injury. He was not even slightly hurt.'[264]

In order to safeguard the status of Valdivia as a community, when friends left following the earthquake the Local Assembly asked the Regional Spiritual Assembly to permit Hermann and Anna Grossmann to remain registered as members of the community, even though they were currently in Germany. The Assembly consented that they were members of this community, which 'is a great honour for us in South

America, where your father was born and spent the early years of his life', wrote Donald Witzel, a long-time Counsellor and veteran pioneer living in South America, to Hartmut Grossmann.[265]

By 1960 there were eight communities in Chile: Santiago, Viña del Mar, Quilpué, Valparaiso, Valdivia, Loncoche, Borno and Punta Arenas. These communities were to be the pillars upon which the National Spiritual Assembly of Chile was to be erected at Riḍván 1961. Therefore, no day of the Grossmanns' visit was to be wasted.

During the first days of Riḍván, from 23 to 25 April 1960, Hermann Grossmann – representing the Hands of the Cause of God – was able to participate in the National Convention of the southern countries, and during the last days of Riḍván, from 29 April to 2 May, he took part in the National Convention of the northern countries in Cali, Colombia. Uruguay had two communities – Montevideo and Minas – and Colombia eight – Cali, Bogotá, Pereira, Medellín, Manizales, Bucaramanga, Cartagena and Baranquilla.

In mid-May, and again in early June, the Grossmanns paid visits to the four communities of Ecuador: Quito, Otavalo, Guayaquil and Cuenca. In Quito and Otavalo the friends took advantage of the presence of the Hand of the Cause, who spoke their language so fluently, to hold an intensive publicity campaign. They organized several well-attended public lectures.

Between these visits, Hermann Grossmann was once again in Cali, Baranquilla and Bogotá, where he gave a radio interview. Not a day passed without one or even several meetings taking place, and, in addition, the Hand of the Cause often had private conversations with believers and inquirers who wished to talk to him.

In Lima the Grossmanns met friends from all over Peru. There were four communities in that country in 1960 – Lima, Huancayo, Arequipa and Callao.

On 14 June Anna and Hermann Grossmann travelled to Chile. In Santiago they consulted with the Spiritual Assembly and in Valparaiso they arranged a meeting with the friends from Viña del Mar and Quilpué.

One of the friends made notes during a lecture given in Valparaiso by Hermann Grossmann on 16 June 1960. The following fragments extracted from these notes are interesting since they reflect the purpose and main theme of his travels:

> Dr Grossmann spoke of Christianity as the misunderstood religion in which Peter was the only 'rock'. After Christ's death, none of his disciples remained faithful to him – even Peter denied him. In the only Christian community and the centre of the Faith, Jerusalem, there were essentially three parties: Christians who, on the basis of Christianity, wished to remain Jewish; Christians who were infused with a new spirit; and the third, and most successful, group whose spiritual centre was Paul, who had not known Christ and had even been his enemy. He was a Hellene and he combined his own ideas with the teachings of Christ ... After two hundred years, Hellenistic Christianity was one of many religions in Rome. After Constantine had declared this doctrine to be the state religion, its influence increased, although it did not have a social order of its own. Hence, the Christians adopted the Roman social order, which was not from God ... In this order, power was in the hands of the citizens of that city alone ... Muhammad, on the other hand, made no such distinction. The same law applied to all, and He expressly ordered that Jews, Christians, Zoroastrians and Sabeans should not be discriminated against in comparison with orthodox Muslims ... In the Crusades, the Christians became acquainted with the new divine order of Muhammad ... The first nations came into being.
>
> The divine order of Bahá'u'lláh contains the idea of neither the empire nor the nation. It speaks only of peoples who make up various parts of the world ...
>
> In the Will and Testament of 'Abdu'l-Bahá, a gap had opened up because the Guardian had not appointed a successor. Shoghi Effendi's testament is *The Dispensation of Bahá'u'lláh*, as he pointed out in a letter to Persia as early as 1937. It contains his last will and his spiritual testament. In his last message in 1957, he appointed the Hands of the Cause of God to act as 'Chief Stewards', his successors and representatives until the establishment of the Universal House of Justice. The state of Israel recognized this message as Shoghi Effendi's testament ... The Hands of the Cause of God set Riḍván 1963 as the date [for the establishment of the Universal House of Justice].
>
> The Guardian's 1957 message also refers to the Covenant-breakers who will arise. Now the words of the Guardian are clearly evident: Mason Remey, during a meeting of the Hands of the Cause declared that he was the Guardian's successor ...[266]

Four days later, Hermann and Anna Grossmann returned to Buenos Aires, the capital of Argentina. There, Dr Grossmann delivered a well-attended public talk and on 1 July they took a hydroplane to Asunción in Paraguay. Hermann Grossmann spent four days conversing with the friends in the Ḥaẓíratu'l-Quds. Many came to talk to him, bringing inquirers with them. Back in Buenos Aires, he again took part in a meeting of the Regional Spiritual Assembly of southern South America. On Sunday 17 July there was a big farewell party with the Bahá'ís and on 21 July Hermann and Anna Grossmann boarded their ship for the journey back to Europe.

The voyage took fourteen days, and their first port of call was Barcelona. There, friends were waiting at the harbour to meet them briefly. Next day they sailed on to Genoa, where they disembarked. They reached their home in Neckargemünd a day later, on 7 August 1960.

Hermann Grossmann and his wife had been travel-teaching for a total of 252 days and had attended 144 events, excluding small-scale events and consultations. This was the longest stay by the Hand of the Cause of God Dr Grossmann in South America.

He was so exhausted as a result of these strenuous journeys that it took him weeks to recover. In September 1960 he was again able to participate in a summer school in Ziegelhausen, near Heidelberg. This summer school was 'bursting at the seams', with 85 participants from 15 countries there to 'revivify their spirits and enrich their knowledge'. The two German Hands of the Cause, Adelbert Mühlschlegel and Hermann Grossmann, held interesting talks which were followed by lively and inspiring discussions. 'A highlight of the delightful week', recounts one participant, 'was the fascinating report by Mrs Anna Grossmann on the historically significant teaching mission covering a number of the South American republics which she took with the Hand of the Cause Hermann Grossmann.'[267]

Some time later, Hermann Grossmann attended a conference in Luxembourg at which Claude Levy presided. In a brief opening address Dr Grossmann reminded the friends of '... those nearly-forgotten days when we Bahá'ís lived a quiet and sleepy life,' as he is quoted in one report. 'But then things began to change, and suddenly we have found it is "ten minutes before midnight".' Now the Bahá'ís must 'put into effect all possible means for filling the goals set for us by the beloved Guardian'. After this, several friends held further talks about teaching. In the evening, Hermann Grossmann showed slides of the believers in South America. Of particular interest were those of the new indigenous communities that had sprung up with such remarkable speed. He told the story of that first farmer who had knocked on the door of the Bahá'í Centre in La Paz, and explained that there were now a thousand indigenous believers and many more preparing to become Bahá'ís. 'Dr Grossmann's great spirit as a revered Hand of the Cause pervaded the whole assemblage,' concludes the report. 'His generous visit, in spite of delicate health ... was an inspiration to all present.'[268]

From mid-October 1960 the Hands of the Cause of God met in Bahjí for a period of six weeks in order to consult on the fulfilment of the Plan.

On 18 November there followed a European Conference in Frankfurt am Main, during which the foundation stone was laid for the House of Worship at Langenhain in the Taunus hills near Frankfurt by the Hand of the Cause Amelia Collins. In the presence of seven Hands and over a thousand other people, Amelia Collins placed a silver plate along with dust from the Shrine of Bahá'u'lláh upon the cornerstone, the foundation of the future Mother Temple of Europe. 'World history had been made indeed,' noted René Steiner in a report for the American *Bahá'í News*:

> It was not the history of material battles of oppression and of fear. It was the beginning of the rebirth of Europe in the realms of the spirit and in the realm of thought ... Future generations will remember that noon hour on a wind-swept hill in the heart of Europe. Was it not Goethe who said at Valmy that history had been made? How much more would this be true here, where the only weapons were those of the spirit and of the mind of man.[269]

The ceremony was followed by an official reception in the grand conference hall at the Zoological Gardens in Frankfurt.

Hermann Grossmann concluded his Bahá'í activities for the year 1960 by attending a conference at The Hague in the Netherlands in late November. He then withdrew to his home in Neckargemünd in order to regain his strength.

The year 1961 began with a Bahá'í conference in Luxembourg. In the second half of January, Hermann Grossmann toured Austria, meeting the friends in Salzburg, Linz, Vienna, Baden, Graz and Innsbruck. His preparations for returning to South America for a third visit fell in the period of the Fast. The aim of this journey was to help with the formation of the National Spiritual Assemblies and to provide assistance to these young institutions as they commenced their activities.

Once again, vaccinations and visits to consulates were required, although his Argentine passport opened the doors to all the other South

American states. His wife Anna, who was again accompanying him, also travelled on an Argentine passport. On 30 March 1961 they departed from the airport at Frankfurt am Main, and after a flight lasting more than twenty-four hours, including an unexpected stop in Dakar, Senegal, they finally landed in Recife, Brazil. After two days in Bahia, they flew on to Rio de Janeiro and then spent several days in São Paulo. Sometimes they took their breakfast alone in the hotel, but often they met friends even at that early hour and continued meeting and talking to people all day, before a meeting with believers and seekers in the evening. Anna Grossmann joyfully noted in her diary each meeting with the indigenous believers, such as those of the Crao tribe in Bahia.

Two days were devoted to consultation with the Regional Spiritual Assembly for northern South America in Lima. Next followed five days in Quito, Ecuador, including a final consultative session with the Local Spiritual Assembly. They were able to send encouraging reports to the Hands of the Cause in Haifa and to the Regional Spiritual Assembly in Lima before flying on to Buenos Aires on 19 April.

In Buenos Aires, the Argentine Bahá'ís came together for their National Convention, during which the first National Spiritual Assembly of Argentina was elected on the third day of Riḍván. Hermann Grossmann conveyed official greetings from the Hands of the Cause of God to the conference. 'Dr Grossmann spoke of the spirit of responsibility, enthusiasm and service that pervaded the meeting and of his confidence that this would be reflected in the activities of the new Bahá'í community of Argentina,' reads one report. 'Inspired by these words and with a feeling of nearness to Bahá'u'lláh ... the assembled friends elected their National Spiritual Assembly.'[270]

On the seventh day of Riḍván the Grossmanns reached Chile, and on the ninth day of Riḍván Hermann Grossmann was able to greet the first National Spiritual Assembly of Chile on behalf of the Hands of the Cause of God.

Reporting on the National Convention, a Bahá'í recalled:

> The colourful city of Santiago with its wonderful parks and gardens set against the snow peaked mountains in the background was the setting for the greatest Bahá'í event in Chilean history; the formation of its first National Spiritual Assembly. On the 29th of April 1961 ... the Convention was opened with due ceremony. This was presided over by Dr Alejandro Reid, the representative of the now dissolved Regional Assembly. He said a few brief words before handing over to Dr Hermann Grossmann, the

representative of the Hands of the Cause in Haifa, who was to officially open this momentous occasion. Dr Grossmann addressed us with simple and kind words, saying: 'Dearly beloved friends, the Hands of the Cause had the idea of sending a Hand of the Cause to every National Convention in South America, and I asked to be permitted to go to Argentina and Chile, since those are the two countries that I know best ... I was with you last year and I can now say that Chile was born, grew up and has already reached maturity. I do not think you need any further help, but I must say that the Hands of the Cause are always at your service and, through them, so am I.' The moving part of the Convention arrived; the election of the members of the National Spiritual Assembly of the Bahá'ís of Chile. Dr Grossmann again addressed the assemblage, saying ... 'A new National Spiritual Assembly is a pillar in the building of the Universal House of Justice. When the first National Spiritual Assemblies were formed, we did not think about that so much, but now it is different because we will soon have the Universal House of Justice. You must therefore hurry to understand what a National Spiritual Assembly is and what great responsibility you bear. It is not just a large-scale Local Spiritual Assembly. It must be a physician and judge and father, and know the problems of the entire country. Latin America has the bounty of providing 21 pillars to support the Universal House of Justice. What is needed now is the strengthening of the Local Assemblies ... We must now consolidate in order to promote the spirit of unity and understand the significance of our Faith in the world. I am sure that you will achieve your goals ... and I know that the Chilean community will make even greater progress than in the past year.'[271]

A visit to Punta Arenas on the Magellan Strait in southern Chile made Hermann Grossmann especially happy because Shoghi Effendi had been particularly fond of that town. After a stay in Puerto Montt he gave a radio interview in Osorno. Hermann and Anna Grossmann then travelled by train to Valdivia and Loncoche, then back to Santiago. In each place they met the friends and their contacts, and every evening Hermann Grossmann spoke at meetings. Their next destinations were Buenos Aires, Bahia Blanca and, in mid-June, Montevideo where they met with the first National Spiritual Assembly of Uruguay. The Hand of the Cause of God 'Alí-Akbar Furútan had been present at the historic occasion of its formation.

In her diary, Anna Grossmann complains about the long delays – sometimes of several hours, sometimes even of days – of flights and train journeys. These often completely upset their plans and left friends waiting in vain at their destination. However, the friends were indefatigable and patiently put up even with fruitless waiting.

The Grossmanns travelled to Rosario and Córdoba by train. In both towns a great many people assembled each day to listen to the Hand of the Cause. At the end of June, they returned to Buenos Aires, where Dr Grossmann was able to support the young National Spiritual Assembly in dealing with many problems. At this time he saw it as his primary duty to strengthen the assemblies and make them immune to the machinations of the enemies of the Cause who sought to attack the successful and rapidly growing Bahá'í communities in South America. Whenever he met the newly created communities, he also pointed out their duty to bring the message of Bahá'u'lláh to the deprived and oppressed indigenous peoples of South America. By 1961 this work had already commenced on the Orinoco in Venezuela, in the Guajira in northern Colombia, and in Chile. In the high-altitude plains of Bolivia the first schools had been founded in order to combat illiteracy and lay the foundation for improving living conditions.

On 7 July Hermann and Anna Grossmann flew to the capital of Paraguay, Asunción. During Riḍván, the Hand of the Cause Dr Muhájir had conveyed greetings from the World Centre to the participants in the election of the first National Spiritual Assembly. Although the friends there had not received the news that the Grossmanns were coming, they quickly came together and took advantage of the presence of the guests to deepen their own knowledge and that of their friends. Some of the meetings with Hermann Grossmann were enhanced with music. He loved the sound of the traditional Paraguayan harp played by one of the young women present. His visit ended with several days of consultation with the members of the National Spiritual Assembly.

On his return to Buenos Aires, a further Assembly meeting took place and on 19 July Anna and Hermann Grossmann said goodbye to the friends in Argentina and travelled on to Bolivia.

In Cochabamba Dr Muhájir had participated in the election of the new National Spiritual Assembly as a representative of the institution of the Hands of the Cause. Again, Hermann Grossmann's visit served to clear up some of the problems that had arisen since then.

In a letter written to Hartmut Grossmann in 1995 Oscar Salazar, a believer living in Salta, Argentina, recounted the fascinating and moving story of how he became a Bahá'í. On a journey from La Paz to Chile he and his wife took a break in Cochabamba. Mr Salazar, who at that time considered himself a revolutionary, bought a local newspaper in order to find out if Chile was still maintaining diplomatic relations with newly communist Cuba rather than breaking them off as most other Latin American states had done. The couple's intention was to obtain permission from the Cuban Consulate in Chile to travel to that 'ostracized and outlawed' Caribbean country. On the last page of the newspaper they noticed an advertisement:

> The Bahá'í community of Cochabamba invites you to a public talk by Dr Hermann Grossmann, who is here on a tour through several American countries, on the way to others of the southern tip of the continent, and is speaking on the subject of the troubles of our times. Hour 7 p.m., at No.12 Ecuador Street ... Admission free.

Oscar Salazar wondered what 'Bahá'í' could be:

> Could it be perhaps the initials of a new group of our comrades, camouflaged as a pseudo-movement? And what about this Grossmann ...? Could he be an imperialist agent, or maybe a fascist-nazi follower of Hitler? The last name was Germanic! We should investigate. The Salazars were the first to arrive at the meeting and were welcomed with such warmth by the lady of the house that it was as if they had known one another for years. The people began to arrive one after the other. They were men, women and children of all ages. At the front some four or six rows of chairs had been kept in reserve. After a while their occupants arrived. They were local farmers dressed in their typical regional costumes. The meeting room was so full that many had to stand in the corners. Although the majority appeared to be Bolivians, one could discern foreigners among those present.
>
> Suddenly those seated rose to their feet. The 'so called' Grossmann had entered accompanied by a lady. The hosts showed them to the seats reserved for them, which were surrounded by beautiful bouquets of flowers with cards of welcome.
>
> The 'revolutionary' [Oscar Salazar] and his wife were facing the 'mysterious' personage. He seemed to be about sixty years of age, of normal height, stocky figure and round face. He was accompanied by his wife who looked younger than him. Brother Hartmut, I am sorry not to be able to remember clearly the sequence of the talk given by your eminent father, but making a mental effort I can tell you that he spoke of the oneness of tangible and intangible existence, of the interrelatedness of all being ... in the eternal movement of the process of creation ... He spoke of Krishna, Moses, Zoroaster, Buddha, Christ, Muhammad, the Báb, and he ended with Bahá'u'lláh, Who he affirmed was the Architect of the unity of mankind.

He spoke of the last days of the 'old world order' and the elimination of all prejudices that still separate human groups, but said that humankind would inevitably attain its unity. Did not Marxist-Leninists wish to accomplish this also? Undoubtedly we had to collect more information. We received different pamphlets ... Hartmut, that was the only moment, the only time, that I had the privilege of knowing that illustrious man of calm speech ... He opened the closed minds of this couple, but most of all the brain of the man (myself) who was a furious and active international agitator, a recalcitrant atheist who had been imprisoned and who had arrived in that country as a fugitive from Brazil, to connect with that angel of the Blessed Beauty – because, 'He Who doeth what He pleaseth', had decided to enrol that crazy man in the ranks of His Hosts.

Before knowing about the Faith, he was convinced that there was no truth but 'dialectical materialism'. Dr Grossmann unbarred the heart of an anti-religionist, and opened a breach in his mind to incite him to search for Truth ... [In] investigation after investigation he met other distinguished teachers of the Cause, and in the end declared himself a Bahá'í on the 4th of November of 1961, also declaring that in order to repay God for turning him again to His path, he would dedicate himself to the teaching and dissemination of His Faith for the rest of his days in the physical world. Who knows how many of the blind, like me, were reached by the Light in their labyrinth of darkness through the power of the words of your illustrious father.[272]

Peru and Ecuador had been visited by the Hand of the Cause Hasan Balyuzi during Riḍván, when the National Spiritual Assemblies were elected. In August, Hermann Grossmann spent several weeks in these two countries helping to clarify administrative issues and deepen the friends in the Faith. He paid visits to Lima and Chiclayo in Peru, and to Guayaquil and Quito in Ecuador. He had intensive discussions with both National Assemblies.

At the end of August, Anna and Hermann Grossmann flew to Colombia, where they visited Cali and Bogotá. Urgent questions were clarified during a two-day meeting with the National Spiritual Assembly in Bogotá.

The last days of their stay in South America were spent in Venezuela, where the Hand of the Cause Ugo Giachery had assisted with the formation of that National Spiritual Assembly. After a meeting with that body in Caracas, they travelled on to Maracay and Sucre. On 5 September 1961 Hermann and Anna Grossmann ended their second joint trip, which had again taken them to all the countries of South America.

Two days later they arrived, exhausted but very happy, at their home in Neckargemünd. The journey had been full of wonderful meetings with friends and strangers alike.

On 15 October the Hands of the Cause assembled for their six-week Conclave in Bahjí. Hermann Grossmann undoubtedly gave an encouraging report concerning the progress of the Faith in South America, as well as speaking of his intensive efforts to ward off the threat posed by the Covenant-breakers.

CHAPTER 22

LAST JOURNEY TO SOUTH AMERICA, 1962[273]

Despite clear signs of great strain, Hermann Grossmann set out one last time to visit South America. 'Once again his own enthusiasm carried him from place to place,' writes Anna Grossmann, 'allowing him, as he himself called it, to bring to a good end one of his most difficult tasks in one of the countries of South America.'

In the late evening of 24 February 1962 Anna and Hermann Grossmann again flew from Frankfurt am Main, arriving the next afternoon in Caracas, the capital of Venezuela. After two days of meetings with the friends, they were taken by car to Barquisimeto, where an interview had been organized with the local newspaper. Three days later they were in Valencia, where Dr Grossmann also gave a fairly long press interview. This was followed by an important meeting with the National Spiritual Assembly of Venezuela. Before travelling on, they visited the Temple site that had been donated by the friends.

On 7 March Anna and Hermann Grossmann flew to Curaçao, an island in the Dutch Antilles, where Dr Grossmann delivered a public talk. The following day saw them in Baranquilla in northern Colombia, and then two days later they were with believers in Cartagena, flying on the same evening to Medellín. The next stop was Bucaramanga, followed by Bogotá, the capital of Colombia. Everywhere he went, Hermann Grossmann instructed the believers and talked to seekers. He was in demand from early in the morning till late at night – in each place the believers brought their German-speaking friends along with them. It was, after all, a unique opportunity to meet a Bahá'í with such thorough knowledge of the Writings, who was able to answer questions on every other subject, too, and could do so equally well in German, English and Spanish, the language of the country. The stay there ended with a three-day consultation with the National Spiritual Assembly of

Colombia. Its members and many other friends, accompanied by their children, were at the airport to say good-bye on 19 March as the couple left for Cali.

In Cali they celebrated Naw-Rúz with the believers, and in Quito Hermann Grossmann spent several days consulting with the National Spiritual Assembly of Ecuador. In addition to Quito, Guayaquil was on the Grossmanns' Ecuadorian itinerary. On 31 March they left that country to go to Peru. Their destination there was Lima. Again, Hermann Grossmann met with the National Spiritual Assembly. He was especially happy to hear that large numbers from the indigenous population had accepted the Cause of Bahá'u'lláh.

On 12 April they flew from Lima for a brief visit to La Paz, the capital of Bolivia, before travelling on to Cochabamba, where Hermann Grossmann was able to see for himself the amazing progress of the Faith in Bolivia. The teaching work among the indigenous population had borne excellent fruit: there were now 60 local Spiritual Assemblies in the country, only five of these being in the towns, all the others in villages. Social work among the agricultural communities was in full swing. Twelve schools had already been established.

This outstanding success posed considerable problems for the National Spiritual Assembly, however. All these people were in need of instruction and deepening, and there were only four travelling teachers available. Nevertheless, Hermann Grossmann was happy. He had always been convinced that the native peoples were waiting for the message of Bahá'u'lláh.

After travelling on to Montevideo, he consulted with the Hand of the Cause William Sears, who was staying there. In a long meeting with the National Spiritual Assembly of Uruguay and in many conversations with individual members of this Assembly, Hermann Grossmann invested all his energy in making it absolutely clear to the friends that they were in danger of breaking the Covenant. Much to his joy and gratitude, seven days later he was able to report to the Hands in Haifa that his mission had been accomplished, and on 1 May it was possible to conduct the election of the Local Spiritual Assembly of Montevideo and that of the delegates to the National Convention. With the aid of Bahá'u'lláh, the Hand of the Cause of God had managed to 'bring to a successful end one of his most difficult tasks ...'

Hermann and Anna Grossmann remained in Uruguay and took part in the three-day Convention of delegates from 18 to 20 May. On 20 May the delegates elected the new National Spiritual Assembly of Uruguay and the Hand of the Cause took the opportunity to consult with them during their first meeting.

On 28 May, after their flight had been postponed for several days, the Grossmanns said goodbye to the friends at the airport. As usual, this delay wasted a lot of time and caused much nervous tension as well as increased costs, since the friends waiting at the destination airport had to be informed and other travel plans altered. The only rapid means of communication in those days was by cable, which was expensive. In her memoirs Anna Grossmann mentions that she would take the mail directly to the airline counter so that it would be transported by air. This was especially important for overseas mail. It would otherwise have been sent by ship, which took weeks. Such duties were her responsibility, and it was a wise decision of the Conclave of the Hands of the Cause to send her along on the trip to assist her husband. As far as possible, she took over the task of planning the itinerary, arranging practical matters and obtaining items that were needed, so that he could concentrate his full attention on the teaching work.

In Asunción Dr Grossmann spent several days in consultation with the National Spiritual Assembly of Paraguay and its committees. Many friends came to the hotel seeking advice, since everywhere in South America there was some uncertainty due to the activities of the Covenant-breakers. They travelled with the friends to the newly-acquired Temple site at Lucke and taught the Faith at meetings in Asunción and among the indigenous people.

On 11 June they landed on Chilean soil, arriving in Santiago. The next day they travelled on to Punta Arenas, the most southerly community of this huge continent. They spent two days there, two days filled with useful discussions. In Santiago Hermann Grossmann again consulted with the National Spiritual Assembly, and then they travelled with friends by train to Viña del Mar and Valparaiso. Thus, they could also use the time of travel for further teaching.

On 23 June Anna and Hermann Grossmann participated in the Nineteen Day Feast in Buenos Aires and were reminded of the Feast exactly two years earlier that they had also attended there. What progress the Cause had made since then – more than they had ever dared to hope! The country was now in its second year with its own National Spiritual Assembly. Latin America had fulfilled the goals of the Ten Year Plan two years earlier than envisaged.

In El Palmar they spent a day with a distant cousin of Annel Grossmann. These were some of the few hours they devoted to their numerous relatives in Argentina.

In Buenos Aires, Hermann Grossmann met once more with the National Spiritual Assembly. He then had two days to bid farewell to Rosario, his childhood hometown. This time it was to be forever, for it was evident that his health would not stand up to the rigours of yet another journey.

A further meeting with the National Spiritual Assembly of Uruguay took place in Montevideo and then, on 9 July, the two Hands Abu'l-Qásim Faizi and Hermann Grossmann linked visits in Montevideo. Anna and Hermann Grossmann delayed their departure and, together with the local Bahá'ís, arranged a meeting for Mr Faizi, who, with a deep sense of love and devotion to the beloved Guardian, had been tirelessly travelling throughout Latin America in 1961 and 1962 for the protection of the Cause.

On 11 July the Grossmanns flew to Brazil, where they saw the friends in Porto Alegre, Curitiba, São Paulo, Santo André and Campinas. In São Paulo the National Spiritual Assembly spent two days in consultation with Dr Grossmann. On 17 July the friends said goodbye to both of them, and they landed back in Germany on 28 July, at Frankfurt am Main. They had been travelling for five eventful and exhausting months.

After the trips to South America were over, Anna Grossmann wrote a report for the German *Bahá'í-Nachrichten,* not only giving a colourful and vivid description of the continent itself and the history of the Bahá'í community in each country, but also recounting her personal experiences:[274]

> After three journeys through South America, I have grown very fond of the continent, a fact that I attribute first and foremost to the friendship and warmth of the Bahá'ís in South America.
>
> If one wishes to write about South America, one must first of all say a few words about the landscape and the people, because both are so different from Europe. The backbone of the continent in the west, stretching from Venezuela in the north down to Punta Arenas in the south, is the Cordillera or Andes mountains, whose highest peaks reach to more than six and seven thousand metres and which provide an ever-changing, always spectacular setting: green in the northern countries – the snow-line is very high – and bare and glistening red, reddish, blue or grey in the sun in Peru and Bolivia. Further south, where they form the border between Chile and

Argentina, they resemble the Alps with their wild peaks and blue lakes. From their eastern slopes down to the Atlantic, there are tropical rainforests extending thousands of kilometres southwards, gradually merging into the pampas, the grasslands, before turning into the endless solitude of the Patagonian plain. The town dwellers are mainly the descendants of the Spanish conquistadors and in Brazil of the Portuguese, as well as people descended from both these and the indigenous people, or Indios. One also finds immigrants from all the countries of Europe, and in some republics there are people of black African, east Asian and South Sea Island descent. One becomes so accustomed to the diversity of the population that one misses it when one no longer meets with it.

The development of the Bahá'í Faith in South America began only recently. Before planned propagation by the North American Bahá'í community started under the first Seven Year Plan (1937–1944), Martha Root, the 'outstanding ambassador of the Faith', had already visited all the major cities of South America and made the Faith known there. There exists an article published by the leading Argentine journal *Caras y Caretas* commemorating Martha Root's visit to that country. We know that she was unable to disembark at Bahia (Brazil) because of an outbreak of yellow fever there, and that this intrepid woman crossed the Andean pass between Argentina and Chile on a mule. Like her, several other pioneers had been inspired by 'Abdu'l-Bahá's Tablets of the Divine Plan to leave their homes and carry the message of Bahá'u'lláh to South America. One of them was Leonora Holsapple Armstrong, who continues to render countless services to the Faith in Brazil. It was during the Seven Year Plan that May Maxwell, the mother of Rúḥíyyih Khánum, left the USA to teach in South America and immediately after arriving in Buenos Aires, suffered a heart attack and passed away ... In 1951, during the second Seven Year Plan (1946–1953), the first Regional Spiritual Assembly for all ten South American republics was formed at the request of our Guardian. Among the goals of the subsequent Ten Year Plan was the doubling of the number of communities and the formation of ten National Spiritual Assemblies in accordance with the number of republics on the continent. As a preliminary stage towards this, the Regional National Spiritual Assembly was divided at Riḍván 1957, at the request of the Guardian, into two separate Regional National Spiritual Assemblies, each of which was responsible for five republics. In 1960, the mighty efforts of the Bahá'ís resulted in the establishment of all the Local Spiritual Assemblies required by the Ten Year Plan, and in some countries of even more, so that at Riḍván 1961 the festive establishment of ten National Spiritual Assemblies could take place. Thus, indeed, it is justified to speak of a young Bahá'í activity in South America, which had been initiated by the service of North American pioneers and the guidance and support of the National Spiritual Assembly of the United States of America.

When we again stepped onto South American soil – this time in Venezuela – in February this year, after an absence of more than six months, we were keen to learn how the work was developing under the new independent National Spiritual Assemblies. Had the friends who were on these Assemblies, very few of whom were experienced, been able to fulfil all their manifold obligations, had they grasped the spirit of consultation and the fundamental principle of the Faith, that of 'unity in diversity'? When we bear in mind that today we are all at the start of the implementation of these principles, it is astounding to observe what has been achieved in these assemblies and under their guidance. In all the countries, new assemblies have been established or important communities opened to the Faith, and everywhere in these years of mass enrolment ways have been sought to reach the indigenous people of this continent, the Indios. The National Administrative Centres (Ḥaẓíratu'l-Quds), which had already been purchased in the capitals of the ten republics during the first years of the Ten Year Plan, have now developed into focal points of community life and centres for teaching activities. Of particular beauty are the buildings in Lima, Santiago, Asunción – in this case a colonial style villa with two courtyards, one with a fountain and overhanging vines – and the enchanting Ḥaẓíra in La Paz with its spectacular location. All of them are lovingly cared for and have been improved and enlarged where necessary.

In Caracas (Venezuela) we were able to visit the Temple site that had been donated shortly before by Venezuelan believers. An excellent road through delightful mountain scenery leads to the site, which is about 30 km from Caracas and lies 1,000 m above the city at around 2,000 m above sea level. The tropical heat of the Caribbean region becomes pleasantly cool up there. The view from the Temple site extends far beyond the coast of Venezuela over the blue Caribbean Sea. It was an unforgettable experience to be up there praying, along with the donors of the land and the pioneer from the island of Margarita, for the progress of the Faith and for the future Mashriqu'l-Adhkár to be built on that site. Every country in South America has a Temple site. Where will the first House of Worship for South America be erected?

Another pleasant experience was our visit to the island of Curaçao to meet the friends there. As far as Bahá'í administration is concerned, this island belongs to Venezuela (although politically it has its own administration whilst being associated with the Netherlands). There is a lovely community there, including Mr and Mrs Kellberg, Knights of Bahá'u'lláh. On one of the neighbouring islands, Margarita, there is also a Knight of Bahá'u'lláh, Katharine Meyer. The islands off the coast of South America that are to be opened as part of the Ten Year Plan are under the auspices of the new National Spiritual Assemblies and demand much attention and great care. A pioneer has recently moved to the Galápagos Islands, which are under the care of the National Spiritual Assembly of Ecuador. The National Spiritual Assembly of Chile is responsible for three groups of islands: Juan Fernández, of Robinson Crusoe fame, where there are a few believers; the Island of Castro in the south, which was severely affected by an earthquake in 1960, where there are also some believers; and the distant Easter Island, which has been difficult to open, even though pioneers have been found who are willing to go there. Then there are the Falkland Islands (Malvinas), which are under the responsibility of the National Spiritual Assembly of Argentina and which have one of those intrepid pioneers who are so abundant in our Faith.

The most attractive and popular of activities in South America is teaching among the indigenous population. Throughout the continent, experience has shown that this work transforms those who engage in it, infusing the whole country with renewed enthusiasm and impulses. Yet one should not imagine this work to be too easy. First of all, there is the tropical rainforest which covers thousands of square kilometres, and the people who are at home in this forest live in relatively small tribal or sub-tribal communities; some of them are good and harmless, like children, some of them are wild and dangerous. How, in this enormous expanse of forest is one to find those who are ready to hear the Word of Bahá'u'lláh? Nevertheless, the friends succeeded in doing just that. They approached the region from four different directions and found some receptive souls, enough to establish four communities. One group of natives in northern Brazil declared their affiliation to the Faith in the following words: 'If this is the Law of God for this age, then we will serve the Law.' Incidentally, few people know that in South America there are deserts and desert-like regions and that there are still remnants of the indigenous population there, too. In order to teach them the Faith, one of our friends took it upon himself to share their life of deprivation and poverty, and has been with them for two years now. How happy these people are about the teachings and the prayers; no one had ever prayed with them before. Three communities have already been established among these people.

However, the pride of South America will always be the mountain campesinos who can rejoice in the fame of having brought the Faith to themselves and carried it over a wide area, even beyond their tribal region, without outside assistance. Today they have 60 spiritual assemblies made up entirely of indigenous believers, and they sent 38 delegates to elect the National Spiritual Assembly, whereas all the other countries in South

America sent only 9 delegates. The pioneers, that is the non-indigenous Bahá'ís, who share their arduous lives in order to help them and deepen them in the Faith, are deeply impressed by their purity of heart. They say that however poor they may be – and by our standards they are unimaginably poor – their hearts are all the more pure. In order to attend a congress held at Naw-Rúz, in which over 300 indigenous believers took part, some of them walked for eight days because they could not afford the small sum required for a standing place on a truck. All over the continent, they are asking for schools so that they can be permitted to learn to read and write and to speak Spanish; or rather, now as Bahá'ís they wish to learn, whereas before they retained their traditional enmity towards the government and its attempts to improve their living standards. The old people nervously ask if they, too, can attend school. The Faith has evidently transformed them, so that they are even learning to laugh, for it is said, and is also noted in books, that they are not accustomed to laughing. Our spiritual obligation towards them is very great!

It is now about six years since the doorbell of a Ḥaẓíra rang and two campesinos were found modestly standing there and wishing to know what the word 'Bahá'í' meant. They were both able to speak Spanish, and after a few words of explanation they departed clutching some books and leaflets. A few months later they returned and asked for some teachers to be sent, because the populations of their two villages had become Bahá'ís. That was the beginning, now there are thousands. When one is with them, one wonders what is special about them that one doesn't have oneself. I have found an answer for myself; it is that they are more 'essential'. Their thinking is focused on the essence of things, whereas we – distracted by so many superficial and minor matters – dissipate our energies without getting to the heart of the matter. Let us remember how 'Abdu'l-Bahá, when He called upon the friends in the Western Hemisphere to 'pay the greatest attention to the native population of America', promised that they, with the right leadership and education, would be like the people of Arabia under Muhammad: 'Through the Divine Teachings they will become so enlightened that the whole earth will be illuminated.' Here we are already experiencing the beginning, not only with regard to people's receptivity – which can be clearly expressed in terms of numbers – but also with regard to that more essential consciousness in which they are superior to us. When one is with these people, one does not wish to leave them. Let us recall the words of Hand of the Cause Dr Muhájir after his sojourn in South America recorded in 'News from the World Centre': 'The forty days that I spent in Bolivia were the most beautiful of my life owing to the love and loyalty of the indigenous people ... My only wish is to return to those countries, to serve those people and sacrifice my life for them.'[275]

Finally, I should like to mention an amusing story such as can also happen on that huge continent. Last Riḍván the National Spiritual Assembly of Brazil received the gift of a new community, quite by surprise, since it had known nothing of it before. It happened thus: several years earlier, a believer had left Brazil and gone to a neighbouring country in order to teach the Faith in a remote area. At Riḍván his work bore fruit and he formed a new community for that country. However, more or less while passing through, he had also spread the Faith across the nearby border and found even more attentive listeners and formed at the same time a second Spiritual Assembly. The Brazilian Bahá'í community deserves such a gift, because it is itself doing its utmost, and a visible sign of that is the fact that this year two new communities were established in the far north of Brazil.

I look back with fondness to the believers in South America, to the indigenous people and their American and Persian helpers. They have grasped the significance of this hour, they are not sitting still but are pushing forward, and through their love for the Faith they are convinced that everything is possible. 'Consider how the wind,' Bahá'u'lláh calls to us, 'faithful to that which God hath ordained, bloweth upon all the regions of the earth, be they inhabited or desolate ... So should be every one that claimeth to be a lover of the one true God.' May these lovers of God be permitted to gather an ever richer harvest for the Cause!

'Many seeds were sown at that time which enabled the Faith to flourish in South America in later years,' wrote Anna Grossmann later in an obituary for the Hand of the Cause Hermann Grossmann. 'The impressions of South America, his spiritual affection for the friends, the progress made there – these were all a source of happiness right up to his last days.'

Jameson Bond, a Knight of Bahá'u'lláh and an illustrious Bahá'í, said in an interview in 1968:

> The role of the Germans in South America was very important during this century, but the role of Hermann Grossmann was different from that of the colonial powers, for he returned there as a Hand of the Cause of God. It is probably unnecessary to point out the spiritual truth that through the presence of one of the Chosen Ones ... a new process was set in motion. His decision to return there, following a suggestion made by Shoghi Effendi, was therefore certainly of historical significance. That will only be clearly recognized in the future.[276]

CHAPTER 23

THE MOST GREAT JUBILEE 1963

The year 1962 ended with a conference called by the Hands of the Cause of God in Europe and held in Luxembourg from 7 to 9 December. Among the participants were Amatu'l-Bahá Rúḥíyyih Khánum along with three Hands of the Cause for Europe, Hasan Balyuzi, Dr Giachery and Dr Mühlschlegel, and the Hand of the Cause for the Western Hemisphere, Dr Grossmann – Shoghi Effendi referred to the American continent as the 'Western Hemisphere' in his messages. Also present were fifteen European Auxiliary Board members and members of various National Assemblies. Their consultations focused on ways and means of carrying the Ten Year Crusade to a victorious conclusion. Rúḥíyyih Khánum gave a talk in English about how happy Shoghi Effendi must be regarding the successes achieved so far. After the passing of 'Abdu'l-Bahá, he had taken over responsibility for executing the Divine Plan, despite his own worries, despite his own broken heart over the death of his beloved grandfather, and despite his sense of inadequacy which 'was in the early days much stronger than the Bahá'ís realize', she said. Nevertheless, he had forged ahead and given us the Bahá'í world as we know it. The German and Persian friends were happy that the talk itself was translated into their own languages, but also that the speaker made additional remarks and gave explanations in perfect German and Persian.[277]

That historic occasion in the annals of the Bahá'í Faith, the election of the Universal House of Justice – the climax that was to bring the Ten Year Crusade to its triumphant conclusion – was announced by the representatives of the Hands in the Holy Land in a letter to all the National Spiritual Assemblies dated 16 August 1962:

THE MOST GREAT JUBILEE, 1963

Beloved Friends,

This letter is to inform you that the Annual Gathering of the Hands of the Cause will be held beginning April 9, 1963, preceding the election of the Universal House of Justice.

The wonderful and thrilling victories throughout the Bahá'í world during the past year have made it possible for the Hands of the Faith to postpone their Annual Meeting and to concentrate their efforts on the all-important teaching work so that the 'vast increase' of new believers envisioned by the beloved Guardian for this fourth and final phase of the Crusade may become a reality ...

We urge each National Spiritual Assembly, as well as every individual Bahá'í, to join the Hands of the Cause in every continent in taking advantage of this rising tide, so that every single believer may make a supreme and unprecedented effort to assure that 'vast increase' in new believers envisioned by our beloved Guardian for this fourth phase of his glorious global Crusade ...

We shall pray earnestly at the sacred Threshold of the Blessed Beauty that each individual believer, each Local Assembly, and each National Assembly will arise during these closing hours of a Crusade, the equal of which mortal eyes will never see again, and enrich their record of services with a sacrifice, selflessness, and dedication unmatched by anything they have done in the past, individually or collectively.

With warmest Bahá'í love,
In the service of the beloved Guardian,
Hands of the Cause in the Holy Land.[278]

On 31 October 1962 the Hands in the Holy Land sent a message to all the Bahá'ís in the East and the West. They reminded the believers that there were only six months left until the 'Most Great Jubilee', the 'King of Festivals', the 'Festival of God', the hundredth anniversary of Bahá'u'lláh's Declaration of His mission on the eve of His banishment from Baghdad to Constantinople.

> The celebration of the Most Great Jubilee marks the end of a century – the greatest century this planet has ever seen, or will see, for a period of five hundred thousand years; a century in which the Promised One of all ages ascended the throne of Prophethood and shed the light of His Revelation from the Day of His Declaration upon mankind for twenty-nine years; a century which witnessed the ministry of that unique Being, the Centre of the Covenant, the Mystery of God, the perfect Man, Who served the Cause of His glorious Father for no less than twenty-nine years; a century during which His beloved eldest grandson, Shoghi Effendi, Guardian of the Faith,

laboured to establish that Cause over the face of the entire planet during the thirty-six years of his office ...

So great an occasion calls for celebrations not only on an international scale, through the holding of a World Congress to take place in London during the Riḍván period, but nationally and locally, in every city, hamlet and village where Bahá'ís are to be found throughout the entire world ...

Now irrevocably associated with the termination of our beloved Guardian's Crusade comes another event of singular historic importance – the election of the Universal House of Justice. On the first day of the 'greatest Bahá'í Festival', in the shadow of the Shrine of the Báb, the election will take place of that august Body Shoghi Effendi said would be regarded by posterity as 'the last refuge of a tottering civilization'.[279]

'Any reference to the holding of an international election in the Holy Land should cover the following points,' states a letter from the Hands in the Holy Land to the National and Regional Spiritual Assemblies dated 25 November 1962:

> That the various national Bahá'í communities are voting for the election of the Supreme Administrative Body of the Bahá'í Faith; that the World Centre of the Bahá'ís is situated in Israel because in 1868 the Founder of the Faith, Bahá'u'lláh, at that time a prisoner of the Turks, was exiled to 'Akká and passed away in that country; that as His tomb and that of His Forerunner, the Báb, are places of visitation for the Bahá'ís throughout the world, the World Centre was located in the vicinity of their resting-places; that it is the Spiritual and Administrative Centre of the Bahá'í Faith, and that its world-wide affairs are administered from this Centre.[280]

The National and Regional Spiritual Assemblies gathered on 21 April 1963 in the House of 'Abdu'l-Bahá in Haifa in order to elect the nine members of the Universal House of Justice. Friends who were unable to attend could submit a ballot by mail. The following day, the tellers announced the nine believers who had received the greatest number of votes.[281]

Immediately, the Universal House of Justice began to consult with the Hands of the Cause of God on the practical and legal steps that needed to be taken to firmly establish its functioning in the Holy Land and on 7 June 1963 the Hands of the Cause Residing in the Holy Land were able to inform the Hands throughout the world that, as anticipated in the declaration made on 25 November 1957, the institution of the Custodians had ceased to exist.[282]

Hermann Grossmann took part in the festivities in Haifa and London.

THE MOST GREAT JUBILEE, 1963

In London, over 6,000 Bahá'ís assembled in the Royal Albert Hall for a magnificent celebration. 'The paeans of joy and gratitude, of love and adoration which we now raise to the throne of Bahá'u'lláh would be inadequate, and the celebrations of this Most Great Jubilee in which, as promised by our beloved Guardian, we are now engaged, would be marred were no tribute paid at this time to the Hands of the Cause of God,' wrote the Universal House of Justice in its first message to the Bahá'ís of the world, delivered at that World Congress on 30 April 1963:

> For they share the victory with their beloved commander, he who raised them up and appointed them. They kept the ship on its course and brought it safe to port. The Universal House of Justice, with pride and love, recalls on this supreme occasion its profound admiration for the heroic work which they have accomplished. We do not wish to dwell on the appalling dangers which faced the infant Cause when it was suddenly deprived of our beloved Shoghi Effendi, but rather to acknowledge with all the love and gratitude of our hearts the reality of the sacrifice, the labour, the self-discipline, the superb stewardship of the Hands of the Cause of God. We can think of no more fitting words to express our tribute to these dearly loved and valiant souls than to recall the Words of Bahá'u'lláh Himself: 'Light and glory, greeting and praise be upon the Hands of His Cause, through whom the light of fortitude hath shone forth and the truth hath been established that the authority to choose rests with God, the Powerful, the Mighty, the Unconstrained, through whom the ocean of bounty hath surged and the fragrance of the gracious favours of God, the Lord of mankind, hath been diffused.'[283]

'The words of the Universal House of Justice', writes Ruḥíyyih Khánum, 'are the best tribute to our role in history.'

> To this unique testimony should be added the fact that although the Hands were firmly established as the ruling and guiding body of the entire Bahá'í world, I can bear witness that never for a single instant were the Hands influenced by either ambition or self-esteem. Our sole objective, the purpose of our every effort, was to succeed in electing in 1963 the Universal House of Justice. The Universal House of Justice itself testified that: 'The entire history of religion shows no comparable record of such strict self-discipline, such absolute loyalty, and such complete self-abnegation by the leaders of a religion finding themselves suddenly deprived of their divinely inspired guide. The debt of gratitude which mankind for generations, nay, ages to come, owes to this handful of grief-stricken, steadfast, heroic souls is beyond estimation.'[284]

Having guided the believers safely through the interregnum following the death of the Guardian, the Hands of the Cause were thenceforth able to concentrate all their endeavours on their specific tasks of protecting and propagating the Faith. As they had done during the lifetime of Shoghi Effendi, the Hands of the Cause of God Residing in the Holy Land coordinated the work of the Hands throughout the world, acting as liaison between them and the Head of the Faith. In 1968 the House of Justice brought the institution of the Counsellors into being to extend into the future the Hands' specific functions of protecting and propagating the Faith and, in 1973, it formally established the International Teaching Centre on which all the Hands of the Cause were to be members, with the addition of three Counsellors, to bring to fruition the work of the Hands of the Cause of God Residing in the Holy Land.

CHAPTER 24

FINAL YEARS AND PASSING

In the years 1963 to 1965 Hermann Grossmann travelled around Europe attending conferences, summer schools, teaching conferences and the meetings of the European Hands of the Cause of God.

> After that, however [writes Anna Grossman], his travel plans became more modest and less frequent, and in 1966 he travelled within Germany. The health of this courageous servant of the Almighty had suffered under the privations and changing altitudes he had experienced in South America. He withdrew more and more into his home and his study. In 1965 he wrote *What the Bahá'í Faith Is* and in 1966 *The Bahá'í Believer and the Bahá'í Community*.[285]

Hermann Grossmann's grand-daughter Andrea recalls that time:

> The visits to Grandpa and Grandma in Neckargemünd, sometimes for a weekend or during the school holidays, were something special. I knew that we children, my sisters and cousins, were supposed to be quiet so as not to disturb Grandpa. I often sat down next to him at his table, which seemed huge to me at the time, in the 'White Room'. There Grandpa would work on his archives, and he used to show me photographs and slides taken during his travels through South America and on his visits to the indigenous people. It was all fascinating to me; after all, not everyone had a grandfather who had been born in Argentina, could speak Spanish, flew in aeroplanes and undertook extensive travels in South America to talk to the people there. What was particularly exciting was that Grandpa had met the aboriginal inhabitants, the Indigenas. In his library there were books about the North American Indians, the Aztecs and Mayas. The books contained a lot of photographs but were, unfortunately, written in English. Although I was eager to know what the captions said, I rarely dared ask Grandpa to translate them for me. My most fervent wish – since I had no talent myself in that line – was that Grandpa should draw me pictures. However, by this time that was no longer possible and I only managed to persuade him once to draw me a little pencil picture.

At the end of January, three of the European Hands of the Cause, John Ferraby, Dr Hermann Grossmann and Dr Adelbert Mühlschlegel, along with their seven Auxiliary Board members, met in Brussels at the invitation of the National Spiritual Assembly of Belgium. In October 1967 Hermann Grossmann was only able to participate as an observer for one day at the International Conference in the Jahrhundert-Halle in Frankfurt am Main-Hoechst.

'He became more and more quiet,' writes Anna Grossmann. 'Release from the mortal world was a harmonious process, although not without physical pain. The peace of his soul as it was transported beyond all worldly concerns eased his departure from the visible realm on 7 July 1968.'[286] On 10 July 1968 he was buried in the cemetery in Neckargemünd.

Over the course of many years, Hermann Grossmann had subjected his often sick and weakly body to great feats of exertion in the service of Bahá'u'lláh. Undoubtedly, the inhuman strain imposed by the First World War had also taken its toll – as was the case with so many who had been in the war. The worst effects were probably those caused by the inhalation of poison gas, which he once suffered in the trenches. All this caused long-term general ill-health and the gradual loss of his physical powers during his final years.

The 'yellow house' in Neckargemünd, which was always open to visitors, had been the place to which he had returned from all his many journeys and in whose peaceful setting he found calm amongst his loved ones. He had spent many fruitful years in this house. Now it was bereft of its focal point. After the funeral, which was attended by so many friends, acquaintances and neighbours, it once again brought together those who had been close to him and meant so much to him.

His friends and wayfarers in the Cause of Bahá'u'lláh, Dr Adelbert Mühlschlegel and Dr Eugen Schmidt, delivered the commemorative addresses in the cemetery chapel, which was decorated with an abundance of flowers and was filled to capacity.

Dr Schmidt began his address with some Words of Bahá'u'lláh and then turned to the deceased:

> Dear Hermann, You were always fully confident in this joyful promise, even as a young man when, in seeking after truth, you opened your heart to the Bahá'í Faith in Leipzig almost 50 years ago.
>
> The death of someone so dear to us and to whom we were personally so close – whether as husband, father, grandfather, brother, or as friend

and comrade working together over many decades to transform and unify the human race – causes us deep grief, but may sorrow at his earthly loss become transfigured in the light of creative impulses in our lives. The spiritual bridge to our friend is rooted in our hearts and is an eternal bond between us. We have yet to complete the task entrusted to us on this earth that is at present so full of menacing darkness. At an hour such as this, we are clearly reminded that the time we have to shape and develop our lives is limited ...

The life of our revered friend and brother over more than 69 years was truly one of fulfilment! He displayed great devotion, loyalty, kindness, faithfulness and love in his dedication to his special and honourable task of promulgating the Faith of Bahá'u'lláh throughout the world. He bore in his heart a deeply felt love for mankind as a whole in the light of God's call for unity among all the races, peoples, nations and continents of what has become a small world.

Hermann Grossmann was a strong pillar of the German Bahá'í community, never losing sight of the ultimate goal and always remaining confident throughout all the trials endured by our people, his certainty never shaken that God doeth as He willeth.

After the Second World War, in 1951, he was called upon by Shoghi Effendi, the Guardian of the Bahá'í Faith, to dedicate his knowledge, experience and skills, his sacrifice and devotion, to the promulgation of the message of Bahá'u'lláh throughout the world as a Hand of the Cause of God. The source of his unshakeable faith was always the New Covenant of God as the focal point of unity among the believers ...

Anyone who, following the outstanding example of Hermann Grossmann, permits the light of the joyful divine message of healing and salvation revealed by Bahá'u'lláh to penetrate his heart, will take this occasion of saying goodbye to a companion, friend and spiritual brother as an opportunity to serve his fellow man and work more courageously and confidently than ever for reconciliation and peace in this torn and shattered world, as our friend would have wished, in commemoration of him and out of sincere love for him.

Dear, revered Hermann, we therefore pledge – in your spirit and out of love for you – to carry out our work in the vineyard of God with even greater decisiveness than ever before.[287]

In his address, Hand of the Cause of God Dr Mühlschlegel said:

Our dear respected friend, who has gone on ahead of us to the eternal world, was entrusted with world-wide tasks on behalf of the Bahá'í Faith. He wrote important books and undertook numerous journeys both far and near, including several visits to his native land, South America, in order to promulgate the Faith. He was a loving friend to many people, and his advice was highly valued. During the years of persecution in Germany, he professed our Faith with courage and steadfastness. He was wholeheartedly devoted to the World Centre of the Bahá'í Faith, especially to the Guardian, Shoghi Effendi. He was one of the first people to be raised by the Guardian to the rank of a Hand of the Cause of God. In these days, loving prayers are being offered at the Holy Shrines to accompany his soul on its journey. His name and his services will shine out from the annals of the Bahá'í Faith far into the future.

Dear Hermann, beloved friend and comrade for almost half a century, our paths were brought together even before we knew each other, when, in completely different locations, we both declared our belief in Bahá'u'lláh in the same month and shortly afterwards each received an important letter from the Master. Then we embraced for the first time. Since then we have often worried together, made plans together, exchanged ideas, and sometimes been in Haifa together. Long is the blessed path that we are privileged to be able to look back upon together – you now from the eternal realm, released from the confines of the mortal frame, raised above earthly veils. Our Faith tells us that we will meet again, that we will be permitted to continue serving the Light together.

And yet, even though this time apart is so short compared with eternity, it is nevertheless not without a secret sense of longing. How short-lived everything is here on this earth! Our soul must pass through the realm of time in order to grow towards maturity in the eternal realm.

The soul that to its Father strives,
Lord of the world and all Creation,
When it in service of goodness lives,
Begins to see through old illusion.
For 'tis only to him who keenly seeks the light
That the heavenward path opens before the sight.
Man, if the real he desires to find,
Must needs leave many things behind.

And so with the guidance of a loving hand
He grows in awareness of the trivial and the great.
Then, ever more freed from the dust and sand,
He sees the eternal Source that fleeting things creates.
And as his view in purity doth expand
His being, too, grows pure and immaculate
And rises up with wings of love
To the exalted eternal Heaven above.

Die Seele, die zu ihrem Vater strebt,
dem Herrn und Schöpfer aller, die hier wohnen,

Anna and Hermann Grossmann

Elsa Maria and Hermann Grossmann, October 1967

*Hermann Grossmann at the door of his
house in Neckargemünd,
near Heidelberg, late summer 1967*

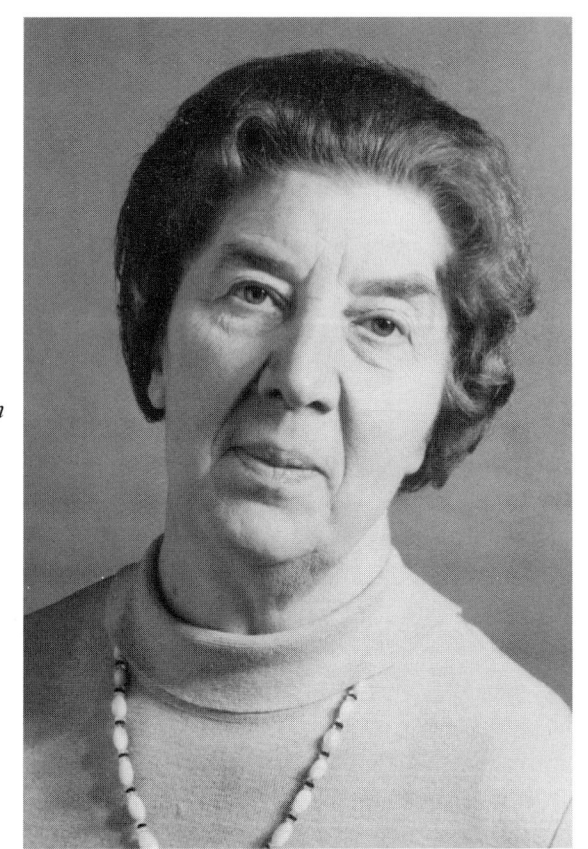

Anna Grossmann

The funeral of Dr Hermann Grossmann, Neckargemüund, 10 July 1968

The gravestone of Dr Hermann Grossmann

The gravestone of Anna Grossmann, Savonlinna, Finland

erkennt, wenn sie dem Guten lebt,
so manche eigene, alte Illusionen.
Denn dem nur, der sich klar zum Licht erhebt,
erschließt die Bahn sich zu den höheren Zonen.
Da muss, um sich zum Echten durchzuringen,
der Mensch noch Abschied sagen vielen Dingen.

Und so von liebevoller Hand geleitet,
wird ihm bewusst, was nichtig und was groß,
und immer herrlicher des Staubs entkleidet,
schaut er der flüchtigen Dinge ewigen Schoß.
Und wie sein Blick sich in der Reinheit weitet,
wird auch sein Wesen rein und makellos
und steigt, beflügelt mit der Liebe Schwingen,
zu ewigen erhabenen Himmelsringen.[288]

In his report on the funeral, René Steiner wrote:

> A large gathering of over one hundred friends took leave of Dr Hermann Grossmann on 10 July 1968 up on the sunlit slopes of the cemetery of Neckargemünd facing the beautiful and peaceful Neckar valley. It was a day of concealed power, of mysterious greatness, not a day of sadness, no, more a day of fulfilment, a day of serious joy strengthened by a firm and deep Faith into [sic] the immortality of the human soul. It was a day of peace and of love, a day of mutual attraction and compassion beyond the reach of words. All of us experienced the pain of personal loss, yet also the joy and the Mercy of new detachment and freedom, of a high and imperishable station now eternally safe. As the children, his loved ones and his closest friends, one by one placed their gift of flowers into the open earth where he was laid to rest, it was an act of symbolic beauty, graciousness and love, a gesture of certitude, of deepest reverence and also thanks. Not long before, in the small chapel below on the hill, music had surrounded the prayers read by friends and words of departure spoken by the Hand of the Cause Dr Adelbert Mühlschlegel and Auxiliary Board member Dr Eugen Schmidt. Flowers in abundance were there reflecting in many a tear.
>
> Now up on the slope the soul seemed free from all suffering and it was as if the heart of him would beat once more whose entire life was dedicated to the establishment of the Faith of God in the heart of Europe, in Latin America and in the whole of mankind. He truly was the establisher of the Faith in these lands, a great educator, a scholar and a true brother. As we looked upon the roses, the snow-white lilies in their prayer-like beauty, upon the crimson-red of the carnations and the last gifts of the Bahá'í institutions, including that of the Universal House of Justice, we realized that our beloved Hand of the Cause was now freed to exercise his influence

as never before and in a way more powerful than all the perishable things of this world.

After a feast of love given by the Grossmann family in their home, we returned once more to the grave and found it covered with flowers of exquisite beauty. How strongly these hours now reminded us of another day in November 1957 on [sic] Great Northern Cemetery when the beloved Guardian was laid to rest and the consciousness of the believers was stirred to greater unity and love.[289]

On 9 July the Universal House of Justice sent a cable to all National Spiritual Assemblies:

DEEPLY REGRET ANNOUNCE PASSING HAND CAUSE HERMANN GROSSMANN GREATLY ADMIRED BELOVED GUARDIAN. HIS GRIEVOUS LOSS DEPRIVES COMPANY HANDS CAUSE OUTSTANDING COLLABORATOR AND BAHÁ'Í WORLD COMMUNITY STAUNCH DEFENDER PROMOTER FAITH. HIS COURAGEOUS LOYALTY DURING CHALLENGING YEARS TESTS PERSECUTIONS GERMANY OUTSTANDING SERVICES SOUTH AMERICA IMMORTALIZED ANNALS FAITH. INVITE ALL NATIONAL SPIRITUAL ASSEMBLIES HOLD MEMORIAL GATHERINGS BEFITTING HIS EXALTED RANK EXEMPLARY SERVICES. REQUEST THOSE RESPONSIBLE MOTHER TEMPLES ARRANGE SERVICES AUDITORIUM.[290]

The Hands of the Cause of God sent the following message of condolence to Anna Grossmann:

GRIEVED NEWS PASSING MUCH BELOVED CO-WORKER DEAR HERMANN; HANDS CONVEY DEEPEST LOVING SYMPATHY ENTIRE FAMILY HIS INDEFATIGABLE OUTSTANDING SERVICES CAUSE EUROPE SOUTH AMERICA HIS STEADFASTNESS FACE GREAT TRIALS CONSTITUTE INSPIRING EXAMPLE PRESENT FUTURE GENERATION BELIEVERS ASSURE FERVENT PRAYERS SHRINES HANDSFAITH.[291]

The Hand of the Cause of God Amatu'l-Bahá Rúḥíyyih Khánum sent a cable with the following words:

DEEPEST SYMPATHY YOU CHILDREN PASSING DEAR HERMANN LONG-STANDING DEVOTED SERVANT FAITH MUCH PRIZED LOVED BY BELOVED GUARDIAN ELEVATED BY HIM RANKS FIRST CONTINGENT HANDS THROUGHOUT WORLD FEEL SURE HIS SOUL REJOICES FREEDOM MORTAL REALM REWARDS RECEIVED ON HIGH, LOVINGLY RÚḤÍYYIH.[292]

A further telegram was received from the Universal House of Justice:

EXTEND LOVING SYMPATHY YOURSELF FAMILY GRIEVOUS LOSS PASSING DEAR HERMANN UNIVERSAL HOUSE OF JUSTICE.[293]

Many Hands of the Cause of God also expressed their personal sympathy: Enoch Olinga, Músá Banání, Collis Featherstone, Dr 'Alí Muḥammad Varqá, Jalál Kházeh, Shu'á'u'lláh 'Alá'i and Dr Ugo Giachery.

The Hand of the Cause of God Zikrullah Khadem sent this cable to Anna Grossmann:

> WITH HEAVY HEART EXPRESS HUMBLE SYMPATHY PASSING DEARLY LOVED CO-WORKER HANDCAUSE HERMANN GROSSMANN ABUNDANT REWARDS STORE FOR HIM BY BLESSED BEAUTY FOR HIS OUTSTANDING HISTORIC SERVICES WHAT A LOSS TO ALL OF US AND JOY TO HIM BEING IN PRESENCE BELOVED ALL HEARTS SHOGHI EFFENDI MAY BAHÁ'U'LLÁH GIVE YOU AND US PATIENCE DEEPEST LOVE KHADEMS.[294]

The Hand of the Cause of God William Sears recalled the difficult days that followed the death of the Guardian, when the Hands of the Cause worked together to ward off the dangers that threatened the Bahá'í community and the life-long and world-wide services Hermann Grossmann had performed, securing him a special place in the hearts of the Bahá'ís and the Hands and also earning him a place in the history of the Faith.[295]

The Hand of the Cause of God John Robarts assured Anna Grossmann of his loving thoughts and continued:

> How greatly dear Hermann was loved! We missed him especially at our recent conclave. His contributions to our consultations have always been wise and loving ... He was a precious friend. Thank God we know something of the great reward he has now entered upon, and which he has richly deserved.[296]

The Hand of the Cause of God John Ferraby recalled the long period during which Hermann Grossmann had served the Faith of Bahá'u'lláh in Germany and the whole of Europe, making it 'difficult to think of the Cause of God ... without him'. He assured Anna Grossmann that her husband's services in preserving the Faith during the days of oppression would never be forgotten, neither would his contributions to Bahá'í literature in German. 'We shall all miss him greatly, but we rest assured that he is able to help the work of the Cause of God on earth more effectively now than ever before ...'[297]

Ian Semple, a member of the Universal House of Justice at the time, also conveyed his condolences, looking back over many years of close association with Hermann Grossmann:

We all knew how seriously ill he was, but my own Bahá'í life has been so closely linked with yours and Hermann's, and so greatly influenced at initial moments by his wise and loving counsel that I feel his loss profoundly.

The beloved Guardian said that Mr Banání's mere presence in Africa was a fountainhead of spiritual strength for that continent, and I am sure the same was true of Hermann in Europe. Even in the days when he was no longer able to be physically active his presence has been a benison for Germany and the entire continent. Now, released from the confines of this material world his mighty spirit will no doubt reinforce a hundred-fold the labours of his fellow believers.[298]

The National Spiritual Assemblies of Germany, Finland, the United States of America, Iran and the British Isles also wrote to Anna Grossmann. The British friends recalled his many visits to their country to participate in summer schools and to meet communities and isolated pioneers there. They mentioned his love and understanding, his encouragement and the steadfastness and courage he inspired in the pioneers. 'Everyone who went to the first summer school held at Mourne Grange in Northern Ireland has vivid memories of the happiness we shared through his presence there.'[299]

In *Noticias Baha'is del Ecuador* an affectionate obituary appeared under the heading, 'Dr Grossmann as I knew him', in which a believer recalled Hermann Grossmann's first visit to Guayaquil:

It was near the end of May 1959 and all of us were eagerly awaiting his arrival. None other than one of the Hands of the Cause of God was soon to come to our town ... He arrived on 3 June, and between fires and gunshots the city was experiencing an atmosphere of [political] unrest, and it had not been possible to hold our reception of welcome in the home of dear Godsea Ashraf [a pioneer in Ecuador]. Other than the hostess, Enrique Serrano and I accompanied the Hand [of the Cause]. That night and through his very short stay we were able to ask questions and receive wise instruction from someone who knew a great deal about life and about the history of mankind. He really knew so much and nervertheless evinced such a spirit of humility, never being arrogant on account of his knowledge. He was truly a blessed soul.

When the hour of his departure came I, who had offered to go to his lodging to accompany him to the airport, overslept. I awoke alarmed at the lateness of the hour, and had to take a taxi directly to the airfield. There I found him sitting with Godsea. She looked at me with reproach due to my failing. (A Bahá'í should not offer that which he cannot fulfil.) When called by my brother, I approached fearfully and said: 'I ask your forgiveness,

Doctor, for not having come on time.' 'You need not apologize,' he replied, 'Come here to my side. I am like you; I am your brother.' I felt very timid before a Hand of the Cause of God, nevertheless I went to him, and he lovingly embraced me. I understood then that true greatness lies in humility. This was Dr Grossmann as I knew him, and since his passing on to the Most Holy Threshold, I shall long for him until my own departure [from this world].

This contribution is followed by a further eulogy:

> The radiant spirit of this precious servant of Bahá'u'lláh, like that of others who have ascended to the exalted and eternal Abhá Kingdom, will continue to illuminate our path, just as they did during their sojourn in this world – united and fused together like one soul in many bodies – as a true example of the Teachings in Bahá'í life.[300]

The Bahá'ís of Bolivia called Hermann Grossmann an outstanding defender of the world-wide Bahá'í community, whose extraordinary services in South America would immortalize him in the annals of the Faith.

'Hermann Grossmann was the most fascinating figure of the German Bahá'í community from its inception.' These were the words in which Bozorg Hemmati expressed his admiration for Dr Grossmann.

> He combined an immensely deep faith with a radiantly warm heart and a brilliant intellect in a unique way. He will remain an exemplary believer for generations. Our dear Master wrote to him on 9 December 1920: 'Thy letter ... indicated that thou hast turned thy face toward the Abhá Kingdom.' Now he has himself ascended to that Abhá Kingdom and, together with other Chosen ones, he has appeared before the Great Master, after having been a source of joy, warmth and love for many people, both Bahá'ís and non-Bahá'ís, throughout his long life ... Dear Annel, I cannot help saying that I still now feel his loving warmth and kindness so strongly that this painful loss seems incredible. As in every close marriage, you helped shape that great life and have brought blessing and happiness to many souls through the message of Bahá'u'lláh. Regardless of whether they accepted the message or not, the people were so fascinated by his warmth and his manner that they were full of admiration for him ... In the Abhá Kingdom, Hermann will be a loving advocate.
> With deep affection, Yours, Bozorg.[301]

Ben Schreibman, who had lived in Germany for some time, sent condolences to the Grossmann family from Luxembourg:

It seems that the precious soul of Dr Grossmann was needed in a greater realm. A place and condition where the service for Bahá'u'lláh will be of greater value and effect. As a 'Hand of the Cause' – it is a permanent title and honour for eternity. His passing will result in a greater number of new believers in Germany and other countries.[302]

The Knight of Bahá'u'lláh Brigitte Lundblade wrote the following to Anna Grossmann:

> When Dr Grossmann visited the Shetland Islands, he restored my wavering faith and showed me such human understanding as I had not experienced since childhood. I am sure that Dr Grossmann came to bring me a message on behalf of our Guardian. Through the years, the wise, loving words of Dr Grossmann have been my companion, have uplifted me and given me strength; his overwhelming love for the suffering souls of his fellow human beings can surely inspire all of us to promulgate the teachings that he so perfectly exemplified.[303]

At the end of 1966, Lise Lotte Walcker, a Bahá'í from Rostock in the GDR (East Germany), had had the opportunity to visit West Germany. In her condolences to Anna Grossmann she mentioned the days she had spent in Neckargemünd and Hermann Grossmann's already delicate state of health at that time.

> I can imagine that death was a release for him and that much patience and sacrifice was demanded of you. His spirit is now freed from the burden of the mortal frame and with His grace it may ascend to the highest heights. What a gift, what a blessing, that we know of His great Plan for mankind. May He be merciful to Hermann and to all of us and grant you and your family the certitude that surpasses all separation. I sincerely hope that this period of suffering will be transformed into blessings for all the family.[304]

'Dearest Anna, My heart is with you dearest friend,' wrote the pioneer to the Republic of Congo, Ola Pawlowska, in response to the news of the death of Hermann Grossmann.

> I thank God that we Bahá'ís have a different attitude toward death, in the case of Dr Grossmann, our dear Hand of the Cause, I am happy that he is released from the bonds of this world and his spirit can soar into the limitless space – the domain of the worlds of God and His presence. I believe that the last years of his life were very difficult both for him and for you especially, so this is a release. We shall all always cherish his memory

and be thankful for what he gave us when he was among us. The last time I saw Dr Grossmann, I think, in '65 at Langenhain. We had lunch together and he was not his old self, I believe he deteriorated since. I did not learn of his passing soon, as news does not travel here quickly ...[305]

In 1995 Katharine Meyer, a devoted pioneer, recorded her memories of Dr Grossmann's travels in South America:

> The tremendous travel schedule that Dr and Mrs Grossmann had set for themselves during the last years of the Ten Year Crusade took a heavy toll on the condition of their health. They arrived in Neckargemünd worn out, really exhausted and were still under medical treatment when both of them wrote to me in January 1963 ... This dedicated servant of God, Dr Hermann Grossmann, was indeed a great soul, a constant worker, respected by all for his profound learning, his wisdom and his firm belief, and his ever showing a gentle and true kindliness.[306]

Martin Aiff wrote to Anna Grossmann:

> We heard about the passing ... of our spiritual father. Despite knowing better, my heart was initially filled with pain ... [but] why shouldn't Hermann go on being our spiritual father, perhaps more intensively than ever since he is now free of earthly limitations.[307]

On Hermann Grossmann's gravestone in the cemetery at Neckargemünd are inscribed the words of Bahá'u'lláh that marked the start of his life's journey as a Bahá'í and that subsequently accompanied him throughout his life: 'Ye are all the leaves of one tree ...

* * *

After the death of her husband, Anna Grossmann was again tirelessly active on behalf of the Cause and served for many years as an Auxiliary Board member for the protection of the Faith. She was able to spend her final years in Savonlinna in Finland, at the home of her son Hartmut Grossmann and her daughter-in-law Ursula, thus serving the young community there as a pioneer. On 12 June 1984 she passed away peacefully and, in accordance with her wishes to be buried in foreign soil, she was laid to rest in the cemetery in Savonlinna, her funeral being attended by her family and many friends. The Universal House of Justice cabled the National Spiritual Assembly of Germany on 14 June 1984 as follows:

Grieved learn passing Anna Grossmann outstanding promoter Faith recall with profound emotion her loving angelic character her stalwart upholding Faith at side her illustrious husband during darkest years Cause Germany, her inspiring services teaching field including extensive travels South America, her tireless labours as member and secretary National Spiritual Assembly and as member Auxiliary Board Finland blessed by her pioneering that land evening her earthly life convey members bereaved family heartfelt sympathy assurance prayers Holy Shrines progress her radiant soul Abhá Kingdom we urge hold befitting memorial meeting Mashriqu'l-Adhkár.

Her gravestone is inscribed with the words of Bahá'u'lláh, *'Niin voimallinen on ykseyden valo, että se voi valaista kaiken maan'* – 'So powerful is the light of unity that it can illuminate the whole earth.'[308]

APPENDIX I

RELIGION AND SCIENCE

A talk by Hermann Grossmann held at Frankfurt am Main in December 1957

Dear friends, an old story relates how a group of people wished to build a tower, a tower that would soar up to the heavens and allow them to communicate with God whenever they wished. What motivated them to build the tower was not their desire to be close to God, but rather their arrogance. For they wished the tower to be a monument, so that their work might be honoured by future generations. And the story goes on to say that after they had made some progress in constructing the tower their languages became confused, so that they could not understand one another and it became impossible to finish the tower. This story has some historical basis. We know that it refers to the time when the Babylonian religion was developing, the period when stepped towers were being constructed, and when superstition was arising. And whenever we find a superstition somewhere and investigate when this superstition first appeared, we can be fairly confident that it existed in Babylon at that time. They were superstitions that, in the form of oracles, augury and other customs, contributed to people's subjugation. It was not free people who built the tower, nor was it in freedom that they had sought a path to God; it was a path not to liberty, but to servitude. The people made themselves dependent on all sorts of things that were not from God.

The 19th century was likewise a time when people believed they could build a tower. They no longer spoke of a tower to help them reach God; rather, this was to be a tower that would help them penetrate the ultimate truth – the tower of Science.

Today we have come to a point where science has itself recognized that it is incapable of reaching the ultimate end using that approach. For science was the science of materialism. Whether that was the fault of scientists or the failure of the guardians of religion is irrelevant here. The fact is evident and we know that this type of science has reached the limits of its knowledge and capabilities, so that the way out is no longer seen as drawing up an image of that which is under investigation, but as relying instead on mathematical models. What is mathematics? If we have an image in mind, we can – perhaps – attain our goal mathematically on the basis of that image. Whether we get our sums right or make some kind of mistake in the calculations is something that we can only assess on the basis of our image, through the result that gives rise to another image or is connected with an image. But if we try to do without the image and understand things – the ultimate wisdom of nature, the ultimate connections – through mathematics alone, this means that we renounce all further research. For working with mathematics without reference to any image opens wide the doors of potential error, since there is nothing else there through which to control it, at least from the point of view of materialism, so that this science ultimately leads to superstition, too.

There are scientists who have drawn consequences from this, men such as Max Planck who have said they can no longer stand apart from religion but must find a bridge between science and religion.

During a discussion with scientists who proudly called themselves materialists, I once heard a chemist say, after three hours of discussion: 'But there is no bridge. It is proven that there is no bridge leading from science, from materialism, to God. And here comes Bahá'u'lláh and says that religion and science should not be in conflict with each other. Where is the bridge, then? Please show me the bridge that science has proved does not exist!'

I replied: 'You are right. I cannot show you this bridge, for you yourself are the bridge.' Bahá'u'lláh speaks of the two wings. 'Abdu'l-Bahá often takes up this image, explaining that we cannot fly with only one wing – not with just the wing of science because we would end up in the quagmire of materialism, and not with just the wing of religion because we would sink in the slough of superstition.

Between the two wings with which I must fly, is me. Hence, the need to seek truth independently. I must seek, only I myself. No one else can seek for me. No one else can teach me how to use these two wings in such a way that I can really soar. I have to try it out for myself, I must experience it, like a little child learning to walk. I cannot prevent the child from bumping its head or falling down. It has to experience things for itself, and in gaining experience it gradually learns to walk properly and to stand safely on the ground.

The Tower of Babel was a tower built out of arrogance. The Tower of Science was also a tower built out of arrogance, an arrogance that believed it had finally created a foundation on which to build and that it had constructed something that would last for eternity and suffice for all time. And this spirit of science is also found in the field of human society: we thought we had established a system of government that would endure forever. Before 1912, no one in Germany would in their wildest dreams have imagined that what we called Germany, the state system known as 'Germany', might ever fall apart, to take just one example. And it was not just Germany that fell apart. Practically the whole world order was brought into disarray.

We cannot interfere with God's purpose. We cannot find our path to God, which is the path to our purpose, a path to the destination determined for us by our Creator, if we tread that path in a spirit of self-consciousness, separating ourselves from the whole. And it is because people's consciousness of self had caused them to become separated from one another, because each individual exalted his own language, speaking only his own tongue, that the Babylonians ended up in a state of confusion, unable to understand one another.

Modern physics has reached the stage where every physicist has his own signs, his own formulae. And if a formula is now found, or a new name decided upon, one must first read an explanation of what is meant by it. There is not even agreement on these matters, let alone in politics, in life in human society or the state. Bahá'u'lláh teaches the principle of unity in diversity. Bahá'u'lláh raises individuality to an unprecedented height. He infuses us with respect for every single individual, such great respect that we may sum it up in Bahá'u'lláh's command: 'Enter not the house of thy friend without his permission.' We must not invade a person's personal sphere. Bahá'u'lláh forbids the confession of sins before human beings. We must not even reach the point where a person discloses his most intimate thoughts and feelings. Instead, we must sense beforehand what he wishes to say and give him the answer before he has exposed his innermost self, so that afterwards he need not feel ashamed or humiliated. It is indeed the highest level of respect for individuality, for the singular qualities of a person that Bahá'u'lláh shows us here, but it is an individuality that completely loses its purpose if it is merely individuality.

And that is the concept of unity in diversity: the individual, the individual organs, the individual cells, everything can only exist because it is not just an individual organ or individual cell in itself but is somehow integrated into a whole, and because when working together in this whole it is able to make use of the energies of all the other parts in an infinite process of mutual exchange. But the concept of unity in diversity, this mutual exchange between the whole and the individual parts, this relationship of dependence – and let us say this relationship of mutual dependence – is not limited just to our little human sphere. Bahá'u'lláh shows us how this is a principle pervading the whole of creation, so that everything is balanced, and balanced in such a way that if we were to cut out or remove only one element, the whole could no longer function. We do not realize how dependent we are, if the sun were to stop shining for just a short while, all living things would die. If the sun were to stand still for just a short while, the law of gravity would be upset and the result would be unimaginable destruction. If even for a moment the plants were to stop producing oxygen, or humans and animals were to stop exhaling carbon dioxide, the relations between the different realms of life would be thrown into turmoil.

And now we can recognize – and we recognize it initially through the achievements of science – that what has brought it to the end, to the edge of the abyss of what was known as progress – namely that matter, the fundamental concern of science and physics – matter, with its mechanistic laws – that this matter is not matter at all, but energy. We know today that matter can be completely transformed into energy and energy can be completely transformed into matter.

Thus, there is no longer any limit to dependence, for then we must admit that the world of the spirit – in which we humans share – and the world of matter are inseparable. Hence, we know that materialism is no longer valid. On the other hand, however, we know that we are placed in this life in a form of spirit, energy, the expression of which is registered by us humans as matter, and that this form of expression also satisfies certain laws. And so we know that we must also pay tribute to this form of spirit.

Hence we are in a world whose origin is one, but which appears to us – in the way we perceive it – to be dual in nature.

And now religion demands of us that we be detached. What is detachment? Bahá'u'lláh does not demand that we renounce the world, on the contrary. He says it is pointless to do so, and we should not renounce it. We have tasks to perform in the world. How can this fit together? Well, if we recognize what the essence of that form of spirit is, that form of energy that we call matter, and if we recognize that it is that form of spirit that is expressed in composition and decomposition – i.e. that it is only something temporary, something that is not eternal – and if we allow that to penetrate our consciousness, then we can become detached. For then we will attach to matter the importance it deserves; that of a fleeting shadow, a fleeting image.

However, Bahá'u'lláh says that if we know it is only a fleeting image, we can enjoy it. For there are many things that we do not enjoy because we live in fear of losing them. But if we know that it is something that we cannot hold on to anyway, even if it lasts a number of years or perhaps even a few generations, then what does it matter in relation to eternity?

Thus, we become a being that at last succeeds in attaining unity. Religion and science, these two wings that we must learn to use equally and in the correct way; these two wings are not really so different. But the difference is that the language of the science wing is oriented towards the fleeting phenomena, and we draw from these fleeting phenomena conclusions about the essence of that which appears through those fleeting phenomena.

The eternal essence does not fit into this category, it relates to that which is beyond the realm of composition and decomposition and is independent of space and time. It is the eternal territory of religion.

I mentioned before two images – those of two towers striving to attain the ultimate wisdom, towers built by human beings.

We can never attain to God, we would never be able to find a path to God, if God did not Himself grant us the opportunity to do so. And He has arranged things in such a way that an infinite abundance of mercy is available, an infinite abundance of opportunities waiting to help us human beings along this path to God – that is, on the path to that which God has chosen for our own best, which we only need to be ready to accept in order to acquire it. 'Love Me that I may love thee. If thou lovest Me not, My love can in no wise reach thee,' says Bahá'u'lláh. He does not give a reason, He simply tells us the causal relationship. It is not an explanation as to why, but a declaration as to how. And in the face of the ultimate questions, the ultimate things, the question 'why' becomes irrelevant; we can only establish 'how'. And only too often we forget when asking 'why' to recognize the 'how'; we fail to see the correlation. 'Love Me' – we must open our hearts, we must permit ourselves to be attracted.

We then realize how everything that flows to us – that must flow to us – really does flow to us. For our life is not a life that exists through our own effort, it is a life that desires to live as determined by the Will of the Creator; namely, as a fully developed individual, a fully developed personality that is not a personality for its own sake but has its role as part of the whole. Thus, our consciousness will eventually be more and more integrated into the whole.

If I realize that I only have the greatest opportunity for myself if I integrate myself into the whole, why should I not go that little bit further and direct all my thoughts and deeds towards service to the whole. Then life will be better for me, too.

Then there is no longer any such thing as altruism or egotism. That distinction vanishes when it is considered in this way. It is simply a life, a life that is meaningful in itself, a life as foreseen in the Plan of Creation. We cannot create the path towards it by our own efforts.

Were it not for the Mediators sent out of God's mercy, as part of that Plan and that provision of divine assistance, coming again and again with their mirrors to show us humans how we should be, both as individuals and as a species, how we should shape our lives – without them we would be unable to connect with the Divine. For all our science and all our deep thoughts, we would be unable to find out the meaning of life and to recognize our tasks in this our earthly life.

And this is perhaps the most profound aspect of what we call religion: that we bow to an authority and permit ourselves to be instructed by this authority, an authority that for the first time in religious history has been explained by Bahá'u'lláh; or rather, let us say that Bahá'u'lláh has given us an image that can be grasped not only by the heart, but also by the intellect. And since we are able to grasp this image intellectually and to take a rational approach, we are able to utilize both these wonderful fields – that of science and that of religion.

Is it not a wonderful thing that for the first time in history we are able not just to believe in religion but to think it, too; and that faith and rationality are not contradictory, that – on the contrary – our faith is strengthened by rational thought, and our thoughts become infinitely fruitful on the basis of our faith. The path to God is not as difficult as we humans have previously thought. But we must first learn to become simple, so simple that we can also understand complicated ideas.

APPENDIX 2

LIST OF PUBLISHED BOOKS, BOOKLETS AND ARTICLES BY HERMANN GROSSMANN: A SELECTION

Die soziale Frage und ihre Lösung im Sinne der Bahá'í-Lehre (The Social Question and its Solution According to the Spirit of the Bahá'í Teachings). Stuttgart: Verlag des Deutschen Bahá'í-Bundes, 1923.

Bahá'í-Erziehung (Bahá'í Education). Wandsbek: Weltgemeinschaft Deutscher Zweig, 1924.

Die Bahá'í-Bewegung, ihre Geschichte, Lehren und Bedeutung (The Bahá'í Movement, its History, Teachings and Significance). Hamburg: Bahá'í-Bewegung, 1926.

Am Morgen einer neuen Zeit: Zusammenbruch oder Neugestaltung, eine kulturelle Diagnose der Gegenwartsnöte (At the Dawn of a New Age: Breakdown or Reorganization? A Cultural Diagnosis of Present-day Exigencies). Stuttgart, Strecker und Schröder Verlag, 1932.

Am Morgen einer neuen Zeit: Zusammenbruch und Neugestaltung, ein Beitrag zur kulturellen Diagnose der Gegenwart. 2nd edition. Stuttgart: August Schröder Verlag, 1948.

Umbruch zur Einheit: Gott Mensch und Welt an der Schwelle einer neuen Ordnung (Breakthrough to Unity: God, Man and World on the Threshold of a New Order). Stuttgart: August Schröder Verlag, 1947.

Was ist die Bahá'í-Religion (What the Bahá'í Faith Is). Frankfurt am Main: Bahá'í-Verlag, 1962, several editions; new title *Was lehrt die Bahá'í-Religion: eine Einführung* (What the Bahá'í Faith Teaches: An Introduction). Hofheim-Langenhain: Bahá'í-Verlag, 1985

Der Bahá'í-Gläubige und die Bahá'í-Gemeinschaft (The Bahá'í Teachings and the Bahá'í Community). Frankfurt am Main: Bahá'í-Verlag, 1966; 2nd edition under the title *Der Bahá'í und die Bahá'í-Gemeinschaft*, a compilation. Oberkalbach: Bahá'í-Verlag, 1973; 3rd edition under the title *Der Bahá'í und die Bahá'í-Gemeinde*. Hofheim: Bahá'í-Verlag, 1994.

Das Bündnis Gottes in der Offenbarungsreligion (God's Covenant in Revealed Religion). Several editions. Hofheim-Langenhain, Bahá'í-Verlag,1981.

HERMANN GROSSMANN

Nähere Erläuterungen zum Buch der Gewissheit, Kitáb-i-Iqán in Bahá'u'lláh, Das Buch der Gewissheit Kitáb-i-Iqán, Frankfurt am Main, Bahá'í-Verlag, 1969, pp 171-195 (Introduction to Kitáb-i-Iqán of Bahá'u'lláh)

Bahá'í Text Compilation (mimeographed; 1945 and later):*A New Day, Knowledge, Man in the Image of God, Community Spirit, Foundation of Civilization, Divine World Order, Being a Bahá'í, The Ma<u>sh</u>riqu'l-A<u>dh</u>kár, Muhammad*

SOME UNPUBLISHED MANUSCRIPTS, ARCHIVES OF DR HERMANN GROSSMANN, HOFHEIM

Religion and Science

Religion as the Constantly Moving Expression of the Divine, The Changeable and the Eternal

Religious History Under the Covenant of God

Independent and Dependent Prophets

Time Periods in Religious History

The True Spirit of Religious History

The Historiography of the Holy Books is not an End in itself

Symbolic Forms of Expression

Overview of Time Periods

From Adam to Joseph, The Mosaic Religious Cycle

History of the Bahá'í Religion in Germany

Zur Geschichte der Bahá'í-Religion 1935 bis 1945 (History of the Bahá'í Faith 1935 to 1945)

TRANSLATIONS

Bahá'u'lláh, Die sieben Täler (The Seven Valleys), Stuttgart, 1950.
— *Verborgene Worte und Worte der Weisheit* (Hidden Words and Words of Wisdom), 1946.

Bahá'í-Gebete (Bahá'í Prayers), eine Auslese aus Gebeten, die Bahá'u'lláh, der Báb und 'Abdu'l-Bahá offenbarten. George Ronald: Oxford, 1948.

ARTICLES

'*Die Bahá'í-Bewegung*' (The Bahá'í Movement), in *Aufstrebende Kulturbewegungen und ihre Vorkämpfer*, edited by Karl Dopf. Hamburg: Signal-Verlag, 1927, pp. 35-8.

LIST OF PUBLISHED BOOKS, BOOKLETS AND ARTICLES

'*Die Ausbreitung und gegenwärtige Aktivität der Bahá'í-Religion, insbesondere in Amerika und Europa*', in *Zeitschrift für Religions- und Geistesgeschichte*, Köln: E.J.Brill-Verlag, Jahrgang X 1958, Heft 4.

ESSAYS IN *THE BAHÁ'Í WORLD*

'Prof. Auguste Forel and the Bahá'í Teaching, A Contibution Towards a Characterization of the Well-Known Swiss Psychologist', in Vol. IV, 1930–1932, p. 393.

'*Der Sinn unserer Zeit*'(The Meaning of the Age in Which We Live), in Vol. V, 1932–1934, p. 571.

'*Ein junger Glaube wird bekannt*'(A Young Faith Gains Recognition), in Vol. VI, 1934–36, p. 689.

'*Neue Arbeit*' (New Work), in Vol. X, 1944–1946, p. 714.

'*Die kleine Welt und der Große Friede*'(The Small World and the Great Peace), in Vol. XI, 1946–1950, p. 785.

VARIOUS ARTICLES

in *Das Rosengärtlein* (The Little Rose Garden) childrens magazine 1924-1928 Hamburg, *La Nova Tago*, *Sonne der Wahrheit*, *Bahá'í News* and other Bahá'í Newspapers

PART II

Reflections on my Father

Hartmut Grossmann

INSTEAD OF AN INTRODUCTION

Why does a son write about his father, why would someone who lives in this world write about parents who are no longer alive?

Love and gratitude for what has been received is a first and natural motive. Later, being a father oneself, one realizes what one owes to one's parents, how much one is influenced by their thinking and acting, and what unconditional love means. Then there are feelings of esteem and respect towards the achievements of one's parents and how they mastered trying times. One compares one's own experience and situation with what one can remember and reflects on their attitude, how they reacted to difficult situations, and one learns from it for one's own life. It is through such comparison that one determines one's identity and attempts to give some account of what has been inherited from our parents.

Man's life has a purpose and a goal, on which strength, thought and action is focused. Part of it serves one's own advancement, the well-being of the family and the education of the children. Some devote their life to service to others. They dedicate themselves to high tasks and ideas, which they try selflessly to translate into deeds. In a time in which ideals and values are decaying and becoming increasingly disregarded, human examples that show us the way and incarnate what we lack become more and more important. Thus the life of my father, as a Bahá'í, who was able to combine retrospection, life in the present and vision of the future, is to me, and possibly to others, an example.

Biographies exist in abundance. They tell us about heroes and conquerors, scientists and founders of companies, whom we may very well admire and respect; however, they leave little impact on our own lives. Many such heroes devoted themselves to an idea which we cannot or do not want to emulate. They materialized their ideals and achieved their aims through means which we do not approve of because they are too selfish.

On the other hand, there are those silent heroes who became an example because they were peace-loving, compassionate and caring for others; however, often we cannot emulate them. We lack the will necessary to follow their example and the strength to achieve the goal they accomplished through gentleness and an attitude of long-suffering.

What about the Manifestation of God, the epitome of suffering, the symbol of love and benevolence, the perfect example for every human being, the incarnation of divine Will? He is eternal, not subject to time. His spirituality, vision, and the divine growth that reveals itself to man, fascinate us.

'Abdu'l-Bahá is the 'Master', the 'Example' for a Bahá'í life. He is close to us, and becomes familiar because of the way He lived His life: in suffering, with forgiveness, kindness, and understanding; in His firmness and adherence to the Faith; in His selflessness and complete service to Bahá'u'lláh. For a Bahá'í, He is the 'Mystery of God', incomprehensible and yet close. His word is guidance and His wisdom is beyond any doubt.

The true being of man consists in his spirituality. It is a connecting power, creates unity, releases creative energies, and empowers for excellence. Thus, the experience of spirituality was for Hermann Grossmann out of the ordinary. He carefully analysed his education, the influence of his environment; he wrestled with 'truth', which he found too incoherent, inhumane and misunderstood. Yet, on the other hand, in an instant, from a few words he realized that he had found 'the' truth. All criticism, all doubts were removed in a 'yes' and his intellect spurred him on to transform from a seeker into a learner, to a 'yes, but ...'.

My father Hermann Grossmann attempted to translate into his own life the divine teachings as he found and internalized them from the Writings of the Faith and the example of 'Abdu'l-Bahá. My father was a human being whose life is of interest because he lived it with all its heights and depths, with perseverance, obedience and steadfastness, with increasing devotion and selflessness. After having accepted the Bahá'í Faith he made it his life. He opened up to the influence of the divine as a creative power – a harmonizing, sustaining power of life – and consistently made it his task to assist this force to have an impact in all spheres of his individual and societal life. His book *Am Morgen einer Neuen Zeit* (The Dawn of a New Age) expresses his intention well, both in its title and its contents. It was his dearest wish to spread the teachings of Bahá'u'lláh, to disseminate the divine remedy and thus revive and strengthen man's belief in God, according to these words of Bahá'u'lláh:

INSTEAD OF AN INTRODUCTION

> The vitality of men's belief in God is dying out in every land; nothing short of His wholesome medicine can ever restore it.[1]

The richer and fuller a human life, the more complex it is. Its richness stems from endeavour, effort, and openness to anything new, different, visionary and daring. In his actions he followed Bahá'u'lláh's advice to always see the end in the beginning. After he became a Bahá'í, service to the Cause was the dominating passion of his life and everything else was made secondary. His activities can be seen as a result of processes in thinking and learning. Not all motivations in his life can be explained, they stay shrouded in his personality; at times they can, however, be elucidated from statements, reactions, his conduct, his ceaseless research and his systematic approach to things.

In the following pages I shall try to highlight certain aspects of the life of Hermann Grossmann. The attempt can be seen as an addendum to the biography that precedes this part. These personal viewpoints are like facets of a polished diamond; they form part of an extraordinary life. They are not an attempt to give a complete picture, but through these reflections to show some of the effects of the light of divine guidance in Hermann Grossmann's life.

THE TABLET FROM 'ABDU'L-BAHÁ

In order to do justice to this life, so rich in its different aspects, it is essential to establish the link between my father's early encounter with the Cause of Bahá'u'lláh and the development of the Faith thus far. In 1920 the believers were oriented towards the personality of 'Abdu'l-Bahá. He was the leader, Who inspired, gave life in the spirit, guided the believers and set an example. At that time Hermann Grossmann may not have felt all the fascination and attraction of 'Abdu'l-Bahá; but he experienced a fraction of it in Grace and Harlan Ober, his spiritual parents who, sent by the Master, taught him the Faith. This was in Leipzig, Germany, in 1920. There can, however, be no doubt that he realized the spiritual greatness of the Master from the words addressed to him. He saw in Him the personality in which 'the incompatible characteristics of a human nature and superhuman knowledge and perfection have been blended and are completely harmonized'. [2]

Thus 'Abdu'l-Bahá's Tablet became, for the life of Hermann Grossmann, a standard and guidance. The message is short but of extraordinary depth. It says:

> O thou who hast been guided by the light of divine guidance:
> Thy letter hath been received. It indicated that thou hast turned thy face toward the Abhá Kingdom. Yield thee thanks unto God that thou hast been enabled to rend the veils asunder, to gaze on the beauty of the Sun of Reality, and to walk in the path of the Kingdom. Thou shouldst be eternally obliged and thankful to those who were the cause of thy guidance, inasmuch as they conferred heavenly life upon thee and enabled thee to be admitted into this resplendent Kingdom.
> Upon thee rest the Glory of the Most Glorious.
>
> abdulBaha abbas Dec. 9, 1920 [3]

To understand my father's life one has to understand the significance of this Tablet. It is addressed to him personally and as personal guidance. It receives a more general significance in connection with the authority of 'Abdu'l-Bahá and the Holy Writings. Hermann Grossmann's statements and reactions, in relation to the Tablet, shed further light on the impact it had on his life.

THE TABLET FROM 'ABDU'L-BAHÁ

The opening sentence stresses that Hermann Grossmann was 'guided by the light of divine guidance'. As stated in other Tablets by 'Abdu'l-Bahá, it is not man who first 'accepts' the Faith of God and then serves it; rather, it is God Who 'chooses' from amongst mankind, opens up the eyes of the believer and has him partake of the light of His guidance:

> From amongst all mankind hath He chosen you, and your eyes have been opened to the light of guidance and your ears attuned to the music of the Company above ... [4]

A condition for man is preparedness and willingness to become an instrument of God. 'Abdu'l-Bahá says in His Tablet that the choice of God is for a human who has certain abilities and capacities. The task for man is then to develop these capacities and serve the Cause of God. As He says elsewhere:

> O thou servant of God!
> Thy letter was received. Thou hast spoken concerning thy lack of ability and capacity. Wert thou without ability and capacity, thou wouldst not have advanced toward the Kingdom of ABHA. [5]

There is little doubt that the Master saw in Hermann Grossmann the ready soul, willing to open up to God and become a servant through a life in the Faith. This is confirmed through the sentence in the Tablet: '... thou hast turned thy face toward the Abhá Kingdom'.

The ensuing sentences in the Tablet from 'Abdu'l-Bahá signify the main purpose of the message and mark the path and task ahead for Hermann Grossmann:

> Yield thee thanks unto God that thou hast been enabled to rend the veils asunder, to gaze on the beauty of the Sun of Reality, and to walk in the path of the Kingdom.

Shoghi Effendi, the Guardian, explained to Hermann Grossmann when he was on pilgrimage in 1937 that the special significance of the first part of the sentence is 'Abdu'l-Bahá's statement: 'thou hast been enabled to rend the veils asunder'. These are the veils of selfish desire, of worldly ties and limitations, of learning and imagination.

During all his life Hermann Grossmann had the much-cherished gift of seeing beauty, loftiness and harmony in diversity. His abilities allowed him to trace this vision in various aspects of human life. As an artist, he expressed natural reality in a personal understanding of nature. As a researcher, he realized that order is the essential principle, which he pursued with great awareness in all manifestations of life. Finally, as a believer, he attempted to stress the links between religious and scientific doctrines.

Before he found the Faith he was a seeker walking many different paths which yet, in the clamour of war and in the lack of solutions apparent thereafter, were proved to be errant ways. Thus, faith in Bahá'u'lláh and the understanding of the truth in His teachings meant more than acceptance of a new religion; it was to him salvation and a path to certitude. He wrote:

> Dreams and desire accompanied me when I started my war diary. The dreams withered away, for the day was too bright, and the desire died in the face of what appeared to be reality. Later I found the truth and new dreams and desire in it and all was accomplished in a miraculous way in You.

This final entry in his wartime diary describing destroyed hope and new trust in the accomplishment of his visions and yearnings, reflects in a few words painful growth and final certitude in his life.

Often enough, before those decisive days of August 1920, he had struggled to receive guidance. In the trenches of a totally destructive stalemate warfare; in the despair of a humiliating return home as a defeated officer; and during his time as a student in an undesired field of studies, it was the dreaming and yearning that kept him alive. He hoped for the light of truth. Then, having found it, the following words of 'Abdu'l-Bahá may have been, unknowingly, a guiding principle:

> From amongst all mankind hath He chosen you, and your eyes have been opened to the light of guidance ... Thank ye and praise ye God that the hand of infinite bestowals hath set upon your heads this gem-studded crown, this crown whose lustrous jewels will forever flash and sparkle down all the reaches of time. To thank Him for this, make ye a mighty effort, and choose for yourselves a noble goal. [6]

And these words of the Master came true in Hermann Grossmann:

> The Sun of Truth hath shone forth in splendour over all the world, and its luminous rising is man's salvation and his eternal life – but only he is of the saved who hath opened wide the eye of his discernment and beheld that glory. [7]

THE TABLET FROM 'ABDU'L-BAHÁ

For Hermann Grossmann the newly found truth in the Bahá'í Faith was a reality which occupied his mind constantly, trying to understand it through ever newer approaches. The words addressed to him by 'Abdu'l-Bahá, 'thou hast been enabled ... to walk in the path of the Kingdom', were a spiritual reality to him. His path in the Faith was a steady progression. 'Development' was a key word. With the coming of Bahá'u'lláh an all-pervasive, irresistible impulse has been released into the world; encrusted and rigid foundations and structures are gradually destroyed through its impact and simultaneously a new order is erected that reveals itself in all aspects of life. Like Shoghi Effendi, Hermann Grossmann saw in history a continuous death and birth, apparent in the ancient cultures of Mesopotamia and described in the works of Oswald Spengler and Arnold Toynbee. He tried to find reasons for such a rise and fall of a culture. In his talks and essays on religious development he traced the thought of progressive divine revelation and the relativity of human knowledge of God and truth. The manifestation of the divine in the world of existence was conceived as a process, an inherent development of the spiritual capacity of man, being evident in all human expressions of mind, in culture, history, arts, science and language. In all aspects of human intelligence, he evidenced development as an expression of creative, divine energy. This was to him progress on the path of God.

In His Tablet 'Abdu'l-Bahá exhorts Hermann Grossmann: 'Thou shouldst be eternally obliged and thankful to those who were the cause of thy guidance.' For years Hermann Grossmann understood this as being the main purport of the Tablet, and expressed deep gratitude to Grace and Harlan Ober as his spiritual parents. One of the names of his son perpetuates the remembrance of those bearers of a spiritual message. There is no doubt that they were, to Hermann Grossmann, a special tool of divine guidance as they, according to the words of 'Abdu'l-Bahá, 'conferred heavenly life' upon him and enabled him 'to walk in the path of the Kingdom'.

At a later date, in the spring of 1957, when Hermann Grossmann and his wife, Anna, came into the presence of Shoghi Effendi during a pilgrimage, he stated in a conversation with the Guardian that he considered this part of the Tablet to be the most important. Shoghi Effendi clarified that this was not the case, but it pays tribute to Hermann Grossmann for his deep gratitude to the Obers for their spiritual guidance.

This issue of divine guidance is stressed twice in the Tablet; through it Hermann Grossmann recognized not only the light of the Faith but he received with its help a directive to the right path of faith. The opening sentence addresses Hermann Grossmann as one who has been 'guided by the light of divine guidance'. To him this first encounter with the Faith was absolute mercy, a divine gift of guidance, which obliged him to serve the Cause of Bahá'u'lláh untiringly.

The Master closes this short but significant Tablet with the following confirmation: 'Upon thee rest the Glory of the Most Glorious.'

'Abdu'l-Bahá signed the Tablet with His own hand. In Western letters He wrote, '*abdul Baha abbas*'. This signature is indicative of the uniqueness and greatness of 'Abdu'l-Bahá. He is an incarnation of humility and selflessness, an example of the meaning of our life, characterized by Him as being Himself the 'Servant of servants'. While the two initial 'a's' in the names 'Abdu'l and Abbás are in small letters, the reference to God in 'Bahá' is written with a capital 'B', so that in His very name the greatest of all men expresses His lowliness in the face of God's majesty. The unequalled servitude of the Master, expressed in this way, released in Hermann Grossmann energies that enabled him to do great deeds in service to Bahá'u'lláh and for the well-being and spiritual growth of his fellow human beings.

'Abdu'l-Bahá's Tablet is a visible example of the special power latent in the Word of God. With a few words it changed Hermann Grossmann from a seeker to a confirmed believer. He received strength and empowerment to make impressive efforts in the service to the Faith; it even assisted him to overcome physical handicaps. The poisonous gas which he had had to breathe during trench warfare influenced his physical health over decades.

When he passed away in 1968 the examining physician still diagnosed the effects of the gas, but what kept him alive and inspired him to cope with unusual hardships and exertions were those few words from the Master, the Mystery of God; words which He Himself had animated with His own powers.

Hermann Grossmann felt the strength and translated it into deeds. In his talks and conversations he mentioned repeatedly the words of the poet that it is the spirit that makes the body. His very life is proof to the transforming power of God's Word, that will transmute a speck of dust into suns and a small moth into a royal falcon.

THE SEEKER

In his book *The Seven Valleys* Bahá'u'lláh depicts the mystic path of a seeker in his quest for truth, certainty and God. The wanderer passes through a number of valleys, goes astray in paths of error and delusion but is finally led by the heavenly light of guidance to the goal of his endeavour. In his burning desire to reach a goal hard to ascertain the seeker wanders through the valleys of search, of love and knowledge, of unity and contentment, of amazement, of true poverty and absolute nothingness. These are the stations on the path of perception, the ones Hermann Grossmann desired to achieve. He translated the *Seven Valleys* and made it available to German-speaking readers. During this mystical journey Hermann Grossmann began to understand his own life with all its heights and depths, its loss of security, its experience of deprivation, suffering and doubt stemming from a shattered concept of this world. What he realized was the assurance that the wayfarer will be guided in his quest if he does not give up but persists. He often referred to his new understanding of Goethe's words (spoken by angels):

> For he whose strivings never cease
> Is ours for his redeeming.
> If, touched by the celestial love,
> His soul has sacred leaven,
> There comes to greet him, from above,
> The company of heaven.
>   (Goethe, *Faust*, Part Two, towards the end of the Fifth Act)

In the years after World War I Hermann Grossmann had not yet partaken of that 'celestial love'. However, his confidence in beauty and truth had prevailed despite all the despair. Painting was his way of expressing his desire for clarity and purity, and his artwork attested to this desire. To him Don Quixote in the classical literature of Spain represented the naïve, yet just embodiment of a misunderstood life; Dante's Purgatory and the catharsis of Aristotle inspired him as a moral support and firm hope. The path was not yet clear, the goal still remained vague, but the readiness to search and the receptivity to something new and superior was there.

Such was the mental situation of the young Hermann Grossmann while studying in Leipzig. His desire to find a purpose in life and moral values was indeed so strong that he accepted the invitation to a talk by two Bahá'ís from the United States, Grace and Harlan Ober, whom 'Abdu'l-Bahá had asked to visit Germany. So open was his heart that he responded to Grace Ober's remark, about the talk and its content being meant for him, with immediate consent. 'Knowledge is a light which God casteth into the heart of whomsoever He willeth,' says the *ḥadith*, and Bahá'u'lláh asserts: 'Wherefore, a man should make ready his heart that it be worthy of the descent of heavenly grace ...' [8]

Hermann Grossmann was a seeker, but after having accepted the Faith his search became re-search of revealed truth and beauty. When presenting the teachings of Bahá'u'lláh he stressed the certitude one finds in the Word of God. The Book of Certitude, the *Kitáb-i-Iqán*, was for him the holy Book second only to the *Kitáb-i-Aqdas*, the Book of Laws. Moreover, Hermann Grossmann became aware of the certainty a believer finds through the study of the Holy Writings. In this way the seeker finds truth despite the limitations of a human mind and the fact that religious truth is relative; God's Word is 'the infallible Balance' and the standard for our understanding; at the same time it is the guide in human search for God.

The tedious path of the seeker who knows not the goal but has the assurance that an end will be found was a valuable experience for Hermann Grossmann. It opened him up to those who were seekers like him. He especially wished to assist those who approached religious truth as he did, those who, however, lacked the divine truth and certainty of a believer in Bahá'u'lláh. His efforts were targeted above all at the youth studying in university and at showing them the bridge between religion and science.

During all his life Hermann Grossmann had an open ear and heart for the interests of young people. His intention was to offer to them something positive in a time of the continued breakdown of order and of negated values and questioned traditions; above all he hoped to open up a new vista to a generation full of doubts. In the years after 1945 he, under difficult conditions, organized youth camps where the participants discussed a new order for the world in the midst of a disastrously hopeless time, and explored means of achieving peace. Hermann Grossmann knew well how to guide and nourish youthful idealism in a constructive manner. His care for young people and his wish to assist them with his experience showed itself in the way he supported the young Iranian Bahá'í students who came to Germany in the years around the middle of the last century. His caution in introducing them to an alien culture and thinking, his compassion for those who were part of a suppressed religious minority and the loving way they were accepted into a western Bahá'í family certainly strengthened these Iranian youth in their faith and helped them to integrate themselves fully into European society.

THE HAND OF THE CAUSE OF GOD

On 24 December 1951 Shoghi Effendi appointed the first contingent of living Hands of the Cause of God.

Bahá'u'lláh characterizes these extraordinary servants of the Cause in a special Tablet. He emphasizes that through the Hands of His Cause '... the light of fortitude hath shone forth and the truth hath been established that the authority to choose rests with God ... [9]

And 'Abdu'l-Bahá is reported to have said:

> The Hands of the Cause are such blessed souls that the evidences of their sanctity and spirituality will be felt in the hearts of people. Their influence must be such that the souls may be carried away by their goodly character, their pure motives, their justice and fairness, that individuals may be enamoured of their praiseworthy character and their virtuous attributes, and that people may turn their faces towards them for their qualities and resplendent signs. 'Hand of the Cause' is not a title which can be given to anybody. Neither is it a position to be handed down to whomsoever may desire it ... The more any soul becomes self-effacing, the more confirmed will he be in the service of the Cause of God; and the more humble, the nearer will he be to Him. [10]

Hermann Grossmann felt this rank was a special favour from God. The high distinction bestowed upon him by Shoghi Effendi was encouragement and a stimulus for him. In his diary he described the situation of the German Bahá'í youth and their thirst for knowledge, during the years after World War II, with these words: '... because they did not wish to stay mid-way but wanted to walk and recognize the path of Bahá'u'lláh with all its consequences for the sake of the needs in this world.' This characterization applies very well to Hermann Grossmann himself. For him the appointment to the rank of Hand of the Cause was a challenge to maturation and insight. He was deeply grateful for this favour which meant shouldering a greater share of responsibility and walking the path outlined by 'Abdu'l-Bahá to its very end; in this way serving mankind according to the high vocation of a Hand of the Cause as stated in the Master's Will and Testament.

The experiences from his youth, wartime and, in particular, the way he mastered situations and dispositions thereafter endowed him with a strength exemplary to others around him. His manifold gifts and his deep knowledge of religion and mysticism, of history, language, painting and poetry, of education, science and administration were the bases on which he was able to approach people of very diverse thinking. Being firm and steadfast in his faith, he was enabled to serve Bahá'u'lláh effectively in the two main functions of a Hand of the Cause, the protection and propagation of the Faith. His scientifically trained mind and his vision made him a strategist, working systematically towards a goal. These were the qualities much needed and used in service to the Faith in Europe and South America. Bahá'u'lláh's words, 'the ocean of bounty hath surged and the fragrance of the gracious favours of God, the Lord of mankind, hath been diffused' [11] were a prop and mainstay for his activities as a Hand of the Cause of God.

Hermann Grossmann cooperated well and closely with the other members of this distinguished institution of the Hands of the Cause of God. He cherished deeply the hope and advice of his colleagues as a support to his own faculties that allowed him to react to situations accordingly. He loved and respected them for their knowledge, strength of character and abilities. He kept up an extensive correspondence and met frequently with many Hands of the Cause at conferences and in his hospitable home.

In his talks Hermann Grossmann stressed the infinite richness of divine knowledge, at the same time admitting his own limitations. He realized that as a human being he depended on the insights and support of others to meet the challenges and demands of his task.

Bahá'u'lláh characterizes the Hands of the Cause in a Tablet as 'the stars of the heaven of Thy knowledge'.[12] Whoever has had the privilege of knowing Hands of the Cause has been deeply impressed by their profound knowledge of the teachings despite their great differences in character and expression. Thus, Hermann Grossmann and Adelbert Mühlschlegel, the other Hand of the Cause of God of German nationality, complemented each other in an unusual way. They expressed the special qualities 'Abdu'l-Bahá and Shoghi Effendi appreciated in Germans in diverse ways. Adelbert Mühlschlegel was an impressive personality because of his charm, poetic abilities, humour and radiant vision. He had the great gift of transmuting depression into hope, sadness into happiness, worldly melancholy into heavenly spirituality. He himself demonstrated how to master tragic situations in life and make the best of them. His spiritual vision enabled him to present mystical truth in a way easy to understand. He thought profoundly about the unfathomable secrets of the universe and the mysterious forces of creation, and he untiringly tried to trace in them the Almighty God.

It is in this attempt that Hermann Grossmann and Adelbert Mühlschlegel met and supported each other. While one showed the greatness and majesty of creation in an objective and logical way, the other did the same through personal and mystical vision. In this manner the two German Hands of the Cause reflected the richness and diversity of this nation of poets and thinkers. In a Tablet to the Bahá'ís in Stuttgart 'Abdu'l-Bahá characterizes Germans saying 'they are endowed with constancy and spiritual perception';[13] these qualities were reflected in these two men in a special and mutually supportive way.

THE ADVOCATE OF GOD

'Abdu'l-Bahá in a talk on 17 November 1912 in New York revealed this prayer ending with the words:

> O Lord! O Lord! Protect them in every test, make every foot firm in the pathway of Thy love, and help them to be as mighty mountains in Thy Cause so that their faith shall not be wavering, their sight shall not be dimmed nor hindered from witnessing the lights emanating from Thy supreme Kingdom. Verily, Thou art the Generous. Thou art the Almighty. Verily, Thou art the Clement, the Merciful. [14]

This prayer depicts a part of Hermann Grossmann's life as a Bahá'í that is typical of his faith – his firmness and valour in defending the Cause of Bahá'u'lláh. That resoluteness was an important and essential part of his being a Bahá'í, from the very first moment of accepting the claim and teachings of Bahá'u'lláh. All his life he was subject to tests and challenges that provoked his firmness; in overcoming them he became a staunch advocate of the Cause. In his communications between 1923 and 1930 he faced a good number of problems and he asked for advice from Shoghi Effendi on how to solve them. He followed the Guardian's advice, obeyed the guidance of the Writings and aspired to clarity in his understanding of what the Faith stands for. This guided him in coping with spiritualistic meetings instead of institutional consultation, with a sectarian and limited view of the teachings, with protecting the Faith from swindlers and, above all, the preservation of the purity and unity of the Faith in cases of Covenant-breaking. Hermann Grossmann suffered because of the imperfections and superficiality of others and made it his task to adhere strictly to the teachings of Bahá'u'lláh and the advice of Shoghi Effendi.

On 13 December 1923 he wrote to the Guardian:

> Enclosed please find a letter we received through ... about the friends in ... We are saddened to realize that spiritism has influenced to a considerable degree even other groups. We have not written to other Bahá'ís about this issue, but we feel it is our duty to let you know about it.

And in another letter to Shoghi Effendi on 20 August 1924:

> We plan here in Hamburg to elect a spiritual study group as [we] believe such a firm structure can more readily withstand opposition from certain unpleasant souls carried into our meetings.

It is appropriate at this point to say something about Hermann Grossmann's relationship to Shoghi Effendi. Most of his letters to the Guardian were reports or information about trends, developments and events; only occasionally did he ask questions or request assistance. His early letters to Shoghi Effendi explain this attitude. He felt difficulties were a means of strengthening oneself; tests were a way of overcoming them through one's own efforts. It was his lifelong principle that mistakes were a means for learning, difficulties were to be overcome, problems had to be solved; any attempt to avoid them meant that they would come back until they were removed. In some letters Hermann Grossmann explained to Shoghi Effendi why he did things in a certain way, asking the Guardian to correct or confirm them on the basis of his being the authorized Interpreter. For Hermann Grossmann the actions of Shoghi Effendi, as Guardian of the Cause of God and as expounder of the revealed Word of God, were the determining factors and the decisive standard. This explains why his correspondence is rather factual, personal issues and any not relevant to the Faith being excluded. Anna Grossmann gives an illuminating example in a letter to Shoghi Effendi dated 19 February 1934:

> He has also to fight for better social conditions for the workers. In this fight he has the full assistance of the economic organization of the German government and together with the *Treuhänder der Arbeit* [someone who is officially entrusted with supervising working conditions] in Frankfurt a. M. he hopes – if the company may get over the financial depression – to realize as much as possible the teachings of our beloved Faith concerning social problems ...'

Hermann Grossmann would hardly have written to the Guardian about such a matter.

Hermann Grossmann's courage in protecting the Faith became especially apparent during the time of Hitler. He was miraculously spared major persecutions, which harassed other Bahá'ís from the time of the interdiction of the Faith on 21 May 1937 and throughout the war. His wife Anna and sister Elsa Maria were interrogated; the latter was threatened with a pistol and imprisoned in Heidelberg for nine days.

That he was spared from all this appeared to Hermann Grossmann like a strange stroke of fate: while a number of believers were facing the special courts of the Gestapo no action was brought against him, even though he had played such a prominent role in the work of the Faith up to 1937 and despite the fact that he staunchly refused to become a member of Hitler's Party. However, what he realized was the service he could render the Cause of Bahá'u'lláh and those believers who were accused. To defend the friends was dangerous, but he succeeded in pleading their case in Darmstadt and Heidelberg. Thus, in the time of interdiction, he was able to present the teachings to the court. He demanded a just treatment of the accused and rejected all accusations. His final speech made its impact; the highly dangerous charge of subversive activities was dropped and changed into the much less serious accusation of having violated the law interdicting meetings. This saved a good number of Bahá'ís from persecution. Hermann Grossmann succeeded beyond any doubt in preserving the believers from further harm through his courage and especially his obedience to the guidance of Shoghi Effendi. The Guardian had, in a letter of 11 February 1934 to Dr Adelbert Mühlschlegel, given clear instructions in case of attacks on the Faith. Hermann Grossmann used the advice, made it part of his defence and succeeded.

His firmness in the Cause was once more challenged during the Custodianship of the Hands of the Cause from autumn 1957 to spring 1963. Again he protected the Faith from being harmed. He was instrumental in thwarting the intrigues of the followers of Mason Remey, first in Europe, then in South America. In this connection it is interesting to study his line of action in an early case of Covenant-breaking in 1930. On 18 April 1930 he wrote to Shoghi Effendi:

> Concerning the troubles caused by Mrs ... I am sure that they will pass again soon as there are only very few souls influenced. I am trying to get in touch with the wavering friends and have offered them every explanation they want to get. The different assemblies have declared their full devotedness. Tomorrow the election of the new National Spiritual Assembly will take place and I confidently hope it will bring forth good results in the future.

In serving the Faith Hermann Grossmann was of exemplary firmness, steadfastness and clarity. His obedience to Shoghi Effendi and his absolute adherence to the Word of God enabled him to defend the Faith with resolution and strength.

THE ADMINISTRATOR

It is pointless to speculate on the way the Faith in Germany might have developed if there had been no Hitler or Third Reich. What can be stated, however, is the fact that this regime abruptly destroyed a positive progression in the unfoldment of the Administrative Order in Germany and on the entire European continent.

Shoghi Effendi, in a letter about the World Order of Bahá'u'lláh addressed to the North American Bahá'í community in 1933, poses a question:

> Will it be America, will it be one of the countries of Europe, who will arise to assume the leadership essential to the shaping of the destinies of this troubled age? [15]

It remained, no doubt, a rhetorical question, for 'Abdu'l-Bahá had chosen the North American Bahá'í community to become the spiritual leader in the establishment of the Administrative Order. The Faith in Germany had, however, achieved a high standard in the years before World War II. There was a national and local structure, the education and training of the friends in summer schools was in place and was far more than an introduction to or deepening in the teachings; in fact, it was the beginning of an early form of systematic training. Public esteem for the Cause of Bahá'u'lláh had led to a kind of public recognition, as attested in 1932 in a book review in *Der Stürmer*, the official political paper of Hitler's Party, which stated that no National Socialist should disregard such ideas. Hermann Grossmann's vision and insight had contributed much to this very positive development of the Faith in Germany.

His grasp of the Administrative Order was extraordinary and from the very beginning of its establishment Hermann Grossmann understood the Covenant at its core and its strength. He was an independent thinker who followed closely the instructions of the Guardian and applied them to the circumstances within the German Bahá'í community. His correspondence with Shoghi Effendi indicates how he scrutinized and analysed the Guardian's advice; in case there were still problems in applying it he would write back to him and ask for further clarification.

In this way Hermann Grossmann learnt about the structure of the Faith in detail; this made him a competent and efficient chairman of the German National Spiritual Assembly. He succeeded in enlarging the believers' understanding of the Administration, and they supported his attempts to develop the system in a way comprehensible to the Bahá'ís. He succeeded in purifying the National Assembly from spiritualistic and other corrupting elements not in agreement with the Covenant. There is little doubt that the German Bahá'í community had the capacity to take the step that Shoghi Effendi had put into effect in the North American Bahá'í community in the mid-1930s, which led to the first national annual plan. Hitler's interdiction of the Faith, however, stopped this development and set back the German believers for many years.

Hermann Grossmann always tried to see and understand developments in their larger context and in their influence on people. The rise of National Socialism, the perfection of a cynical system and the reconstructive forces of a new religion were understood to be opposing processes destined to finally coincide in one result, the destruction of the old order and the disintegration of its values, and the establishment of a new order based on a divinely inspired Revelation. In history and philosophy Hermann Grossmann traced parallel developments and attempted explanations for the rise and fall of cultures. Shoghi Effendi supported such efforts, as he himself saw in history a constant 'rise and fall, integration and disintegration, order and chaos'. Hermann Grossmann reports how he asked the Guardian in 1957 while on pilgrimage about the two processes and their inevitability and explained them in the context of an inescapable dualism. The issue of the conversation centered on Hitler as the quintessence of evil. Had God cursed him to act evil and why? Shoghi Effendi explained that in principle God wishes the education of man to choose good by realizing evil. Hitler was willing to be destructive and become a symbol of evil by his own choice; had he not accepted such a role voluntarily, God would have found someone else.

The passing of 'Abdu'l-Bahá and the appointment of Shoghi Effendi as the Guardian meant for the believers a change to a new age in the development of the Faith. They learnt to transfer their loyalty from the Master to the Guardian, the 'sacred and youthful branch'. Hermann Grossmann had become a Bahá'í in the time of 'Abdu'l-Bahá and had been distinguished by Him in receiving a Tablet that was his guidance for life. He still had the privilege of knowing what the Heroic Age had achieved, with its heroes inspired by the three Central Figures of the Faith. 'Abdu'l-Bahá was an impulse, a guidance and an example to Hermann Grossmann. Other outstanding believers such as Martha Root left their mark and were a proof to what extent an individual can serve the Faith when led by devotion, willpower and selflessness. On the other hand, Hermann Grossmann knew from the early beginnings of the Formative Age how precious was the leadership of the Guardian. Shoghi Effendi was to him authority, guideline and standard. He accepted the authority of the Guardian without the slightest hesitation; he sought his advice and became a willing tool in the service of the Faith. From its very beginning Hermann Grossmann accepted the spirit of the Cause of Bahá'u'lláh as developing the form and creation of a new order. He did not ask 'why' such a process took place but 'how'. From the early beginnings of the time of Shoghi Effendi, Hermann Grossmann reported to him the stages of development of the Faith in Germany, the trends and attitudes of individual believers and institutions, and offered his own opinions. These letters, written by Hermann Grossmann in the 1920s and early 1930s indicate an interesting development in his relation to Shoghi Effendi; initially he addressed him as 'my brother' whom he informed – but soon it was the much-respected 'beloved Guardian' to whom he pledged obedience and allegiance, hoping to receive guidance.

Another illuminating characteristic that throws some light on Hermann Grossmann's understanding of the Faith is his early and sustained efforts to communicate and connect with Bahá'ís on an international level. An extensive correspondence with believers in numerous countries and especially through the means of Esperanto helped to exchange opinions and express the universal character of the Cause of God. Unfortunately this too was stopped by the actions of the National Socialists.

Immediately after World War II he restarted the previously interrupted communications with Bahá'ís in many countries of the world. His thinking was liberal, cosmopolitan and tolerant and apparent in his talks, which stressed the main tenets of Bahá'u'lláh's message: unity of humankind and universal peace. His letters confirm that he was indeed someone who clearly thought in terms of global society.

Living as a Bahá'í in the Fourth and Fifth Epochs of the Formative Age, one is struck by the way Hermann Grossmann was a kind of pioneer in the field of spiritual training. He intended to develop the summer schools in the mid-1930s to become training institutes with a systematic programme, a well planned curriculum, a sequence of courses, harmonized course materials, lectures and seminars based on consultation in groups. Shoghi Effendi supported these efforts through advice on how to develop the concept and turn the training in schools and institutes into future Bahá'í universities, and made available literature as a basis for systematic instruction. Again, the further development of these trail-blazing attempts was shattered by the National Socialists in 1937; however, Hermann Grossmann energetically again took up the idea of training the believers after the war.

THE SYSTEMATIST

Already in his early years of being a Bahá'í, Hermann Grossmann recognized the significance of administration and acted accordingly, as indicated in a letter to Shoghi Effendi dated 6 April 1926:

> From the beginning, when I took in hand the work of a German World Fellowship Branch [an early form of Bahá'í organization] I was convinced that in some sense a special World Fellowship organization could be a danger for the unity of the Cause if led by men not sufficiently devoted to the Cause and that therefore it was necessary to connect the work of World Fellowship with that of the National Spiritual Assembly ...

Structural order within the Faith was for him a means of establishing unity, a way of harmonizing various processes of development and a possibility of disciplining personal endeavours for the benefit of society.

For Hermann Grossmann the existence of an order was a central principle. It signified for him the framework within which a methodical process unfolds. His studies show a researcher who systematically investigates how the various facets of a puzzle fit together into an orderly scheme. In this, what especially interested him were the start of an event, its unfolding from a single original cause, its development in ever more complex bifurcations. Sequence, the manner in which things are linked with each other, the arrangement in a continuous and complex development, were processes he tried to define in science, especially in the history of cultures and religions. He traced the conditions under which an order or an event presents itself like a chain where everything falls into place and has its specific function. Hermann Grossmann understood as a gradual unfoldment the Covenant of God with man; the purpose of divine law; the idea of a Lesser and a Universal Peace which allow for the maintenance of an orderly life in society; the rules, regulations and structures of future civilization; the development from the core of an administrative order into the pattern of the World Order of Bahá'u'lláh, established by Shoghi Effendi: such processes were to him manifestations of a moral and spiritual system and a guiding principle in creation. In his talks he presented the establishment of a divine civilization, the coming of the Kingdom of God on earth, the World Order of Bahá'u'lláh, as the result of the establishment of a unique system. He recognized the administrative structure in the Faith, gradually and painstakingly created by Shoghi Effendi, as a well-ordered, complex and unified organization to guarantee the establishment of a lasting social unification of humankind.

Shoghi Effendi recognized Hermann Grossmann's merits in promoting a sustained and systematic development of the Faith in Germany. On 12 November 1935 he wrote:

> I am confident that as a result of your strenuous endeavours the administrative institutions in your land will be further consolidated and extended and the cause of teaching receive an added impetus.

In a letter to Shoghi Effendi dated 5 March 1930, Hermann Grossmann describes as his main objective to focus his 'energy on the establishment of a scientific appreciation of the Cause'. The relationship between religion and science was for him complementary, each stimulating the other, each promoting the attainment of truth in a different way. Tirelessly he tried, in studies, talks and articles, to present what was common between them and how to link them with each other. In his talks the bird that soars upward with its two wings was a frequently used example. The progress and development of the individual and of society as a whole can come about only with the help of those forces that unite to form a new society. With such thoughts Hermann Grossmann attracted the youth, and he hoped they would become the generation that would prevent religious fanaticism and guarantee a faith-oriented mentality and ethical disposition in science and research. Before World War II he was mainly concerned with the presentation of the Faith in a way that would do justice to both religion and science. His intention was twofold; to catch the ear of intellectuals and academics and to protect the Cause of God from misrepresentation. In his letter to Shoghi Effendi of 14 December 1931 he explains:

> Much success we attained by a new scientific method of teaching, a method which has in view to lead even free-thinkers, by strictly logical proofs, to the reality of Religion and even to recognition of the Manifestation in Bahá'u'lláh.

And again, in a letter to the Guardian of 9 May 1932:

> It is our hope that this attempt of systematic training will deepen the understanding and make the friends more able to spread and teach the Beloved Cause in a worthy way ... there are no friends who can spend time enough for travelling and also because of the difficult economic conditions. Therefore we are trying to train the friends at the different places, that they themselves may learn to teach.

In his books and talks Hermann Grossmann considered subjects and issues in ever-new approaches. The principles of unity in diversity and of organic development were of greatest significance to him. In history, culture and sciences he traced ruptures and transitions and explained the forces causing them as the results of the renewal of religion. The principles of order are focus and direction that orient the diversity in creation towards its single origin. Religion is the one means to guide the individual and society in a sustained process to ever-higher civilization. In this the Covenant between God, His Manifestation and man is the main motivating force. From it stem all its manifestations in human life, education, administration, philosophy and the arts.

The diversity of Hermann Grossmann's interests and the systematic approach in his studies when he prepared his addresses and publications are apparent in a multitude of filing cards. He wrote down on them what was of interest to him, put it in a logical order and transformed it into an easy-to-understand text. The materials thus collected are a witness to the extent to which Hermann Grossmann followed trends and developments and a tribute to his ability to link these processes to the greatness and growth of the Faith.

Hermann Grossmann's opinion was much valued by others for this ability to present the Cause of God in a clear, scientific way and his capacity to be an objective observer. One example was the request in the mid-1950s from a member of the Jesuit Order who asked for a comprehensive introduction to the Administrative Order of the Faith. He wanted this for his Order. Hermann Grossmann obtained the Guardian's approval and set out for a joint study of the Bahá'í system in ten meetings in a monastery close to Heidelberg. The Jesuit followed the instructions in a receptive and objective manner, and did not hide his respect for that divinely ordained Order. On the other hand, Hermann Grossmann was impressed by the seriousness and frankness of his student. He mentioned later that the last meeting ended with the Jesuit's frank and commending realization of this divine system that would lead to the establishment of Bahá'u'lláh's World Order and the erection of the long-desired Kingdom of God on earth. The clergyman admitted, however, that the Church would study the system of the Bahá'ís carefully and adopt it to such an extent as would enable that institution to beat the Faith on its own ground. Whenever Hermann recounted this meeting he added with an amused twinkle in his eye that it was impressive for him as a Bahá'í to introduce a Jesuit in a Benedictine monastery into the deeper correlations of the World Order of Bahá'u'lláh, an Order that intended to abolish the priesthood once and for all.

Hermann Grossmann presented religion and science as complementary forces, mutually supporting each other to help establish the basis for society, truth and justice. In religious history this subject had been a dichotomy which he tried to overcome. An illustrative example is a talk Hermann gave in Frankfurt, Germany in December 1957 (see Appendix I).

THE VISIONARY ARTIST AND THINKER

The Tablet from 'Abdu'l-Bahá to Hermann Grossmann contains a significant sentence that relates to one of his special talents, that of expressing beauty:

> Yield thee thanks unto God that thou hast been enabled ... to gaze on the beauty of the Sun of Reality ...

My father's far-sightedness, vision and perspective of a goal were indeed impressive. His marked imaginative powers allowed him to follow Bahá'u'lláh's exhortation to not only see the end in the beginning but see the end and beginning as one.

> Yet those who journey in the garden land of knowledge, because they see the end in the beginning ... but the people of the Valleys above this see the end and the beginning as one; nay, they see neither beginning nor end ... [16]

This special gift of visionary perspective combined with a love of detail and accuracy enabled him to trace and present developments and processes in a systematic and precise way, for example in the Administrative Order of the Faith, in the World Order of Bahá'u'lláh and in the history of religion. In Hermann Grossmann's writings and talks 'development' is a key word. He traced development in the course of religious progress as organic growth in nature; human maturation was to him characterized by an impulse from God, a moving principle of growth. As early as the beginning of the 1920s he understood the World Order of Bahá'u'lláh as unfoldment of society-building forces. The Bahá'í Administrative Order is the nucleus and pattern for a future divine civilization that the grassroots believers will bring to fruition. Hermann Grossmann loved to talk about that subject, especially in the Catholic south of Germany where people live in expectation of the coming of God's Kingdom on earth.

Another significant concept for Hermann Grossmann was that of 'impulse', initiating religious renewal, a proof for a new religion and its forces motivating a positive process and creating the basis for an ever-advancing civilization. He saw this renewal especially in the arts and in poetry, for he was exceptionally gifted in these fields of human expression. In William Blake and Lessing, especially the famous Parable of the Rings in Lessing's *Nathan der Weise*, he traced the divinely inspired impulse; in Kant's philosophy he perceived it as the idea of a world-encompassing universal peace. The philosophy of the Greeks and the poetry of the German Classics were idealistic expressions of his own understanding of beauty, harmony, symmetry and right proportion.

Hermann Grossmann had a vision of the future of the individual and of human progress based on suffering and tests. In his talks he often expressed this idea in the symbol of the phoenix that resurrects from the ashes into which it has flung itself to gain renewed and more perfect beauty. The Bahá'í Faith is renewed beauty and truth, born out of chaos into a continuous perfecting the human race has never yet experienced. His approach in teaching was positive and constructive, moderated by a concern over the way that man received divine impulse and translated it into action, even perverted it into negative human peculiarities. He was saddened by the fact that the new Order would be established through the destruction of the old. However, the assurance in the Bahá'í Writings that whatever is good will prevail and remain in this world for its benefit became for him a source of confirmation and encouragement.

A focal approach Hermann Grossmann took in ever-new ways was that of the idea of unity in the Bahá'í Faith. He would not accept unity in uniformity. In Communism he saw a system that would destroy itself because of its levelling tendencies. Unity is diversity, the beauty of a diverse garden, the harmonious blending of colours in a rainbow and the manifold facets of a cut diamond. In his book *The Dawn of a New Day* he explains how important that principle is for the enrichment of our lives. Unity in diversity was for Hermann Grossmann the main guarantee for the eventual success of the idea of order in the Faith. The divine Order is not a levelling system but a complex diversity in which everything has its place and purpose in mutual complement. Shoghi Effendi characterizes that process with the term 'fermentation', a process which Hermann Grossmann understood as spirit permeating all spheres of human life. He describes this process as a 'reversal' of values and explains that this is not an abandonment of existing virtues and qualities but a new appreciation of them.

Another expression of the blessing that 'Abdu'l-Bahá bestowed upon Hermann Grossmann through the words that he was to see the 'beauty of the Sun of Reality' was how he translated beauty in his oil and watercolour paintings. The attraction of these pictures lies in the expression of life in landscapes, in the stroke of the brush, the delicacy and shades of the colours. His watercolours express inner harmony and happiness. In 1937, while on pilgrimage, Hermann Grossmann painted a number of pictures which he presented to Shoghi Effendi. Their beauty may have moved the Guardian to exhibit three of the paintings (reproduced here between pages 52 and 53) in the Holy Places where Bahá'u'lláh lived, in the House of 'Abbúd and in the Mansion of Mazra'ih.

Hermann Grossmann was a gifted speaker who used this ability with tact and refinement. The exposition of his talks, moving straight from the simple to the complex, from the general basics to the essential, the art of captivating the interest by giving lively and clear examples, using repetition and variation and different intensity of voice – these were the means he used to fascinate his audience. At the same time he well knew about the demagogic misuse of speech in which a speaker heats up emotions a way he warned of as not to be used by a Bahá'í. In this cautious expression of his deep thoughts he showed discipline and self-restraint. Hermann Grossmann had the rare gift of seeing himself critically; this gave him the possibility of excelling in objectivity and candour. In His Writings Bahá'u'lláh states that selfishness is one of the dense veils that separates man from God. Hermann Grossmann attempted to tear apart those veils through his eloquence in service to the Cause. He spoke his mind about service and self-sacrifice, particularly in the relationship God–Manifestation–man. A human is determined, being on the level of a servant, in his relation to God by the subordination of the weak one who desires the protection of the Strong and Almighty. His own servitude he expressed in his love and immediate obedience to the mediator of divine sovereignty. Service to other human beings was to him the offering up of personal aspirations that would limit and infringe on others' personal spheres of freedom. An example was when in his younger years he abandoned his hopes of becoming an artist and accepted training for business life instead. Hermann Grossmann understood this as submission to the Will of God and service to the Faith. In much the same spirit he defended the endangered believers fearlessly before the public prosecutors of the Nazis. This same spirit assisted him in overcoming his deep grief over the passing of Shoghi Effendi and serving selflessly as one of the 'Chief Stewards of the embryonic world commonwealth of Bahá'u'lláh'. And again it was that spirit that enabled him, despite all physical frailties, to travel several times and during many months all over the South American continent from north to south, in the heights of the Andes and the damp heat of the Amazons. Hermann Grossmann's life was characterized by self-denial and devotion.

THE EDUCATOR

A special field in which Hermann Grossmann excelled from his early days as a Bahá'í was that of education. He was excellent both in theory and in practical application. 'Uncle Hermann' was well known among Bahá'í children and their friends in the years before World War II because of his attractive children's classes. Together with his wife Anna and sister Elsa Maria he started the children's group 'Little Rosegarden, Children of the Sun', with 20 children in Hamburg, Wandsbek in 1924. After two years he was able to report to Shoghi Effendi on 24 November 1926:

> During all that time it was our endeavour to make the garden a real Bahá'í school by teaching the children methodically all those branches which are suitable for promoting the ideas of progress, unity, and harmony, according to the teachings of Bahá'u'lláh. Among the branches now taught are: History of the divers religions, Bahá'í history, philosophy, ethics and history of civilization. We have good results and the children like the lessons to which they listen very attentively. All our experiences at this school are noted and studied in order to obtain new and well proved methods of children's education.

The way the Grossmanns taught children the Faith shows that they intended the lessons for non-Bahá'í children right from the start. The curriculum as drawn up by Hermann Grossmann in the manner outlined above is a proof of flexibility and an effort to convey universal knowledge and moral values. In another letter to the Guardian he reports of his plan to develop a teaching method which would allow children to find out all that they are supposed to learn by themselves.

Lesson Plan
Little Rosegarden, Children of the Sun, Wandsbek
from 6 September 1925 to 14 March 1926 = 28 Sundays, 10:30–12:00
    Subjects 30 min. teacher's lesson
    Tenets of Perception (philosophy) 11
    History of Religion 5
    Teachings for Living the Life 2

Morals (ethics) 7
Esperanto 8
Handicraft lessons 22
Singing
Playtime

Additional parts were: homework (writing letters, learning prayers by heart)

It is worth noting in this lesson plan how manifold the fields of knowledge were and how well each subject was blended with others. Interesting is the intention to not only teach the children but also involve at the same time their often sceptical non-Bahá'í parents. He explains this in a letter to Shoghi Effendi, dated 26 March 1924, saying that he tried to adapt the character and content of the lessons to the expectations of German parents. To reach both children and parents in a more direct way Hermann and Elsa Maria Grossmann published from 1924 the magazine *Das Rosengärtlein* (The Little Rosegarden). The educational purpose is apparent in the first edition: international thinking, mutual assistance, supporting each other. The magazine was bi-monthly and offered prayers, poems, simple texts, fairy tales, narrative descriptions and drawings. The first edition was introduced with the following words:

> Dear Children,
> The small magazine which you hold in your hands today for the first time would hope to become a very close friend of yours. Do you know what made me have it printed for you? In America lives a dear aunt, all children call her 'Aunty Victoria', she loves children and publishes a journal for them. I read it and thought, it is a pity that it is all only written in English and our boys and girls cannot understand it. They deserve just as beautiful a magazine in German. So I went to the printer and asked him to print me such a publication. I wanted so much to have the magazine for you. I was sure there would be a number of other friends ready to support me, so I asked dear friends in Berlin for assistance. They were thrilled by the idea that you should have a magazine of your own, and they regularly send some money to have it printed. Now it reaches you for the first time and requests that it be received as a good friend. It is planned that this beautiful journal is to reach you nine times a year, and should we have enough money we hope to print some pictures next time. I ask you to share it with all your friends so that they can enjoy it as much as you do. And Aunty Victoria gave me yet another very good idea. Write some nice letters and I am going to print them in the magazine.

HERMANN GROSSMANN

So, now you and dear friends all over the world can get to know each other. Is this not a really beautiful thought? So write to me and offer the magazine to others. I pray that you may become radiant stars in the heaven of divine love and greet each one of you warmly,
 your Uncle Hermann

A GERMAN BAHÁ'Í TEACHER IN FRANCE

As mentioned in Part 1, his childhood in Argentina where Hermann Grossmann grew up with people of all parts of the world made him open and unprejudiced. Neither the narrow-mindedness nor meanness of mind in school education in the years before World War I nor the painful experience of the war itself changed that attitude. The Message of Bahá'u'lláh confirmed his cosmopolitan way of thinking and inspired him to present in his talks and books such ideas without the slightest hesitation. This approach is reflected in the following lecture Hermann Grossmann gave in Paris in 1930, published in the international magazine *Star of the West* in an English translation.

> We are pleased to publish an article sent us by an earnest thinker, our Bahá'í friend of Germany, Dr Grossmann. Here he gives us a bit of philosophy such as could come only from one who had been through the deep travail of war. At the request of Dr Grossmann the article has been kindly translated for us by his friend, Mr. H.G. Pauli, of Brooklyn.

'Abdu'l-Bahá has many times pointed out how useful and how necessary it would be to travel for the diffusion of Unity.

As a matter of fact, Bahá'ís travel a great deal, frequently under great financial sacrifices. Is it the result of a desire to undertake journeys, which urges us on? Many are attracted, it is true, to study new landscapes, new people, their habits and customs, because these are interesting. But only for that reason? No, a Bahá'í has not the time to pursue his interests only. Are there not endless duties to perform? Does there not rest upon each single one of us the heavy responsibility of a new and better age? Are we to think that because others are working for this great purpose, we may now and then take it easy? Did 'Abdu'l-Bahá ever permit Himself to take leisure and leave others to do the work?

The world exists for our happiness. O surely, that is one of the most beautiful of the Bahá'í Teachings, this sincerely [sic] wish for joy. We would and we should be joyful! But joyful in giving thanks to God and in feeling that we are united with Him. That is the specific in the Bahá'í happiness. And that is what I mean when I say that a Bahá'í has not time for enjoyment only.

To be united with God in every hour, in every moment, to love Him, to give thanks to Him, means to love His creatures, to show our thankfulness to Him in showing kindness to them. That is the first duty of a Bahá'í; that is his constant duty. Everything we do should attest our love, that it comes from Him.

It does not help us much to familiarize ourselves with other people and to learn of foreign customs, if we do not possess the right spirit and if this knowledge does not lead to understanding and to prayer.

'O God, I thank Thee, that Thou hast taught me to see when my eyes were blind. I give Thee thanks, that Thou hast taught me not only to recognize matter, but the spirit in matter. The Spirit cries for humanity, that we surrender prejudice and that we enlarge our hearts and open them. The Spirit cries for unity, for love, and understanding. O God, suffer me to be filled with this spirit, suffer me to be a tool for the sake of Holy Peace amongst nations and humanity.'

Should you travel thus, then obey the command as a Bahá'í in foreign countries and go to other peoples.

But duty does not exist only in regard to the distant lands. Perhaps it may be easier for us Occidentals to find unity with the Orient since the Orientals appear to us to be so distant and so foreign, that we find ourselves attracted to learn to know them. But are we also ready to love and to learn to know those more like our own people, those near to us whose names are familiar? Can we also welcome these nearer neighbors with an open heart and without prejudice?

Are the Germans ready to try to feel for the French in every respect as for their brothers? Are the English ready to receive the Americans as sons of their own people? Not only with outward politeness and acceptable and obliging manners, but from the very heart? Let us be honest. Maybe it would be better to travel less, and to supplicate for the Spirit of God as a companion on our journeys. We can do that, even as business men and in the midst of the world.

And another thing: let us not always believe that we have to perform as an educational mission as we journey through other countries. Admittedly, our particular country has a great culture. But whatever our country may have, other countries also possess a great culture. And we shall find at least in every country something that is of value for us to acquire. Is it the result of pride, that we so readily put our country above all the others as regards its customs and achievements? Let us observe with an understanding heart. We love our country. Its customs, and its peculiarities are familiar to us. We have recognized its usefulness and its purpose and its orderliness. Therefore we believe that in our country everything is the best possible. But just so other nations are of the same opinion. Is not that a reason to become more thoughtful? God has created a world of diversities, and of a purpose not only just one correct type.

In Germany the telegraph poles are in a straight line on the railroad beds. That appears to us to be correct and intelligent. In France the poles incline in the opposite direction of the curves of the roadbed in order that they may resist the better pull on the wires. Does not that appear as self-evident? Which is the better? Every country has its experience and will insist that its way is the best! And perhaps both are right. Therefore, we must not insist that we are right in every instance. That is also tolerance and appreciation.

Humanity has been guilty in the past – they knew not what they did. But since the war humanity has, as it were, matured. And there rests upon us a terrific obligation: to work, work, work, that never again war should be, not here nor anywhere on earth. Do we recall how we stood facing each other in arms; do we remember how the shells furrowed the earth at Verdun, in the Champagne, in Flanders? How it seemed when comrades cried out under the splinters that tore them to pieces? How we stood by, bit our teeth together and shuddered within: 'Lord, Lord, help.' But we could not help and were forced to look on while their lives ebbed out in contortions!

In front of me in the railroad train compartment a French soldier is asleep. He wears the uniform against which I stood in the field out there to fight; and the scenery through which we pass is the same in which we years ago – not so very long ago – had dug ourselves in and to which earth we clung when the machine guns let their hail fire sweep over us so low.

Did we not all of us do our duty? At least we were told that it was our duty. Today we recognize another duty, and it is a peculiar feeling of brotherhood, which overcomes me, a feeling that would cause me to weep for joy as I walk through the streets of Paris and read and hear so much about the constructive work for peace.

Many of us in Germany are beginning to realize in the quietness an unintentional protection in our forced defenseless state by the Versailles Agreement, which will protect us, we hope, from taking part in a possible war-like complication. We are happy, therefore, that we may pursue the path of freedom without interference instead of to be obliged to turn our penetrative mind and our strength to the means of war in the first instance. A new war of the great nations will draw all countries into sufferings and is it not our kind that would then destroy itself? Let us desist from the narrow point of view to visualize the happenings of the past. War is horror for humanity, even so wherever it is furious. We must ban the ghost of war, or we shall never be master of it. For even while we are resting in the sleep of peace the torch of war may enkindle our home again in flames.

Should we not as 'Abdu'l-Bahá instructed, concentrate all of our thoughts on love and unity? 'A thought of hatred must be destroyed by a more powerful thought of love.' Should the workers for peace be less inspired and less active, less steadfast, and less convinced than the devotees of war? Should we wait until a new and more horrifying world war demolishes humanity, with all kinds of horror, before we cry for peace?

Before us appears Father Time as a sage, who says: 'Under my toga I hide both war and peace – choose!' [17]

MY PARENTS

In our family the relationship of the children to their parents was characterized by the Faith being a priority in daily life. With warmth and care my father and my mother nourished in us children the love for Bahá'u'lláh. My father did this in a unique way, combining imagination and an abundance of thought, detailed narrative and logic with a sense for the extraordinary. The fairytale of the King of Dwarfs, Flowerpot, was a never-ending story for us children, a bonus on Sunday mornings. A dwarf is damaged by a flowerpot thrown at him which leaves a deep dent in his head and makes him an outsider, but at the same time he enchants his environment because he grows in this dent various beautiful and fragrant flowers. He uses this as a charm and his friendliness to attract the hearts of people. He is made king, delights his subjects through his love, justice and benevolence. This gets him into all kinds of situations in which he can prove these qualities. Goodness always wins, for sympathy and understanding are the powers that overcome evil. We children were introduced to a violence-free fairytale world, which was a healthy anti-world to reality. Our father succeeded in this way in conveying to us the principles of the Bahá'í Faith at a time when the Cause of Bahá'u'lláh was persecuted and violence and fear of a destructive war gripped the lives of all.

A precious document of the love and care of my father is a letter, dated 11 March 1954, sent to me on the occasion of my secondary school finals. It is a letter that permits an insight into his inner being and appears like an evaluation of his own life. It is guidance and advice that my father hoped to convey for my life and that reflects his own sorrowful experience.

> Westerland, 11 March 1954
>
> My dear little grown-up boy,
> These are a few last sentences from a long, long letter, which I conceived in my thoughts this morning when your mother told me about your oral exams. I wrote part on the beach, another part in my room. I wish I could be with you now but before you receive this letter you will have written

your exams. Thus, I am far away from home, so far as never after our visit to Haifa, and this at a time when I had really hoped to be with you. Earlier, you were still a little boy, so small that your mother and I felt we should not take you along [to Haifa]; today you have reached the first significant part in your life where you have, in the eyes of the world, become an adult; only for your parents, secretly, so that others may not become aware of it, you are still the small grown-up boy.

I think it is always the case at this particular point in the development of their children that fathers, grandfathers and great-grandparents repeat in their imagination the days when they left school. They deeply hope to save their children from all that burden of inadequacy which they carried within themselves. This is a continuous hope for growth and it is a good one, but it is bad if there is no such hope. When I left school I had received a final certificate to further my studies, now being on my own; but what I would have needed desperately was a certificate that would have given me the trust to go through life accounting for my own life. Instead I had to realize that it was the world of dreams into which I had placed myself and that the world around me had no room for dreams. This was a troublesome, most disturbing perception. I praise destiny that led me to Bahá'u'lláh and changed my world of dreams into a world of faith and knowledge. Thus, I perceived a path in the pathless and assisting mercy when inadequacy threatened to paralyse my endeavours. I do hope I may have received a final certificate in the Faith, in the art of living; however, I may most probably never ever achieve the aim in school.

My dear one, you have inherited what may make it easier and what may make it more difficult for you. It will be easier as you know about the path which I had to look for so long; easier also as you were able to realize early that the transition to a time when our dreams will come true is steadily coming nearer. It is more difficult, however, as it is hard to have patience in that final battle. When the church steeples seem rather close and one thinks they cannot be far, one tends to forget that they are surrounded by little houses that grow bigger the closer we get, and we lose sight of the towers because of the narrow lanes. At present the goals set by Bahá'u'lláh are far away but we come closer and fast. The narrow lanes do not yet allow the true vision; keep this in mind for your own and other people's sake; be patient with them and yourself. Lately, in my talks, I have mentioned often the word 'mercy', the mercy offered by Bahá'u'lláh. This is what the new race of men and the new order, which is still in the world of so many dreams, desire; and because it is desired it will become reality. I wish for you that you will enter that new part in your life and be assured of that mercy which you yourself have often experienced; see what is in front of you and do not reach for the unachievable, neither within yourself nor in others; remember that mercy was at the beginning of your life path while your father recognized it late, only very late with certainty. This knowledge will facilitate your path of self-responsibility, my dear grown-up boy.

I kiss you as your loving father.

His caring way of introducing us children to nature will always be remembered. His garden was unique in variation, design and diversity and allowed him to show us the harmony of the world of rock, plant and animal. Lizards were a symbol of beauty for us and we learned to approach them with caution.

Of great significance for me was the fact that I could accompany my father to spend my vacations in his firm in Waldmichelbach, a place not far from our home. It was a small enterprise manufacturing cardboard, idyllically situated in the Odenwald in southern Germany. My father never had a driver's licence and had, therefore, a chauffeur. He was a tall, strong man who liked and loved me; he had great respect for my father as well. At that time it was rather unusual to see the way my father treated him and how natural it was that the boss sat at the same table with his driver. The same good relationship characterized my father and the workers in his firm. Therefore they liked and spoiled me and introduced me to the secrets of paper and cardboard production. My father's open-mindedness, inherited from his childhood in South America, free from any prejudice, assisted me significantly in understanding the implications of fundamental principles of the Faith. Most important, however, was the example he gave me as teacher of the Cause of Bahá'u'lláh. One of the responsibilities he had as a Hand of the Cause of God was to assist the development of the Faith in Germany.

When visiting various Bahá'í communities my father preferred to travel by car. Over the weekends I was his driver. On the way he deepened me in the teachings of Bahá'u'lláh, pointing out the historical relationship between religion and civilization, the interrelation between religion and science, everything that was on his mind. He loved to analyse his talks and their effect when we had met with the Bahá'ís and their friends. He was a brilliant speaker who knew how to impress his audience; he had the gift of focusing on the listeners, to adapt his talk to their capacity, and he used excellently the means of language and style to do so. These hours were precious as an invaluable introduction into the art of teaching the Faith. I owe my father in this respect very, very much; he became for me the example to an extent that people feel

HERMANN GROSSMANN

I am like him in gestures and way of presentation.

To draw a complete picture of the life of my father necessitates that the part my mother played in it be included. She was his partner for life, his companion, his complement, a source of support and protection. In the truest sense of the word she put herself in front of him as a shield, and as a helpmate she enabled him to serve the Faith to the best of his capacity. My mother was a selfless and sacrificial person, ready to serve the Cause of God. She knew well my father's strength and weakness, supported the one with love and devotion and softened the other through her understanding and kindness. Earlier I have mentioned that my father was miraculously spared imprisonment during the time of the Third Reich. It was his task, possibly decreed by God, to assist His Faith and the believers in their time of need. During all these trials my mother and my aunt Elsa Maria Grossmann protected and shielded my father from afflictions. Imprisonment would have been detrimental in view of his poor health. My mother's letters to Shoghi Effendi, especially in the years before World War II, throw some light on this. They attest to her self-denial, humility, self-sacrificing spirit and devotion and to her warmth, humaneness and her strength and steadfastness in the Faith.

On 31 December 1935 she wrote to the Guardian:

> On this last day of the year 1935 I send you my deepest love and greetings, my heartfelt devotion. I pray to the Beloved that He may bless and guide Shoghi Effendi, the precious head of the Cause of God. And I ask the Beloved to accept my life as a service to Him, and at its end which He may grant, as a sacrifice in His path. It is my heart's deepest desire that I may become worthy enough to be a martyr of the Faith of God. Alláh-u-Abhá!

The Universal House of Justice in honour of my deceased mother and in a loving and touching way characterizes her as an 'outstanding promoter [of the] Faith'. It is interesting to compare the service of my father in the administrative work in Germany with that of my mother. For years he was the chairman of the National Spiritual Assembly and served that institution with clarity, discipline and effectiveness in the promotion and consolidation of the Faith. My mother served in a similar way as secretary of the National Spiritual Assembly. While he harmonized contending opinions in clear-cut decisions, she translated the decisions into actions tempered by empathy and insight into what was doable. She served the Cause in yet another special way, deeply devoted and selflessly. When the institution of the Auxiliary Board was established in 1954 she was its member, first for Propagation, then for Protection. She served in an exemplary manner in both capacities for many years.

My mother was a fitting complement to my father in the promotion of the Cause of Bahá'u'lláh. While my father concentrated on certain subjects in his presentations and appealed especially to the intellect of his audience, my mother touched above all the hearts of people. Where he convinced through logic and clear proof, she complemented him through well-balanced harmony of thought and action. Where the one impressed because of his spirited and objective clarity and conclusive presentation of truth, the other enchanted the audience through warm feeling and personal sympathy.

In later years Amatu'l-Bahá Rúḥíyyih Khánum used to stress her friendship with my parents; she always emphasized the harmonious complement of their characters.

The radiant personality of my mother influenced many seekers who remember fondly her intuitive grasp, warmth and understanding. During the months-long visits to South America she accompanied my father, took care of the planning and organization, provided for his health and studied Spanish to be able to facilitate the meetings and converse with the believers in their mother tongue. In this context I would like to mention a characteristic of my father that is indicative of his attitude. Whenever he addressed and spoke to a German audience he would present the profound and essential verities in the teachings of Bahá'u'lláh in a way intellectual and logical consistency dictated, even the choice of words; however, the reports about his teaching methods in South America describe a very different attitude. They speak of deep warmth, feelings, a graceful intuitive capacity and personal heart-warming encouragement. The language of his childhood, the environment and the situation in South America clearly inspired another, somewhat hidden side in his character. My father's sympathy and loving care expressed themselves differently and adapted, factually in a German and emotionally in a Spanish environment.

In the education of their children my mother was a highly sensitive partner of my father. From earliest childhood the Bahá'í Faith took priority and spiritual steadfastness was not only a basis but protection in afflictions. I remember not one Goodbye from my mother, even for the shortest time of absence, which she would not link to a request that God would guide and protect me on my way. During the war, and afterwards when hunger and want prevailed and our home was crowded with the two families of her sisters, my mother was a tower of strength to all. It was she who started out with a handcart and in daylong marches to exchange something we owned for potatoes or vegetables from a farmer. As a young teenager I was allowed to accompany her. She was exemplary in courage, strength and loving care whatever the situation was: pushing the heavily loaded cart through the soggy forest soil, sitting on the cart and going down the hill at breakneck speed or hiding in the furrows of fields or road-side ditches from becoming targets for low-flying fighter-planes' machine guns.

Today I cherish even more the way and manner in which my mother brought close to me the love for Bahá'u'lláh and the realization of the depth and beauty of His teachings with the clarity and firmness typical of her; this became all the more impressive and lasting when we spent all our energies in these long and arduous marches through forsaken forests. Her example of active service to others showed to me the way for the spirit to express itself in deeds to manifest its transforming powers. For my personal appreciation of what the Bahá'í Faith stands for my mother gave me all that I needed in addition to what my father provided.

In the obituary on my mother the Universal House of Justice emphasizes: 'Finland [is] blessed by her pioneering [to] that land [in] the evening [of] her earthly life.' A strong motivation for her pioneering was to save a local Spiritual Assembly under number in this northern country, the language of which she did not understand and to which the only links were my family and I who lived at that time in Savonlinna close to the Russian border. Another reason may also have been the suggestion of Shoghi Effendi that a Bahá'í can serve the Cause of Bahá'u'lláh well, even at a great age, if he or she buries his or her bones in foreign soil. Thus my mother became an example to her family and the Finnish believers in her service. Her grave in Savonlinna is indeed a blessing for this community and the entire country.

The Universal House of Justice states that the members of that institution remember the 'loving angelic character' of my mother. This description is most apt in portraying why so many people, especially in Germany, remember her so well, many years after her passing. A fine testimony to her humility and gratitude for a life of fulfilment is her last Will.

MY PARENTS

Last will regarding my burial

I wish to be buried where I die. Should I die within one hour's journey from Neckargemünd or in Neckargemünd I would like to be buried in the same grave as my husband. As an epitaph I wish my name, the year of birth and death only.

I wish to be buried as a Bahá'í; if need be a prayer read from my prayer book will do.

I thank my children, my son- and daughter-in-law, the members of my family, my grandchildren and all the friends for their love, kindness and friendship.

My deepest gratitude goes to the Universal House of Justice and the Hands of the Cause of God, they were extremely kind to me.

    Anna Grossmann, née Hartmuth

We children honoured her Will in all but one point. Anna had been all her life a devoted and warm-hearted teacher of the Faith; we were certain she would not have objected to have on her tombstone in Savonlinna in the Finnish language the following words of Bahá'u'lláh: *'So powerful is the light of unity that it can illuminate the whole earth.'*[18]

We hope to make known this wonderful truth from the Writings of Bahá'u'lláh to all those who pass by her grave.

It was the harmony between two deeply devoted souls to the Cause of Bahá'u'lláh which opened up to us children the wondrous power and beauty of the Word of God. It is at the same time a legacy – a better one parents cannot request from God. The House of Justice expressed this sentiment in a loving way, stating in a cable to the family on 14 June 1984:

> ... your esteemed and much-loved mother whose soul [is] undoubtedly rejoicing [over the] services [to the] Cause [by] her children [and] grandchildren ...[19]

May Hermann and Anna Grossmann be in the future examples of abiding guidance and encouragement.

GLOSSARY

Ages: Shoghi Effendi used the term 'ages' to designate the three stages in the evolution of the Bahá'í community: the Heroic Age was from 1844 to 1921; the Formative Age began in 1921 and will continue until the Golden Age. This will last until the end of the Bahá'í Dispensation which will endure for at least one thousand years.

Aymara: Indigenous South Americans, who flourished before the Incas. Today (2009) they live mainly in the region of Lake Titicaca and make up the majority of the rural population of Bolivia with a few remaining in Peru. Their language, also called Aymara, is one of the family of languages known as Aymaran, one of the chief linguistic groups of the region. (See also Quechua).

Chief Stewards: In his last message in October 1957, Shoghi Effendi referred to the Hands of the Cause of God as 'the Chief Stewards of Bahá'u'lláh's Embryonic World Commonwealth, who have been invested by the unerring Pen of the Centre of His Covenant with the dual function of guarding over the security, and of ensuring the propagation of His Father's Faith'. This message contained strong indications regarding the future destiny of the Faith of God and led the Bahá'í community to rally around the Hands of the Cause of God after the passing of Shoghi Effendi.

Cold War: The state of diplomatic tension between the Communist world and the West arising from the struggle to win political and economic advantages without precipitating a major war, especially in the years from 1947 to 1962.

Conclave: Annual meeting of the Hands of the Cause of God, held in the Holy Land, after the passing of Shoghi Effendi until the establishment of the International Teaching Centre in 1973.

Custodians: Nine Hands of the Cause of God who were appointed by the body of the Hands on 25 November 1957 'to exercise – subject to such directions and decisions as may be given from time to time by us as the Chief Stewards of the Bahá'í World Faith – all such functions, rights and powers in succession to the Guardian of the Bahá'í Faith, His

Eminence the late Shoghi Effendi Rabbani, as are necessary to serve the interests of the Bahá'í World Faith, and this until such time as the Universal House of Justice, upon being duly established and elected in conformity with the Sacred Writings of Bahá'u'lláh and the Will and Testament of 'Abdu'l-Bahá, may otherwise determine'. In pursuance of the above, the Universal House of Justice decided on 7 June 1963 that 'the office of the Custodians of the Bahá'í World Faith ceases to exist', and this was endorsed in a declaration by the Custodians on the same date.

Epochs: This term was used by Shoghi Effendi to designate subdivisions of the three Ages of the Bahá'í Faith. The Heroic Age contained three epochs: the Ministries of the Báb, Bahá'u'lláh and 'Abdu'l-Bahá. The first epoch of the Formative Age began in 1921 and the fifth epoch in 2006. Shoghi Effendi also used the word 'epoch' to designate stages in the implementation of 'Abdu'l-Bahá's Divine Plan for the propagation of the Bahá'í Faith. The first epoch of the Divine Plan was from 1937 to 1963. We are now (in 2009) in the fifth epoch of the Formative Age and the second epoch of the Divine Plan.

European Teaching Committee: A committee of the National Spiritual Assembly of the United States and Canada appointed to build up Bahá'í communities, in accordance with the Second Seven Year Plan, in the goal countries of the 'sorrow stricken, war lacerated, sorely bewildered nations and peoples' of Europe after World War II. These were the Iberian Peninsula (Portugal and Spain), the Low Countries (Belgium and the Netherlands), the Scandinavian states (Norway, Sweden and Denmark), and Italy, to which Luxembourg and Switzerland were added constituting what came to be known as 'the Ten Goal Countries', to which Finland was later added.

Gestapo: The secret state police of Nazi Germany (*Geheime Staatspolizei*).

Hadíth: Traditions of Islam; utterances attributed to Muhammad, next to the Qur'án a source of religious decrees. In Shí'í Islam utterances of the Imáms are also regarded as *hadíth.*

Ḥaẓíratu'l-Quds (Arabic: 'Sacred Fold'): Bahá'í administrative headquarters and seats of National and Local Spiritual Assemblies.

Holy Years: The twelve months from 15 October 1952 to 15 October 1953 constituted a Holy Year, declared by Shoghi Effendi to commemorate the centenary of the intimation of Bahá'u'lláh's mission in the Síyáh-Chál. The Universal House of Justice declared the period from Riḍván 1992 to Riḍván 1993 to be a Holy Year, marking the centenary of Bahá'u'lláh's passing and the inauguration of the Lesser Covenant.

Indios, also called **Campesinos** *or* **Indigenas**: indigenous peoples of Latin America and their descendants. They usually speak an indigenous American language and often still live in a traditional and united group.

International Bahá'í Bureau: Office established in 1925 with the approval of Shoghi Effendi to promote Bahá'í teaching activities in Europe and as a communication centre between Bahá'í groups internationally; closed in 1957.

International Bahá'í Council: Created as an institution by Shoghi Effendi and formally announced to the Bahá'í world in January 1951 as the forerunner of the Universal House of Justice; its purposes were to forge links with the Israeli authorities, to assist the Guardian in the work of completing the superstructure of the Shrine of the Báb and to serve as an international Bahá'í secretariat. It became an elected body at Riḍván 1961, at which time its services to the Custodians were extended to include assisting with preparations for the International Bahá'í Convention at Riḍván 1963 and for the Bahá'í World Congress to be held in London following the International Convention. It ceased to exist in 1963 upon the formation of the Universal House of Justice.

Interregnum: In Bahá'í history, the period from the passing of Shoghi Effendi until the establishment of the Universal House of Justice (November 1957–April 1963) during which the Hands of the Cause of God exercised direction of the Bahá'í Faith.

Knights of Bahá'u'lláh: Shoghi Effendi conferred this title on all pioneers who opened designated virgin territories to the Faith during the first year of the Ten Year Crusade (Riḍván 1953 to Riḍván 1954), and on the first to do so in each such territory thereafter.

Mashriqu'l-Adhkár: (Arabic: 'Dawning Place of the Mention of God'): Bahá'í House of Worship and the surrounding complex of buildings of philanthropic institutions.

Mother Temple: Name used for the first House of Worship built in a specified area, indicating that it will be the first of many in that area.

NSDAP: Abbreviation of *Nationalsozialistische Deutsche Arbeiterpartei* (National Socialist German Workers' Party); a political party led by Hitler, based on aggressive militarism, anti-Semitism, and the assertion of the racial superiority of the 'Aryans'.

Quechua: A group of indigenous inhabitants of South America mainly occupying Peru and Ecuador. The language, also called Quechua, is the principal one of a family of languages known as Quechuan and, under the rule of the Incas, was the official language of their empire. (See also Aymara).

Reichsarbeitsdienst: During the Third Reich a 6-month compulsory labour service for male and female youth aged 18–25: dressed in uniform, they were increasingly trained and used in pre-military service.

Sabean Religion: An ancient Middle Eastern religion accepted by Bahá'ís as one of nine known, still existing, revealed religions.

Wilhelminian period: A seemingly brilliant epoch of German history under Wilhelm II (1888–1918), Emperor of Germany. It concealed serious inner tensions.

BIBLIOGRAPHY

'Abdu'l-Bahá. *The Promulgation of Universal Peace*. Wilmette, IL: Bahá'í Publishing Trust, 1995.
— *Selections from the Writings of 'Abdu'l-Bahá*. Haifa: Bahá'í World Centre, 1978; Wilmette, IL: Bahá'í Publishing Trust, 2000.
— *Tablets of Abdul Baha Abbas*. Chicago, New York: Bahai Publishing Society, 3 vols. 1909–1915.
— *The Will and Testament of 'Abdu'l-Bahá*. Wilmette, IL: Bahá'í Publishing Trust, 1971.
Bahá'í-Nachrichten. National Spiritual Assembly of the Bahá'ís of Germany and Austria.
Bahá'í News. National Spiritual Assembly of the United States, 1924– . Various issues.
The Bahá'í World. Vol. IV (1930–1932), Vol. V (1932–1934), Vol. VI (1934–1936), Vol. X (1944–1946), RP Wilmette, IL : Bahá'í Publishing Trust, 1981; Vol. XIII (1954–1963), Haifa: The Universal House of Justice, 1970; Vol. XV (1968–1973), Haifa: Bahá'í World Centre, 1976; Vol. XVII (1976–1979), Haifa: Bahá'í World Centre, 1981; Vol.XIX ((1983–1986), Haifa: Bahá'í World Centre, 1994.
Bahá'u'lláh. *Epistle to the Son of the Wolf*. Wilmette, IL: Bahá'í Publishing Trust, 1988.
— *Gleanings from the Writings of Bahá'u'lláh*. Translated by Shoghi Effendi. Wilmette, IL: Bahá'í Publishing Trust, 1982.
— *The Seven Valleys and the Four Valleys*. Wilmette, IL: Bahá'í Publishing Trust, rev. ed. 1991.
—*Tablets of Bahá'u'lláh Revealed after the Kitáb-i-Aqdas*. Haifa: Bahá'í World Centre, 1978.
A Compendium of Volumes of the Bahá'í World, an International Record, I-XII, 82–110 of the Bahá'í Era (1925–1954). Compiled by Roger White. Oxford: George Ronald, 1981.
Groschek, Iris. *Wilhelm Heydorn und die Anfänge der Bahá'í in Hamburg*. Zeitschrift des Vereins für Hamburgische Geschichte. Band 84. 1998.
Grossmann, Anna. 'Memories'. Unpublished. Archives of the National Spiritual Assembly of Germany, Hofheim
—'Notes'. Unpublished. Archives of the National Spiritual Assembly of Germany, Hofheim.
Grossmann, Elsa Maria. 'Memories of Elsa Maria Grossmann. Notes by Foruhar Khabirpour and Elsa Maria Grossmann.' Hofheim: Archives of the National Spiritual Assembly of the Bahá'ís of Germany.
Grossmann, Hermann. See also Appendix 2.

— *Am Morgen einer neuen Zeit*. Stuttgart, 1932, 1948.
— *Umbruch zur Einheit*. Stuttgart, 1947.
— *Zur Geschichte der Bahá'í-Religion 1935 bis 1945* (History of the Bahá'í Faith 1935 to 1945). Unpublished manuscript. Hofheim: Archives of Hermann Grossmann.
Harper, Barron. *Lights of Fortitude*. Oxford: George Ronald, 1997, 2007.
Heller, Wendy. *Lidia*. Oxford: George Ronald, 1985.
Hofman, David. *George Townshend: Hand of the Cause of God*. Oxford, George Ronald, 1983, 2002.
Jahresbericht 1980–1982. Hamburg: Joachim Jangius-Gesellschaft des Wissenschaften.
Lights of Guidance: *A Bahá'í Reference File*. Compiled by Helen Basset Hornby. Rev. ed. New Delhi: Bahá'í Publishing Trust, 1999.
Momen, Moojan. *Dr. J. E. Esslemont, Hand of the Cause of God*. London: Bahá'í Publishing Trust, 1975.
Noticias Bahá'ís. Organo de la Asamblea Espiritual National Bahá'í de Argentina, Bolivia, Chile, Paraguay y Uruguay.
Rabbani, Rúḥíyyih (Amatu'l-Bahá Rúḥíyyih Khánum). *The Passing of Shoghi Effendi*. In collaboration with John Ferraby. London, Bahá'í Publishing Trust, 1958.
— *The Priceless Pearl*. London: Bahá'í Publishing Trust, 1969.
Romanische Jahrbücher. Hamburg, 1966, 1980.
Das Rosengärtlein. Eine Neunteljahresschrift für die Bahá'í-Jugend und ihre Freunde. Hamburg, 1924–1928
Shoghi Effendi. *The Bahá'í Faith 1844–1952: Information Statistical and Comparative*. London: Bahá'í Publishing Trust, 1952.
— *Citadel of Faith: Messages to America 1947–1957*. Wilmette, IL: Bahá'í Publishing Trust, 1965.
— *The World Order of Bahá'u'lláh*. Wilmette, IL: Bahá'í Publishing Trust, 1965.
— *God Passes By*. Wilmette, IL: Bahá'í Publishing Trust, 1970.
—*The Light of Divine Guidance*. Vol. 1: *The Messages from the Guardian of the Bahá'í Faith to the Bahá'ís of Germany and Austria*. Hofheim: Bahá'í-Verlag, 1982. Vol. 2: *Letters from the Guardian of the Bahá'í Faith to Individual Believers, Groups and Bahá'í Communities in Germany and Austria*. Hofheim: Bahá'í-Verlag, 1985.
— *Messages to the Bahá'í World 1950–1957*. Wilmette, IL: Bahá'í Publishing Trust, 1958.
Sonne der Wahrheit. Organ der Bahá'í in Deutschand und Österreich. 1921–1937.
Star of the West, A Bahá'í Magazine. Chicago, 1910–1935. Issues 1910 to 1924, RP 8 vols. Oxford: George Ronald, 1978.
Taherzadeh, Adib. *The Revelation of Bahá'u'lláh*. Vol. 4. Oxford: George Ronald, 1987
The Universal House of Justice. *The Ministry of the Custodians 1957–1963: An Account of the Stewardship of the Hands of the Cause*. Haifa: Bahá'í World Centre, 1992.

REFERENCES

PART I

PREFACE
1. Abdu'l-Bahá, Will and Testament, para. 21, p. 13.

2 THE FIRST WORLD WAR
2. Elsa Maria Grossmann, 'Notes by Foruhar Khabirpour and Elsa Maria Grossmann', Diary, Archives of the National Spiritual Assembly of Germany, Hofheim.

3 ENCOUNTER WITH THE BAHÁ'Í FAITH
3. Anna Grossmann, 'Notes', Archives of the National Spiritual Assembly of Germany, Hofheim.
4. Elsa Maria Grossmann, 'Notes by Foruhar Khabirpour', Archives of the National Spiritual Assembly of Germany, Hofheim.
5. Anna Grossmann, 'Notes', op. cit.
6. *Compendium*, p. 585.
7. Elsa Maria Grossmann, 'Notes by Foruhar Khabirpour', op. cit.
8. Anna Grossmann in a letter.

5 FIRST ENDEAVOURS ON BEHALF OF THE BELOVED CAUSE
9. *Bahá'í World*, Vol. XV, p. 417.
10. *Star of the West*, November 1923, p. 249.
11. *Bahá'í News*, August 1927, p. 7.
12. Shoghi Effendi, *God Passes By*, p. 386.
13. *Bahá'í News*, August 1927, p. 7.
14. See also: Momen, *Esslemont*, p. 34.
15. Elsa Maria Grossmann, 'Notes', see also: Groschek, *Wilhelm Heydorn*.
16. Letter from Hermann Grossmann to Shoghi Effendi, 17 November 1926.
17. Letter from Hermann Grossmann to Shoghi Effendi, 13 December 1923.
18. *Das Rosengärtlein*.
19. *Bahá'í News Letter*, October 1929, p. 8 and November 1929, p. 3.

20. *Star of the West*, Vol. 20, No. 6, September 1929, p. 193.
21. Letter from Hermann Grossmann to Shoghi Effendi, 18 February 1929.
22. Letter from Hermann Grossmann to Shoghi Effendi, 24 November 1926.
23. *Sonne der Wahrheit*, November 1922 and Shoghi Effendi, *The Bahá'í Faith 1842–1952*, p. 12.
24. Letter from Hermann Grossmann to Shoghi Effendi, 6 April 1926.
25. Anna Grossmann, 'Notes', op. cit.

6 ESPERANTO

26. Heller, *Lidia*, p. 248.
27. Shoghi Effendi, *The Light of Divine Guidance*, Vol. 1, p. 25.
28. *Bahá'í-Nachrichten*, October 1935, p. 6.
29. Report of Adolf Lorey about the dissolution of the Esperanto Association in Germany, dated 2 June 1946, Archives of Dr Hermann Grossmann, National Spiritual Assembly of the Bahá'ís of Germany, Hofheim.

7 THE YEARS UP TO 1937

30. Archives of Dr Hermann Grossmann, Hofheim.
31. *Bahá'í World*, Vol. IV, p. 67.
32. *Bahá'í-Nachrichten*, April 1936, p. 11.
33. Archives of Dr Hermann Grossmann, Hofheim.
34. Letter from Shoghi Effendi to Hermann Grossmann, 12 November 1935, Archives of the National Spiritual Assembly of the Bahá'ís of Germany, Hofheim.
35. With the kind assistance of Professor Margot Kruse, Reinbek near Hamburg, according to *Romanische Jahrbücher*, Hamburg 1966 and 1980; and the *Jahresbericht 1980–1982* of the Joachim Jangius-Gesellschaft der Wissenschaften, Hamburg.

8 PILGRIMAGE TO HAIFA

36. *Bahá'í World*, Vol. XVII, p. 406.
37. Anna Grossmann, 'Memories', unpublished. Archives of the National Spiritual Assembly of Germany, Hofheim.
38. Elsa Maria Grossmann, 'Pilgrimage to the Holy Places of the Bahá'ís', unpublished.

9 INTERDICTION UNDER THE NATIONAL SOCIALISTS

39. This chapter is supported by Hermann Grossmann's unpublished manuscript *Zur Geschichte der Bahá'í-Religion 1935 bis 1945* (History of the Bahá'í Religion 1935 to 1945), Archives of Dr Hermann Grossmann, Hofheim.

REFERENCES

40. Letter from Amatu'l-Bahá Rúḥíyyih Khánum to Elsa Maria Grossmann and Anna Grossmann, 24 February 1937, Archives of the National Spiritual Assembly of Germany, Hofheim.
41. Letter from Anna Grossmann to Shoghi Effendi, 29 April 1937.
42. 'Mitteilungen der Geheimen Staatspolizei Hamburg an die Bahá'í-Bewegung Hamburg vom 5. Juni 1937', Archives of Dr Hermann Grossmann, Hofheim.
43. Letter from Anna Grossmann to Shoghi Effendi, 9 June 1937.
44. Letter from Shoghi Effendi to Anna Grossmann, 20 March 1938, Archives of the National Spiritual Assembly of the Bahá'ís of Germany, Hofheim.
45. Shoghi Effendi, *The Light of Divine Guidance*, Vol. 1, pp. 54–5.
46. *Bahá'í World*, Vol. XIII, pp. 909–11.
47. According to a letter addressed to Shoghi Effendi, 17 November 1938.
48. Shoghi Effendi, *The Light of Divine Guidance*, Vol. 2, p. 50.
49. Emil Jörn, 1953, Archives of Dr Hermann Grossmann, Hofheim.
50. Notes from 1946 and 1961: 'Entstehung der Bahá'í-Gemeinde Schwerin' (Beginning of the Bahá'í Community in Schwerin), Archives of Dr Hermann Grossmann, Hofheim.
51. Karla Gerber, 'Notes'.
52. Anna Grossmann in a letter to Wendy Heller; see Heller, *Lidia*, pp. 240–41.
53. Private archives.
54. Memories of Charlotta Koehler, Colmar, February 1999.
55. Anna Grossmann, Report, Archives of Dr Hermann Grossmann, Hofheim; and *Bahá'í World*, Vol. X, p. 25.
56. Letters from Ruth Espenlaub-Schnizler to Susanne Pfaff-Grossmann, 22 September 1999 and December 2000.
57. ibid.
58. Reports from newspapers, Archives of Dr Hermann Grossmann, Hofheim.
59. Archives of Dr Hermann Grossmann, Hofheim.
60. Dr Hermann Grossmann, 'Notes', Archives of Dr Hermann Grossmann, Hofheim.

10 THE RENEWAL OF BAHÁ'Í ACTIVITIES, 1945–1948

61. Archives of Dr Hermann Grossmann, Hofheim.
62. Martin Aiff, tape recording, 22 June 1999.
63. Letter from Hermine and Massoud Berdjis to Hartmut Grossmann, 14 February 1996.
64. Hermann Grossmann, *Geschichte der Bahá'í-Religion in Deutschland nach dem Zusammenbruch der nationalsozialistischen, Herrschaft*

(History of the Bahá'í Religion in Germany). Unpublished manuscript, Archives of Dr Hermann Grossmann, Hofheim.
65. ibid.
66. ibid.
67. *Sonne der Wahrheit*, October 1947, p. 95.
68. Letter from Rúḥíyyih Khánum to Anna Grossmann, 9 February 1947, in Shoghi Effendi, *The Light of Divine Guidance*, Vol. 2, p. 57.
69. Martin Aiff, tape recording, 22 June 1999.
70. E-mail from Christopher Sprung to Susanne Pfaff-Grossmann, 22 June 1999.
71. Archives of Dr Hermann Grossmann, Hofheim.
72. Hermann Grossmann, *Geschichte der Bahá'í-Religion in Deutschland nach dem Zusammenbruch der nationalsozialistischen Herrschaft*, (History of the Bahá'í Religion in Germany), op. cit.
73. ibid.
74. Martin Aiff, tape recording, 22 June 1999.
75. Hermann Grossmann, *Geschichte der Bahá'í-Religion in Deutschland nach dem Zusammenbruch der nationalsozialistischen Herrschaft*, History of the Bahá'í Religion, Manuscript, Archives Hermann Grossmann, Hofheim is this the same as in note 39 and notes 64, 75, 78 etc?
76. *Bahá'í World*, Vol. X, p. 734.
77. *Bahá'í News*, February 1946, p. 2.
78. Hermann Grossmann, *Geschichte der Bahá'í-Religion in Deutschland nach dem Zusammenbruch der nationalsozialistischen Herrschaft,* (History of the Bahá'í Religion in Germany), op. cit.
79. ibid.
80. ibid.
81. Jean Sévin, 'Brève souvenance d'une grande figure de la Foi', letter of 27 June 1996.
82. Hermann Grossmann, *Geschichte der Bahá'í-Religion in Deutschland nach dem Zusammenbruch der nationalsozialistischen Herrschaft,* (History of the Bahá'í Religion in Germany), op. cit.
83. *Bahá'í World*, Vol. X, p. 26.
84. Martin Aiff, tape recording, 22 June 1999.
85. Hermann Grossmann, *Geschichte der Bahá'í-Religion in Deutschland nach dem Zusammenbruch der nationalsozialistischen Herrschaft,* (History of the Bahá'í Religion in Germany), op. cit.
86. ibid.
87. Shoghi Effendi, *The Light of Divine Guidance*, Vol. 2, pp. 75–6.
88. Letter from Rúḥíyyih Khánum to Anna Grossmann, 14 April 1948, written in German, Archives of the National Spiritual Assembly of Germany, Hofheim.

REFERENCES

89. Shoghi Effendi, *The Light of Divine Guidance*, Vol. 1, pp. 154 and 156.
90. *Bahá'í-Nachrichten*, April 1949, p. 5.
91. Letter from Liese Lotte Walcker to Anna Grossmann, 13 August 1968.
92. Shoghi Effendi, *Citadel of Faith*, p. 125.

11 THE FIVE YEAR PLAN, 1948–1953

93. *Bahá'í-Nachrichten*, September 1948, p. 11.
94. Letter from Hand of the Cause of God 'Alí-Muḥammad Varqá to Hartmut Grossmann, 2 September 1995.
95. *Bahá'í-Nachrichten*, September 1951, pp. 2–3.
96. *Bahá'í-Nachrichten*, September 1948, p. 6.
97. Ian Semple, 'Notes for Anke Grossmann', 1 July 1995.
98. Ian Semple to Anke Grossmann, tape recording, June 1995.
99. Letter from Dr Mokhtar Afscharian to Susanne Pfaff-Grossmann, 28 September 1999.
100. Fax from Dr Parviz Eschraghi to Susanne Pfaff-Grossmann, 16 June 1999.
101. Letter from Eunice Braun to Susanne Pfaff-Grossmann, 16 July 1997.
102. *Bahá'í-Nachrichten*, May 1949.
103. Shoghi Effendi, *The Light of Divine Guidance*, Vol.1, p. 164.
104. *Compendium*, pp. 482 and 657, and Anna Grossmann 'In Memory of Lina Benke', private archives.
105. Shoghi Effendi, *The Light of Divine Guidance*, Vol. 1, pp. 170–71.
106. *Bahá'í News*, December 1951, p. 4.
107. Shoghi Effendi, *The Light of Divine Guidance*, Vol. 1, p. 177.
108. ibid. p. 179.
109. Ian Semple, 'Notes for Anke Grossmann', 1 July 1995.
110. Shoghi Effendi, *The Light of Divine Guidance*, Vol. 1, p. 185.

12 APPOINTMENT AS A HAND OF THE CAUSE OF GOD

111. 'Abdu'l-Bahá, Will and Testament, paras. 20–22, pp. 12–13.
112. Rúḥíyyih Rabbani, *The Priceless Pearl*.
113. 'Cablegram from the Guardian Shoghi Effendi via International Bahá'í Bureau', Geneva, 23 December 1951, private archives.
114. Letter from the secretary of the National Spritual Assembly of the Bahá'ís of Germany and Austria to Hermann Grossmann, 9 January 1952.
115. Letter from the secretary of the National Spiritual Assembly of the Bahá'ís of India, Pakistan and Burma to Hermann Grossmann, 9 January 1952.
116. Letter from the secretary of the National Spiritual Assembly of the Bahá'ís of Iran to Hermann Grossmann, 21 January 1952.

117. Letter from the secretary of the National Spiritual Assembly of the Bahá'ís of the British Isles to Hermann Grossmann, 23 January 1952.
118. Undated letter from the Kampala Bahá'í Group, Kampala, Uganda to Hermann Grossmann.
119. Letter from the secretary of the National Spiritual Assembly of the Bahá'ís of Canada to Hermann Grossmann, 15 May 1952.
120. Letter from the Assemblee Spirituelle Bahá'ie de Luxembourg to Hermann Grossmann, 18 January 1952.
121. Letter from Hand of the Cause of God Agnes B. Alexander, Tokyo, Japan to Hermann Grossmann, 27 January 1952.
122. See also Barron Harper, *Lights of Fortitude*, rev. ed. p. 364.
123. Letter from Beatrice Ashton, Evanston, IL, USA, to Hermann Grossmann, 31 December 1951.
124. Letter from Ian Semple to Hermann Grossmann, 7 January 1952.
125. Ian Semple, 'Notes for Anke Grossmann', 1 July 1995.
126. Letter from Dr M. Zabih, Tehran, to Hermann Grossmann, 19 January 1952.
127. Martin Aiff, tape recording, 22 June 1999.
128. *Bahá'í News*, November 1952, p. 11.

13 ANNA GROSSMANN

129. Letter from Amatu'l-Bahá Rúḥíyyih Khánum to Anna Grossmann, 20 August 1939, Archives of the National Spiritual Assembly of the Bahá'ís of Germany, Hofheim.
130. Letter from Hand of the Cause of God Amatu'l-Bahá Rúḥíyyih Khánum to Hartmut Grossmann, 3 September 1984, Archives of the National Spiritual Assembly of Germany, Hofheim.
131. Ian Semple, 'Memories of Dr Hermann Grossmann'.
132. Hartmut Grossmann, 'Memories of Anna Grossmann'.
133. Letter from Harry Liedtke to Hartmut Grossmann, 12 April 1996.
134. Letter from René Steiner to Hartmut and Ursula Grossmann, 1998.
135. Letter from Hermine Berdjis to Susanne Pfaff-Grossmann, 17 November 1997.
136. Badieh Poostchi, 'Notes to Anna Grossmann', letter to Susanne Pfaff-Grossmann. 1 April 2001.
137. Letter from Ola Pawlowska to Ursula Grossmann, 6 December 1995.
138. Letter from Hermine Berdjis to Susanne Pfaff-Grossmann, 17 November 1997.
139. Letter from Ursula von Brunn to Hartmut and Ursula Grossmann, 10 October 1995.
140. Hand of the Cause of God 'Alí-Akbar Furútan to Hartmut Grossmann, July 1995.

REFERENCES

141. E-mail from Gisela von Brunn to Susanne Pfaff-Grossmann, 16 July 2000; and letter from Ursula von Brunn to Kerstin Poschmann, 10 October 1995.
142. Fred Schechter to Anke Grossmann, tape recording.
143. Anneliese Bopp to Susanne Pfaff-Grossmann, April 2000.
144. Wolfgang Peter Loehndorf, e-mail to Susanne Pfaff-Grossmann, 28 April 2002.
145. Letter from Anna Grossmann to Annemarie Krüger-Brauns, 9 May 1979.

14 THE TIRELESS SCHOLAR

146. Hanna Guckeisen, Foreword to Hermann Grossmann, *Am Morgen einer neuen Zeit.*
147. Hermann Grossmann, *Umbruch zur Einheit*, p. 7.
148. Shoghi Effendi, *The Light of Divine Guidance*, Vol. 2, p. 84.
149. Fax from Dr Udo Schaefer, 5 February 1996.
150. Archives of Dr Hermann Grossmann, Hofheim.
151. ibid.
152. Ben Levy, tape recording.
153. *Bahá'í-Nachrichten*, September 1948, p. 11.
154. Archives of Dr Hermann Grossmann, Hofheim.
155. Archives of Dr Hermann Grossmann, Hofheim.

15 LAUNCHING THE TEN YEAR CRUSADE

156. Shoghi Effendi, Cablegram 5 August 1952, in *Messages to the Bahá'í World*, p. 40.
157. ibid. p. 42.
158. Shoghi Effendi, Message to the American Intercontinental Conference, 4 May 1953, Archives of Dr Hermann Grossmann, Hofheim.
159. Archives of Dr Hermann Grossmann, Hofheim.
160. ibid.
161. Brigitte Lundblade, 'Memories of Dr Hermann Grossmann, Hand of the Cause of God', in letter to Hartmut and Ursula Grossmann, 16 December 1995.

16 ELSA MARIA GROSSMANN

162. The following quotations are taken from 'Memories of Elsa Maria Grossmann, Notes by Foruhar Khabirpour and Elsa Maria Grossmann', 'In Memoriam', Archives of the National Spiritual Assembly of Germany, Hofheim.
163. Elsa Maria Grossmann, poems, private archives.
164. Lottchen Wernicke, Notes to Susanne Pfaff-Grossmann, October 2000.

165. Notes of Karla Gerber to Susanne Pfaff-Grossmann, 1996.
166. Lottchen Wernicke, Notes to Susanne Pfaff-Grossmann, October 2000.
167. *Bahá'í News*, August 1958, p. 9.
168. Letter from Amatu'l-Bahá Rúḥíyyih Khánum to Elsa Maria Grossmann, 28 March 1958, Archives of the National Spiritual Assembly of Germany, Hofheim.
169. Letter from Amatu'l-Bahá Rúḥíyyih Khánum to Elsa Maria Grossmann, 16 February 1958, Archives of the National Spiritual Assembly of Germany, Hofheim.
170. Lottchen Wernicke, Notes to Susanne Pfaff-Grossmann, October 2000.
171. Elsa Maria Grossmann, poems, private archives.

17 THE FIRST FIVE YEARS OF THE TEN YEAR CRUSADE, 1953-1957

172. *Bahá'í-Nachrichten*, March/April 1954, p. 4 and May 1954, p. 11; also *Bahá'í News*, December 1954, pp. 3–4.
173. *Bahá'í-Nachrichten*, May 1954, p. 24; and *Bahá'í News*, December 1954, p. 4.
174. *Bahá'í-Nachrichten*, May 1954, p. 35.
175. Letter from the National Spiritual Assembly of the Bahá'ís of the British Isles, 28 September 1954.
176. *Bahá'í News*, December 1954, p. 3.
177. Letter from Hermann Grossmann to Geertrui Ankersmit, 14 April 1955; and Archives of Dr Hermann Grossmann, Hofheim.
178. Letter from Hermine Berdjis to Susanne Pfaff-Grossmann, 17 November 1997; and in David Hofman, *George Townshend*, p. 363.
179. *Bahá'í-Nachrichten*, April 1955, p. 7.
180. Memoirs of Anna Grossmann; and *Bahá'í News*, September 1955.
181. Archives of Dr Hermann Grossmann, Hofheim.
182. Letter from Ursula von Brunn to Hartmut and Ursula Grossmann, 11 October 1995.
183. Hermann Grossmann, travel diary 1955, private archives.
184. *Bahá'í-Nachrichten*, January/March 1955, p. 2.
185. ibid. December 1955 and January/February 1956, pp. 14–15.
186. ibid. March 1956, p. 8.
187. *Bahá'í World*, Vol. XVI, p. 537.
188. Hermann Grossmann, travel diary 1956, private archives.
189. *Bahá'í-Nachrichten*, June 1956, p. 18.
190. ibid., also *Bahá'í News*, August 1956, p. 5.
191. *Bahá'í-Nachrichten*, June 1956, p. 18.
192. E-mail from Alex Käfer to Susanne Pfaff-Grossmann, 8 May 1999.

REFERENCES

193. Letter from Hermine and Massoud Berdjis to Hartmut Grossmann, 14 February 1996.
194. Letter from Nahid Aschari to Susanne Pfaff-Grossmann, August 2003.
195. Hermann Grossmann, travel diary 1957, private archives.
196. *Bahá'í News*, June 1957, p. 11.
197. Letter from Brigitte Lundblade to Hartmut and Ursula Grossmann, 16 December 1995.
198. *Bahá'í News*, February 1958, p. 11.

18 SECOND PILGRIMAGE, 1957

199. Martin Aiff, tape recording, 22 June 1999.
200. Letter from Änni Blackmer-Langenhorst to Hartmut Grossmann, 3 October 1996.
201. Letter from Ezzat Zahrai to Hartmut Grossmann, 5 February 1997.
202. Anna Grossmann in *Bahá'í-Nachrichten*, June 1957, p. 10.
203. Ian Semple, 'Notes for Anke Grossmann', 1 July 1995.
204. ibid.
205. ibid.
206. Anna Grossmann in *Bahá'í-Nachrichten*, June 1957, p. 10; and 'Anna Grossmann Pilgrim Notes', and 'Anna Grossmann Notes', Archives of Dr Hermann Grossmann, Hofheim.
207. Letter from Nahid Aschari to Susanne Pfaff-Grossmann, August 2003.
208. Anna Grossmann in *Bahá'í-Nachrichten*, June 1957, p. 10.
209. Ian Semple, 'Notes for Anke Grossmann', 1 July 1995.
210. *Bahá'í-Nachrichten*, June 1957, pp. 2–4.
211. Martin Aiff, tape recording, 22 June 1999.

19 THE PASSING OF THE GUARDIAN, SHOGHI EFFENDI

212. Amatu'l-Bahá Rúḥíyyih Khánum, *The Passing of Shoghi Effendi*.
213. *Ministry of the Custodians*, p. 8.
214. Amatu'l-Bahá Rúḥíyyih Khánum, *The Passing of Shoghi Effendi*.
215. Martin Aiff, tape recording, 22 June 1999.
216. Hermann Grossmann, travel diary 1957, private archives.
217. *Ministry of the Custodians*, p. 7; and *Bahá'í News*, July 1957, p. 2.
218. Letter from René Steiner to Susanne Pfaff-Grossmann, August 1998.
219. Archives of Dr Hermann Grossmann, Hofheim.
220. Letter from Evelyn Marks to Barbara Grossmann, July 1995.
221. Letter from Hand of the Cause of God 'Alí-Akbar Furútan to Hartmut Grossmann, July 1995.
222. Martin Aiff, tape recording, 22 June 1999.
223. Archives of Dr Hermann Grossmann, Hofheim.

224. 'Abdu'l-Bahá, Will and Testament, para. 54.
225. *Bahá'í News*, July 1958, p. 17.
226. *Österreichische Bahá'í-Mitteilungen*, July 2000.
227. *Bahá'í-Nachrichten*, June/July 1958, p. 11.
228. *Bahá'í News*, October 1958, p. 2.
229. *Bahá'í News*, January 1959, p. 14.
230. *Ministry of the Custodians*, pp. 118–21.
231. ibid. p. 124.

20 RETURN TO SOUTH AMERICA, 1959

232. This chapter is based on the travel diary of Dr Hermann Grossmann, private archives.
233. Anna Grossmann, in *Bahá'í-Briefe*, No. 38, pp. 1037–44.
234. Anna Grossmann, in *Bahá'í-Nachrichten*, March 1959, p. 8.
235. ibid.
236. Letter from Mas'úd Khamsí to Hartmut and Ursula Grossmann, 20 April 1998.
237. *Compendium*, p. 516.
238. *Bahá'í News*, July 1959, p. 13.
239. Letter from Katharine Meyer to Hartmut Grossmann, 29 December 1995.
240. *Noticias Bahá'ís* (Argentina, Bolivia, Chile, Paraguay and Uruguay), May/ July 1959, p. 5.
241. Letter from an unidentified lady, sent to the Grossmann family by Ursula von Brunn in 1995.
242. Letter from an unidentified lady, sent to the Grossmann family by Ursula von Brunn in 1995.
243. Letter from Athos Costas, 23 September 1995, sent to the Grossmann family by Ursula von Brunn.
244. Letter dated 21 May 1995, sent to the Grossmann family by Ursula von Brunn.
245. *Bahá'í News*, July 1959, p. 10.
246. Reported by Marlies Reitz to Susanne Pfaff-Grossmann, March 2000.
247. Memories of Yolanda Claros R., October 1995, sent by Ursula von Brunn.
248. *Noticias Bahá'ís* (Argentina, Bolivia, Chile, Paraguay and Uruguay), May/July 1959, p. 2; and *Bahá'í News*, July 1959, p. 13.
249. Letter from Katharine Meyer to Hartmut Grossmann, 29 December 1995.
250. Anna Grossmann, in *Bahá'í-Nachrichten*, August 1959, pp. 1–2; and also Ian Semple, tape recording.
251. Ian Semple, conversation with Anke Grossmann, tape recording, June 1995.

REFERENCES

252. *Bahá'í-Nachrichten*, October 1959, p. 10.
253. *Ministry of the Custodians*, pp. 167–8.

21 SOUTH AMERICAN PILLARS OF THE UNIVERSAL HOUSE OF JUSTICE

254. This chapter is based on the diaries of Anna Grossmann and Hermann Grossmann, private archives.
255. Anna Grossmann, in *Bahá'í-Nachrichten*, 21 March 1960.
256. Memoirs of Renate Modern, São Paulo, Brazil, October 1995.
257. Anna Grossmann, in *Bahá'í-Nachrichten*, 21 March 1960.
258. E-mail from Gilbert Grasselly to Hartmut Grossmann, 15 December 1995.
259. Anna Grossmann, in *Bahá'í-Nachrichten*, 21 March 1960.
260. *Bahá'í News*, August 1960, p. 5.
261. *Bahá'í News*, September 1960, p. 14.
262. Report, 'Visitas a Comunidad Bahá'í de Valdivia (Chile) efectuadas por Mano de la Causa de Dios Dr Hermann Grossmann', 10 November 1995.
263. Letter from Hermann Grossmann copied by the Local Spiritual Assembly of Valdivia, 30 September 1960.
264. *Bahá'í-Nachrichten*, September 1960, p. 4.
265. E-mail from Donald Witzel, 18 November 1997.
266. Notes on a lecture of Hermann Grossmann, by an unidentified Bahá'í.
267. *Bahá'í News*, January 1961, p. 6.
268. *Bahá'í News*, December 1960, p. 16.
269. *Bahá'í News*, February 1961, p. 1.
270. *Noticias Bahá'ís* (Argentina), May/August 1961.
271. Written by an unidentified author.
272. Letter from Oscar Salazar, Salta, Argentina, to Hartmut Grossmann, 12 December 1994.

22 LAST JOURNEY TO SOUTH AMERICA, 1962

273. This chapter is based on the diary and the memories of Anna Grossmann, private archives.
274. *Bahá'í-Nachrichten*, October 1962, p. 9.
275. Dr Muhájir did in fact lay down his life in South America; he passed away in 1979 while participating in a teaching conference in Quito, Ecuador.
276. Jameson Bond, conversation with Anke Grossmann, tape recording.

23 THE MOST GREAT JUBILEE, 1963

277. *Bahá'í News*, March 1963, p. 5.
278. *Ministry of the Custodians*, pp. 365–6.
279. ibid. pp. 381–5.
280. ibid. p. 396.
281. ibid. pp. 429–30.
282. ibid. p. 433.
283. *Messages from the Universal House of Justice 1963–1986*, p. 6.
284. *Ministry of the Custodians*, p. 2.

24 FINAL YEARS AND PASSING

285. Anna Grossmann, 'Memories'.
286. ibid.
287. *Bahá'í-Nachrichten*, 1 August 1968, pp. 8–10.
288. ibid. pp. 10–11.
289. ibid. p. 11; and letter from René Steiner to Anna Grossmann.
290. Cable from the Universal House of Justice, in *Bahá'í-Nachrichten*, 1 August 1968, p. 11; also *Bahá'í News*, September 1968, p. 3; and Harper, *Lights of Fortitude*, p. 183.
291. Cable from the Hands of the Cause of God to Anna Grossmann, 9 July 1968.
292. Cable from the Hand of the Cause of God Amatu'l-Bahá Rúḥíyyih Khánum to Anna Grossmann, 9 July 1968.
293. Cable from the Universal House of Justice to Anna Grossmann, 9 July 1968.
294. Cable from the Hand of the Cause of God Zikrullah Khadem to Anna Grossmann, 12 July 1968.
295. Letter from the Hand of the Cause of God William Sears to Anna Grossmann, 9 August 1968.
296. Letter from the Hand of the Cause of God John Robarts to Anna Grossmann, 26 July 1968.
297. Letter from the Hand of the Cause of God John Ferraby to Anna Grossmann, 16 July 1968.
298. Letter from Ian Semple, Member of the Universal House of Justice, 12 July 1968.
299. Letter from the National Spiritual Assembly of the British Isles, 15 July 1968.
300. *Noticias Bahá'ís del Ecuador*, September/October 1968.
301. Letter from Bozorg Hemmati to Anna Grossmann, 9 July 1968.
302. Letter from Ben Schreibman, Luxembourg, to the Grossmann family, undated.

REFERENCES

303. Letter from Brigitte Lundblade to Anna Grossmann, 26 July 1968.
304. Letter from Lise Lotte Walcker, Rostock, to Anna Grossmann, 13 August 1968.
305. Letter from Ola Pawlowska to Anna Grossmann, 3 September 1968.
306. Letter from Katharine Meyer to Hartmut Grossmann, 29 December 1995.
307. Letter from Martin Aiff to Anna Grossmann, 17 September 1968.
308. Bahá'u'lláh, *Gleanings*, CXXXII, p. 288.

PART II

INSTEAD OF AN INTRODUCTION

1. Bahá'u'lláh, *Gleanings*, XCIX, p. 200.

THE TABLET FROM 'ABDU'L-BAHÁ

2. Shoghi Effendi, 'The Dispensation of Bahá'u'lláh', in *The World Order of Bahá'u'lláh*, p. 134.
3. *Bahá'í World*, Vol. XV, p. 417, signature and date from the original Tablet.
4. 'Abdu'l-Bahá, *Selections* 17:2, p. 35.
5. 'Abdu'l-Bahá, *Tablets*, p. 109.
6. 'Abdu'l-Bahá, *Selections* 17:2–3, p. 35.
7. ibid. 160:5, p. 191.

THE SEEKER

8. Bahá'u'lláh, *Four Valleys*, Second Valley, paras. 6–7, p. 54.

THE HAND OF THE CAUSE OF GOD

9. Bahá'u'lláh, Lawḥ-i-Dunyá, para. 2, in *Tablets*, p. 83.
10. Taherzadeh, *Revelation of Bahá'u'lláh*, Vol. 4, p. 285.
11. Bahá'u'lláh, Lawḥ-i-Dunyá, para. 2, in *Tablets*, p. 83.
12. Tablet of Bahá'u'lláh cited in *Lights of Guidance*, No. 1080.
13. Translated from the Persian and provided to the author by the Bahá'í World Centre.

THE ADVOCATE OF GOD

14. 'Abdu'l-Bahá, *Promulgation of Universal Peace*, p. 442.

HERMANN GROSSMANN

THE ADMINISTRATOR

15. Shoghi Effendi, 'America and the Most Great Peace', in *The World Order of Bahá'u'lláh*, p. 94.

THE VISIONARY ARTIST AND THINKER

16. Bahá'u'lláh, The Valley of Knowledge, *Seven Valleys*, p. 15.

A GERMAN BAHÁ'Í TEACHER IN FRANCE

17. *Star of the West*, Vol. 21, May 1930, p. 51.

MY PARENTS

18. Bahá'u'lláh, *Epistle to the Son of the Wolf*, p. 14.
19. *Bahá'í World*, Vol. XIX, pp. 640–41.

INDEX

'Abdu'l-Bahá viii, 23, 35, 62-3, 64, 141, 165, 201, 294
  Divine Plan (and Tablets of) 22, 110, 136-7, 170, 175, 215, 218
  Exemplar 37, 250, 268
  and German Bahá'ís 13, 14, 24, 84, 258, 261-2
  visits to Stuttgart and Esslingen 25
  photograph of 71
  Tablet to Hermann Grossmann 21, 63, 252-6, 267, 274, 276
  Will and Testament viii, 32, 64, 105-6, 111, 136, 174-5, 294
  Writings and talks 25, 31, 35, 37, 42, 56, 57, 73, 99, 107, 124, 143, 156, 260, 263
  on Hands of the Cause 71
Adams, Paul, Knight of Bahá'u'lláh 121, 191
Administrative Order, Bahá'í 31-2, 49, 73, 87, 95, 174, 191, 266, 270, 274
  and North American Bahá'í community 174, 266
  training in 49, 79, 104, 113, 137, 267, 272-3
  see also Bahá'í administration
Afscharian, Dr Mokhtar 98-100
Ahmedzadeh, Dr Aminulláh, 125
Ahmedzadeh, Helga 177-8
Aiff, Martin 73-5, 80, 83, 90, 112, 170-71, 173, 235
  and Gerda Aiff 163, 168, 170
'Akká vii, 51-2, 156, 164-5, 170, 173, 222
  Most Great Prison 164-5
'Alá'í, Shu'á'u'lláh, Hand of the Cause of God 231
Alexander, Agnes, Hand of the Cause of God 110
Amsterdam, Netherlands 156
Ankersmit, Geertrui (Bates) 153
Antwerp, Belgium 156
Arequipa, Peru 190, 201
Argentina
  Bahá'í community 186-7, 196-7, 198, 205, 207

and Grossmann family 3-6, 45, 69, 140
and Hartmuth family 17
National Spiritual Assembly 198, 205, 213-14
travels of Anna and Hermann Grossmann 184-5, 195-6, 202, 205, 206, 207
see also Buenos Aires; Rosario
Aschari, Nahid 158-9, 166-7
Ashraf, Godsea 232-3
Ashton, Beatrice 98, 110
Asunción, Paraguay 185, 202-3, 207, 213
Austria
  Bahá'í community 42, 91, 153, 155, 158, 167
  National Spiritual Assembly 158, 192
  National Spiritual Assembly of Germany and Austria 53, 86, 107, 115, 138, 153, 173, 178
  travels of Dr Grossmann 42, 155, 158-9, 167, 177-8, 179, 204
Auxiliary Board 115-16, 151-2, 177, 189, 191, 198, 220, 226, 236, 289
  instituted by Shoghi Effendi 115

Báb, the 31, 51, 74, 124, 126, 129, 132, 208, 294
  Dispensation of 147
  portrait 137, 138
  Shrine 50, 51, 163-4, 222, 295
Baden, Austria 204
Bahá'í administration 196-7, 216, 267, 270
  interdiction in Germany and Austria 54-7
  see also Administrative Order
Bahá'í community in Germany *see* German Bahá'í community
Bahá'i history 67, 106, 135, 152, 294-5
Bahá'í-Nachrichten 89-90, 101, 163-4, 168, 192, 214
Bahá'í-Vereinigung (Bahá'í Association) 24
Bahá'í publishing
  in Germany 24, 36-8, 56, 72-3, 125-6, 128, 143
  in Argentina 186
Bahá'í World, The 25, 42, 126, 245

313

Bahá'í World Centre 4, 106, 122, 135-6, 186, 207, 222, 228
Bahá'í World Congress (London 1963) 175, 221-3, 295
Bahia, Brazil 184, 205, 215
Bahá'u'lláh 31, 50-51, 58-9, 74, 80, 118, 141, 164-5, 200, 208-9, 219, 222
  introduction to His Cause vii-ix
  Covenant 31, 66, 128-30 *see also* Covenant
  Declaration 176, 221
  portrait 179
  Shrine 50, 51, 164-5, 166, 204
  significance of His Revelation 49, 127, 255, 268
    Bahá'í Dispensation 293
    Bahá'í World Commonwealth viii, 277, 293
    Kingdom of God on earth 271, 273
    Lesser Peace 127, 172-3
    Most Great Peace 127
    World Order of Bahá'u'lláh 49, 69, 85, 166, 174-5, 176-7, 202, 266, 270-71, 272-3, 274
  teachings vii-viii, 23, 32, 42, 44, 72, 116-18, 125, 128, 131, 158, 238-42, 268, 276-8, 286-7
  Testament viii, 52
  Writings 31, 35, 37, 43, 44, 51, 73, 83, 90, 95, 124, 294
    translations *see* translation
  see also specific titles
Bahíyyih Khánum, Greatest Holy Leaf 20, 50
Bahjí, Mansion of vii, 51, 54, 165, 173, 179, 200
  Shrine of Bahá'u'lláh *see* Bahá'u'lláh
Balyuzi, Hasan, Hand of the Cause of God 169, 209, 220
Banání, Músá, Hand of the Cause of God 231, 232
Barquisemeto, Venezuela 190, 211
Barranquilla, Colombia 191, 201, 211
Bauer, Bruno 96
Bender, Hugo and Kläre 57
Belgium 100-01, 156-7, 158-159, 226, 294
Benelux countries 132, 151, 156-7, 159, 294
Benke, Adam and Lina 14, 42, 101-3
Berdjis, Hermine and Massoud 75, 118, 121, 158
Berlin 22, 43, 58, 83, 103-4, 127, 279
Bogotá, Colombia 191, 201, 209, 211
Bolles, Jeanne 41-2

Bolivia 122, 155, 186, 187, 189-90, 197, 198, 207-9, 212, 214, 218, 233, 293
  National Spiritual Assembly 207
  Temple land 198
  travels of Anna and Hermann Grossmann 122, 187-90, 207-9, 212, 214
Bond, Jameson, Knight of Bahá'u'lláh 219-20
Bopp, Anneliese 115, 122-3, 171
Bordeaux, France 156
Borno, Chile 201
Braun, Eunice 100-01
Brauns, Jörg 62
Brauns-Forel, Marta 57, 58
Brazil 183-4, 190, 194-5, 197, 205, 214, 217-18
  National Spiritual Assembly 198, 214, 215, 218
Bremen 56
Britain 83
  British Empire 87
  British zones in Germany 60, 72, 83, 88, 92, 103
British Bahá'í Community 143, 151-2, 153, 154, 160-61, 164, 180, 232, 234
  National Spiritual Assembly 108, 138, 151-2, 232
Brunn, Gisela von 121-2, 154-5
Brunn, Ursula von, Knight of Bahá'u'lláh 121, 138, 154-5, 190
Brussels, Belgium 38, 100-01, 156-7, 158, 159, 226
Bucaramanga, Colombia 201, 211
Budapest Congress 39
Buenos Aires, Argentina 184-8 passim, 191, 195-7, 202-7 passim, 213-14, 215

Cali, Colombia 191, 198, 201, 209, 212
Callao, Peru 187, 201
Campinas, Brazil 214
Caracas, Venezuela 190, 209, 211, 216
Cartagena, Colombia 201, 211
centres, early Bahá'í in Germany, *see* German Bahá'í community; Berlin; Esslingen; Gera; Leipzig; Rostock; Schwerin; Stuttgart; Warnemünde; Weinheim
Channel Islands 112
Charleroi, Belgium 156
Chateauroux, France 156
Chatellerault, France 156
Chiclayo, Peru 187, 209
Chief Stewards *see* Hands of the Cause of God

INDEX

Chile 185-7, 197, 198, 199-202, 205-6, 207-8, 213, 214-15, 216
  National Spiritual Assembly 201, 205-6, 213, 217
Christaller, Professor 37
Claros, Yolanda 189-90
Cochabamba, Bolivia 187, 189-90, 207-9, 212 Cold War 93-4, 103, 293
Cold War 93-4, 103, 293
Collins, Amelia, Hand of the Cause of God 137, 169, 179, 204
Colmar, France 65
Colombia 190-91, 197, 198, 201, 207, 209, 211-12
  National Spiritual Assembly 209, 211-12
conferences, Bahá'í
  European
    All-Swiss (1950) 103
    Benelux (Arnhem 1954) 132-3, 151
    Benelux (The Hague 1956) 157
    Bex-les Bains (1957) 161-2
    Birmingham (1952) 110-11
    Brussels (1949) 100-01
    The Hague (1960) 204
    Luxembourg (1952) 112-13
    Luxembourg (1961) 204
    Lyon (1958) 179
  in Germany
    Neckargemünd (1949) 101
    Berlin (1951) 103-4
    Esslingen (1955) 154
    Frankfurt (1952) 136-7
    Frankfurt (1955) 154
    Frankfurt (1960) 204
    Munich (1959) 178
    Nuremberg (1959) 178
  of Hands of the Cause
    Bern (1958) 177
    Copenhagen (1959) 191
    Frankfurt (Riḍván 1954) 151-2
    Frankfurt (October 1954) 152
    Frankfurt (1958) 179-80
    Luxembourg (1962) 220
  International, Intercontinental
    Frankfurt (1958) 178-9
    Frankfurt (1967) 226
    Kampala (1953) 108, 135, 137
    New Delhi (1953) 135, 139
    Palermo (1968) 122-3
    Stockholm (1953) 113, 135, 138, 139, 146
    Wilmette, Ill., (1953) 135-6, 137-8
  regional 113, 185-7

South America
  Chile (1959) 185-7
  Quito (1979) 311
  see also Bahá'í World Congress
Cordóba, Argentina 185, 197
Costas, Athos 187-8, 190
Council, International Bahá'í 105-6, 137, 166, 176, 295
Covenant 31, 66, 74, 98, 104, 113, 128-30, 131, 221, 227,266, 267, 270, 272, 293, 295
  Covenant-breaking 66, 166, 171, 173, 177, 196, 202, 210, 212, 123, 263, 265
  talks and writings by Hermann Grossmann 101, 103, 104, 126, 127-9, 131-2, 136-7
Crao tribe, Brazil 205
Cuenca, Ecuador 201
Curituba, Brazil 183, 204

Darmstadt 38, 68, 73, 81
  Special Court case under National Socialism 65-6, 67, 70, 78, 265
Davison, Robert Bruce 72, 81, 84
Deutscher Bahá'í-Bund 142
Döring family 30
Dreyfus, Hippolyte 156
Dreyfus-Barney, Laura 156

Ecuador 190, 191, 197, 198, 201, 205, 209, 296, 311
  National Spiritual Assembly 209, 212, 217
  Noticias Baha'is del Ecuador 232-3
  travels of Anna and Germann Grossmann 191, 201, 205, 209, 232-3
Echtner, Vuk 42
Ehlers, August and Mariechen 65
Eichenauer, John C. 72, 83, 84, 85, 88
Eichler, Frieda 64, 66
English (language) 21, 35, 65, 98, 126, 138, 183, 192, 211, 225, 279, 281
  and Elsa Maria Grossmann 4, 140-3, 146
Eschraghi, Dr Parviz 100
Espenlaub-Schnizler, Ruth 66-7
Esperanto 23, 31, 34-9
  Bahaa Esperanto Eldonejo 37
  Bahaa Esperanto-Ligo 38, 39
  Congresses 34, 35, 37, 38
  and Dr Esslemont 35
  and Dr Grossmann 36-8
  Esperantists 23, 34, 81
  literature 29, 35, 37

315

and Martha Root 34
La Nova Tago 23, 35-8
prohibition 36, 37-8
Esslemont, Dr John E., Hand of the Cause of God 23, 35, 37, 95, 111, 133
Esslingen 30, 31, 43, 57, 73, 83, 85, 95, 127
'Häusle' 41, 57, 73, 75, 86, 88, 154
summer schools 56, 86-8, 101, 109, 154, 158
training institute 86, 269
visit of 'Abdu'l-Bahá 25
European Teaching Committee 100-01, 112-13, 138, 152, 157, 294
Ezeiza, Argentina 197

Faroe Islands 160
Featherstone, Collis, Hand of the Cause of God 231
Ferraby, John, Hand of the Cause of God 169, 226, 231
Five Year Plan (1948-1953) 32, 95-104, 127, 133
Finland 232, 236, 290, 294
Forel, Professor Auguste 37, 57, 126, 133
Frankfurt am Main
Bahá'í community 43, 57, 63, 65-6, 81, 84, 85, 98, 103, 122, 151, 159
Ḥaẓíratu'l-Quds 73, 86, 91, 95-7, 115, 122-3, 136, 152
and passing of Shoghi Effendi 170-71, 174-5
House of Worship 66, 138, 167-8, 179, 180, 204
meetings of Hands of the Cause 115, 151-2, 179, 180
see also conferences; Dr Hermann Grossmann: travels
France 9-11, 50, 65, 74, 83, 156, 164, 192, 281-4
National Spiritual Assembly 177
Frisian Islands 4, 138, 140, 146-7, 153, 154, 158
Fujita, Saichiro 50, 52
Furútan, 'Ali-Akbar, Hand of the Cause of God 121, 172-3, 206

Gera 30
Gerber, Karla 60-61
Gericke, Else 62
German Bahá'í community
in early 20th century 14-15, 22-5, 29-32, 42-3, 270, 278
visit of 'Abdu'l-Bahá 25

visits of Martha Root 22-3, 29
in 1930s 40-45, 48, 266-7, 271-2
interdiction and persecution under National Socialism 54-70, 81-7, 126, 145-6, 230, 266-7
National Spiritual Assembly
before World War II 30-31, 36-8, 52-3, 56, 133, 265, 267, 270, 288
first election 30
and German Democratic Republic 93-4, 104
post World War II 77, 81, 85-6, 89, 95-6, 104, 107, 115, 120, 122-3, 155
pioneers
German 101-3, 104, 120, 121-2, 140, 146-7, 154-5, 158, 168
Persian 98-100, 107, 111-12, 259
post World War II
aftermath (1945-1948) 38-9, 72-94, 109, 110, 121, 127, 268-9
Five Year Plan (1948-53) 32, 95-104, 127, 133
Ten Year Crusade (1953-1963) 136, 151, 154-5, 158-9, 180
Shoghi Effendi on 50, 55, 77, 80, 84-5, 91, 92, 96, 103-4, 261-2
and passing 170-71, 174-5
youth 73-80, 97-8, 99-100, 258-9
see also Bahá'í-Verlag; Esperanto; Frankfurt am Main; Hofheim-Langenhain; Stuttgart; *and individual place names*
Germany 239, 261-2, 283, 296
and Grossmann family 3, 6-7, 8-9, 45, 181
and Hartmuth family 17-18
Gerst, Gestapo officer 58, 67
Gerstner, Friedrich 23, 34-6
Gestapo 43, 54, 55-6, 57-61, 64-7, 143, 145, 265, 294
Giachery Dr Ugo, Hand of the Cause of God 112, 138, 151-2, 154, 169, 179, 180, 191, 192, 193, 194, 209, 220, 221
Gleanings from the Writings of Bahá'u'lláh 95, 143
Goethe 257
Gollmer, Paul 85
Gollmer, Wilhelm 62
Göppingen 30, 43, 57, 63, 66, 83
Grasselly, Gilbert 196
Graz, Austria 158, 167, 177, 204
Great Britain *see* Britain; British Bahá'í Community

INDEX

Greeven, Max 56-7
Grimsehl, Ernst 8
Grossmann, Anke ix, 98, 192
Grossmann, Anna
  birth and early life 17-20
  diaries, letters, notes and memoirs 14, 31-2, 51, 52, 58, 62, 66, 93, 116-17, 123, 225, 226, 264, 288
    on South America 163-8 passim, 195-6, 197, 203, 205, 206, 211, 213, 214-19
  friendship with Amatu'l-Bahá Rúḥíyyih Khánum 54, 80, 91-2, 114, 165, 289
  investigated by Gestapo 58, 60-61, 65, 68, 264
  marriage and family life 18, 20, 40-41, 46, 61, 114-15, 117-19, 120, 122, 196, 288-9
  passing 236, 290-91
  pilgrimages 48-53, 159, 163-8
  services to Bahá'í Cause
    Auxiliary Board 115-16, 121, 236, 289
    in Germany 20, 23, 25, 31, 37, 40, 55, 60, 69, 72, 82, 89, 97, 99, 103, 115-16, 119-20, 121, 123, 131, 278, 288
    pioneering in Finland 236, 290
    Secretary of the National Spiritual Assembly of the Bahá'ís of Germany 115, 288-9
    as a speaker 97, 121, 222, 131
    travels with Dr Grossmann 122, 159, 163-8, 194-203, 205-10, 211-19
Grossmann, Dr Hermann
  appointment as Hand of the Cause of God 106-12, 114, 260-61
  archives 61, 64, 127, 133, 244
  artist 4, 16, 19, 130, 195, 253-4, 257, 274, 276
  birth and early life 3-17, 281
    First World War 6, 8-11, 254, 256, 283
    see also Rosario, Argentina
  and Covenant 101, 103, 104, 127-8, 265-6, 270
  declaration as a Bahá'í 13-15, 141
  and education of children 23, 25-9, 37, 278-80
  and Esperanto 35-7, 268
  and establishment of Administrative Order 31-2, 43-4, 49-50, 79-80, 87, 104, 174-7, 191, 197, 209, 261, 266-74, 288
  interest in science 8, 52, 121, 132, 134, 178, 183, 237-42, 254, 258
  marriage and family life 18-20, 40, 45-7, 71, 114, 117-18, 120, 122, 142, 225, 285-91
    letters to his children 15, 285-7
    see also Neckargemünd
  and National Socialist regime 60-70, 71, 267
    defence of Bahá'ís 67, 264-5, 276
    prosecuted 61, 67-70
    review 85-8
  passing and funeral 122-3, 226-35
  personality 96, 98, 104, 120, 138, 160-61, 167-9, 171, 173-4, 187, 188-90, 196, 199, 233, 250-51, 261-2, 281
  pilgrimages 48-53, 163-8, 253, 255
  professional work 15-16, 17, 40-41, 70, 264, 287
  scholarship 44, 124-34, 254
    Institute for Religion and Science 32, 133-4
    library 30, 124
    systematic approach 130, 261, 270-73
  service to Bahá'í Cause 249-51, 263, 276-7
    early, in Hamburg 22-32, 35-7, 265-9
    before and during World War II 40-45, 60-70
    following World War II 84, 258, 268
    National Spiritual Assembly of the Bahá'ís of Germany 43, 85, 86, 267, 288
    as Hand of the Cause 261-2
    Chief Stewards 171-2, 277
    Conclaves 171, 173, 179-80, 193, 210
    in Europe 115, 136-7, 138, 151-62, 177-80, 192, 203, 220, 225-6
    and passing of Guardian 169-73, 277
    in South America 181-91, 194-203, 204-9, 211-14, 219, 225, 277
  and Shoghi Effendi 24, 43, 49, 51-3, 124, 181, 253, 255, 264, 266-9, 271
    passing of Shoghi Effendi 169-73, 277, 293
    see also Hermann Grossman: pilgrimages
  spiritual path 250-52, 254-8, 262, 286
  Tablet of 'Abdu'l-Bahá 21, 51, 252-6, 267, 274

317

talks 8, 24, 43, 44 72-3, 76, 81-3, 127-8, 132, 153-5, 156, 192, 208, 254, 256, 261, 275
  advice on speaking, method 44, 121, 276, 287, 288-9
  subjects:
    Administrative Order 79, 87, 104, 174-7, 274
    Christianity 202
    Covenant 101, 103, 104, 127-8
    Ḥaẓíratu'l-Quds 157, 161-2
    National Spiritual Assembly 206
    religion and science 237-42
    passing of Shoghi Effendi 174-7
    situation of Bahá'ís under National Socialism 85-8
    Ten Year Plan 136-7, 138, 175-6
    travel 281-4
    World Order of Bahá'u'lláh 85, 202, 274
as teacher 73-80, 88-9, 131, 208-9, 287
  and Administrative Order 32, 79-80, 90, 104, 191, 197, 209, 267, 268-9, 271
  and youth 73-80, 97-8, 99-100, 258-9
travels:
  Argentina 184-6, 195-6, 197, 202, 205, 206, 207, 213-14
  Austria 15, 42, 155-6, 158-9, 167, 177-8, 179, 204
  Belgium 100-01, 156-7, 158-9, 226
  Benelux 132, 151, 156-7, 159
  Bolivia 122, 187-90, 207-9, 212, 214
  Brazil 183-4, 194-5, 205, 214
  Chile 185-7, 199-202, 205-6, 213, 214-15, 216
  Colombia 190-91, 198, 201, 209, 211-12
  Czechoslovakia
  British Isles 151-2, 153, 154, 160-61, 234
  Ecuador 191, 201, 205, 209, 232-3
  France 156, 192, 281-4
  Frisian Islands (Sylt) 154, 158
  German towns
    Altena 159
    Bamberg 43
    Berlin 43, 103-4, 127
    Bonn 127, 158, 159
    Braunschweig 159
    Cologne 37, 158, 159
    Dusseldorf 158, 159
    Ebingen 127
    Esslingen 43, 73, 75, 86-8, 101, 109, 127, 154, 158
    Frankfurt am Main 43, 81, 103, 127, 132, 136, 154, 157, 159, 237, 273
      International Conferences 178, 204, 226
      meetings of Hands of the Cause 115, 151-3, 179
      passing of Shoghi Effendi 170-71, 174-7
    Freiburg 127, 173-4
    Friedberg 43
    Gera 30
    Gießen 81, 127
    Göppingen 43, 83
    Hamburg 43, 127, 159
    Hanover 159
    Heilbronn 43
    Heppenheim 75, 77, 81, 127
    Karlsruhe 43, 81, 127
    Leipzig 43
    Ludwigsburg 83
    Mannheim 43, 82
    Munich 127, 155, 158, 178, 179
    Nuremberg 158, 178
    Plochingen 83
    Reutlingen 127
    Rostock 24, 43
    Schwerin 24, 43
    Stuttgart 85, 127
    Tübingen 127
    Ulm 127, 155, 158
    Warnemünde 24, 30, 43
    Weinheim 43, 81, 127
    Wiesbaden 81, 127
    Würzburg 43
  Ireland 153, 154
  Luxembourg 156, 159, 161, 192, 203-4, 220
  Netherlands 132-3, 153, 156-7, 204
  Paraguay 185, 186, 202-3, 207, 213
  Peru 187, 190, 197, 198, 201, 209, 212
  Switzerland 103, 153, 192
  Uruguay 184, 198, 206, 212-13, 214
  Venezuela 190, 209, 211, 216
vision 262, 274-7, 286
writings
  books 37, 42-3, 95, 124-6, 128-9, 131-2, 243-4, 275
  diaries and letters 10, 11, 15, 78-9, 86, 153, 183, 200, 254, 260, 279-80

INDEX

essays and articles 25, 29, 36, 126-7, 245
poems and verse 9, 19-20, 46-7, 63-4
stories 28-9, 46, 285
translations 35, 43, 125, 143, 244
Grossmann, Elsa Maria
  birth and early life 4-6, 140
  courage under National Socialism 61, 64, 145-6, 288
    arrest and imprisonment 65, 68, 145, 264
  declaration as a Bahá'í 4, 140-41, 142
  and Esperanto 23, 142
    Lydia Zamenhof 35, 62, 142
  and Hermann Grossmann 11, 13-14, 154-5, 288
  passing 147
  pilgrimage 48-52, 144
  poems 25-6, 144-5, 147-50
  services to Bahá'í Cause 22-3, 142, 143
    child education 23, 25-6, 278-9
    Knight of Bahá'u'lláh to Frisian Islands 4, 138, 140, 146-7
    Westerland auf Sylt 147, 154
    translations 4, 95, 143
  and Shoghi Effendi 143-4, 146
Grossmann, Hartmut vii, 4, 40-41, 61-2, 96, 114, 201, 207-9, 236
  and Hermann Grossmann 249, 285-7
Grossmann, Johanna and Curt 3-4, 6, 8, 14, 141-3
Grossmann, Professor Dr Rudolf 4, 45
Grossmann, Susanne (Pfaff-) 15, 20, 48
Grünewald, Berta 146
Guajira, Colombia 207
Guayaquil, Ecuador 191, 201, 209, 212, 232-3

Hague, The, Netherlands 156-7, 172, 204
Hahn (Pfaff), Andrea 119
Haifa
  and 'Abdu'l-Bahá 13, 21, 23, 49
  Bahá'í Holy Places vii, 23, 50, 51-2, 163-5, 170, 222
    House of 'Abdu'l-Bahá 222
    Shrine of the Báb 50, 51, 163-4
  Bahá'í World Centre 4
  Conclaves of Hands of the Cause 171, 173, 179-80, 193, 210
  Hands of the Cause Resident in the Holy Land 205, 206, 212, 222
  International Bahá'í Archives 51
  International Bahá'í Council 105-6, 137, 166
  International Teaching Centre vii, ix
  pilgrimages 48-53, 54, 56, 65, 115, 159, 163-8, 170, 286
  Pilgrim House, Western 48-9, 50, 52, 166, 168
  Universal House of Justice 50, 222
  see also Shoghi Effendi
Hamburg 6, 8, 11, 15, 20
  Bahá'í community
    early centre 14, 22-3
    in 1920s 20, 22-3, 29, 34, 40, 142, 264
      magazines and newsletters 23, 25, 29
    following World War II 83
    Spiritual Assembly 29
  and Grossmann family 4-8, 14, 15, 45, 140, 142, 264
  University 4, 15, 29, 45, 124
  visits of Dr Grossmann 43, 127, 159
Hands of the Cause of God
  appointment viii, 105-6, 110-11, 112, 260
  and Auxiliary Board 115-16, 152, 191, 226
  character, duties and functions viii-ix, 105, 184-5, 196, 260-61
  Chief Stewards viii-ix, 171-2, 177, 202, 293
  Conclaves 171, 172, 179-80, 193, 204, 210, 213
  and election of Universal House of Justice 180, 181, 193, 202, 220-22
  European 106, 115-16, 151, 152, 169, 173, 177, 179, 180, 220, 225, 226
  funeral of Shoghi Effendi 169-70
  German 132-3, 151, 169, 203, 261-2
  and Interregnum 295
  and Mason Remey 177, 202
  messages of condolence to Grossmann family 230-2
  and Most Great Jubilee 221-2
  Resident in the Holy Land 89, 137, 224
    Custodians 181, 205-6, 212, 220-22, 265, 293-4
  travels 137-8, 178, 180, 193, 194
  see also conferences
  tribute to 223-4
  of the Western Hemisphere 193, 198, 220
Hartmuth, Anna and Wilhelm 17-18
Haug, Rolf, Knight of Bahá'u'lláh 138
Ḥaẓíratu'l-Quds *see* Frankfurt am Main; Hofheim-Langenhain; Stuttgart
Hebrides 160

Heidelberg
  Bahá'í community 40, 41, 57, 61, 72, 78-9, 82, 96, 98-9, 147
    harassment and arrests under National Socialism 57, 58, 61, 65, 145, 264
    Court proceedings 66-7
    sentences revoked 68, 145
    National Convention (1937) 84-5
    Spiritual Assembly 41, 85
    registration 155
    visits by Dr Grossmann 38, 43, 127, 203
    youth 78-9
  University 82, 98-9, 183
Heilbronn 30, 43
Hemmati, Dr Bozorg 111-12, 233
Heppenheim 57, 65, 81, 127
  youth meetings 73, 75-8
Herrigel, Wilhelm 23-4, 59
Heydorn, Pastor Wilhelm 23-4
Holy Year 106, 135, 137, 295-6
Hofheim-Langenhain vii, 167, 178, 189, 204
House of Worship *see* Mother Temple
Hofman, Marion 152
Holsapple Armstrong, Leonora 215
Horn, Edith 65-6, 81
Huancayo, Peru 201

indigenous peoples
  Africa 137
  South America 122, 186, 187-9, 190, 197-8, 203-13 passim, 215-19, 225, 293, 295, 296
  Indios 122, 295
Innsbruck, Austria 158, 177, 204
Institute of Religion and Science 32, 133-4
Intercontinental Conference *see* conferences
interdiction of Bahá'í Faith
  by the National Socialists 54-70, 82, 85-8, 94, 102, 126, 130, 143-4, 264-5
  by the Soviets 60, 93-4, 103
  confiscation of Bahá'í books 56-7, 59, 64, 66
International Bahá'í Archives 51
International Bahá'í Bureau 107, 143, 295
International Bahá'í Council 105-6, 137, 166, 176, 295
International Conference *see* conferences
International Teaching Centre vii, ix, 224, 293
Ioas, Leroy, Hand of the Cause of God 137, 153, 155
Ireland 153, 154
  Northern 232

Jachakollo, Andrés, Carmelo and Isidro 187-8
Jack, Marion 102
Jankullo, Bolivia 186
Jarvis, Henry 84
Jerusalem, 52, 202
  Hebrew University 52
Jörn, Emil 30, 59-60, 112
Jubilee
  Great (1952) 106
  Most Great, King of Festivals (1963) 220-24

Käfer, Alex 158
Karlsruhe 30, 43, 57, 62, 81, 102, 127
Khadem, Zikrullah, Hand of the Cause of God 112, 161-2, 231
Kházeh, Jalal, Hand of the Cause of God 231
Kellberg, Mr and Mrs, Knights of Bahá'u'lláh 216-17
Khamsí, Mas'ud 184-5, 190
Kitáb-i-Aqdas (Most Holy Book) 258
Kitáb-i-Íqán (Book of Certitude) 35, 126, 258
Klitzing, Karl 30, 60
Knights of Bahá'u'lláh 4, 89, 120, 121, 146-7, 153, 154, 160-61, 186, 191, 216-17, 219, 234, 295
Köhler, Paul and family 58-9, 62
Köstlin, Anna 31
Knobloch, Alma 14
Kohler, Alfred 85
Kohler, Hansjörg 62
Koller-Jäger, Heide 83

La Paz, Bolivia, 187, 190
Lawḥ-i-Karmil (Tablet of Carmel) 136
Lehne, Rosel and Theo 58-9
Leidinger, Theodor 62
Levy, Ben 109, 132
Leipzig
  Bahá'í community 13-14, 37, 43, 62, 93
  Spiritual Assembly 30, 93
  and Hermann Grossmann's encounter with the Bahá'í Faith 13-14, 141, 226, 252, 258
  University 13, 15-16, 45, 258
Liedtke, Harry 117
Liège, France 156
Lima, Peru 187, 201, 209, 212
Linz, Austria 158-9, 177-8, 204
Loehndorf, Peter 123 (note 144)
Loncoche, Chile 201, 206

INDEX

Lorey, Adolf 36-8
Lundblade, Brigitte (Hasselblatt), Knight of Bahá'u'lláh 160-61, 234
Luxembourg 108, 112, 156, 159, 161, 192, 203-4, 220, 233-4, 294
  see also Benelux countries
Lynch, Anne 107
Lyon, France 156, 179

Macco, Carla 61, 65, 66-7
Macco, Fritz 61-2
Mannheim 43, 61, 75, 82
Manizales, Colombia 201
Maracay, Venezuela 190, 209
Marseilles, France 156
Maxwell, Mary, see Rúḥíyyih Khánum
Maxwell, May 41, 52, 110, 185, 215
Maxwell, Sutherland, Hand of the Cause of God 52, 137
Medellín, Colombia 191, 201, 211
Meyer, Katharine, Knight of Bahá'u'lláh 186, 217, 235
Minas, Uruguay 261
Monaco, Monte Carlo 156
Montevideo, Uruguay 184, 198, 201, 206, 212-13, 214
Mother Temple 179, 295
  of Europe 66, 179, 189
    architectural plans 167-8
    foundation stone 204
  of the West 137
Muhájir, Raḥmatu'lláh, Hand of the Cause of God 207, 218, 311
Mühlschlegel, Dr Adelbert, Hand of the Cause of God 15, 23, 37, 38-9, 44, 56, 89, 99, 112, 131, 132-3, 151-2, 169, 180, 203, 220, 226, 227-9, 261-2, 265
Mühlschlegel, Herma 54-5, 118
Munich 38, 41-2, 45, 127, 142, 155, 158, 178, 179

National Socialists 54-70, 71, 82, 145-6, 266, 267
  and Esperanto 35-6, 38, 55, 57, 268, 269
  NSDAP 69-70, 265, 296
  persecution of Bahá'ís 57-61, 63-9, 72, 86-7, 104, 126, 145, 228, 230, 264-5
  Special Court in Darmstadt 65-6, 67, 70, 78, 265
  Heidelberg case see Heidelberg
Neckargemünd
  Bahá'í activities 37, 72-3, 74-5, 78-80, 82, 90, 95, 101, 115, 127, 133-4, 173

Grossmann family home 37, 40, 45, 88, 103, 110, 115, 117-19, 120, 143, 147, 191, 204, 225, 226
  and World War II 58, 60-62, 71, 72, 78, 145-6
  resting-place of Dr Grossmann 147, 226, 229-30, 235, 291
Netherlands 132-3, 153, 156-7, 159, 204, 216, 294
Nice, France 156
Nova Tago, La (Esperanto magazine) 23, 35-8, 55
NSDAP see National Socialists

Ober, Harlan and Grace 13-14, 41, 102, 252, 255, 258
Olinga, Enoch, Hand of the Cause of God 231
Orkney Isles 112, 160
Orleans, France 156
Orloff, Roan 38
Ortega, Sabino 188-9
Oruro, Bolivia 187, 190
Otavalo, Ecuador 201

Paraguay 185-7 passim, 195-8 passim, 202-3
  National Spiritual Assembly 207, 213
Paris, France 156, 177, 281-3
Pawlowska, Ola, Knight of Bahá'u'lláh 120, 234-5
Pereira, Colombia 201
persecution see National Socialists
Petersen, Martha 146
Petit, François 192
Peru 187, 190, 198, 201, 214, 293, 296
  National Spiritual Assembly 209, 212
pilgrimage see Hermann Grossmann
pioneering, pioneers 14, 87, 89, 136-8, 140, 153, 157, 160-61, 163, 164, 172, 178, 179, 183-4, 190, 196-9, 215-18, 234, 295
  American 156, 157, 159, 181, 187, 195, 196, 198, 199, 201, 215-16
  British 154, 232
  German ix, 42, 73-4, 87, 101-4, 112, 120, 121-2, 138, 140, 146-7, 155, 158, 159, 168, 186, 190, 235-6, 290
  Persian 98-100, 107, 111-12, 166-7, 178, 181, 184-5, 194-5, 198, 232
  training courses in Germany 95, 101, 102
  see also Knights of Bahá'u'lláh
Pirmasens 15, 17-20, 58
Poitiers, France 156
Poostchi, Badieh 119-20

321

Porto Alegre, Brazil 183, 214
Prague, Czechoslovakia 42
Preisendanz, Professor 64
Punta Arenas, Chile 185, 201, 206, 213, 214

Quilpué, Chile 201
Quito, Ecuador 191, 201, 209, 212, 311

Recife, Brazil 183-4, 205
religion and science 32, 36, 132, 134, 178, 244, 255, 258, 270-73, 287
  Institute of Religion and Science 32, 133-4
  talk by Hermann Grossmann (App. 2) 132, 237-42
Remey, Charles Mason, Hand of the Cause of God 137, 165, 166, 177, 196, 202, 265
Riḍván (various years) 30, 41, 82, 99, 115, 133, 137, 147, 151, 159, 166-7, 184, 186, 190, 193, 198, 200, 201, 202, 205, 207, 209, 215, 219, 222-3, 295
  Garden (Holy Land) 51-2, 165
Rio de Janeiro, Brazil 183, 195, 205
Robarts, John, Hand of the Cause of God 231
Rocholl, Teuto 167, 168
Root, Martha 22-3, 29, 34-5, 37, 60, 110, 133, 142, 215, 268
Rosario, Argentina 3-7, 140, 185-6, 197, 207, 214
Rosengärtlein, Das 25-9, 142, 279-80
Rostock 22, 24, 30, 43, 59, 93, 234
Rothschild, Sophie 63, 66
Rúḥíyyih Khánum, Amatu'l-Bahá (Mary Maxwell) 48-9, 52, 54, 77, 80, 91, 105, 128, 137, 147, 165, 166, 167-8, 185, 191-2, 215, 220, 223, 230
  friendship with Anna Grossmann 114, 165, 289
  in Germany 41-2, 191-2
  passing of Shoghi Effendi 169-70, 173

Salazar, Oscar 207-9
Salvador, Brazil 183
Salzburg, Austria 155, 158, 177, 204
Santa Clara, Brazil 183
Santiago, Chile 185, 201, 205-6, 213, 216
Santo André, Brazil 183, 214
Santos, Brazil, 183, 195
São Caetano, Brazil 183
São Paulo, Brazil 183-4, 205, 214
São Vicente, Brazil, 183
Schaefer, Dr Udo 99, 130-31
Schechter, Fred 122

Schenk, Marie 65
Schmidt, Dr Eugen, and family 43, 65, 89, 97, 99, 131, 226-7, 229
Schmidt, Gaius and Margarete 65
Schoch-Häcker, Anna 66
Schreibman, Ben 233-4
Schubert, Hede 82, 85, 89
Schwarz, Alice 54
Schweizer, Alfred 62
Schweizer, Annemarie and Albert 20, 31
Schweizer, Mariele 65, 83
Schwedler, Mrs 30
Schwerin 22, 24, 30, 43, 60, 93
Sears, William, Hand of the Cause of God 194, 195, 197, 212, 231
Semple, Ian 97-8, 110-11, 115, 165, 167-8, 192, 231-2
Seven Valleys (of Bahá'u'lláh) 43, 125, 257, 279
Sévin, Jean, Knight of Bahá'u'lláh 88-9
Shetland Islands 160-61, 234
Shoghi Effendi, Guardian of the Cause of God
  appoints Hands of the Cause viii-ix, 23, 105-8, 110, 111, 112, 260, 267
  Chief Stewards 171-2, 293
  and building of Administrative Order in Germany 30-32, 35-6, 43, 49-50, 77, 84-5, 95, 103, 104, 115, 263-4, 266-7, 271
  National Spiritual Assembly 86, 96
  summer schools 56-7, 269
  displays paintings by Hermann Grossmann 276 *see also* between pages 52-3
  on German Bahá'ís 50, 55, 77, 80, 84-5, 91, 92, 104, 140, 261-2
  Guardianship viii, 52, 79, 105, 170, 174-6, 184, 202, 264, 267-8
  and Hermann Grossmann *see* Grossmann, Hermann
  and interdiction of Faith in Germany 55-7, 69
  marriage 48-9, 52
  meetings of Grossmann family with 48-53, 166, 172, 181, 253, 255
  and military serice 61
  Mother Temple of Europe, plans for 167-8
  passing and funeral 168, 169-73, 277, 293
  and Persian students 100
  and pioneers 101-2, 104, 166-7, 168, 290

INDEX

talk by Hermann Grossmann 174-7
Ten Year Plan 135-8, 151, 175-7 *see also* Ten Year Plan
   and youth 77
   see also Grossmann, Anna; Grossmann, Elsa Maria; International Bahá'í Council; Universal House of Justice; World Order of Bahá'u'lláh
Sofia, Bulgaria 14, 42, 102
Sonne der Wahrheit 55, 79, 85, 90, 95, 142
Special Court *see* National Socialists
spiritualism 24, 263, 267
Spiritual Assemblies
   local 155, 179, 199, 206, 217, 221
     see also specific place names
   National 30, 35, 86, 106, 115, 135, 136, 138, 152, 159, 171, 173, 176, 178, 179, 180, 1814, 186, 193, 198, 204, 206-7, 215-17, 220-22, 230, 294
     Austria 158, 192
     Argentina 196, 205, 207, 213-14, 217
     Belgium 226
     Bolivia 189, 207, 212
     Brazil 214, 219
     British Isles 108, 138, 151-2, 282
     Canada 108
     Chile 200, 201, 205-6, 213, 217
     Colombia 209, 211-12
     Ecuador 209, 212, 217
     Finland 232
     Germany *see* German Bahá'í community
     Germany and Austria 138, 173, 178
     India, Pakistan and Burma 107-8
     Iran 108, 232
     Iran and Iraq 138
     Italy 122-3
     Italy and Switzerland 138, 173
     Paraguay 207, 213
     Peru 209, 212
     United States 100, 138, 193, 216
     United States and Canada 84-5, 174, 294
     Uruguay 206, 213, 214
     Venezuela 198, 209, 211
   Regional 138, 178, 180, 184, 193, 197, 215, 222
     South America (north): Brazil, Peru, Colombia, Ecuador and Venezuela 197, 198, 205
     South America (south): Argentina, Bolivia, Chile, Paraguay and Uruguay 196-8, 200-01, 203

Sprung, Christopher 81
Steiner, René 44, 117-18, 171-2, 204, 229-30
Stockholm 113, 135, 137-8, 140, 146
Stuttgart
   early centre 14, 20, 23, 24, 30, 38, 56, 59-60
   Tablet of 'Abdu'l-Bahá 262
   visit of 'Abdu'l-Bahá 25
   and National Socialist regime 57, 62-3, 65
   post World War II 66, 73, 82-3, 85, 98, 127, 155
   seat of National Spiritual Assembly 82-3, 85, 96
Sucre, Venezuela 190, 209
summer schools 56, 77, 97-8, 99, 101, 112, 121, 134, 142, 151-2, 154, 161, 179, 192, 197, 203, 225, 232, 266, 269
   Esslingen 41, 86-8, 154, 158
   youth summer schools 75, 77-80, 97-8, 110, 192
Switzerland 44, 91, 96, 103, 138, 143, 153, 173, 192, 294

Tablet of Carmel *see* Lawḥ-i-Karmil
teaching conferences *see* conferences, Bahá'í
Ten Year Plan (Ten Year Crusade) 94, 115, 135-9, 140, 151-62, 166, 173, 175-6, 178-9, 191, 220-23, 295
   in Latin America 181, 184, 186, 191, 193, 194, 197, 199, 204, 213, 215-17, 235
Theosophical Society 13, 24
Tobey, Mark 55
Townshend, George, Hand of the Cause of God 151, 153-4
translation of Bahá'í literature 23, 31, 35, 37, 83, 90
   by Elsa Maria Grossmann 4, 95, 140, 143
   by Hermann Grossmann 43, 1225, 143, 244, 257
True, Edna 100-01

Universal House of Justice ix, 39, 50, 89, 105-6, 111, 119, 122, 136, 172, 175-6, 177, 180, 181, 193, 202, 206, 293, 295
   first election 220-222
   and International Bahá'í Council 106, 295
   Peace Message 80-81
   tribute to Anna Grossmann 235-6, 288, 290
   tribute to Hermann Grossmann 230

tribute to Hands of the Cause 223
Uruguay 184, 186, 196, 197, 198, 201, 206
   National Spiritual Assembly 206, 212-13, 214

Valdivia, Chile 199-201, 206
Valencia, Venezuela 190, 211
Valparaiso, Chile 201-2, 213
Varqá, Dr 'Ali-Muhámmad, Hand of the Cause of God 96, 231
Venezuela 190, 197, 198-9, 207, 209, 211, 214, 216
   National Spiritual Assembly 198, 209, 211
   Temple site 211, 216
Vienna, Austria 15, 20, 91, 155-6, 158, 177, 204
Villakollo, Bolivia 187-9
Viña del Mar, Chile 186, 201, 213
Vorarlberg, Austria 119

Walcker, Lise Lotte 234
Walcker, Mrs 30, 59
Wandsbek 6, 20, 25, 36, 37, 40, 278
   reading room 29-30, 124
Warnemünde 22, 24, 30, 43, 59-60, 93, 112

Weber, Klaus 62
Weinheim 43, 66, 71, 81, 127
Wernicke, Lottchen 145 (note 164)
Wertheimer, Berta, Thekla and Thea 63, 66
Westerhoff, Bernhard ix
Westerland auf Sylt 138, 146, 147, 154-5, 158
Witzel, Donald 200-01
World Fellowship Organization 31, 270
World Order (of Bahá'u'lláh) 32, 44, 49, 69, 73, 82-3, 85-8, 125, 130, 136, 166, 172, 174-7, 202, 255, 258, 266-73, 274-5, 286
World War I 8-12, 14, 18, 22, 42, 72, 102, 140, 226, 254, 256, 281, 283
World War II 57, 59-63, 70-72, 73-4, 77-8, 80-81, 91-2, 100-01, 104, 145-6, 260, 264-5, 285, 290, 294
   see also German Bahá'í community; National Socialists; Neckargemünd

Zabih, Manutschehr 88, 111
Zahrai, Ezzat 163 (note 201)
Zamenhof, Lidia 34-5, 37, 62, 133, 142
Zamenhof, Dr Ludwig L. 34, 38
Zonneveld, Arnold 121-2